MW00533098

Pitch the Perfect Investment

THE ESSENTIAL GUIDE TO WINNING ON WALL STREET

Paul D. Sonkin and Paul Johnson

WILEY

Published by John Wiley & Sons, Inc., Hoboken, New Jersey.
Published simultaneously in Canada.

For general information on our other products and services or for technical support, please contact our Customer Care Department within the United States at (800) 762-2974, outside the United States at (317) 572-3993 or fax (317) 572-4002.

Wiley publishes in a variety of print and electronic formats and by print-on-demand. Some material included with standard print versions of this book may not be included in e-books or in print-on-demand. If this book refers to media such as a CD or DVD that is not included in the version you purchased, you may download this material at http://booksupport.wiley.com. For more information about Wiley products, visit www.wiley.com.

Library of Congress Cataloging-in-Publication Data:

Names: Sonkin, Paul D., 1968-author. | Johnson, Paul, 1960-author.
Title: Pitch the perfect investment : the essential guide to winning on wall street/Paul D. Sonkin, Paul Johnson.
Description: Hoboken : Wiley, 2017. | Includes index. |
Identifiers: LCCN 2017013999 (print) | LCCN 2017025132 (ebook) | ISBN 9781119280965 (pdf) | ISBN 9781119280972 (epub) | ISBN 9781119051787 (hardback) | ISBN 9781119280965 (ePDF)
Subjects: LCSH: Investments. | Securities. | BISAC: BUSINESS & ECONOMICS/ Investments & Securities.
Classification: LCC HG4521 (ebook) | LCC HG4521 .S71196 2017 (print) | DDC 332.6–dc23
LC record available at https://lccn.loc.gov/2017013999

Printed in the United States of America.

10 9 8 7 6 5 4 3 2 1

PS dedicates the book to the next generation—Zev, Zoe, and Paris.

PJ dedicates the book to his two near-perfect children, Charlotte and Henry.

Contents

Preface

A picture is not thought out and settled beforehand. While it is being done it changes as one's thoughts change. And when it is finished, it still goes on changing, according to the state of mind of whoever is looking at it. A picture lives a life like a living creature, undergoing the changes imposed on us by our life from day to day. This is natural enough, as the picture lives only through the man who is looking at it.

—Pablo Picasso[1]

The quote by Picasso captures how we feel about this book, as our thoughts changed considerably over the three years it took us to write it. In the many conversations we had with our patient acquisition editor, Bill Falloon, once again explaining why the book was going to miss yet *another* deadline, we reassured him, "You are going to get a much different, but better book than you initially signed up for."

Now that the book is finally finished, we are excited to see what happens as our creation is "released into the wild." Like Picasso's picture, our book will take on a life of its own as the concepts we present are assessed and scrutinized, adopted by some and refuted by others. We know that certain of our ideas will undergo changes as our readers either build upon or discard and replace them

---

[1] Conversation with Christian Zervos, 1935, reprinted in *Picasso on Art*, ed. Dore Ashton (New York: Viking, 1972).

through the process of creative destruction.[2] *We welcome both.* It is our desire to educate and stretch people's minds in the fields of security analysis and fundamental investing. We hope that, like Picasso's pictures, the book lives a long life through those who are looking at it.

As Paul S. is fond of saying, "Being listed as a co-author and writing a book are two completely different things." While we both have been *listed* as co-authors before, this is the first book that we have actually *written*. We both had wanted to write a book for years, but life kept intervening and we never found the time to pursue the idea. During the summer of 2013, with significant prodding from his friend Alejandra, Paul S. finally decided to write a book.

Like so many events in life, the spark of this collaboration was random. On Friday, October 4, 2013, just after the conclusion of the 23rd annual Graham & Dodd Breakfast at the Pierre Hotel in New York City, Paul S. and Paul J. were talking when Paul S. mentioned that he was planning to write a book. Paul J. asked, "What is the title of your book?" Paul S. replied, "*The Perfect Pitch.*" Paul J. responded, "Funny. I had always planned on writing a book called *The Perfect Investment.*" We began emailing each other after returning to our offices later that morning and quickly discovered that our books were complementary. While Paul S. was fascinated with the role pitching played in getting an investment idea adopted, Paul J. was focused on finding the right idea to pitch. It became increasingly clear that the two books were different sides of the same coin and obvious that we should combine efforts to write a single book together.

In addition to our complementary views, we had known each other for almost 20 years, had similar approaches to investing, and a lot of mutual respect. Besides, we thought it would be fun to work together. The book began to take shape over the next several weeks as we fleshed out the proposal for our publisher and settled on the title *Pitch the Perfect Investment.*

The gestation of our friendship began in September 1994 when Paul S., then a student at Columbia Business School, took Paul J.'s Security Analysis class. Paul S. and about 20 other students loved Paul J.'s content and teaching style so much that they persuaded

---

[2] In the words of Paul Samuelson, "Inexact sciences . . . advance funeral by funeral."

him to teach a second class the following semester. When Paul S. approached Paul J. about teaching this class, Paul J. said, "I already taught you all the material I have." Paul S. responded, "That's okay, just teach the same stuff again." Of course, Paul J. created new material and the class was a smashing success.

Over the following summer, Paul S. offered to help Paul J. with his Security Analysis class and became his teaching assistant in the fall of 1995. Then, in the spring of 1996, Paul S. became an adjunct professor and taught at Columbia Business School for the next 16 years, eventually teaching over 450 students. As of the writing of this book, Paul J. has been an adjunct professor for 25 years and has taught over 40 investment courses to more than 2,000 students.

For Paul S., the journey to writing this book began when he started working as a research analyst for legendary microcap value investor Chuck Royce after graduating in May 1995. On his first day at work, he found out abruptly that he was not adequately prepared for the job. While he felt that he had a pretty good handle on the mechanics of the research process, he was unequipped to present the information in a way that would persuade a portfolio manager to follow his recommendation. He quickly discovered that many of his classmates were in a similar position. Paul S. remembers a call from one of his former classmates, who told him, "It's my first day on the job and my boss came over to say hello, and see how I was settling in, then threw an annual report on my desk, said 'tell me what you think,' leaving before I had a chance to ask him anything. What do I do now?"

To address that deficiency, when Paul S. taught his first class, Advanced Seminar in Fundamental Research Techniques, in the spring of 1996, his goal was to teach students the essential skills they would need to do their job as a securities analyst. He told his students on the first day of class, "You go to Apex Technical School to learn how to weld. This class will teach you how to be a research analyst. It's a *vocational* class that will teach you how to do the job." Paul structured his lectures originally to teach fundamental research techniques, with the course culminating in a final project where each student gave a 20-minute presentation on a stock they had worked on during the term. The presentations were painfully boring, and to Paul, who was diagnosed with attention deficit disorder at the age of five, the experience of sitting through them was simply unbearable. Because of his impatience, he interrupted students after a minute or two into their presentation and started peppering them with questions.

As a result of this experience, Paul completely inverted the structure of the course. The final project remained a presentation, but research was now performed to support the pitch, not the other way around. Paul figured that if the students could support and defend their pitch, then it indicated that they had done an appropriate amount of research. This exercise cemented Paul's belief that the pitch is the backbone of any good investment recommendation.

There was a parallel influence for Paul structuring his class this way. In the fall of 1995, Paul audited Pat Duff's Advanced Security Analysis course,[3] in which students were assigned an industry and required to pitch stocks from that industry to guest portfolio managers Duff invited to class. These portfolio managers, like legendary investor Dick Gilder, would mercilessly punch holes in the students' presentations. Paul adopted this structure in his Security Analysis class the next time he taught the course. Then, in the spring of 1999, Paul conceived the idea of melding Duff's class with Bruce Greenwald's Value Investing class[4] to create a new course, which he titled Advanced Seminar in Applied Value Investing and then taught for the next 13 years. The new course focused on having the students pitch investment ideas with a value discipline. Applied Value Investing is one of the most popular courses at Columbia Business School, with multiple sections taught each semester.

Paul J.'s journey was different. Paul became an adjunct professor at Columbia Business School in the fall of 1992 on the recommendation of Charlie Wolf, with whom Paul worked at Credit Suisse First Boston. Charlie had been a tenured professor at Columbia since 1966, teaching courses on debt markets and credit instruments. Roger Murray, who began teaching Security Analysis at Columbia when Benjamin Graham retired in 1956, had himself

---

[3] Advanced Security Analysis originally was taught by Jimmy Rogers, then handed over to Pat Duff, then to John Griffin, and then to David Greenspan.

[4] Paul S. was the teaching assistant and graded final papers for Bruce Greenwald's Value Investing class for several years and co-taught the class in 1997 with Paul J. while Bruce was on sabbatical.

retired in 1978. After several years without offering a course in security analysis, the Business School asked Charlie to take over teaching the class. At the age of 51, to learn more about how an equity analyst did his job, Charlie took a sabbatical year off from teaching to work as a rookie analyst at First Boston Corp. (which was eventually acquired by Credit Suisse). Charlie began his Wall Street career writing research reports on a small technology company called Apple Computer. He was so enthralled with being a Wall Street analyst that he gave up his tenure and never returned to academia. Charlie agreed with the school to teach security analysis as an adjunct professor, usually in the fall term, and to recruit other Wall Street analysts to teach the same course in the spring. Charlie was unable to teach the course in the fall of 1992 and walked across the hall to Paul's office to see if he had any interest in teaching the course for him. The conversation took place in early August and the fall term was scheduled to start only four weeks later. Although Paul was amenable to the idea of teaching someday, he was concerned that he would not have enough time to prep for the term or enough material to fill a semester-long course. Further to the point, Paul had received his MBA only the spring before and was a little concerned that he was too inexperienced to teach an investment course to MBA students at a top-ranked business school. But Charlie was persuasive and Paul agreed to teach the class. Paul loved the experience so much that he continued to teach (off and on) for the next 25 years.

Paul J.'s interest in writing a book stemmed from his hope of one day publishing his classroom material, although he recognized that there was a big difference between creating lecture notes and writing a thoughtful investment book. Paul knew that the main challenge would be finding the time to convert his notes into a book while he pursued his career and raised his family. It took the nudge from Paul S. in late 2013 to get the ball rolling.

This book ultimately is the product of our frustration. We have had no book to assign for our courses that covered all of the main topics that we teach and wanted to rectify the situation. There is *The Intelligent Investor* by Ben Graham, *The Most Important Thing, Illuminated* by Howard Marks, *You Can Be a Stock Market Genius* by Joel Greenblatt, pirated copies of *Margin of Safety* by Seth Klarman, and photocopies of the Buffett Partnerships letters, but there is no single source of material to augment classroom lectures and homework assignments. In fact, Paul J. distributes to his students a "bulk pack" of readings that is more than 400 pages long and contains copies of book chapters, journal articles, research reports, newspaper clippings, and other interesting published items he has collected during his career.

Over the years, we have each read thousands of books, journal articles, and other publications. Paul S. has taught more than 450 students and Paul J. more than 2,000. We have each listened to literally thousands of stock pitches not only from students but from corporate executives, investor relations personnel, institutional salesmen, sell side analysts, and other professional investors. We have learned what elements are required to pitch the perfect investment and have tried to distill this knowledge and experience into a single, easy-to-understand volume.

Originally, and without much thought, we planned to write this book for Wall Street practitioners. However, the more we wrote, the more we realized that the true audience was our students. Most seasoned practitioners had already learned the lessons we wanted to present and we knew that they would not find the book as valuable as would a younger, less experienced newcomer to the industry.[5] We began to focus our writing exclusively on this demographic and that focus allowed us to emphasize the issues we thought most essential for a young analyst to learn.

Since training for new research analysts is basically nonexistent on Wall Street,[6] our goal was to write a "survival" guide for someone embarking on a career as an investment professional. We thought of John "Lofty" Wiseman's *SAS Survival Handbook: The Ultimate Guide to Surviving Anywhere,* which has sold over a million copies, as a model. Wiseman's book is comprehensive and addresses many different disaster scenarios in varying climates, in wild or urban settings, on land or at sea. The author states in the introduction that "Survival depends on applying basic principles and adopting them to the circumstances" and discusses the three elements that are necessary to survival: the will to live, knowledge, and a "kit."

---

[5] This is a polite way of saying that seasoned practitioners are incredibly stubborn and set in their ways. In other words, it's hard to teach old dogs new tricks.

[6] In fact, Steve Cohen started his own Point72 University because of "the lack of talent" on Wall Street.

If you are embarking on a Wall Street career, you must have a will to live, as you are throwing yourself into an incredibly challenging career and one that will test your will to survive on a regular basis. In terms of the kit, Wiseman says, "We keep this to a minimum and have a thorough knowledge of its uses and capabilities." On Wall Street, the kit includes your computer, phone, and access to data sources such as CapitalIQ, Factset, and Bloomberg, as well as sell-side research and other similar resources.

The critical element in survival is *having knowledge.* As Wiseman's guide states, "The more we know the easier it is to survive. Knowledge dispels fear. Look at the locals and see how they survive. Talk to people who have endured and learn from their experiences." Wiseman further states that "by sharing the survival knowledge that I and my colleagues have gained through experience, I aim to help you make those decisions correctly. These methods and skills have helped save our lives and they will help you to be a survivor too."

In this spirit, **Pitch the Perfect Investment** **provides you with the knowledge you need to survive (and thrive) as a Wall Street analyst**.

Whereas the *SAS Survival Handbook* has 672 pages, our publisher informed us that the ideal size for a book of this type is approximately 320 pages. Obviously, we missed that mark with our book weighing in at 496 pages, but we could have easily written a book many times that length. The page constraint forced us to distill our content to what we felt were the most critical elements in our "survival guide." Through this culling process, we sought to keep the resolution of concepts consistent throughout the book. For example, in an early draft we wrote five pages on the limitations of EBITDA.

While the material was excellent, it was overkill for what we were trying to communicate in the chapter and we truncated the discussion accordingly. Please keep in mind that many (actually all) of the topics we discuss can be expanded upon significantly.

Accordingly, unlike the *SAS Survival Handbook,* which attempts to address *every* conceivable scenario, we seek to explain most situations rather than trying to explain every exception, nuance, and possible outcome. One frustration with teaching is that in every class there seems to be "that guy." He (it is usually a he) seems to challenge just about every statement we make, possibly only to hear his own voice as he attempts to look smart in front of the professor and his fellow classmates. Paul S. remembers an incident when he was Paul J.'s teaching assistant involving a particularly persistent student. Paul J. asked the class, "Why does anyone buy a stock?" The answer was, "Because they expect it to go up." Clearly no one buys a stock with the expectation of losing money. However, there was one student, who, for some unknown reason, insisted on searching for a "corner case"[7] to prove Paul J. wrong.[8] The student challenged Paul J. for 10 minutes, offering scenario after scenario under which one might purchase a stock for a reason other than to make money, each of which Paul J. gracefully parried and proved to be flawed, until the student finally found a case involving an elaborate options hedge that seemed to be an exception. While the student appeared to be technically correct, the discussion seemed to be an incredible waste of time, as, in the vast majority of situations, an investor buys a stock because he expects it to go up.

This example is like the standard approach in physics stating that mass is constant. While this convention holds in most cases, it is not a true law as mass actually increases with velocity, although the change is imperceptible until the velocity exceeds 360,000 miles per hour. To put this extreme speed in perspective, a 250-grain bullet shot from a Sako TRG-42 .338 Lapua rifle travels at 2,045 miles per hour, whereas the escape velocity from earth is 25,000 miles per hour and the space shuttle flies at 17,500 miles per hour once out

---

[7] A corner case is a situation that occurs only outside normal parameters—specifically, where the cause is due to multiple variables at extreme levels.

[8] Clearly, the student had not read Phil Fisher's book *Common Stocks and Uncommon Profits,* where the author states, "For one reason or another, through one method or another, you buy common stock in order to make money."

of Earth's gravitational pull. Therefore, one can state that mass *is constant* without the need to qualify the statement to account for extreme velocities. Similarly, we discuss concepts that hold *most* of the time, although not in every single corner case.

Another motivating factor in our writing the book is that there is a wealth of information, mainly contained in academic journals, that is too complicated for most investors to access easily. For example, we attempt to translate concepts like market efficiency, behavioral finance, and risk into language that is understandable while retaining the critical subtleties underlying these ideas. Unfortunately, we have found that many of the concepts that have made it into the mainstream investment community suffer from the "telephone game" when they are "communicated" to a broader audience. Unfortunately, the message has become a distorted version of the author's original meaning. Also, many concepts lose much of their significance when truncated to appeal to the masses. A prime example occurred on CNBC when Eugene Fama was asked to encapsulate the efficient market hypothesis in a 30-second soundbite. Clearly, the body of work that won Fama a Nobel Prize in Economics[9] cannot be fully articulated in a brief sound bite.

In addition to being complicated, the sheer volume of material is absolutely staggering, which made the culling process that much more challenging. We have read innumerable books and journal articles in which we found a few sentences, paragraphs, or pages that we felt were relevant, offered an important insight, made a critical point, or were just plain interesting. While oftentimes it felt like herding cats, we have sought to collect these insights and present them in a straightforward way in a single volume. However, in some cases our effort to accomplish this goal has come at the expense of nuance. Although we tried as best we could to achieve the delicate balance of accuracy versus clarity (and brevity), we expect some readers will find fault with our choices. We only ask that they accept that precision is often the enemy of clarity and understanding.

Given that we have different backgrounds, experiences, and styles of thinking, over the three years of writing the book together,

---

[9] Although we refer to the Nobel Prize in Economics on several occasions in the book, the official title is "The Sveriges Riksbank Prize in Economic Sciences in Memory of Alfred Nobel," which has been awarded 48 times to 78 laureates between 1969 and 2016.

we have had countless spirited discussions regarding concepts in the book.[10] Coupled with the fact that many of the topics are challenging to conceptualize and often difficult to explain, while at times controversial, several chapters went through 40-plus drafts and were completely rewritten multiple times. There was also a lot of material that wound up on the cutting-room floor. We believe that the final product benefited greatly from these efforts.

Like many people with the "gift" of ADD, Paul S. uses a lot of metaphors and is a creative, visual thinker. For Paul J., this creativity made the process sometimes frustrating,[11] often challenging, but always instructive and, in the end, a highly rewarding experience. Paul S. would come up with "crazy ideas" and Paul J. would work to bring them down to earth.

As part of this process and because he is extremely metaphorical in his thinking, Paul S. used diagrams and charts (which you will see throughout the book) to sort through various issues in his mind that he was trying to explain before attempting to write the accompanying text. He would often send these images to Paul J. as an email attachment, saying, "I think I might be going down a rabbit hole. I want to bounce this idea off you to make sure I'm going in the right direction before I spend too much time running down this thread." The diagrams proved to be an effective way for us to discuss, debate, argue, and, ultimately, reach clarity on numerous particularly slippery concepts and important insights.

The interesting part of the exercise was that the visual representation often explained the concepts better than either of us could articulate in writing. We soon realized that we should include these visual aids in the book as part of our presentation because we thought they might also be useful to the reader. Paul S. had been reading about the concept of cognitive load and the fact that pictures and diagrams not only explain concepts better than words (the proverbial picture is worth a thousand words), but graphic images also give the reader's brain a break, which reduces the buildup of cognitive load.

---

[10] More accurately described as "knock-down, drag-out" fights.

[11] For Paul J., the phrase "sometimes frustrating" is a polite understatement. Perhaps this feeling is more appropriately expressed as, "For Paul J., dealing with Paul S.'s convoluted rat's-nest of a brain and stubbornness made him want to reach through the phone and strangle him more than once."

While we created the diagrams ourselves, since neither of us is an artist, our use of illustrations raised a critical issue as we felt the look and feel of the images needed to be consistent throughout the book. We determined that the only way to achieve that goal would be to find an illustrator who could create consistent images. In March 2016, Paul S. stumbled upon an illustrator, Charlie Pendergraft, on Instagram (@drawmecharlie), who was very creative and reasonably priced. Over the course of a year, Charlie produced more than 300 images that we have used in the book.

We feel that the diagrams and charts make our book unique in terms of presenting complicated financial concepts in an easy-to-read, understandable form. We appreciate that there is a fine line between corny and clever, and are unsure as to where some of the images in the book fall—we figure some will be the former, while others will be the latter, although the ultimate balance will reside in the mind of each reader.

Derek Thompson, in his book *Hit Makers*, discusses how new products, songs, and concepts become popular. For example, in industrial design, hits are partly the result of a concept developed by Raymond Loewy called "most advanced, yet acceptable." This insight can be thought of as a "familiar surprise," in which there is a certain amount of "new" coupled with an underlying familiarity. While the presentation format in the book is new, the content is familiar because all the concepts have their roots in hard science or rigorous finance theory.

If I have seen further, it is by standing on the shoulders of giants.

—Isaac Newton

We should stress that most of the ideas in the book are not our own. In many cases, we have simply repackaged well-vetted concepts into what we believe is a much more user-friendly format. As Paul S. has said, think of the book's building blocks as Legos. We did not invent the Legos in our book, although we feel we have built something unique with them.

This book is divided into two primary sections. We selected this structure because an analyst has two distinctively different responsibilities. The analyst's first assignment is to find a good investment, one where there is a large spread between the market price and intrinsic value. This part of the process requires the analyst to calculate the stock's intrinsic value, determine whether a genuine mispricing exists, and identify a catalyst that will close the gap between the stock's price and its intrinsic value, thus correcting the stock's mispricing.

The second part of the process is communicating (pitching) the idea to the portfolio manager. This step requires a completely different set of skills. We have structured the book accordingly, as shown in Figure P.1. (Note: the numbers in the circles correspond with chapter numbers in the book.)

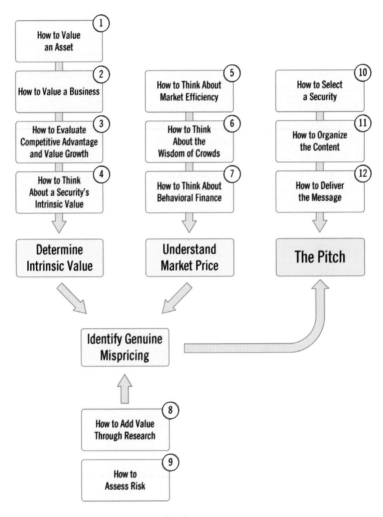

Figure P.1   Pitch the Perfect Investment Roadmap

The first four chapters of the book layout the process of determining a company's intrinsic value. This explanation begins with valuing an asset using a discounted cash flow model in Chapter 1, then uses this approach to value a business in Chapter 2. Because assessing competitive advantage is critical to determining the value of growth, we discuss these topics in depth in Chapter 3. Chapter 4 uses those tools to value a security.

The primary building blocks for these four chapters are based on the work of Warren Buffett, Aswath Damodaran, David Dodd, Mario Gabelli, Benjamin Graham, Bruce Greenwald, Seth Klarman, Michael Mauboussin, Roger Murray, and John Burr Williams.

We then explain how investors set stock prices, which entails a detailed discussion of market efficiency. We begin in Chapter 5 with an examination of Eugene Fama's efficient market hypothesis, where we establish the rules the market follows to set prices. We discuss the wisdom of crowds in Chapter 6 and show how these rules are implemented in the market. We then discuss behavioral finance in Chapter 7 to show how these rules can become strained or broken.

The primary building blocks for these three chapters are based on the work of John Bogel, Nolan Dalla, Eugene Fama, Sir Francis Galton, Benjamin Graham, Daniel Kahneman, Andrew Lo, Michael Mauboussin, Roger Murray, Scott Page, William Sharpe, Robert Shiller, Andrei Shleifer, Ned Smith, James Surowiecki, Amos Tversky, and Robert Vishny.

In Chapter 8 we discuss how to add value through the research process. We show that the investor must develop an **informational advantage**, an **analytical advantage**, or a **trading advantage** to be able to claim that a stock is genuinely mispriced. If the investor cannot identify why other investors are wrong, show why he is right, and articulate what advantage he has, then it is unlikely that he has identified a true mispricing. We end the chapter by defining a catalyst as any event that begins to close the gap between the stock price and your estimate of intrinsic value. The primary building blocks for this chapter come from Eugene Fama and Michael Steinhardt.

In Chapter 9 we demonstrate that risk and uncertainty are not synonymous and show that their difference is misunderstood by most investors. We then highlight the components of an investment's return and emphasize that while most investors focus on their estimate of intrinsic value, time is a critical, although often overlooked, factor. We demonstrate how an investor can significantly reduce risk by increasing the accuracy and precision of both their estimate of intrinsic value and the investment's time horizon. The primary building blocks for this chapter are based on the work of Howard Marks and Nassim Nicholas Taleb.

At this point in the book we will have shown how to vet the perfect investment. The next part discusses the key elements of pitching that investment to a portfolio manager.

We explain in Chapter 10 that for the analyst to select the proper security to pitch, he must know the portfolio manager's selection criteria. We demonstrate that the manager will not even listen, much less adopt, an investment idea unless it matches his investment criteria. We show in Chapter 11 how to organize the content of the pitch to maximize its impact. Finally, we discuss in Chapter 12 the different elements necessary to ensure the effectiveness of the delivery, while minimizing extraneous factors.

The primary building blocks for these three chapters are based on the work of Milo Frank, Marianne LaFrance, John T. Malloy, Alfred Mehrabian, and Stephen Toulmin.

There are other people whose work and ideas were less identifiable as discrete building blocks, but were critical in the development of certain concepts, helped shape our thought process, or simply stretched our thinking. This list includes Per Bak, Sornette Didier, David Dreman, Nancy Duarte, Paul Ekman, David Epstein, D. Craig Fecel, Philip A. Fisher, Richard Gabriel, Malcom Gladwell, Steve Johnson, Gary Klein, Cole Nussbaumer Knaflic, Maria Konnikova, Pierre-Simon Laplace, Daniel J. Levitin, Tim Loughran, Douglas S. Lavine, David Matsumoto, Alfred Rappaport, Antonin Scalia, Nate Silver, Keith E. Stanovitch, Philip E. Tetlock, Richard Thaler, Chris Voss, Duncan Watts, Holly White, and Timothy D. Wilson.

It is not our intention to take credit for anyone else's work. The people mentioned here are individuals whose work contributed to our understanding of the concepts we present in the book. In addition to all the individuals we have previously mentioned, there are numerous other people who have provided an insight or relevant subtlety that we included in the book. In some cases, we make reference to them in the text or in a footnote, but in other cases we may have inadvertently left them out. Any oversight is unintentional and we apologize in advance for not being more diligent with our notes. We will seek to correct this deficiency over time as we assemble a reading list of books and journal papers that we feel were relevant and important in our writing the book, which we will make available on our website, www.pitchtheperfectinvestment.com.

In the words of Judd Kahn, paraphrasing Samuel Johnson, "You never finish a book, you just stop writing." There is a lot more we could have written, but we had to stop somewhere. Please keep in mind that we do not view this book as a definitive treatise. Rather, we have tried to advance the discussion and add to the overall mosaic of available investment literature. For us, writing the book has generated more questions in our minds than it has answered, which we found both exhilarating and terrifying. One can imagine the world as an infinitely long hallway with doors on either side. To us it felt that we were exposed to other worlds we never knew existed every time we opened one of the doors to look inside, which we found exhilarating. The terrifying part is our recognition that there are many more doors in the hallway that we did not have the time to even open.

There are numerous topics that we have not done justice to in this book, some of which will be subjects for us to write about in the future, including: signal detection theory, cognitive psychology, situational awareness, information foraging, and trial advocacy, as well as many areas of decision making, information theory, and storytelling. Stay tuned.

The authors take the position that everyone bleeds the same color blood and are therefore equal. However, for environmental reasons (which we discuss in the next paragraph), economy in writing, and consistency, we wrote primarily in the masculine gender.[12] While our preference would be to use a single pronoun throughout the book, unfortunately, this option does not exist in the English language.

We ask readers to weigh the benefits to the environment when evaluating this decision. By our calculation[13], if we use "he or she" and "him or her" instead of "he" and "him," the book will be longer by approximately four pages. If the book sells 100,000 physical copies over its life (perhaps optimistic), this choice would result in 200,000 extra pages printed (front and back). Since each page

---

[12] Women comprise only 11% of the total number of portfolio managers in the United States. We were surprised when we learned that this number has remained constant over the past twenty years. The low representation is unfortunate because the academic research shows that women generally are better investors than men.

[13] We used the 'Fermi estimation' technique. The classic example of this technique is estimating the number of piano tuners there are in Chicago.

weighs roughly 1.8 grams, the extra pages would total almost 800 pounds of paper. Following math from the Sierra Club, these extra pages would equal approximately four trees. A typical tree absorbs 48 pounds of carbon dioxide (imagine a 48-pound block of dry ice which is solid CO_2) and produces 260 pounds of oxygen per year. If a tree lives for an average of 75 years, and we save four trees, then our choice equals 14,400 pounds of carbon dioxide and 78,000 pounds of oxygen. Although we sometimes struggled with our choice, we justified it for environmental reasons. We could think of no better cognitive dissonance!

A few "housekeeping" items: For economy of writing we primarily use the term "stock" in reference to whatever financial asset we are discussing. However, any security (or any asset, for that matter) can be substituted, including but not limited to a bond, an option, a building, raw land, gold, stamps, and rare snow globes. For the same reason, we usually refer to "purchasing" or "buying" a stock although "selling" or "shorting" can easily be substituted. In some footnotes, rather than providing a link like: https://www.youtube.com/watch?v=pz6ZwIlGfw4 we put "You can google 'Clarence fifth Beatle' to see the full interview" in the footnote. We felt that these types of references will make it easier for the reader by eliminating the possibility of dead links and transcription errors. Throughout the book, we denote **key words** in bold. In certain chapters, we use colors for text that corresponds to colors in diagrams. There will be notes in the relevant chapters conveying this information. In some instances, numbers in tables or figures might not add up. Rest assured that these "errors" are not careless mistakes, but the result of rounding. We could have avoided this issue by using numbers with cents throughout the book, but we thought that the extra "precision" would only add unnecessary clutter to an already complicated set of calculations.

Because of the litigious nature of our society we are compelled to include the following disclaimer: **The views, opinions, and interpretations expressed are those of the authors and do not necessarily represent the views of their respective firms, the individuals who have been referenced, nor any firms with whom they may be affiliated**.

Finally, as is convention, we take full responsibility for the many errors, omissions, and compromises that remain.

If you are new to the investment business, we hope this book prepares you for what you will encounter. You are at the beginning of a journey that will never end. Buckle up and enjoy the ride.

Introduction

Whether you are a portfolio manager pitching on CNBC or a young analyst just out of school pitching a stock in a job interview,[1] the stakes are extremely high. Everyone in the investment business needs to find great ideas and then pitch them to their audience to succeed on Wall Street.

The title of this book contains two critical components—**pitching** and **the perfect investment**. In it, we provide a detailed road map to help you identify great investment ideas and a set of guidelines to pitch those ideas with the goal of *getting your audience to act*. If you don't have a great investment idea, there is nothing to pitch. If you have a great idea but cannot communicate it, your pitch will fall on deaf ears.

The person making the buy or sell decision is the person to whom you are pitching. That person is most often a portfolio manager whose goal is to beat the market, which means he needs to earn an investment return above the market return after fees and adjusting for risk. The portfolio manager's most important concern is performance and, to generate good performance, the manager needs to find **ideas** to put into his portfolio that will beat the market. If a portfolio manager hears a compelling pitch and believes that the idea will outperform, he will begin salivating like one of Pavlov's dogs.

---

[1] It is important to recognize that *all* job interviews in the investment business are essentially stock pitches. A stock pitch gives the portfolio manager an idea of how you think and whether you can do the job. The interview may start with a question like, "Tell me about your favorite class in college." However, the manager is biding his time until he can ask his primary interest, "So, what's your best idea?"

The ideal outcome of a stock pitch is that your idea is so captivating in both its **content** and **delivery** that the portfolio manager feels compelled to immediately "clear his desk" and begin work for fear of missing an opportunity to help him outperform the market.

One of the primary challenges all analysts face is determining the value of a stock, which represents a fractional ownership of a business. The book begins by laying the foundation of how to value an asset, where we discuss the different subcomponents of cash flow: **timing**, **duration**, **magnitude**, and **growth**, as well as **uncertainty** and the **time value of money**, all of which impact an asset's value, as we show in Figure I.1.

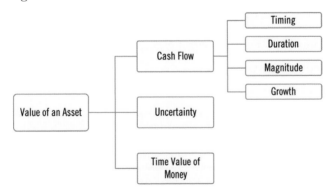

Figure I.1   Factors Influencing the Value of an Asset

We then address the importance of discounting future cash flows in determining an asset's value, which is also a critical component in the foundation of valuing a business, as illustrated in Figure I.2:

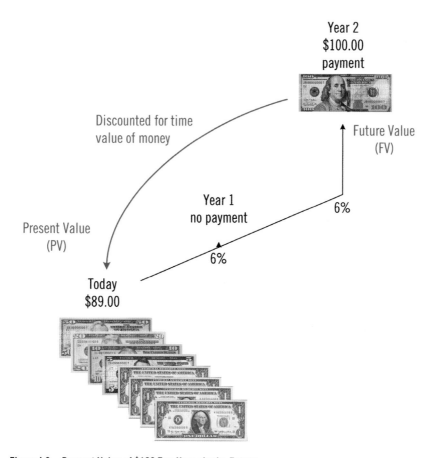

Figure I.2   Present Value of $100 Two Years in the Future

With the goal of ultimately determining the value of a stock, we start the process with simple examples, and then relax constraints, adding more complexity to the analysis, while building up to real-world examples. We use a simple DCF to value a "plain vanilla" bond, then a perpetuity, and then a stream of cash flows, as we show in Figure I.3.

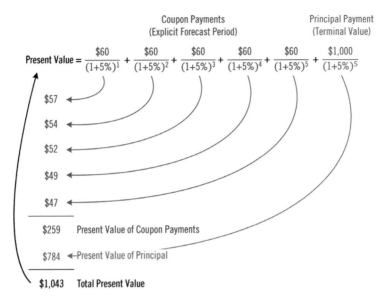

$$\text{Present Value} = \frac{\$60}{(1+5\%)^1} + \frac{\$60}{(1+5\%)^2} + \frac{\$60}{(1+5\%)^3} + \frac{\$60}{(1+5\%)^4} + \frac{\$60}{(1+5\%)^5} + \frac{\$1,000}{(1+5\%)^5}$$

Coupon Payments (Explicit Forecast Period)

Principal Payment (Terminal Value)

$57
$54
$52
$49
$47

$259   Present Value of Coupon Payments

$784   ← Present Value of Principal

$1,043   Total Present Value

Figure I.3   Present Value of a Plain-Vanilla Bond

With these tools, we then take on the challenge of calculating the value of a simple business—a neighborhood lemonade stand. We start the analysis with the assumption that the lemonade stand does not grow or face competition, which makes the initial valuation task much simpler.

However, since all businesses face competition in the real world, we need to relax this assumption and assess the company's competitive advantage, as it is a critical component when estimating future cash flows and determining the value of growth. We show that without an identifiable barrier that prevents other companies from entering the market, competitive pressures will erode the lemonade stand's excess returns, which we show will have a significant negative impact on its future cash flow and overall valuation, as seen in Figure I.4.

Figure I.4   Competitive Pressure Drives Excess Returns to Zero

Once we explain how competitive advantage impacts a company's future cash flow and return on invested capital, we turn to the very real challenges of valuing growth. Most people believe that *all* growth is good. We show that the perceived value of growth can be misleading, as not all growth produces *actual value*. We use several examples to illustrate the difference between good growth, bad growth, and worthless growth, which we suspect might surprise some readers.

We culminate the valuation section by discussing the concept of intrinsic value and defer to Warren Buffett, Professor Roger Murray, and Seth Klarman to explain why it is important to think about the stock's intrinsic value as a range of values rather than a single-point estimate or number.

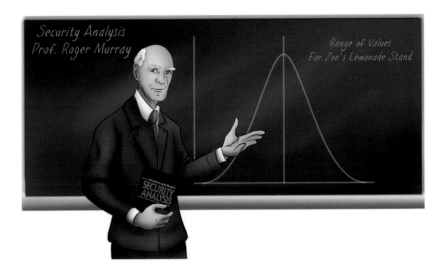

We have found that most analysts spend an inordinate amount of time conducting exhaustive research believing the goal is to arrive at a precise and accurate estimate of a company's intrinsic value. They then compare their estimates of the company's value with the market price and, if there is a large enough disparity between them, declare the security as mispriced, which they then claim represents a significant opportunity to make money. When the analyst finally pitches the stock to a portfolio manager, they are left dumbfounded that the idea is rejected. The analyst does not know what went wrong with the pitch and usually is perplexed as to why the portfolio manager did not adopt the idea.

INCOMPLETE INFORMATION

Paul S. and Paul J. participated at a recent stock pitch competition as judges. There were four presentations. It was apparent that the students performed exhaustive research on the companies they pitched and demonstrated successfully why their estimate of intrinsic value was correct. Based on their price targets, each investment idea promised a return that would generate significant return.

Nonetheless, Paul and Paul felt uneasy with each analyst's recommendation. What caused their discomfort? Several times during the presentations, Paul leaned over and whispered to Paul, "Yeah, it sounds like a great business and seems cheap, but is it *mispriced*? Are other investors missing something or are we?"

The fact remains that all the research in the world will not matter if the analyst cannot articulate why the stock is mispriced. While the analyst might present a convincing argument that his estimate for the value of a stock is correct, the portfolio manager will never feel comfortable adopting the idea without a complete understanding of what other investors are missing.

To address this concern, we begin the discussion of market efficiency by providing tools to more fully understand how the market prices stocks and identify whether a genuine mispricing exists. We first highlight the difficulty of beating the market, discuss the efficient market hypothesis, and then explain what it means for a stock to be efficiently priced. This framework stresses the role information plays in market efficiency and shows that an efficiently priced stock is one that "fully reflects all available information." From here we establish the conditions or **rules** required for market efficiency (Figure I.5).

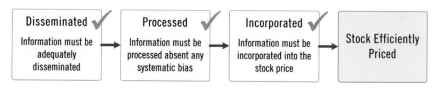

Figure I.5   The Three Rules of Market Efficiency

We then demonstrate that the wisdom of crowds is the mechanism governing the tenets of market efficiency. Although many investors claim to understand the wisdom of crowds, the concept is often articulated simply as "The crowd will arrive at a better answer than the individual." This oversimplification misses critical elements of what makes a crowd wise and what factors drive it to madness. We present several examples that highlight different facets to explain how the wisdom of crowds functions. We use stories like the Beatles' forgotten *Aloha from Hawaii* album, featuring the infamous fifth

Beatle, Clarence Walker,[2] to show that the crowd does not need much information to arrive at the correct answer, although we also show that false or wrong information can skew the outcome and result in a systematic error.

After establishing a firm understanding of the wisdom of crowds, we discuss how the process applies to the stock market. We explain that for the consensus (the crowd) to arrive at an accurate estimate of value, the following four conditions must be met:

1. Information must be available and noticed by a sufficient number of investors.
2. The group of investors must be diverse.
3. Investors must act independently from one another.
4. Investors cannot face significant impediments to trading, otherwise information will not be incorporated into the stock price.

---

[2] Those who did not grow up with *Saturday Night Live* might not know that Clarence was in fact the fifth Beatle. Simply Google "Clarence fifth Beatle" to see the full interview where he tells his story.

We then show that the consensus can arrive at the wrong estimate of a stock's value when errors occur in the **dissemination, processing,** or **incorporation** of information, which alone or together
can cause mispricings.

We then turn attention to behavioral finance, which is believed
by many people to be an alternative to the efficient market hypothesis.
We discuss how human behavior can turn the wisdom of crowds into
the madness of crowds, but *only* if the collective's behavior produces
a systematic error causing the market to lose its diversity or suffer a
breakdown in independence, which are two crucial conditions that
make crowds wise. We also explain how human behavior can limit
the incorporation of information, which can also cause a stock to be
mispriced.

By this point in the book, we will have established the rules of
market efficiency and shown how the wisdom of crowds implements
those rules. We also will have demonstrated how human behavior
(behavioral finance) can muck up the works and cause the wisdom
of crowds to lose its effectiveness. This section ends by demonstrating why **behavioral finance is not an alternative to the efficient market hypothesis; rather, is a part of the efficient market hypothesis**,
as we illustrate in Figure I.6.

Figure I.6   Market Efficiency and Behavioral Finance Coexist

Armed with these insights, we show the analyst how to begin
his research process with the goal of finding situations where

genuine mispricings exist. The book establishes the importance of having a variant perspective, a concept created by legendary investor Michael Steinhardt. We show that developing a variant perspective helps the analyst identify the source of the mispricing and provides a process to establish an advantage or edge in the market. The discussion describes the three potential advantages an investor can develop, which mirror the three tenets of market efficiency:

1. An **informational advantage** is when the investor has information other investors do not have that has not been adequately **disseminated** in the market. With an informational advantage the investor can state, "I know this will happen."
2. An **analytical advantage** is when the investor looks at the exact same data set as other investors but sees things that other investors don't see. However, with an analytical advantage the investor can only state, "I think this will happen."
3. A **trading advantage** is when the investor can trade or hold the security when other investors are unable or unwilling to take or hold a position.[3]

We also discuss the concept of a **catalyst**, which we show is defined as any event that begins to correct the stock's mispricing. By the end of this section, you will have the tools to determine if you have a true variant perspective, if the perceived mispricing is genuine, and if you possess an advantage or edge over other investors.

We then focus the discussion on risk. The terms *risk* and *uncertainty* are used interchangeably in the investment business and often are misunderstood. We discuss the difference between the two terms and explain that **uncertainty** is defined as a situation where the potential outcome is indeterminate, while **risk** is defined as the possibility of loss or injury. We then show that financial risk is present *only* when capital is committed, which is the *only* time an investor has the possibility of financial loss. We further demonstrate that there are *two* types of risk when an investor commits capital—being wrong in estimating intrinsic value or in estimating the time it takes for the mispricing to correct, as we show in Figure I.7.

---

[3] Many people mistakenly believe that the third advantage is behavioral in nature. It is not. Drawing a different conclusion from observing the behavior of other investors clearly falls in the **analytical advantage** category.

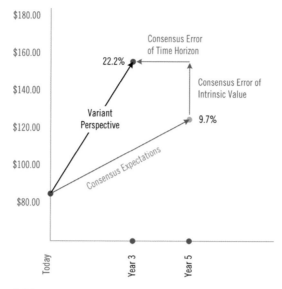

Figure I.7   Two Potential Errors to the Consensus Expectations

We also highlight how one can mitigate these risks by increasing the precision and accuracy of the estimates of value and time, using the targets in Figure I.8 to illustrate the point and show how the two measures can reduce investment risk, as seen in Figure I.9.

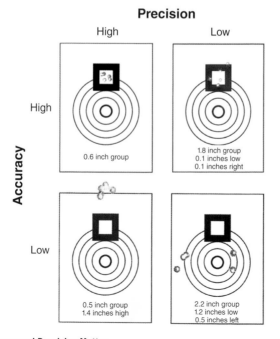

Figure I.8   Accuracy and Precision Matter

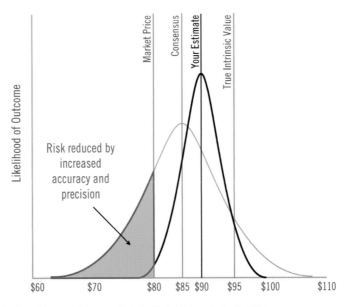

Figure I.9   Precision and Accuracy Substantially Reduce Potential Risk

At this point in the book, we will have explained how to:

1. Calculate the range of intrinsic values for a stock.
2. Articulate why the stock is mispriced.
3. Determine whether you have a variant perspective and an advantage over other investors.
4. Assess the investment's level of risk.

In other words, you will have all the tools you need to vet *the perfect investment.*

The book then turns to pitching. We show that the portfolio manager has four key investment questions he needs answered concerning any idea he is pitched before he will take action. We explain that the manager's first instinct, when hearing a new idea, is *greed,* and the question that comes to mind is, "How much money can I make?" However, *fear* begins to get the better of him as he shifts his thinking from "How much can I make?" to "How much can I lose?," which becomes the second question he needs answered.

If the idea offers sufficient return given the level of risk, there is a third factor that needs to be addressed, which reflects the portfolio manager's unease that the opportunity looks too good to be true. The question the manager asks himself at this point is, "Why me, O Lord?"[4] and the analyst will need to convince him that a genuine mispricing exists to answer this question successfully.

Once this concern is put to rest, the portfolio manager most-likely will raise one final issue—"How and when will the next guy figure it out?"—knowing that he will only make money if other investors eventually recognize and correct the mispricing.

The portfolio manager will adopt an idea only if the four questions are answered to his satisfaction. We show how to use Steinhardt's framework to structure answers to address the manager's four key questions and arrive at the *perfect pitch*, as demonstrated in Figure I.10.

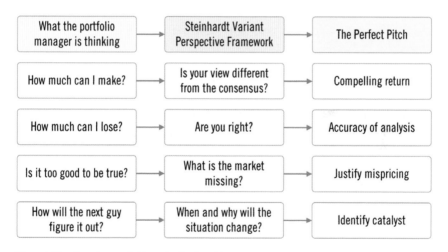

Figure I.10   Questions to Achieve the Perfect Pitch

Because portfolio managers expect analysts to supply them with compelling investment opportunities, the analyst's primary role is to find and present ideas that will beat the market.

---

[4] This is the question Judd Kahn always asked when he challenged Paul S. on an investment idea.

Analyst   Portfolio Manager

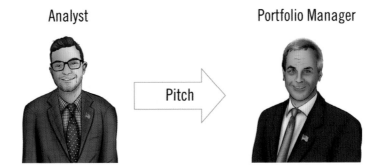

Pitch

However, since the portfolio manager's success depends on his investment performance, he will be *extremely selective* about which ideas he selects for his portfolio and will put any new idea under intense scrutiny to identify its flaws. The analyst must be able to defend his analysis to survive this grilling.

Portfolio managers are also extremely busy. They are inundated with information and pitched new ideas throughout the day, and are always short on time. To the portfolio manager, his time is a finite resource and most precious asset. Therefore, he will be also *extremely selective* in allocating his time and, if the analyst is given an opportunity to pitch his idea, the analyst must be quick, concise, and persuasive.[5]

We provide the tools to overcome these challenges. We show that the most effective pitch is organized into three segments: a **30-second hook**, a **2-minute drill**, and a **longer period of Q&A**. The hook must be simple, succinct, and extremely compelling. The goal of the 30-second hook is to capture the portfolio manager's attention and leave him wanting to know more about the idea, which leads naturally into the 2-minute drill. The 2-minute drill allows the analyst to articulate his main arguments, address the manager's four questions, and further express the attractiveness of the investment. The objective of the 2-minute drill is to draw the portfolio manager further into the idea and entice him to engage in Q&A, which allows him to ask questions concerning issues and topics the analyst did not address in the first two stages. We have found that this three-segment structure makes the most efficient use of the portfolio manager's time and maximizes the chance that the analyst's idea gets adopted.

---

[5] According to Lindsay Previdi, who screens investment talent for billionaire investor Steven Schonfeld, most interviewees repeatedly make the mistake of failing to state their recommendation upfront when pitching their idea. Her advice: "Don't bury the lede!"

Most portfolio managers will have their guard up concerning any new investment idea they are pitched. Imagine that they have a highly alert, slightly paranoid, heavily armed[6] sentinel in their head to protect them from bad investment ideas and from individuals wanting to waste their time. We can call this guard Dr. No.[7] This layer of protection produces obstacles that the analyst must overcome to get her idea adopted.

We show there are three primary components to the structure of a pitch: **security selection**, the **content of the message**, and the **delivery of the message**.

Overcome Obstacles

A typical pitch plays out like a scene from the movie *Wall Street*, when a young Bud Fox finagles his way into Gordon Gekko's office and gets a precious few minutes of Gekko's time. Gekko quickly gets down to business, stating, as he looks up at Fox, "So what's on your mind, kemosabe? Why am I listening to you?" In the movie, Fox pitches his first idea: "Chart breakout on this one here. Whitewood-Young Industries. Low P/E, explosive earnings,

---

[6] In fact, the sentinel is armed with an Eliseo RTS Tubegun, chambered in a 6.5 × 47 Lapua, was the rifle used to shoot the targets in Figure I.8.

[7] A portfolio manager usually defaults to "no" when hearing a new investment idea. As Chris Flynn, one of Paul S.'s co-workers at Royce, often said, "Owning a stock is usually painful and something I seek to avoid. I do exhaustive research to find reasons why I *shouldn't* buy a stock. If, in the end, I can't find a good reason *not* to own it, I will reluctantly buy it." Bill Ackman once said that he tries to think of anything and everything that could possibly go wrong and if, at the end of the process, all that is left is nuclear war, he buys the stock.

30% discount to book value, great cash flow, strong management and a couple of 5% holders." Gekko shuts him down, "It's a dog. What else you got, sport?"[8]

Interestingly, art imitating life as this scene is all too common in the investment business. Fox may have done extensive research on Whitewood-Young, but it was clearly not the right stock to pitch to Gekko.

Portfolio managers have a template in their mind of what *their* perfect investment looks like, called a **schema**. A schema is a type of mental model comprised of the manager's implicit checklist of investment criteria. The manager's investment schemas are shaped by their **domain-specific knowledge**, which is comprised of the facts and experiences they have accumulated over their lifetime.

When evaluating a new idea, the portfolio manager compares it to their schema through the process of **pattern recognition**[9] to see if the idea matches a favorable pattern or should be rejected.

---

[8] *Wall Street*. Directed by Oliver Stone. Twentieth Century Fox Film Corporation, 1987.

[9] The true process is called "Recognition-Primed Decision-Making," where individuals use their experience to form patterns. When making a decision, an individual attempts to match the situation to patterns they have learned and experienced from the past. Doing this comparison allows them to make rapid decisions. This theory was developed in the 1980s by Gary A. Klein and is discussed in his book "*Sources of Power: How People Make Decisions.*"

The critical first step in the analyst's process is to find an idea that fits the portfolio manager's schema. Determining if an investment idea will appeal to a portfolio manager is like determining if the portfolio manager would find a bacon sundae appealing.[10] Similar to a schema of the perfect investment idea, the manager probably has a schema for the perfect sundae. When the manager is presented with a "new idea" such as a bacon sundae, they use their "sundae schema" to decide if the new sundae appeals to them, as we show in Figure I.11.

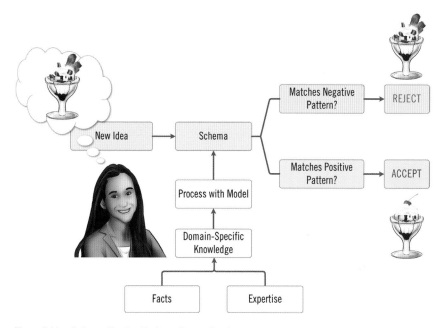

Figure I.11   Schema Used to Evaluate Bacon Sundae

As we emphasize throughout the book, it is critical for the analyst to find an idea that fits the portfolio manager's schema. Most young analysts make the understandable mistake of pitching an idea that *they* like rather than one that the portfolio manager will like. This approach is like concluding, "I like bacon sundaes, so the portfolio manager will like them, too." However, whether you like bacon or bacon sundaes

---

[10] We did not fabricate this story. During the summer of 2012, Burger King offered a bacon sundae with soft vanilla ice cream, topped with hot fudge, caramel, bacon crumbles, and a slice of bacon. Neither author tried one.

is irrelevant. The only question you need to answer is, "Does the portfolio manager likes bacon sundaes?" This insight stresses the importance of identifying and understanding the criteria that comprise the portfolio manager's investment schema, which we show in Figure I.12, and then selecting an appropriate stock to match it.

Figure I.12   Portfolio Manager's Stated Criteria

Unfortunately, achieving this insight is not an easy task. We explain that while some of the manager's criteria will be **objective** and articulated clearly, other criteria will be **subjective** and open to interpretation. Making the task even more challenging is the fact that the manager often has additional criteria that are **unstated**. The lack of specificity in the **subjective** criteria makes it difficult for the analyst to uncover, decipher, and satisfy all the requirements in the manager's schema. The fact that some of the criteria remains unstated makes the task all that more challenging.

An experienced portfolio manager's schemas have been refined through decades of investing and become more complex and nuanced as the manager gains additional experience. Over time, a manager's investment criteria get so ingrained in his mind that it becomes second nature and almost impossible to articulate fully.

Because the criteria have become second nature, there is no *explicit* checklist in the manager's mind that the idea must match; rather, he gets a certain "feeling" when he hears a good idea. Consequentially, most seasoned portfolio managers often are unable to fully articulate their criteria. A quote from legendary investor Leon Cooperman epitomizes this phenomenon perfectly:

> We try to find some set of statistics that motivate us to act. The analogy I have always used is that when you go into the beer section of the supermarket, you see 25 different brands of beer. There's something that makes you reach for one particular brew. In the parlance of the stock market, there's some combination of return-on-equity, growth rate, P/E ratio, dividend yield, and asset value that makes you act.[11]

Although satisfying the portfolio manager's objective criteria will get him to at least listen to the pitch, the manager will reject the idea if it fails to satisfy his stated subjective *and* any unstated criteria, as shown in Figure I.13. We show the analyst how to assess the different criteria necessary to get the portfolio manager to adopt his idea, with careful attention paid to cracking the code of his subjective criteria.

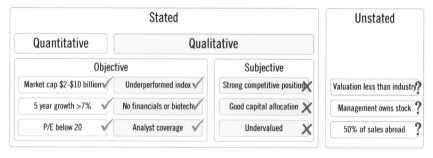

Figure I.13   Subjective Criteria Not Satisfied and Unstated Criteria Unknown

---

[11] "Lee Cooperman—Buying Straw Hats in the Winter," *Graham & Doddsville*, Fall 2011, 5.

Once the analyst has selected an idea appropriate for the portfolio manager and completed the necessary research to fully understand the opportunity, the information must be organized carefully into the **content** of the message. Using the Toulmin model of argumentation, we show how to structure this information to create persuasive and convincing arguments. We then walk through the most effective way to stress test, and then present, these arguments to maximize their impact when presented.

Finally, once the analyst has organized the message, constructed the arguments, and battle-hardened all elements of the content, he is ready to deliver his pitch.

We stress the importance of keeping presentation materials simple and focused on answering the portfolio manager's four key investment questions. We also show that most information gathered through the research process is extraneous and unnecessary *to the pitch*.[12] Despite this fact, most analysts insist on packing too much content onto their slides. They are either trying to demonstrate the exhaustive research they have performed or do not know what information is most relevant to their pitch. This approach often results in the analyst losing the forest for the trees as their main arguments become lost in a sea of data. Unfortunately, a presentation that contains superfluous information increases the portfolio manager's cognitive load significantly and forces them to extract the relevant message themselves. Faced with a disorganized, albeit data intensive presentation, most managers will throw up their hands in frustration, abandon the pitch, and lose interest in the idea.

---

[12] While the information gathered through the research process is of vital importance in fully *vetting* the idea, it is not necessary to include in the actual pitch.

We emphasize the fact that multitasking is a myth and explain that a portfolio manager can pay attention to only one thing at a time. Therefore, if his attention is absorbed in trying to decipher a data-packed slide, he is not listening to the analyst, which undermines the effectiveness of the pitch. Therefore, when choosing accompanying information to present, the analyst should stay focused on keeping the slides simple and addressing only the key points to the message, as seen in Figure I.14. We encourage the analyst to heed the sage words of Judd Kahn, "Less is more."

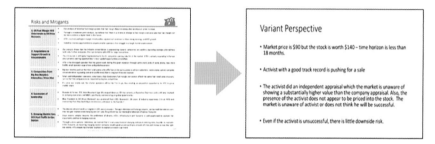

Figure I.14   Less is More

Since the analyst is the one delivering the content of the message, the impression he makes can have a significant impact on the portfolio manager's receptivity to his recommendation. We use envelopes to illustrate this point. Imagine the manager has asked you to send a write-up of your analysis and recommendation ahead of the meeting. You can choose either of the following two envelopes. Which one would make a better impression?

You might ask, "Why should the envelope matter? They both contain the *exact* same message. Isn't it the content that is most important?" The answer is, "Yes, but ..."

It is obvious which of the two envelopes makes a better impression. We use the example to bring attention to the numerous non-verbal factors that will affect the portfolio manager's receptivity to the analyst and his pitch. While having nothing to do with the content of the message, these additional considerations will influence the portfolio manager's perception of the analyst's capability and credibility. We discuss important factors such as eye contact, physical gestures, posture, dress, hair style, and, believe it or not, how the wearing of glasses makes you look intelligent. After all, if the content of the message is the same, whose recommendation would you take?

Let's begin the journey. We hope you find that this book helps you succeed on Wall Street.

THE PERFECT INVESTMENT

The goal in Part I of the book is to show how to identify the perfect investment, which we explain is one where a stock has been mispriced. We also show that the investor must identify a path for the mispricing to correct and be able to exploit the opportunity. To determine if a stock is mispriced, the analyst needs to calculate the stock's intrinsic value, which we cover in detail in the first four chapters of the book.

We define the value of an asset in Chapter 1 and show how it is valued using a discounted cash flow model. We use this approach to value a business in Chapter 2. Because assessing competitive advantage is critical to determining the value of growth, we discuss these topics in depth in Chapter 3. Finally, we use these tools in Chapter 4 to show how to think about a security's intrinsic value.

To determine if a genuine mispricing exists, we need to define the conditions under which a stock will be efficiently priced, which requires a detailed discussion of market efficiency. We begin in Chapter 5 with an explanation of Eugene Fama's efficient market hypothesis, which we show are the rules the market follows to set prices. We then discuss the wisdom of crowds in Chapter 6 and show it as the mechanism that implements the rules in the market. We then explore behavioral finance in Chapter 7 and show how the rules can become strained or broken when a systematic error skews the crowd's view.

To establish if a mispricing is genuine, the investor must demonstrate that he has either an informational advantage, an analytical advantage, or a trading advantage. If the investor cannot identify specifically why other investors are wrong, show why he is right, and articulate what advantage he has, then it is unlikely he has identified a stock that is truly mispriced. We discuss these topics in Chapter 8 and then define a catalyst as any event that begins to close the gap between the stock price and your estimate of intrinsic value.

In Chapter 9 we show that risk and uncertainty are not the same thing and that the difference is often misunderstood. We then discuss the three components of investment return—the price you pay, your estimate of intrinsic value, and the estimated time horizon. It is the authors' experience that most investors spend the bulk of their time focusing on calculating their estimate of intrinsic value, while failing to estimate accurately an investment's time horizon. We feel this focus is a mistake as time is a critical factor in determining the investment's ultimate return. We then move the discussion to how through research an investor can significantly reduce risk by increasing the accuracy and precision of both the estimates of intrinsic value and the investment's time horizon.

By the end of Part I we will have shown how to vet the perfect investment.

C H A P T E R

How to Value an Asset

Pearls of Wisdom

Valuing an asset is a relatively simple concept: The value of an asset is the cash flows produced by that asset, over its useful life, discounted for the time value of money and the uncertainty of receiving those cash flows.

Three Primary Components of Value

In this chapter, we discuss the three main components necessary to calculate the value of an asset: the cash flows, the uncertainty of receiving the cash flows, and the time value of money. We show these components in Figure 1.1.

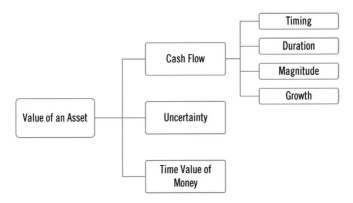

Figure 1.1   Primary Components to the Value of an Asset

Four Subcomponents of Cash Flow

The first part of the definition, "Cash flows produced by that asset, over its useful life," includes four subcomponents: **timing**, **duration**, **magnitude**, and **growth**, as shown in Figure 1.2.

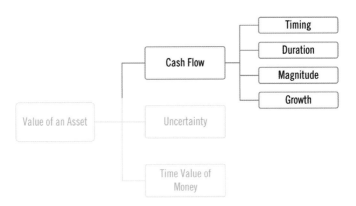

Figure 1.2   Four Cash Flow Subcomponents

The first subcomponent, **timing**, addresses the question, "When will we get the cash?" Will we get the cash flow next year or in five years? While the amount of the cash flow is the same in Figures 1.3A and B, the cash flow is received sooner in A than in B. All else being equal, getting cash sooner is better than getting it later.

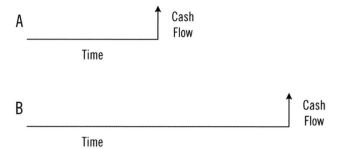

Figure 1.3   Getting Cash Sooner Is Preferable

The second subcomponent, **duration**, addresses the question, "How long will the cash flows last?" **Duration**[1] can be thought of as an asset's estimated useful life. For example, an annuity that pays each year for eight years is more valuable than one that pays for only four years, as shown in Figure 1.4. A longer duration of cash flows is better than a shorter one.

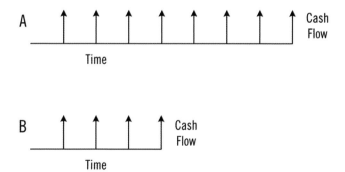

Figure 1.4   A Longer Duration of Cash Flows Is Preferable

The third subcomponent, **magnitude**, addresses the question, "How much cash will we get?" Figure 1.5 shows a stream of $4 payments versus a similar stream of $2 payments. It should be obvious that larger cash flows are better than smaller ones.

---

[1] The term *duration* is used to indicate how long the cash flows will last and should not be confused with the same term's use in discussing bond valuations.

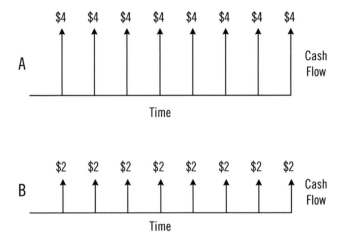

Figure 1.5   A Greater Magnitude in Cash Flows Is Preferable

The fourth subcomponent, **growth**, addresses the questions, "Will the cash flows grow over time?" or "How fast will the cash flow grow over time?" A growing stream of cash flow is preferable to one that is not growing (A versus B), as shown in Figure 1.6.

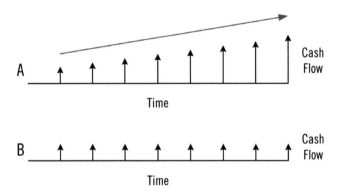

Figure 1.6   Growing Cash Flows Are Preferable

When starting at the same level, a stream of cash flows with a faster growth rate is preferable to one with a slower growth rate (A versus B), as shown in Figure 1.7.

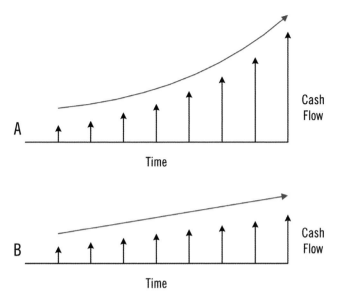

Figure 1.7   Faster Growing Cash Flows Are Preferable

A stable cash flow is preferable to one with a negative growth rate or losses, as shown in Figure 1.8. (Note: Arrows pointing down in B represent cash *outflows* reflecting losses.)

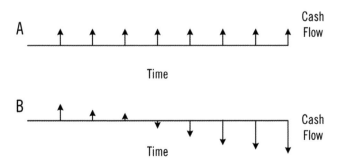

Figure 1.8   Stable Cash Flows Are Preferable to Negative or Declining Cash Flows

It is important to note that it is necessary to make estimates for *all* four subcomponents—**timing**, **duration**, **magnitude**, and **growth**—to calculate the asset's future cash flow.

Uncertainty

The second part of the definition states that the cash flows need to be "discounted for . . . the uncertainty of receiving those cash flows." There was no uncertainty to the cash flows up to this point in the discussion as we assumed that they were *known* and guaranteed (similar to the coupon payments from a U.S. Treasury Bond). However, an asset's cash flows will be dependent on events that will happen in the future, and because the future is inherently uncertain, we must take **uncertainty** into account when addressing the question, "How certain are the future cash flows?"

It is important to note that *uncertainty* will have an impact on all four cash flow subcomponents and, in turn, affect the asset's value, as shown in Figure 1.9.

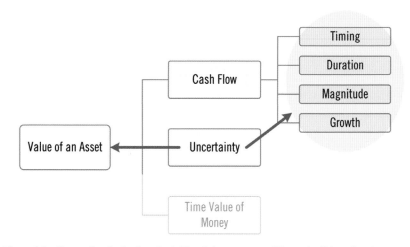

Figure 1.9   Uncertainty in the Four Cash Flow Subcomponents Affects the Value of an Asset

Even the most predictable cash flows have some degree of uncertainty to them, however. Therefore, we need to think of any cash flow we calculate as an *estimate* of the *expected* cash flow rather than a guaranteed amount.

Before we proceed further we need to alter slightly the definition of an asset's value to reflect this observation:

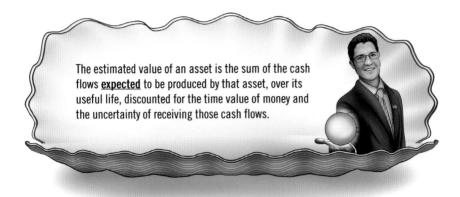

The estimated value of an asset is the sum of the cash flows **expected** to be produced by that asset, over its useful life, discounted for the time value of money and the uncertainty of receiving those cash flows.

Rather than thinking about future cash flows as single-point estimates, as shown in Figure 1.10, it is more appropriate to think about a *range of cash flow estimates,* around a single-point estimate.

Figure 1.10   Single-Point Cash Flow Estimate

For instance, while we *expect* the cash flow to equal $4 in this example, we need to recognize that there is a possibility that the actual cash flow will be greater or less than $4, within a *forecasted range* of $2 to $6, as shown in Figure 1.11.

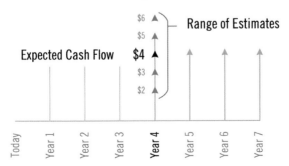

Figure 1.11   Range of Cash Flow Estimates

Another way of depicting the full range of possible estimates is to think of it as a **distribution** of potential cash flow estimates spreading out, in both directions, around a single-point estimate, as shown in Figure 1.12. The graph shows the range of possible outcomes, with values closest to the single-point estimate representing the outcomes with higher probabilities of being the true cash flow received, while cash flow estimates in the tails of the distribution represent outcomes that have lower probabilities of occurring.

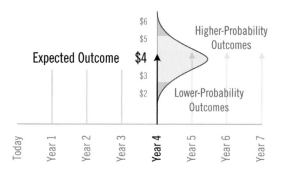

Figure 1.12   Distribution of Cash Flow Estimates

It is hard to predict the future. The charts in Figure 1.13 show how the distributions of possible outcomes widen and the expected point estimates become less predictable as uncertainty increases the further we forecast cash flows into the future. We use the increasingly blurry $100 bill to provide a visual representation of this reality.

(Note: We rotated the diagram to create a 3D image so that the probability distribution of the estimate can be seen on the z-axis, while time remains on the x-axis and estimated cash flows on the y-axis.)

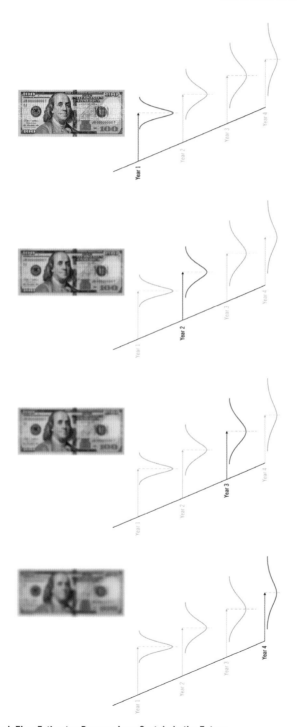

Figure 1.13   Cash Flow Estimates Become Less Certain in the Future

Figure 1.14 combines the individual cash flow distributions from Figure 1.13 into a single chart, showing how the uncertainty of estimating cash flow increases as we look further into the future.

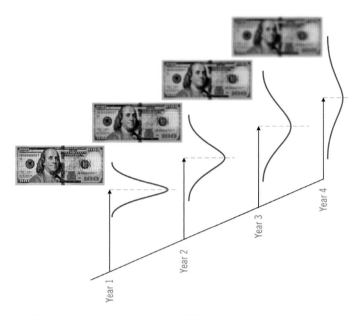

Figure 1.14   The Range of Cash Flows Estimates Widens in the Future

The Time Value of Money

The final component of the definition of an asset's value states that its cash flows must be "discounted for the time value of money." Discounting for time is a straightforward concept: A dollar today is worth more than a dollar in the future, or thought of another way, "A bird in the hand is worth two in the bush."[2] The value of cash flows today is referred to as their **present value**.

It is often easier for most people to understand the concept of **present value** after a discussion of **future value**, which is based on **compounding**. For example, with a 6% annual rate of return, $100 today increases in value to $106.00 in one year and $112.36 in two years, as shown in Figure 1.15.

---

[2] As finance professors, we have always been intrigued by this comment. For a "bird in hand" to be "worth two in the bush" suggests either a very high discount rate or great uncertainty that there are, in fact, two birds in the bush. It might also reflect the fact that birds are very difficult to catch with your hands. So maybe the high discount rate is appropriate.

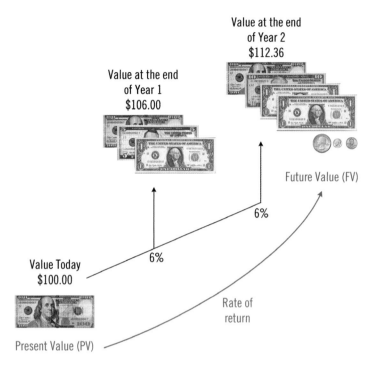

Figure 1.15   Future Value of $100

The value of $100 in one year is calculated by compounding the initial value by 6%, as shown in the following computation:

Future value at end of year 1 = $100.00 * (1 + 6%) = $106.00

The value at the end of the second year is calculated the same way, by compounding the value at the end of the first year by the same 6% for the second year:

Future value at the end of year 2 = $106.00 * (1 + 6%) = $112.36

Alternatively, the value at the end of year 2 can be calculated by compounding the initial cash flow by two periods of 6% interest, as shown in the following calculation:

Future value at the end of year 2 = $100.00 * (1 + 6%) * (1 + 6%) = $112.36

The following formulas can be used to calculate the future value of any amount of money:

Future value at the end of year 1 = $\$_1 = \$_0 * (1 + i)$

Future value at the end of year 2 = $\$_2 = \$_1 * (1 + i)$

Or, alternatively:

$$\text{Future value at the end of year } 2 = \$_2 = \$_0 * (1 + i) * (1 + i)$$

Which is the equivalent of (using simpler notation):

$$\text{Future value at the end of year } 2 = \$_2 = \$_0 (1 + i)^2$$

Where:

$\$_0$ equals the value of cash today
$\$_1$ equals the value of cash in one year
$\$_2$ equals the value of cash in two years
i represents the return on investment

To calculate the **present value** of a future $100 payment, we need to **discount** it to find its value in today's dollars, which is essentially compounding in reverse. For simplicity, we use the same 6% rate and show that a cash payment of $100 one year from now discounted at 6% is worth $94.34 today, as shown in Figure 1.16.

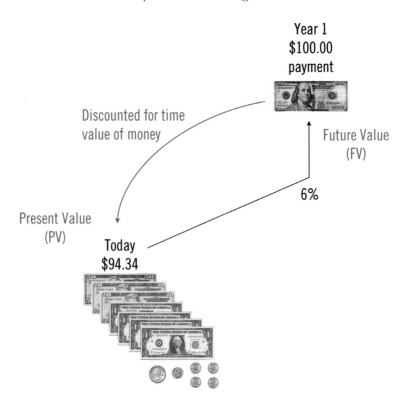

Figure 1.16   Present Value of $100 One Year in the Future

The formula for discounting future payments is similar to the one used to calculate the future value of cash, with the components in the formula rearranged:

$$\text{Present Value}\,(PV) = \frac{\$_1}{(1+i)^1} + \frac{\$_2}{(1+i)^2}$$

Therefore, the present value of $100 at a 6% discount rate is calculated as follows:

$$\text{Present Value}\,(PV) = \frac{\$100.00}{(1+6\%)^1}$$

$$PV = \frac{\$100.00}{1.06} = \$94.34$$

It should be straightforward to show that a cash payment of $100 two years from now discounted at 6% is worth $89.00 today, as shown in Figure 1.17.

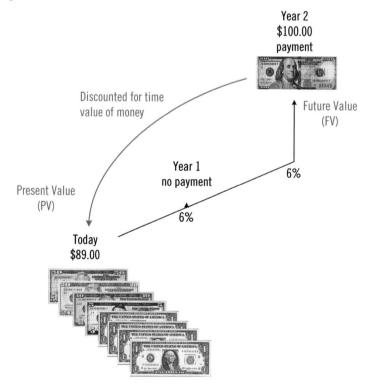

Figure 1.17   Present Value of $100 Two Years in the Future

Using the same formula from above:

$$\text{Present Value (PV)} = \frac{\$100.00}{\left(1+6\%\right)^2}$$

$$PV = \frac{\$100.00}{1.124} = \$89.00$$

Alternatively, if we assume that there is a $100 payment in year 2, but no payment in year 1, then we can use the slightly more complicated formula to show that the present value of the two payments at a 6% discount rate also equals $89.00, as the following calculation shows:

$$\text{Present Value (PV)} = \frac{\$_1}{\left(1+i\right)^1} + \frac{\$_2}{\left(1+i\right)^2}$$

$$\text{Present Value (PV)} = \frac{\$0.00}{\left(1+6\%\right)^1} + \frac{\$100.00}{\left(1+6\%\right)^2}$$

$$\text{Present Value (PV)} = \frac{\$0.00}{1.06} + \frac{\$100.00}{1.124}$$

$$PV = \$0.00 + \$89.00 = \$89.00$$

To calculate the present value of a stream of future cash payments, we need to discount each expected payment separately, as we did with the two-period stream of payments. We use a stream of four annual payments as an example in Figure 1.18.

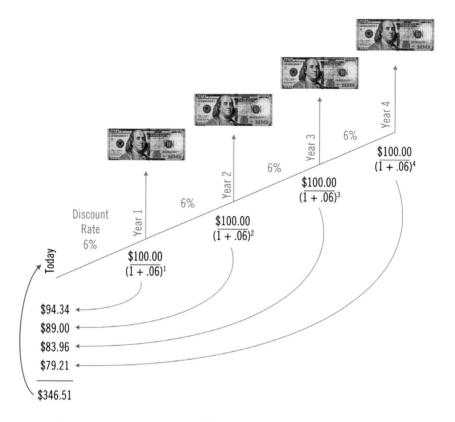

Figure 1.18   Present Value of a Stream of $100s

The calculation is the same, only with more years represented:

$$\text{Present Value (PV)} = \frac{\$_1}{\left(1+i\right)^1} + \frac{\$_2}{\left(1+i\right)^2} + \frac{\$_3}{\left(1+i\right)^3} + \frac{\$_4}{\left(1+i\right)^4}$$

$$\text{PV} = \frac{\$100.00}{\left(1+6\%\right)^1} + \frac{\$100.00}{\left(1+6\%\right)^2} + \frac{\$100.00}{\left(1+6\%\right)^3} + \frac{\$100.00}{\left(1+6\%\right)^4}$$

$$PV = \frac{\$100.00}{1.06} + \frac{\$100.00}{1.124} + \frac{\$100.00}{1.19} + \frac{\$100.00}{1.26}$$

$$PV = \$94.34 + \$89.00 + \$83.96 + \$79.21 = \$346.51$$

We use future cash *payments* throughout the compounding and discounting examples to simplify the discussion. It should be easy to see that the future payments can be replaced with the asset's future cash flows and that the present value formula for four years of cash flow is the following:

$$\text{Present Value} \left(PV\right) = \frac{CF_1}{\left(1+i\right)^1} + \frac{CF_2}{\left(1+i\right)^2} + \frac{CF_3}{\left(1+i\right)^3} + \frac{CF_4}{\left(1+i\right)^4}$$

Where:
    CF_1 equals cash flow in year 1
    CF_2 equals cash flow in year 2
    CF_3 equals cash flow in year 3
    CF_4 equals cash flow in year 4
    i represents the discount return

Some people argue that the **timing** of cash flow and the **time value of money** are the same thing. Although we agree, we believe there is significant value in discussing the concepts separately to show the different roles they play when evaluating future cash flows.[3] **Timing** is *when* you get the money, for example, next year or in five years. The time value of money is *the rate used to discount* the cash flows in the future back to today's value, which is their **present value**.

Now that we have established the framework for valuing an asset, we increase the complexity in the next chapter, and use these tools to value a simple business: the proverbial lemonade stand.

---

[3] Two individuals we respect—Michael Mauboussin and Judd Kahn—argued that there is no need to separate the two concepts, as the time value of money captures the timing of cash flows. Although we agree intellectually with their point of view, we think it easier to comprehend the importance when they are separated.

Zoe will not operate her lemonade stand alone, as she will receive help from legendary investor Bill Ackman, who is an expert on the finances of lemonade stands.[4]

Gems:
- ♦ Valuing an asset is a relatively simple concept: The **value of an asset** is the sum of cash flows produced by that asset, over its useful life, discounted for the time value of money and the uncertainty of receiving those cash flows.
- ♦ Regarding cash flows:
  - ♦ Getting cash sooner is better than getting it later.
  - ♦ A longer duration of cash flows is better than a shorter one.
  - ♦ Larger cash flows are better than smaller ones.
  - ♦ A stream of cash flows with a faster growth rate is preferable to one with a slower growth rate.

---

[4] You can Google "Bill Ackman lemonade stand" to find the Floating University's excellent video: "William Ackman: Everything You Need to Know about Finance and Investing in under an Hour."

- A growing stream of cash flows is preferable to one that is not growing.
- A stable stream of cash flows is preferable to one with a negative growth rate or losses.
- **Uncertainty** will have an impact on all four cash flow subcomponents and, in turn, affect the asset's value.
- The definition of the value of an asset must be altered to account for the inherent uncertainty of future cash flows: The *estimated* value of an asset is the sum of the cash flows *expected* to be produced by that asset, over its useful life, discounted for the time value of money and the uncertainty of receiving those cash flows.
  - It is hard to predict the future as uncertainty increases the further we forecast cash flows into the future.
  - An asset's cash flows must be "discounted for the time value of money." Discounting for time is a straightforward concept: A dollar today is worth more than a dollar in the future, or thought of another way, "A bird in the hand is worth two in the bush." The value of cash flows today is referred to as their **present value**.

How to Value a Business

To figure out what Zoe's Lemonade Stand is worth today (its **present value**), we need to estimate the cash flows it will generate over its useful life and then discount those cash flows back to the present to account for the time value of money and uncertainty of the cash flow estimates, as we show here:

$$\text{Present Value}\left(\text{PV}\right) = \frac{CF_1}{\left(1+i\right)^1} + \frac{CF_2}{\left(1+i\right)^2} + \frac{CF_3}{\left(1+i\right)^3} + \frac{CF_4}{\left(1+i\right)^4}$$

Defining Cash Flow

We first need a definition for the cash flow the business generates. Unfortunately, like many other terms in finance, there is no single definition; rather, there are many. In the interest of simplicity, we defer to Warren Buffett's definition, which he calls **owner earnings**, as outlined in the 1986 Berkshire Hathaway Chairman's Letter:

Net Income
  + Depreciation and amortization
  − Maintenance cap-ex
  = Owner earnings

To calculate the net income for Zoe's Lemonade Stand, we need to build a financial model for her business. This exercise entails forecasting sales, cost of goods sold, SG&A (selling, general, and administrative) expenses, depreciation, and taxes. We must perform this calculation for each year in the forecast period, which in this example is four years, as shown in Table 2.1. To keep the model simple, we will not forecast any growth in revenues in this example.

Table 2.1   Income Statement for Zoe's Lemonade Stand

	Year 1	Year 2	Year 3	Year 4
Revenues	1,200	1,200	1,200	1,200
Cost of Good Sold	-540	-540	-540	-540
Gross Profit	660	660	660	660
Selling General and Admin	-492	-492	-492	-492
Operating Income	168	168	168	168
Income Taxes	-59	-59	-59	-59
Net Income	109	109	109	109
Depreciation and Amortization	63	63	63	63
Maintenance Capex	-52	-52	-52	-52
Owner Earnings	**120**	**120**	**120**	**120**

WHY EBITDA IS *NOT* A DEFINITION OF FREE CASH FLOW

While EBITDA (**E**arnings **B**efore **I**nterest, **T**axes, **D**epreciation, and **A**mortization) appears to be a ubiquitous term on Wall Street, it is a relatively new financial concept. It was not until the LBO (leveraged buyout) boom in the 1980s that EBITDA was adopted widely as a financial measure. A leveraged buyout is a financial transaction where a group of investors, such as a private equity firm, acquires a public company (or division of a company) using a small amount of equity and a lot of debt to buy the company's outstanding shares. To win in a competitive auction, the buyout investors need to determine the amount of debt a takeover candidate can support in order to maximize their bid for the target company. Because EBITDA is a good proxy of the level of debt a company can service, at least in the short term, it quickly became the key financial metric for the private equity industry and has been associated with LBOs ever since.

Despite its merits, EBITDA is potentially a poor measure of a company's true financial performance and can be misleading when used to estimate what a company is worth. We show in the following discussion that owner earnings is a more accurate metric in both situations.

We compare owner earnings and EBITDA for Zoe's Lemonade Stand in Table 2.2 to illustrate the difference between the two measures of her financial performance. As the comparison shows, Zoe's Lemonade Stand produced owner earnings of $120 during the year, which represents the free cash flow the business generated and the amount of cash Zoe can take out of the business with no adverse effect on its future operations. On the other hand, Zoe's Lemonade Stand generated significantly greater EBITDA than owner earnings, as the analysis

Table 2.2   First-Year Owner Earnings versus EBITDA for Zoe's Lemonade Stand

	Owner Earnings	EBITDA
Revenues	1,200	1,200
Cost of Good Sold	-540	-540
Gross Profit	660	660
Selling General and Admin	-492	-492
Operating Income	168	168
Income Taxes	-59	
Net Income	109	
Depreciation and Amortization	63	63
Maintenance Capex	-52	
Owner Earnings	120	231

shows. However, the $231 in EBITDA is not a true measure of the lemonade stand's free cash flow or the amount of cash Zoe can take out of the business without potentially harming its future. For instance, the lemonade stand will fall into disrepair over time if Zoe does not spend money on maintaining and repairing her facilities (maintenance capex). Interest would also be a real expense if Zoe borrows money, and the bank can take possession of the lemonade stand if she is unable to pay what she owes her creditors. And, finally, Zoe could wind up in jail if she fails to pay her taxes. EBITDA does not consider any of these cash requirements despite the obvious fact that they are real financial obligations and there are significant consequences to not paying them.

While EBITDA may be a reasonable proxy of the maximum amount of debt a business can support, which was its original use, it is not an accurate measure of the company's true financial performance because it fails to account for major, unavoidable cash expenses that are necessary to maintain the business. Owner earnings, on the other hand, is more representative of how much cash the business generates after accounting for *all* expenses (assuming no growth), the cash left over that can be taken out of the business (or invested in growth), and the most appropriate measure to use when calculating the value of the business.

How to Calculate Present Value Using a Discounted Cash Flow Model

We use 8.5% as the discount rate (which incorporates both uncertainty and the time value of money) to calculate the present value, or the value in today's dollars, of Zoe's Lemonade Stand's estimated cash flows, as shown in Figure 2.1.

$$\text{Present Value} = \frac{\$120}{(1+8.5\%)^1} + \frac{\$120}{(1+8.5\%)^2} + \frac{\$120}{(1+8.5\%)^3} + \frac{\$120}{(1+8.5\%)^4}$$

$111
$102
$94
$87
———
$393

$$\text{Present Value (PV)} = \frac{CF_1}{(1+i)^1} + \frac{CF_2}{(1+i)^2} + \frac{CF_3}{(1+i)^3} + \frac{CF_4}{(1+i)^4}$$

Present Value of Zoe's Lemonade Stand $= \$393$

Figure 2.1   Present Value of Four Years of Cash Flows from Zoe's Lemonade Stand

Although this calculation is relatively straightforward, it raises a couple of obvious questions: Why do we estimate and value only four years of cash flow? Why would the lemonade stand not generate cash flow beyond the four-year forecast period? Unless we are going to operate the business for only four years, it makes sense to include the cash flow from year 5 in the valuation analysis. And the same goes for year 6. We show the calculation with the two additional years included in Figure 2.2.

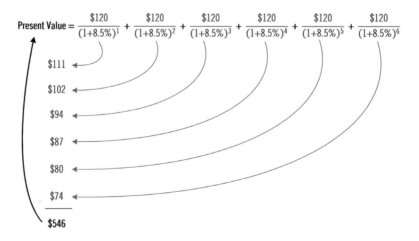

$$\text{Present Value} = \frac{\$120}{(1+8.5\%)^1} + \frac{\$120}{(1+8.5\%)^2} + \frac{\$120}{(1+8.5\%)^3} + \frac{\$120}{(1+8.5\%)^4} + \frac{\$120}{(1+8.5\%)^5} + \frac{\$120}{(1+8.5\%)^6}$$

$111
$102
$94
$87
$80
$74
———
$546

Figure 2.2   Present Value of Six Years of Cash Flows from Zoe's Lemonade Stand

$$\text{Present Value (PV)} = \frac{CF_1}{(1+i)^1} + \frac{CF_2}{(1+i)^2} + \frac{CF_3}{(1+i)^3} + \frac{CF_4}{(1+i)^4} + \frac{CF_5}{(1+i)^5} + \frac{CF_6}{(1+i)^6}$$

Present Value of Zoe's Lemonade Stand = $546

In fact, it should be apparent that we need to include all of the cash flows the business will generate, over its entire useful life, in the analysis. Therefore, we need to extend the forecast period in the calculation to include *all* future years, which we designate as year *n* in the equation shown here:

$$PV = \frac{CF_1}{(1+i)^1} + \frac{CF_2}{(1+i)^2} + \frac{CF_3}{(1+i)^3} + \frac{CF_4}{(1+i)^4} + \frac{CF_5}{(1+i)^5} + \frac{CF_6}{(1+i)^6} + \ldots + \frac{CF_n}{(1+i)^n}$$

The following formula is the formal way the discounted cash flow (DCF) model is usually presented:

$$\text{Present Value (PV)} = \sum_{t=0}^{T} \frac{CF_t}{(1+i)^t}$$

Although more intimidating in this form, the formula merely states that the **present value** equals the sum of all cash flows the business will generate, over its useful life, discounted back to the current period. It is important to note that the time period in the equation extends from the present until time *t*, which, in theory, is the end of all time.

While the formula is straightforward, the challenge is estimating the future cash flows to be used as inputs. As we discuss in the previous chapter, there are four subcomponents that we need to consider when estimating future cash flows—**timing, duration, magnitude**, and **growth**. Also, it is important to recognize that the formula requires that we estimate cash flows many years into the future. In fact, the formula, in its truest sense, calls for an *infinite* number of future cash flow estimates.

We also need to consider the time value of money and the level of uncertainty in the cash flow estimates. Unfortunately, the discount rate is not a number one can look up in the newspaper. Although the concept is simple—a dollar today is worth more than a dollar in the future, as we discuss in the prior chapter—the challenge is determining the appropriate discount rate to use.

In practice, most analysts use the interest rate of U.S. government fixed-income securities as a proxy for the time value of money and generally select the rate on a long-dated security, such as a 10-year government note, to match the long duration of the company's cash flow estimates.

Capturing the uncertainty of future cash flows is more challenging. Less predictable cash flows are less valuable in today's dollars than are more predictable ones; therefore, we need to discount them at a higher rate. Determining how much higher the discount rate needs to be takes domain-specific knowledge concerning the nature of the business and degree of uncertainty to the future cash flows.

Although using a DCF is the correct way to value future cash flows, the formula is challenging in practice because of the difficulty in estimating all six of the independent components for a time period extended well into the future. Consequentially, few investors use the model in its entirety, with most of them using only an abridged version, which we demonstrate later in the chapter.

BUT I DON'T DO THAT!

Most professional portfolio managers dismiss the value of the DCF model and scoff at the idea of using one in their investment analysis, often reacting with, "But I don't do that—that's not the way the stock market works." In fact, no matter what valuation method portfolio managers use, they are actually performing a DCF calculation implicitly and relying on the model without acknowledging it.

For instance, when a money manager states, "With a P/E (price / earnings ratio) of 6 on 2018 earnings, Apple is cheap," he is effectively performing a discounted cash flow analysis. When he says, "GM is a good buy at 7 times 2017 EBITDA," he is doing a discounted cash flow analysis. If he values a company on its liquidation, sum of the parts, or breakup value, he is performing a discounted cash flow analysis. If he values a company using Private Market Value (PMV),[1] which is "the value an informed industrialist would pay to purchase assets with similar characteristics," he is relying on discounted cash flow analysis.

If the portfolio manager says, "The company is a good acquisition candidate," he assumes that it will be less expensive or more expeditious for another company to buy the target company than to build a comparable business on their own (the buy-versus-build decision).

---

[1] "Private Market Value" is a term coined by Mario J. Gabelli, which we discuss in the Chapter 3.

In this case, the portfolio manager is relying on an estimate of the company's Private Market Value, which is, at its core, a DCF. If the portfolio manager values a security using a P/E ratio, an EBITDA multiple, an earnings yield, or a cap rate, he is using a discounted cash flow model. Despite the manager's assertions that he is not using a DCF, in reality he is because *each of these ratios uses a proxy for the business's market value divided by a proxy for its cash flow* and is the equivalent to calculating the present value of a stream of cash flows in perpetuity (which is a simplified version of the discounted cash flow model, as we discuss in the chapter).

The two most popular ratios used in investment analysis—a P/E ratio and an EBITDA multiple—are simply modified versions of the present value of a perpetuity, which is the steady-state cash flow divided by the required discount rate.

The formula for a present value of a perpetuity is:

$$\text{PV of Perpetuity} = \frac{CF}{i} = \text{Market Value of Business}$$

where i = discount rate

We can show that a P/E ratio is equivalent to a perpetuity by rearranging the factors used in the formula:

$$\text{Price / Earnings Ratio} = \frac{\text{Stock Price}}{\text{Earnings Per Share}} = \frac{P}{E}$$

$$\text{Earnings Yield} = \frac{E}{P} = i$$

We can demonstrate this analysis for a company with earnings of $8.66 per share and a stock price of $117.16:

$$\text{Earnings Yield} = \frac{E}{P} = \frac{\$8.66}{\$117.16} = 7.4\%$$

$$\text{PV of Perpetuity} = \frac{CF}{i} = \frac{\$8.66}{7.4\%} = \$117.16$$

$$\frac{P}{E} = \frac{\text{Stock Price}}{\text{Earnings Per Share}} = \frac{\text{Market Value of Business}}{\text{Cash Flow}}$$

(Continued)

(*Continued*)

An EBITDA multiple is basically a modified P/E and is nothing more than another version of the business value divided by its cash flow:

$$\text{EBITDA Multiple} = \frac{\text{Enterprise Value}}{\text{EBITDA}} = \frac{\text{Business Value}}{\text{Cash Flow}}$$

The valuation in all these cases assumes that the cash flow—EPS (earnings per share) and EBITDA—continues in perpetuity, which is the same assumption used with the perpetuity valuation formula and is nothing more than an abbreviated DCF.

If the portfolio manager values a company using a breakup, liquidation, or replacement value calculation, he assumes that the assets will convert to cash in a future liquidation or when a third party acquires the business in a buyout or M&A transaction. However, the acquirer will make the purchase only if he believes he can generate enough cash flow from the business to justify the purchase price. Since the estimate of value in each of these cases is based on what someone else is willing to pay for the business, the valuation, ultimately, is based on a DCF.

Even if the portfolio manager invests based on changes in investor expectations, he is relying on someone else placing value on the business's future cash flows, which follows the preceding logic. Once again, the underlying valuation assumption is based on a DCF.

Despite what portfolio managers claim is their preferred valuation method—enterprise value to EBITDA multiple, P/E ratio, price to sales, caprate, Private Market Value, sum of parts or liquidation value—they are performing, at the core, a discounted cash flow analysis, either explicitly or implicitly, whether they admit it or not.

Predicting the Future Is Not Easy

Predicting events in the future is difficult and highlights the biggest challenge in using a DCF to value a business. Because the analyst cannot know with certainty what events will transpire, he is forced to make numerous assumptions when predicting future cash flows. For instance, there are a litany of different scenarios that could unfold even with a simple business like Zoe's Lemonade Stand, each with differing probabilities of occurring, and all resulting in different cash flow predictions.

For example, one future scenario could be that sugar prices increase sharply in a short period of time, without Zoe being able to pass the higher cost on to her customers. As a result, her margins get squeezed (pun intended), which lowers the magnitude of future cash flows. In another scenario, it rains every weekend during the summer, causing lemonade sales to be disappointing because of reduced foot traffic. In yet another scenario, the lemonade stand is damaged in a storm, resulting in higher maintenance expenses to repair the damage. There are an infinite number of such possible scenarios, each with its own probability, making it challenging to predict future cash flows with a high degree of confidence. We show several external factors and their relationship to the four cash flow subcomponents in Figure 2.3.

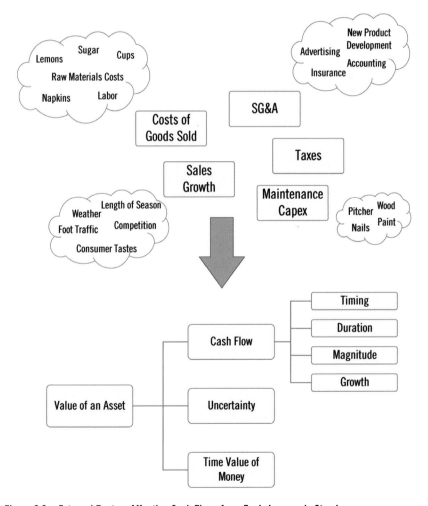

Figure 2.3   External Factors Affecting Cash Flows from Zoe's Lemonade Stand

Because of the challenges in forecasting future cash flows for even a simple business like a lemonade stand, let alone the significantly greater challenges in forecasting future cash flows for a more complex business, we start with a straight-forward example of valuing a "plain vanilla" bond and then add complexity as we move toward valuing an operating business. The goal is to show how to use a DCF effectively to calculate the value of a business, while recognizing the model's inherent limitations.

How to Calculate the Present Value of a Bond

We need the following information to value a "plain vanilla" bond using a DCF model:

- Timing—timing of coupon payments and repayment of principal
- Duration—number of payments (time to the bond's maturity)
- Magnitude—coupon payment amount
- Growth—not applicable since the coupons will not change
- Uncertainty—probability of default (ability to pay)
- Time value of money

Valuing a bond is straightforward because most of the variables are contractually set: the timing of the payments is fixed; duration, which is the number of coupon payments, is fixed; the magnitude, which is the amount of the coupon payment, is fixed; and growth is not applicable since each coupon payment is the same over the life of the bond (in this example). The discount rate used will incorporate the time value of money and capture the uncertainty of the issuing entity's ability to pay the coupons and repay the principal amount at maturity. We use the following parameters in the example:

- Timing—coupon payments: *annual*; principal: *upon maturity*
- Duration—number of payments: *five years*
- Magnitude—coupon payment rate: *6%*
- Growth—not applicable: *payments fixed*
- Uncertainty—probability of default (ability to pay): *low in the example*
- Time value of money: *5%*[2]

---

[2] Please note, there is no rhyme or reason to why we use 5% as the discount rate in this example. It is the concept that is important, not the actual numbers used.

Because we know each of the components just listed, we can use a five-year DCF to calculate the present value of the cash flows to determine the bond's value, as shown in Figure 2.4. (NOTE: we will use blue to signify the forecast period and red to signify the principal amount.)

$$PV = \frac{CF_1}{(1+i)^1} + \frac{CF_2}{(1+i)^2} + \frac{CF_3}{(1+i)^3} + \frac{CF_4}{(1+i)^4} + \frac{CF_5}{(1+i)^5} + \frac{Principal}{(1+i)^5}$$

Or:

$$Present\ Value = \sum_{t=0}^{5} \frac{CF_t}{(1+i)^t} + \frac{Principal}{(1+i)^5}$$

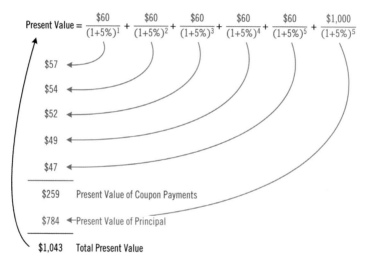

$$Present\ Value = \frac{\$60}{(1+5\%)^1} + \frac{\$60}{(1+5\%)^2} + \frac{\$60}{(1+5\%)^3} + \frac{\$60}{(1+5\%)^4} + \frac{\$60}{(1+5\%)^5} + \frac{\$1,000}{(1+5\%)^5}$$

$57

$54

$52

$49

$47

———

$259   Present Value of Coupon Payments

$784 ←Present Value of Principal

———

$1,043   Total Present Value

PV = Present value of coupon payment + Present value of principal

PV = $260 + $784

Present value of bond = $1,043

Figure 2.4   Present Value of a "Plain Vanilla" Bond

The example shows that calculating the present value of a bond is similar to how we calculate the present value of Zoe's Lemonade Stand in Figure 2.2 above, except the duration is five years instead of six years, and we receive two payments in the final year—the fifth coupon payment and the repayment of the principal amount.

How to Calculate the Present Value of a Perpetuity

Bonds that have no set maturity date are called perpetual bonds, or **perpetuities** for short. Perpetuities pay regular coupon payments like a bond, except perpetual bonds never mature, as the name implies. As a result, the coupon payments continue forever and the principal is never paid back. Because perpetuities have no maturity date, the duration is infinite. We use the following parameters to value the perpetuity:

- Timing—coupon payments: *annual*
- Duration—number of payments: *infinite*
- Magnitude—coupon payment rate: *6%*
- Growth—not applicable: *payments fixed*
- Uncertainty—probability of default (ability to pay): *extremely low*
- Time value of money: *5%*

Interestingly, calculating the value of a perpetuity is simpler than the DCF model used to value a standard bond because there is no maturity to the cash flows, as we show with the following formula.

$$\text{Present Value of Perpetuity} = \frac{CF}{i}$$

$$\text{Present Value of Perpetuity} = \frac{\$60}{5\%}$$

$$\text{Present Value of Perpetuity} = \$1,200$$

How to Calculate the Present Value of a Business

Valuing a business is similar to valuing a perpetuity because the cash flows the business generates last forever (at least in theory), which matches the duration of the coupon payments from a perpetuity. We will, therefore, use the perpetuity valuation formula as the first step in valuing a business. The main difference between the two entities is that the coupon payments (cash flows) are contractually set with a bond (even with a perpetuity) and are usually the same amount each period. This condition is not the case with a lemonade stand, or any other business, for that matter, because the business's future cash flows can, and will, vary from year to year—greatly in some cases.

We show the differences in the parameters used in a DCF to value a bond, a perpetuity, and an operating business in Table 2.3.

Table 2.3   Comparison of the Primary Components to the Value of a Bond, Perpetuity, and Zoe's Lemonade Stand

	"Plain Vanilla" Bond	Perpetuity	Lemonade Stand
Timing: frequency of payments	Annual	Annual	Uncertain
Duration: number of payments	5 years	Infinite	Uncertain
Magnitude: coupon payment rate	6%	6%	Uncertain
Growth	N/A fixed payments	N/A fixed payments	Uncertain
Uncertainty: probability of default (ability to pay)	Extremely low	Extremely low	Uncertain
Time value of money	5%	5%	Uncertain

While many of the variables in a bond or perpetuity are contractually set, those factors are usually unknown and uncertain in an operating business, as the table shows.

Valuing any asset using the perpetuity formula requires that the cash flows remain constant over time. Although this assumption is unrealistic for an ongoing business, the exercise offers valuable insights and is an important step in ultimately understanding how to value an ongoing operating company. We can use the perpetuity formula to value a business by substituting the coupon payment with the business's annual cash flows, as we show in the following.

$$\text{Present Value of Perpetuity} = \frac{CF}{i}$$

Where:

CF = estimated annual cash flow
i = discount rate

Zoe's Lemonade Stand generates $120 of cash flow each year, as we show in Table 2.1. The present value of the lemonade stand using the perpetuity formula, with a discount rate of 8.5%, equals $1,412, as shown here:

$$\text{Present Value of Zoe's Lemonade Stand} = \frac{\$120}{8.5\%} = \$1,412$$

The calculation captures the six valuation components we discuss in the prior chapter. For instance, because we are using estimated annual cash flows and have set them to be the same each year, the estimates capture timing and magnitude. Also, because we assume the business will generate cash flow every year in the future, the estimates capture duration. And, as with the perpetuity, the discount rate captures the time value of money and uncertainty. What is not captured with this formula is growth, which we discuss in further detail in the next section.

How to Calculate the Present Value of a Growing Cash Flow Stream Using a Two-Stage DCF Model

The valuation process up to this point has been relatively straightforward, mostly because we either knew all the inputs to the DCF model or made simplifying assumptions. And, in all cases, we ignored growth. However, since practically all businesses try to grow over time, growth is an important factor when calculating a company's present value. Unfortunately, valuing growth is challenging because any formula used to value growth is highly sensitive to the assumptions employed.

A standard method used to value growth is to split the cash flow estimates into multiple stages, which allows the analyst to apply a different growth rate to each stage, and then value each stage separately, with the most common approach using a two-stage model. Using a two-stage model, individual cash flow estimates are made for each year in the first stage, which is called the **explicit forecast period**, and then each cash flow estimate is discounted back to its present value, as we have done in each example up to this point. The second stage, called the **terminal value**, captures the value of all cash flows beyond the explicit forecast period, although we then need to discount it back to calculate its present value.

To demonstrate how a two-stage model works, we can use it to value a standard bond. The coupon payments represent the cash flow from the explicit forecast period and the bond's principal amount represent the terminal value, as we show in Figure 2.5. Not surprisingly, the calculation confirms that we reach the same valuation as when we used the simpler DCF above.

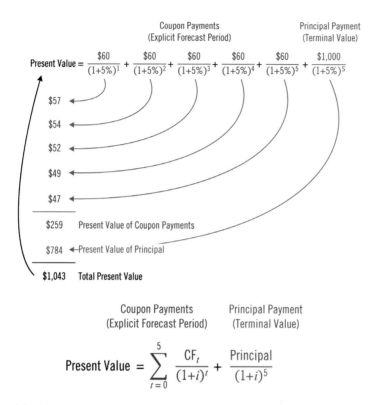

Figure 2.5   Present Value Formula Used to Value a Bond

As we show with the bond valuation in Figure 2.5, it follows that the present value of the present value of the business is the sum of the present value of the cash flows from the explicit forecast period and the present value of the terminal value, as the following equation shows:

PV = present value of cash flows during forecast period
+ present value of terminal value

The cash flow estimates for the lemonade stand from the explicit forecast period replace the bond's coupon payments and the lemonade stand's terminal value replaces the bond's principal payment. We calculate the present value of the cash flows in the first stage as we have in all the examples and then use the perpetuity formula to represent the lemonade stand's terminal value as we show in Figure 2.6.

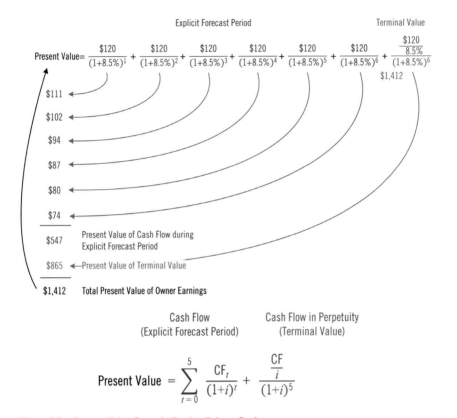

Figure 2.6   Present Value Formula Used to Value a Business

We use a two-stage model to value growth in the next three examples. We vary the growth in the first stage, the explicit forecast period, starting with no growth in the first case, 10% growth in the second case, and 15% growth in the third case. We assume no growth in the terminal value in all three cases.

Two Stage DCF Model with No Growth

The first case assumes no growth during the six-year forecast period, as we show with the explicit cash flow forecasts in Table 2.4.

Table 2.4   Abbreviate Six-Year Forecast of Owner Earnings for Zoe's Lemonade Stand with No Growth

	Year 1	Year 2	Year 3	Year 4	Year 5	Year 6
Revenues	1,200	1,200	1,200	1,200	1,200	1,200
Net Income	109	109	109	109	109	109
Owner Earnings	120	120	120	120	120	120

We can use a DCF model to calculate the present value of the individual cash flows and the terminal value, as demonstrated in Figure 2.7. The calculation shows that the present value of the cash flows from the six-year explicit forecast period totals $547 and the present value of the terminal value equals $865, with the total present value for Zoe's Lemonade Stand, assuming no growth, totaling $1,412.

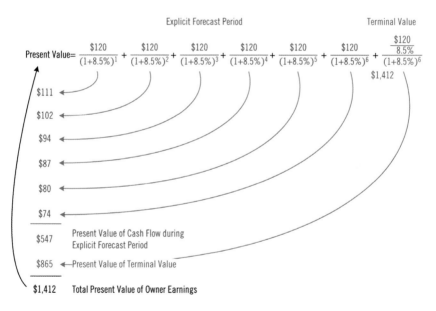

$$PV = \text{Present Value of Cash Flows during Forecast Period}$$
$$+ \text{ Present Value of Terminal Value}$$

$$\text{Present Value of Zoe's Lemonade Stand} \left(\text{No Growth}\right) = \$547 + \$865$$

$$\text{Present Value of Zoe's Lemonade Stand} \left(\text{No Growth}\right) = \$1,412$$

Figure 2.7   Present Value of Zoe's Lemonade Stand with No Growth

Since the cash flows are constant throughout the company's life in this example, the value we derive from the two-stage model equals the perpetuity value, as the flowing calculation demonstrates:

$$PV = \frac{CF}{i}$$

$$\text{Present Value of Zoe's Lemonade Stand (No Growth)} = \frac{\$120}{8.5\%} = \$1,412$$

Two-Stage DCF Model with 10% Growth

The second case assumes 10% growth in annual cash flow during the explicit forecast period, which we illustrate in Table 2.5, and no growth in perpetuity thereafter.

Table 2.5   Abbreviated Six-Year Forecast of Owner Earnings for Zoe's Lemonade Stand with 10% Annual Growth

	Year 1	Year 2	Year 3	Year 4	Year 5	Year 6
Revenues	1,200	1,320	1,452	1,597	1,757	1,933
Net Income	109	120	132	145	160	175
Owner Earnings	120	132	145	160	176	193

We calculate that the present value of the cash flows from the six-year explicit forecast period equals $687, and the present value of the terminal value equals $1,394. The two values sum to $2,081, which is the total present value of Zoe's Lemonade Stand in this example, as shown in Figure 2.8.

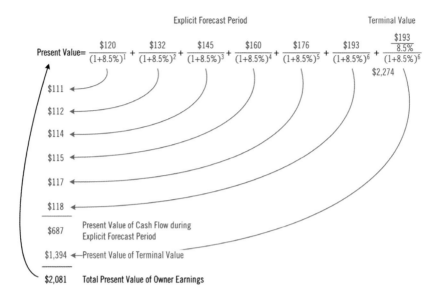

$$PV = \text{Present Value of Cash Flows During Forecast Period}$$
$$+ \text{Present Value of Terminal Value}$$

$$\text{Present Value of Zoe's Lemonade Stand} = \$687 + \$1,394$$

$$\text{Present Value of Zoe's Lemonade Stand} = \$2,081$$

Figure 2.8   Present Value of Zoe's Lemonade Stand with 10% Annual Growth

Not surprisingly, the present value of the lemonade stand with 10% cash flow growth is higher than the no-growth scenario, as higher growth is more valuable than lower growth, as we outline in Chapter 1.

Two-Stage DCF Model with 15% Growth

The third case assumes 15% growth in annual cash flow during the six-year explicit forecast period, as shown in Table 2.6, and no growth in perpetuity thereafter.

Table 2.6   Abbreviated Six-Year Forecast of Owner Earnings for Zoe's Lemonade Stand with 15% Annual Growth

	Year 1	Year 2	Year 3	Year 4	Year 5	Year 6
Revenues	1,200	1,380	1,587	1,825	2,099	2,414
Net Income	109	126	144	166	191	219
Owner Earnings	**120**	**138**	**159**	**183**	**210**	**241**

We calculate that the present value of the cash flows from the explicit six-year forecast period equals \$772 and the present value of the terminal value equals \$1,739. The two values sum to \$2,511, which is the present value of Zoe's Lemonade Stand in this example, as shown in Figure 2.9.

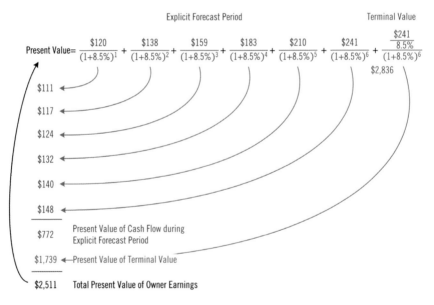

$$PV = \text{Present Value of cash flows during forecast period}$$
$$+ \text{ Present Value of terminal value}$$

$$\text{Present Value of Zoe's Lemonade stand} = \$772 + \$1,739$$

$$\text{Present Value of Zoe's Lemonade stand} = \$2,511$$

Figure 2.9   Present Value of Zoe's Lemonade Stand with 15% Annual Growth

The present value of Zoe's Lemonade Stand with 15% growth is higher than in the two prior examples, which is consistent with the claim that higher growth is more valuable than lower growth, as we discuss in Chapter 1.

How to Think About the Discount Rate

We have used a discount rate of 8.5% in all examples up to this point. We need to address the question, "Is 8.5% the proper discount rate to use?" or what we think is an even better question, "How do we determine what is the appropriate discount rate?"

An in-depth discussion of discount rates is beyond the scope of this book, as academics in finance and investment professionals have published hundreds of books and thousands of journal articles debating the topic. We discuss ways to *think* about what might be a proper discount rate instead.

Calculating the Cost of Capital

The "correct" rate to use in the discounting process is the company's **cost of capital**, which also represents investors' **opportunity cost**, making the two returns opposite sides of the same coin. The **cost of capital** is the rate of return an investor demands to make an investment, while the **opportunity cost** is the foregone return the investor gives up when he chooses one investment opportunity over another one. A company's cost of capital has three main components:

1. The ratio between debt and equity financing
2. The after-tax interest on the company's borrowings (cost of debt)
3. The cost of equity

Because the cost of capital is weighted by the ratio of debt to equity, it is called the Weighted Average Cost of Capital, which is known as WACC and calculated using the following formula:

$$WACC = \frac{Debt}{Debt + Equity}\left(r_{debt}\right)*\left(1-t\right) + \frac{Equity}{Debt + Equity}\left(r_{equity}\right)$$

Where:

$$
\begin{aligned}
Debt &= \text{value of debt} \\
Equity &= \text{market value of equity} \\
r_{debt} &= \text{cost of debt} \\
r_{equity} &= \text{cost of equity} \\
t &= \text{corporate tax rate}
\end{aligned}
$$

Calculating a company's cost of debt is straightforward, as we show later in the chapter. Calculating a company's cost of equity, on the other hand, is complicated and requires further explanation. A company's cost of equity is the return that is required to compensate individuals for investing in the company and is the rate of return investors expect to receive for owning the stock. The return must compensate the individual for the **time value of money** as well as for the **uncertainty** of the company's future financial performance. In other words, **the company's cost of equity is the rate of return necessary to entice investors to purchase the company's stock**.

The Capital Asset Pricing Model[3]   The basic model used in theoretical finance to calculate a stock's expected return, and in turn, the company's cost of equity, is called the capital asset pricing model (CAPM), which was first proposed by William Sharpe and John Litner in the 1960s and is written as follows:

$$r_e = r_f + \beta \left(r_m - r_f \right)$$

Where:

r_e = expected return

r_f = risk-free rate

β = the stock's beta

r_m = expected market return

$\left(r_m - r_f \right)$ = market premium—the return of the market in excess of the risk-free rate

Although a bit intimidating, the CAPM states that the expected return for a security equals the risk-free rate plus a risk premium. The risk-free rate compensates the investor for the time value of

---

[3] Note: The authors want to stress that they *do not* feel that using the CAPM model is the proper way to determine a company's cost of equity. Because beta is used ubiquitously throughout the investment community (particularly in investment banking) to calculate the cost of equity we felt it necessary to include it in the discussion of the cost of capital. One cannot dismiss a concept unless one understands it fully. In fact, Paul Samuelson is quoted as saying, "Inexact sciences like economics advance funeral by funeral." In the author's opinion, the concept of beta needs a stake driven through its heart.

money and is customarily represented by the yield on long-term government bonds, such as U.S. Treasuries, while the rest of the equation represents how the investor is compensated for the uncertainty in the business, which requires further explanation.

The Beta Delusion[4]   A stock's **beta** measures its volatility relative to the market and, according to academic finance, represents the stock's market-related risk. The market premium is the expected market return plus the risk-free rate and is the additional return necessary to compensate investors for holding stocks rather than risk-free assets such as government bonds. The CAPM combines a stock's beta with the market premium to produce the expected return of the stock given its relative volatility to the market, which is how the capital asset pricing model defines a company's **cost of equity**.

BETA IS *NOT* AN ACCURATE MEASURE OF RISK (DESPITE WHAT YOU MIGHT HAVE BEEN TAUGHT!)

Beta measures the volatility of an individual stock compared with the volatility of the overall stock market and is used in academic finance as the main measure of a stock's risk. A stock with a beta greater than 1 is more volatile than the overall market and is viewed as a riskier asset, at least in theoretical finance, while a stock with a beta less than 1 is less volatile than the market and is viewed as less risky.

Academics in finance argue that beta is important because it represents the stock's market-related risk, which cannot be reduced by diversification and, therefore, is the only risk for which investors should be compensated above the risk-free rate. Theoretical finance further states that because a stock's beta is the appropriate measure of the stock's risk, the capital asset pricing model can be used to determine a company's expected return, which is equivalent to the company's cost of equity.

Professional investors rarely view a stock's volatility as the primary risk of investing in a company and, in turn, dismiss beta's relevancy to investing because it is calculated without regard to the fundamentals of the business. Seth Klarman wrote in *Margin of Safety*, "I find it preposterous that a single number reflecting past price fluctuations could be thought to completely describe the risk in a security. Beta views risk solely from the perspective of market prices, failing to take into consideration specific business fundamentals or economic developments. The reality is that past security price volatility does not reliably predict future investment performance (or even future volatility) and therefore is a poor measure of risk."[5]

[5] Seth A. Klarman, *Margin of Safety: Risk-Averse Value Investing Strategies for the Thoughtful Investor* (New York: HarperCollins, 1991).

[4] This is a play on Richard Dawkins's book, *The God Delusion*.

Calculating the Weighted Average Cost of Capital for Chemtura

In the following example, we use Chemtura, a specialty chemical company, to show how to calculate a public company's weighted average cost of capital, using the CAPM. Calculating the company's cost of debt is relatively easy. At the time of this analysis in 2016, Chemtura had a single bond issue maturing in July 2021 with $450 million outstanding and an interest rate of 5.93%, in addition to a term loan of $82 million, with an interest rate of 3.78%. The cost of debt is calculated after tax[6] because interest is tax deductible (all dollar amounts are in millions). Chemtura's after-tax cost of debt equals 3.6%, as we show in the following calculation:

$$\text{Interest Expense} = \left(\$450 * 5.93\%\right) + \left(\$82 * 3.78\%\right)$$
$$= \$26.7 + \$3.1 = \$29.8$$

$$r_{debt} = \frac{\text{Interest Expense} * \left(1 - \text{tax rate}\right)}{\text{Total Debt}}$$

$$r_{debt} = \frac{\$29.8 * \left(1 - 35\%\right)}{\$450 + \$82}$$

$$r_{debt} = \frac{\$19.3}{\$532}$$

$$r_{debt} = 3.6\%$$

Chemtura's cost of equity is a bit trickier to calculate. Although there are explicit interest rates with Chemtura's debt, this is not the case with Chemtura's equity. We can use the capital asset pricing model to estimate the company's cost of equity. We selected the 10-year U.S. Treasury Note yielding 2.2% at the time of this writing in May 2016, to represent the risk-free rate; the S&P 500's long-term

[6] We assume a 35% tax rate throughout the chapter, which we believe is a reasonable proxy of the U.S. statutory corporate tax rate at the time of this writing in May 2016.

historical return of 9.7% for the expected market return; and the number provided on Yahoo! Finance for the stock's beta.[7] We estimate Chemtura's cost of equity to equal 11.2%, as we show in the following calculation:

$$r_{equity} = r_f + \beta\left(r_m - r_f\right)$$

$$r_{equity} = 2.2\% + 1.2\left(9.7\% - 2.2\%\right)$$

$$r_{equity} = 2.2\% + 1.2\left(7.5\%\right)$$

$$r_{equity} = 2.2\% + 9.0\%$$

$$r_{equity} = 11.2\%$$

We calculate Chemtura's WACC using the company's cost of debt of 3.6% and cost of equity of 11.2% (all dollar amounts in billions):

$$WACC = \frac{Debt}{Debt + Equity}\left(r_{debt}\right) + \frac{Equity}{Debt + Equity}\left(r_{equity}\right)$$

$$WACC = \frac{\$0.532}{\$2.532}\left(3.6\%\right) + \frac{\$2.0}{\$2.532}\left(11.2\%\right)$$

$$WACC = 21.0\%\left(3.6\%\right) + 79.0\%\left(11.2\%\right)$$

$$WACC = 0.8\% + 8.8\% = 9.6\%$$

These formulas may seem impressive, particularly in their implied precision, but it is important to note that the only fundamental aspect of the business that is factored into the calculation is Chemtura's **capital structure**. The outlook for the business, level of competition, quality of management, and all other fundamental factors are ignored, which is why most professional portfolio managers dismiss using the CAPM to calculate a company's cost of capital. Although analysts need to understand how companies and investors think about and, in turn, estimate a firm's weighted average cost of capital, **it is important to recognize that the standard approach using CAPM has significant shortcomings**.

---

[7] We do not know how Yahoo! calculates the betas it publishes on Yahoo! Finance or if they are accurate. Because this discussion is meant to illustrate the concept, the accuracy of the number does not matter.

The Discount Rate Stack

There are numerous factors other than the stock's relative volatility that should to be considered when determining a company's cost of capital. These factors are the building blocks of the discount rate stack, which we show in Figure 2.10.

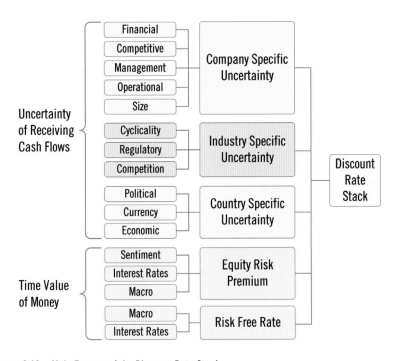

Figure 2.10   Main Factors of the Discount Rate Stack

The discount rate stack is not a formula. It should be viewed more like a checklist of uncertainties that need to be considered when estimating a company's cost of equity.

When in Doubt, Just Use 10%

Although the cost of capital is vital to every investment decision that an executive must make, calculating a precise cost of equity is probably an impossible task and one that forces investors and business managers alike to settle for an imprecise estimate.

Warren Buffett and Charlie Munger, two of the greatest investors in history, seem to agree with the challenges we outline above, as is reflected in their comments on the topic during the Berkshire Hathaway 2003 annual meeting:

> **Buffett:** Charlie and I don't know our cost of capital. It's taught in business schools, but we're skeptical. We just look to do the most intelligent thing we can with the capital that we have. We measure everything against our alternatives. I've never seen a cost of capital calculation that made sense to me. Have you, Charlie?

> **Munger:** Never. If you take the best text in economics by Mankiw, he says intelligent people make decisions based on opportunity costs—in other words, it's your alternatives that matter. That's how we make all of our decisions. The rest of the world has gone off on some kick—there's even a cost of equity capital— perfectly amazing mental malfunction.[8]

Buffett and Munger acknowledge that calculating a company's cost of capital, at best, is an inexact art and one that will not result in reaching a precise estimate.

We fear that readers must be asking themselves at this point why we made them suffer through the calculation of Chemtura's WACC when most professional investors, including Buffett and Munger, feel that beta and the CAPM are inadequate methods for calculating a company's cost of equity. We presented the example for two reasons. The first was to explain the method taught most often in business schools around the world. The second was to demonstrate that despite the implied precision in the formulas taught, in the end, we calculated Chemtura's WACC to equal 9.6%, which is essentially the same rate as the S&P's long-term annual return of 9.7%, and what we believe is an excellent proxy for investors' long-term **opportunity cost**.

Professor Bruce Greenwald instructs the students in his value investing class to "Just use 10%. It's close enough and it makes the math easy." We agree that it is reasonably safe to use 10% as an estimate for the cost of capital when calculating a company's value. The analyst can always adjust the rate (up or down) as he gains additional insight into the uncertainties facing the company.

[8] Whitney Tilson. "Notes from the 2003 Berkshire Hathaway Annual Meeting." Annual Meeting of the Shareholders of Berkshire Hathaway Inc., Omaha, Nebraska, May 3, 2003.

Gems:

- ▽ Despite its merits, EBITDA is potentially a poor measure of a company's true financial performance and can be misleading when used to estimate what a company is worth. Owner earnings is a more accurate metric in both situations.
- ▽ Although a DCF is the economically correct way to value future cash flows, the formula is challenging to use in practice because of the difficulty in estimating all six of the independent components for a period of time extended well into the future. Consequentially, few investors use the model in its entirety, with most using an abridged version.
- ▽ Despite what portfolio managers claim is their preferred valuation method—enterprise value to EBITDA multiple, P/E ratio, price to sales, caprate, private market value, sum of parts, or liquidation value—they are performing, at the core, a discounted cash flow analysis, either explicitly or implicitly, whether they believe it or not.
- ▽ Calculating a company's cost of debt is straightforward. Calculating a company's cost of equity, on the other hand, is complicated. A company's cost of equity is the return required to compensate individuals for investing in the company and is the rate of return investors expect to receive from owning the stock. The return must compensate the individual for the time value of money as well as the uncertainty of the company's future financial performance. In other words, the company's cost of equity is the rate of return necessary to entice investors to purchase the company's stock.
- ▽ Professional investors rarely view a stock's volatility as the primary fundamental risk of investing in a company and, in turn, dismiss the relevancy of beta and CAPM to investing because the methodology ignores important fundamentals of the business.
- ▽ Although the cost of capital is vital to every investment decision that an executive must make, calculating a precise cost of equity is probably an impossible goal and one that forces investors and business managers alike to settle for an imprecise estimate.
    - ▽ At the end of the day, heed the words of Columbia Business School Professor Bruce Greenwald, "Just use 10%. It's close enough and it makes the math easy."

How to Evaluate Competitive Advantage and Value Growth

In each example up to this point in the book, we assumed that the business we were analyzing operates as a **going concern** and calculated the company's value based on estimates of its future cash flows. While it is most common for a business to *operate* its assets with the specific goal of generating cash flow, the business can also generate cash flow by *selling* its assets, as we show in Figure 3.1.

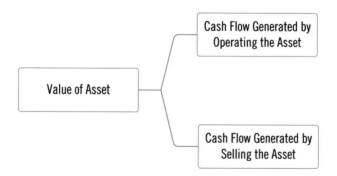

Figure 3.1 Cash Flow is Generated by Operating an Asset or Selling an Asset

Cash Flow Generated by Selling Assets

There are instances when a company may decide to cease operations and sell its assets outright, rather than continuing to operate them, generating cash in the process. The value of the business in this case is calculated by estimating how much cash the company would receive from liquidating its assets. This analysis is referred to as a company's **liquidation value**.

WHAT IS A DESK WORTH?

When Paul S. ran his investment partnership, The Hummingbird Value Fund, his office with Judd Kahn was on the 55th floor at Citicorp Center in midtown Manhattan. That is where he met legendary investor Jeff Doe.[1] Jeff walked into Paul's office one day and said, "We are redecorating our office and getting new desks. Would you have any interest in purchasing our old stuff?" While Paul had a desk he liked, he figured he would take a look. He said to Jeff, "Out of curiosity, how much would you take?" Jeff's answer, "$300." Paul replied, "Well, they are really nice but I'm happy with my old desk." Jeff then said, "How about $100?" Paul said, "Thanks, but no." Then Jeff said, "Well, if you want them, you can just take them." Paul thought about it, decided that he in fact liked the desk he had, and said to Jeff, "Why don't you donate it to Goodwill and have them pick it up?" Jeff replied, "I called them and they ask for a $300 donation for each desk they take. They have to use union movers in the building, which are expensive. And the building charges a similar fee if I just want to throw them out."

This story illustrates that an asset is only worth the cash flow it can produce and can actually have a negative value, as was the case with Jeff's old desks.

---
[1] Jeff's real last name is unimportant to the story, although he knows who he is.

There are also situations where a company may decide to sell part or all of its operating entities to a financial or strategic buyer. Valuing the company based on its value to a potential buyer is referred to as a company's **Private Market Value**. We show these two approaches in Figure 3.2.

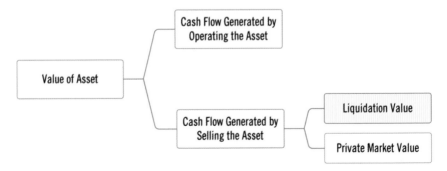

Figure 3.2   Value from Selling an Asset: Liquidation Value and Private Market Value

We can illustrate the distinction between generating cash flow by operating an asset versus selling the asset with a simple example. Mystery Ranch, a backpack manufacturer based in Bozeman, Montana, owns lots of sewing machines. Dana Gleason, the company's founder, might use one of the company's sewing machines, perhaps a Juki 1541S, to manufacture backpacks that the company would then sell to customers to generate revenue and produce cash flow. Alternatively, the company could generate cash by liquidating the same sewing machine by listing it on eBay and selling it for cash, as illustrated in Figure 3.3.

Operating an Asset to Generate Cash Flow

Selling an Asset to Generate Cash Flow

Figure 3.3   Operating or Selling an Asset to Generate Cash Flow

To calculate the sewing machine's **liquidation value**, we need to perform research to find out how much other used Juki 1541S sewing machines have sold for. From that information, we might conclude that Mystery Ranch could receive approximately $1,300 for the machine, if they elected to sell it.

If a company decides to liquidate all its assets, we would need to calculate the value of each asset separately, just as we did with one of Mystery Ranch's used Juki sewing machines, to figure out the company's full liquidation value.

Liquidation Value

To illustrate this process further, we will liquidate Sevcon, Inc., a public company that makes motor controllers for electric vehicles, including motorcycles, cars, and forklifts. To complete this exercise, we need to estimate what we will receive in the liquidation process for each of the company's different assets. We can value liquid assets, such as cash and marketable securities, at 100 cents on the dollar[2] because these assets are generally easy to sell and should be worth approximately their stated value. On the other hand, we will need to discount the value of less liquid assets, such as inventories and accounts receivable, because it is unlikely we will recover 100% of their stated value in a liquidation. For instance, we might collect close to full value for finished goods inventory, although it is unlikely we will get much more than scrap value for any work in process inventory and raw materials such as wire, magnets, and power supplies. Although we would expect to collect close to full value for all accounts receivable as a going concern, we might not be able to convince all the company's *former* customers (remember, the company is exiting the business) to pay what they owe in a liquidation without incurring additional costs to force collection. On the other hand, the company will need to honor all its liabilities and obligations, which must be subtracted from the amount we receive from the sale of its assets, giving us an estimate of the final net proceeds, or cash flow, from the liquidation. We show three liquidation values, based on different recovery assumptions, in Table 3.1.

---

[2] Although liquid assets such as cash *should* be valued close to 100 cents on the dollar, there are plenty of times in the real world where such an assumption would be a mistake. For instance, a simple example is Apple, a company that reported cash on its balance sheet of $233 billion in March 2016. Given that that the vast majority of Apple's cash is outside the United States, the company would have to pay U.S. taxes to repatriate it. Technically, although Apple has $233 billion in cash, it is highly unlikely that the cash would actually total $233 billion in a liquidation, at least in U.S. dollars.

Table 3.1 Sevcon Liquidation Analysis

Sevcon Inc. Balance Sheet	July 4, 2015	Liquidation Value					
		Low		Base		High	
		Percent	Value	Percent	Value	Percent	Value
Cash and cash equivalents	8,548	95%	8,121	100%	8,548	100%	8,548
Receivables	8,328	70%	5,830	80%	6,662	90%	7,495
Inventories	6,596	30%	1,979	40%	2,638	50%	3,298
Prepaid expenses and other current assets	2,573	5%	129	10%	257	15%	386
Total current assets	26,045						
Long-term assets	7,821	10%	782	20%	1,564	30%	2,346
Total assets	33,866		16,840		19,670		22,073
Current liabilities	7,112	100%	7,112	90%	6,401	80%	5,690
Liability for pension benefits	8,674	62%	5,378	62%	5,378	62%	5,378
Other long-term liabilities	500	100%	500	90%	450	80%	400
Total liabilities	16,286		12,990		12,229		11,467
Stockholders' equity	17,492						
Non-controlling interest	88						
Total liabilities and stockholders' equity	33,866						
Net Liquidation Value			3,850		7,442		10,606
Shares Outstanding			4,959		4,959		4,959
Net per share liquidation value			**$ 0.78**		**$ 1.50**		**$ 2.14**

We can create a distribution of potential liquidation values for Sevcon using the three point estimates we calculated in the analysis in Table 3.1, as we show in Figure 3.4. It is interesting to note that the estimates of net cash we would receive from liquidating all Sevcon's assets, even under the most favorable assumptions, yield a value well below the market price of $7.60 for the company's stock in August 2015.

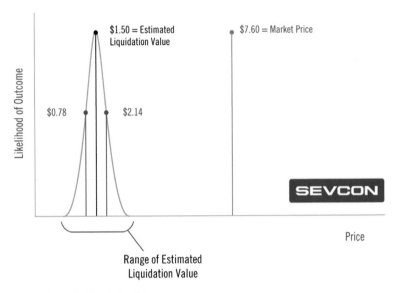

Figure 3.4   Sevcon's Liquidation Value

It is important to note that carrying out a liquidation analysis is often of limited practical value unless a company is actually going to liquidate some or all of its assets. However, calculating a realistic liquidation value can provide an *indication* of a minimum level of value for the business if it is no longer viable as a going concern.

Private Market Value

A company can also generate cash flow by selling some or all of its assets to a buyer who intends on operating the assets. This valuation method is referred to as **Private Market Value** (PMV), a term coined by Mario Gabelli when he started his firm in 1977. A company's Private Market Value represents the price an informed industrialist (a rational buyer) would be willing to pay to control a company's assets.

In his first appearance on Louis Rukeyser's *Wall $treet Week*, on March 5, 1982, Gabelli stated:

> The idea is what is the private market value of the company, looking at a company not from an earnings dynamic but from the point of view of what an industrialist would pay for the company....
>
> My approach is a bottoms-up approach. If we were sitting around this room with ten industrialists, I would say to them, "What would you pay me for this company if I would give you one bid, winner takes all? What would I get for it?" I would take the company apart, piece by piece and try to understand where the private market value of that company is versus the public market.[3]

Whether they know it or not, investors are referring to a company's PMV when they say, "The company is a good acquisition candidate."

---

[3] Mario J. Gabelli interview with Louis Rukeyser, *Wall $treet Week*. Maryland Public Television. Owings Mills, Maryland, March 5, 1982.

Roger Murray provided a more comprehensive definition of Private Market Value during his lecture series in early 1993:

> If I say to myself how would I define private market value, I would say it is likely to be intrinsic value plus, potentially, a control premium, because, by definition, being private I can turn over my business … to a private entity, and I can use a longer time horizon than if I got those ridiculous analysts and shareholders out there giving me a hard time. So, potentially there can be a control premium of value, and there may be a patience factor. We will talk about this. The greatest deficiency in the market's pricing of corporate America is its lack of patience. So maybe if we have it private, we have a better ability to exercise patience.
>
> But there is one negative. I always like to be able to maximize the flexibility and effectiveness of a company by public financing of the enterprise, and I like to have access to the capital markets right at hand. I will even register those huge bond issues that I can take down in 24 hours, and I do not have to negotiate, enter into loan agreements or any of those kinds of restrictive features. So, I would take that as a subtraction.[4]

To paraphrase, Murray defines Private Market Value as the business's value plus a control premium and a "patience factor," minus market access.[5]

There are two different types of private market buyers: financial buyers such as private equity firms like Kohlberg Kravis and Roberts (KKR) and the Blackstone Group, to name two, and strategic buyers, such as Roper Technologies and Illinois Tool Works, two public companies that are active acquirers.

---

[4] Roger F. Murray, and Gabelli Asset Management Company "Lecture #1. Value Versus Price." Roger F. Murray lecture series, Museum of Television & Radio, New York, January 22, 1993.

[5] To further clarify, the "control premium" is defined as the premium a buyer would have to pay to gain control of the assets. Murray's "patience factor" is the luxury of time that management has when making decisions without the scrutiny of public shareholders. "Market access" is a company's ability to raise capital in the equity or debt markets because, all else being equal, a public company would, in most cases, have easier access to the capital markets than a similar private company.

Financial buyers target publicly held companies that they feel are undervalued by other investors and look specifically for situations where they believe they can improve the financial performance to increase the company's value. These buyers aim to take companies private so that they can employ Murray's patience factor to focus on implementing potentially dramatic improvements to the company's operational efficiency, often with a longer time horizon than management feels they have as a publicly held entity. The financial buyer believes that these actions will generate a significant increase in the company's value, from which the buyer will reap the benefit.

On the other hand, a strategic buyer, which can be either an existing competitor or a company wanting to enter the market, often wants to expand its market position and is faced with a buy-versus-build decision. In these situations, the acquirer must choose either to reproduce the incumbent's assets or, alternatively, to simply buy the incumbent to gain control of its assets. The potential acquirer must weigh whether it is cheaper to buy the company "as is" or attempt to reproduce its market position, a calculation that needs to balance time to market against the cost to acquire. As most assets can be reproduced over time, the majority of the control premium paid in these deals is driven by the acquirer's desire to reduce its time to market.

Cash Flow Generated by Operating the Assets: Return on Invested Capital, Cost of Capital, and Excess Returns

Generating cash flows almost always requires some sort of outlay of capital because it is exceedingly rare for a business to be able to produce positive cash flows without some kind of prior capital investment. The capital outlay in business is generally referred to as a business's **invested capital**, and the return on that capital is usually referred to as the business's **return on invested capital**, or **ROIC**. Invested capital also has a cost, however, as we discuss in Chapter 2, which is usually referred to as the business's **cost of capital**.

A company generates what economists call **excess returns when its return on invested capital (ROIC) is greater than its cost of capital (WACC)**. It is excess returns that attract competition, not a company's cash flows, because other companies know they will have to invest capital to capture the cash flows. Therefore, a potential competitor will be interested in entering the market only if they are confident that the incremental cash flows generated by the incremental investment will produce a return greater than the incremental cost of capital for that investment.

To determine if a company earns excess returns, we need to know two numbers: The company's **cost of capital** and its **return on invested capital**.

For instance, if Zoe decides to invest money in a lemonade stand, that capital has to come from somewhere, either from her savings or from borrowing. If she has her savings invested in Charlie Dreifus's Royce Special Equity Fund (that has returned 8.5% per annum over the past 10 years at the time of this writing in March 2017), she would forgo this return to make the investment in the lemonade stand.[6] Presumably, Zoe wants to earn the highest possible return on her money. Therefore, she will invest in the lemonade stand only if she expects it to deliver a return higher than her

---

[6] We assume that the fund continues to earn 8.5% per annum in the future.

current investment; otherwise, she would be financially better off leaving her savings in Charlie's fund. The return she forgoes is her **opportunity cost** and, in this case, also is the lemonade stand's **cost of capital**, as we explain in Chapter 2.

Zoe needs to compare the *potential return* she could earn investing in the lemonade stand against her 8.5% cost of capital to see if investing in the business makes sense. In other words, Zoe needs to calculate the lemonade stand's expected ROIC to decide whether to move forward with the investment. It should make sense that the lemonade stand's return on invested capital needs to exceed the cost of capital for Zoe to be better off financially by making the investment.

Calculating a return on invested capital is similar to calculating a return on any investment. For example, if Zoe has $1,000 invested in a triple tax-free bond[7] and receives checks for $40 in the mail each year,[8] then the return on her investment is 4%, as the following calculation demonstrates:

$$\text{Return on Investment} = \frac{\text{After-Tax Income}}{\text{Capital Invested}}$$

$$\text{Return on Investment} = \frac{\$40}{\$1,000} = 4\%$$

Similarly, the lemonade stand's return on invested capital will equal the cash the business generates divided by the capital invested in the business, as the following formula shows:

$$\text{Return on Invested Capital (ROIC)} = \frac{\text{Owner Earnings}}{\text{Invested Capital}}$$

We define owner earnings in Chapter 2 and, therefore, we will not repeat the explanation here. However, we need to define **invested capital** in more detail to move forward with the analysis.

Zoe knows how much she has invested in her tax-free bond; therefore, calculating her return on invested capital is easy. Although conceptually similar, determining the amount of invested capital in a real business can be trickier in practice. For simplicity, invested capital is equivalent to the amount of cash invested in the business,

---

[7] Free from local, state, and federal tax.
[8] Municipal bonds actually pay semi-annually, so Zoe would receive two checks of $20 each per year.

which in Zoe's case is all the different items she needs to purchase to get the business up and running. More formally, invested capital is defined as follows:[9]

$$\text{Invested Capital} = \text{Current Assets} - \text{Current Liabilities}$$
$$+ \text{Net PP\&E (property, plant, and equipment)}$$

The invested capital of Zoe's Lemonade Stand is shown in Table 3.2.

Table 3.2   Zoe's Lemonade Stand Balance Sheet

Cash for change	50.00	
Inventory		
Lemons - 3 bags	21.00	
Solo 16 oz cups - 100	21.94	
Color Straws - 250 count	3.04	
Domino Sugar - 4lb bag	4.19	
Total Inventory	50.17	
Total Current Assets	$ 100.17	
Accounts Payable	18.19	
Accrued Salaries and Expenses	35.00	
Total Current Liabilities	$ 53.19	
Net Working Capital		$ 46.98
Fixed Assets		
Cost to build Lemonade Stand	398.96	
Pitcher x 2	28.16	
Ice cube trays	8.94	
Cash Register	63.99	
28 quart cooler	38.99	
Stainless Steel Juicer	13.98	
Net Property Plant and Equipment	$ 553.02	$ 553.02
Total Invested Capital		$ 600.00

[9] The intricacies and mechanics of calculating return on invested capital are beyond the scope of this book. A great place to start is Michael Mauboussin's June 4, 2014, report, *Calculating Return on Invested Capital.* Google "Mauboussin calculating return on invested capital" to obtain a copy of the report online.

We show in the previous chapter that Zoe estimates the lemonade stand will produce $120 of owner earnings in her first year of operation, which means the business would generate a return on invested capital of 20.0%, as the following calculation shows:

$$\text{Return on Invested Capital (ROIC)} = \frac{\text{Owner Earnings}}{\text{Invested Capital}}$$

$$\text{Return on Invested Capital (ROIC)} = \frac{\$120}{\$600} = 20.0\%$$

Zoe can perform a similar analysis on her investment in the Royce Special Equity Fund:

$$\text{Return on Invested Capital in Royce Special Equity Fund} = \frac{\text{Investment Return}}{\text{Invested Capital}}$$

$$\text{Return on Invested Capital in Royce Special Equity Fund} = \frac{\$51}{\$600} = 8.5\%$$

As mentioned above, the expected return from investing in the Royce Fund is Zoe's **opportunity cost** and the lemonade stand's **cost of capital**, which, as the calculation shows, equals 8.5% on her $600 investment, or $51 per year. The following analysis shows that Zoe would generate excess returns by investing in the lemonade stand, which we can show as both a percent and a dollar amount.

(Note: We will signify excess returns in orange, cost of capital in purple, and incremental growth in green throughout this chapter.)

We can calculate the lemonade stand's excess return as a *percent* using the following formula:

$$\text{Excess Returns in Percent} = (\text{Return on Invested Capital} - \text{Cost of Capital})$$

$$\text{Excess Returns in Percent} = (\text{ROIC} - \text{WACC})$$

$$\text{Excess Returns in Percent} = (20.0\% - 8.5\%) = 11.5\%$$

We can calculate the excess return as a *dollar amount* by multiplying each percentage in the preceding formula by the amount of capital invested in the business, as the following calculation demonstrates:

$$\text{Excess Returns in Dollars} = (\text{ROIC} - \text{WACC}) * \text{Invested Capital}$$

$$\text{Excess Returns in Dollars} = (20.0\% - 8.5\%) * \$600$$

$$\text{Excess Returns in Dollars} = 11.5\% * \$600 = \$69$$

We can define owner earnings in terms of its return on invested capital if we rearrange the earlier ROIC formula:

$$\text{Return on Invested Capital (ROIC)} = \frac{\text{Owner Earnings}}{\text{Invested Capital}}$$

$$\text{Owner Earnings} = (\text{ROIC} * \text{Invested Capital})$$

Which, for the lemonade stand, equals:

$$\text{Owner Earnings} = 20.0\% * \$600 = \$120$$

We can split owner earnings into its two components—excess returns in dollars and cost of capital in dollars—using the following formula:

$$\text{Owner Earnings} = (\text{ROIC} * \text{Invested Capital})$$

$$= (\text{Excess Returns} + \text{Cost of Capital}) * \text{Invested Capital}$$

$$\text{Owner Earnings} = (\text{Excess Returns} * \text{Invested Capital})$$

$$+ (\text{Cost of Capital} * \text{Invested Capital})$$

$$\text{Owner Earnings} = (20.0\% * \$600) = (11.5\% * \$600) + (8.5\% * \$600)$$

$$\text{Owner Earnings} = \$120 = \$69 + \$51$$

The dollar amount of the cost of capital is called a **capital charge**, which equals the company's cost of capital times the amount of capital invested in the business. The capital charge is the cash flow the lemonade stand must generate to cover its cost of equity capital. The analysis shows that Zoe would expect to earn excess returns of $69 each year by making the investment in the lemonade stand.

WHAT EXACTLY IS A CAPITAL CHARGE?

It is important to fully understand the concept of a capital charge to follow the examples in the rest of the chapter.

A capital charge is nothing more than the *dollar* equivalent of the cost of capital and is calculated by multiplying the amount of invested capital by the cost of capital. For instance, if Zoe's cost of capital is 8.5% (as we assume throughout the book), then the capital charge on the $600 of capital she invested in the business would be $51 per year.

If Zoe funds the lemonade stand exclusively from borrowing money at a rate of 8.5%, her cost of capital would be a real cash expense and it would be easy to identify the capital charge because interest expense is a line item on the income statement.

On the other hand, Zoe will still have a capital charge if she funds the business entirely with equity. However, unlike interest expense, the equity capital charge is a noncash expense and there is no explicit line item on the income statement reflecting the charge. Although there is an obvious financial cost with equity, we have found that it is hard for many investors (and most senior executives) to comprehend its importance because there is no actual cash or corresponding accounting expense associated with the capital charge.

Businesses with Excess Returns Attract Competition

The lemonade stand's return on invested capital of 20.0% will likely attract competitors, however. For example, let's say that the weather is very nice during the first few weeks of summer and business is booming. In fact, the lemonade stand's business is so good that Zoe has enough profits at the end of the month to buy a new bicycle. Charlotte, who lives across the street from Zoe's house, notices Zoe's newfound riches and thinks to herself, "I want a new bicycle, too. Since Zoe is making so much money, so quickly, I think I will start a lemonade stand as well."

As the only person selling lemonade in her neighborhood, Zoe has a monopoly on the market. She is providing a product to customers that no one else is offering and has generated an impressive financial return of 20.0% in the process (see Table 3.3).

Table 3.3   Zoe's Lemonade Stand: Monopoly Returns

	Zoe
Cups sold	600
Price per cup	$ 2.00
Revenues	1,200
Costs	1,080
Owner Earnings	120
Invested Capital	600
ROIC	20.0%

However, long-lasting monopolies are rare because sooner or later competitors figure out how to replicate the product, enter the market, and compete for customers. The uniqueness of the product proves to be temporary over time. Unless Zoe has some way to prevent Charlotte from entering her market, Charlotte will begin selling lemonade, and take revenues and profits away from Zoe, and the reduced profits will decrease the lemonade stand's return on invested capital. For example, if Charlotte captures half of Zoe's sales, then Zoe's return on invested capital would fall to 10.0%, as the analysis in Table 3.4 shows.

Table 3.4   Zoe's Lemonade Stand: No Competitive Advantage

	Zoe	Charlotte
Cups sold	300	300
Price per cup	$ 2.00	$ 2.00
Revenues	600	600
Costs	540	540
Owner earnings	60	60
Invested capital	600	600
ROIC	**10.0%**	**10.0%**

To prevent Charlotte from entering the market and negatively impacting her profitability, Zoe needs some type of **competitive advantage**.[10]

Competitive Advantage Defined

We see from the ROIC formula that the only way for a company to generate a return on invested capital greater than its cost of capital is to command higher prices, achieve lower costs, or use capital more efficiently than its competitors, as we demonstrate in Table 3.5.

Table 3.5   Sources of Excess Return

		Year 1	
	Revenues	1200	← Higher Prices
	Cost of goods sold	-535	
Owner Earnings	Gross profit	665	Lower
	Selling, general and administrative	-453	← Costs
	Operating income	212	
	Income taxes	-80	
	Net income	131	
	+ Depreciation and amortization	52	
	- Maintenance capex	-63	
	= **Owner earnings**	120	

Return on Invested Capital =

		Year 1	
	Current assets	100	
Invested Capital	Current liabilities	-53	More Efficient use
	Net working capital	47	← of Capital
	Net property plant and equipment	553	
	Invested capital	600	

For instance, we see the benefit of a price advantage in Table 3.6, where Zoe generates a higher return on capital than Charlotte because Zoe charges a higher price for each cup of lemonade sold.

---

[10] This discussion is meant to be a brief overview of competitive advantage, as an in-depth review of the topic is beyond the scope of this book. There are hundreds of books and articles written on the subject, although *Competition Demystified*, by Bruce Greenwald and Judd Kahn, is our favorite full-length treatment.

Table 3.6   Zoe's Lemonade Stand: Price Advantage

	Zoe	Charlotte
Cups sold	300	300
Price per cup	**$ 3.00**	**$ 2.00**
Revenues	900	600
Costs	810	540
Owner earnings	90	60
Invested capital	600	600
ROIC	**15.0%**	**10.0%**

Alternatively, we see the benefit of a **cost advantage** in Table 3.7, where Zoe generates a higher return on capital than Charlotte because Zoe has lower operating costs.

Table 3.7   Zoe's Lemonade Stand: Cost Advantage

	Zoe	Charlotte
Cups sold	300	300
Price per cup	$ 2.00	$ 2.00
Revenues	600	600
Costs	**450**	**540**
Owner earnings	150	60
Invested capital	600	600
ROIC	**25.0%**	**10.0%**

And, finally, we see the effect of using capital more efficiently in Table 3.8, where Zoe generates a higher return on capital than Charlotte because her business uses capital more efficiently.

Table 3.8   Zoe's Lemonade Stand: Capital Efficiency

	Zoe	Charlotte
Cups sold	300	300
Price per cup	$ 2.00	$ 2.00
Revenues	600	600
Costs	540	540
Owner earnings	60	60
Invested capital	**295**	**600**
ROIC	**20.3%**	**10.0%**

Sources of Competitive Advantage

There are four main sources of competitive advantage: customer-facing advantages, production advantages, efficiency advantages, and advantages due to government policy.

Competitive advantage is defined as a company's ability to generate excess returns. A sustainable competitive advantage is defined as a company's ability to generate excess returns over an extended period of time in the future, which requires barriers to entry to prevent competitors from entering the market and eroding away the excess returns.

Competitive advantages that allow a company to charge a higher price are generally referred to as **customer-facing advantages**, which implies that the customer is willing to stick with their current supplier and pay the higher price rather than pay a lower price by switching to a new supplier. These advantages exist when the customer is faced with search costs, switching costs, or buying habits.

Customer captivity based on **search costs** occurs when a consumer cannot or will not take the time to compare competing products or services. This customer behavior is generally found with purchases that are infrequent and involve decisions that are critically important. For example, if your car breaks down on a rainy night, you probably won't call four different towing companies to see which one is the cheapest.

Customer captivity based on **switching costs** arises in situations when there is a prohibitively high cost in terms of time or money to switch from one product to another. For example, if you bank with Chase and have all your payees set up in its online system, have direct deposit for your paycheck, and know the most convenient ATM locations in your neighborhood, you will be hesitant to switch to Citibank because the change would be time-consuming and require your learning a new online banking system.

If the search costs and switching costs are low, yet the customer remains captive, it is most likely that their decision is based on a well-ingrained **habit**. Habit-based purchase decisions generally include routine purchases for products such as shampoo, toothpaste, beer, laundry detergent, or cigarettes.

Many people believe that **brands** are a source of competitive advantage. However, unless the brand reinforces the search costs, switching costs, or consumer's buying habit, it is not an advantage by itself. Virtually every product available has a brand, even if it is a house brand such as Whole Foods' 365 Everyday Value set of products. One cannot argue that brands are a source of competitive advantage if *every* product has one. On the other hand, a simple example of a brand that *is* a source of competitive advantage is Tylenol. If you walk into a CVS with a headache, you have the option to purchase the CVS-brand acetaminophen for $6 and the same-sized bottle of Tylenol for $9. Even though the two medicines are the same chemically, Tylenol's brand commands a higher price that people are willing to pay.

Advantages based on **customer captivity** often erodes over time as individual tastes, needs, and desires change. Consumer preferences also shift with changes in social norms, pop culture, or new information based on health and safety concerns or efficacy of a product or service. New technologies change rapidly, bringing innovative products and services to market that often obliterate the demand for other products, even if the products have enjoyed strong customer captivity in the past. Finally, the proliferation of information can weaken customer-based advantages because the additional information allows consumers to be better informed in their purchasing decisions. For instance, the Internet allows consumers to perform in-depth research before buying a product and allows consumers to compare products more easily before making a purchase decision.

Production advantages provide a company with lower manufacturing costs than its competitors. A company with a cost advantage can either charge the same price for its products as competitors, generating higher profitability and return on capital; or, charge a lower price for its products than competitors, potentially gaining market share, yet still maintaining its profitability and high return on capital.

We show the financial results from these two choices in Table 3.9. As the example illustrates, Zoe charges the same price as Charlotte in the example on the left, although she has a higher return on invested capital because of her lower costs. In the example on the right, Zoe cut her price, but maintains a higher return on invested capital than Charlotte, also because of her lower costs.

Production advantages come from three primary sources: **proprietary production technology**, **lower cost of inputs**, or **superior distribution**.

Table 3.9   Zoe's Lemonade Stand: Pricing Alternatives

	Zoe	Charlotte		Zoe	Charlotte
Cups sold	300	300	Cups sold	300	300
Price per cup	$ 2.00	$ 2.00	Price per cup	$ 1.25	$ 1.25
Revenues	600	600	Revenues	375	375
Costs	450	540	Costs	281	338
Cost as % of revenue	**75%**	**90%**	**Cost as % of revenue**	**75%**	**90%**
Owner earnings	150	60	Owner earnings	94	38
Invested capital	600	600	Invested capital	600	600
ROIC	**25.0%**	**10.0%**	**ROIC**	**15.6%**	**6.3%**

A company with **proprietary production technology** manufactures products that are hard for competitors to replicate. For example, Intel's advanced production technology allows it to produce microprocessors that no other semiconductor manufacturer can reproduce, resulting in a significantly higher return on capital than any of its competitors.

Most production advantages erode over time, however, because it is hard for any company to maintain its proprietary technology for very long before its competitors successfully replicate or re-create the process.

A company will have a **structural cost advantage** if it has **lower cost of inputs** or possesses **unique resources**. For example, if Zoe was the only one in the neighborhood to have a lemon tree in her backyard and therefore did not have to pay for lemons, she would have lower costs in producing her lemonade than her competitors.

However, excess returns accrue to the *suppliers* of the unique resource over time, not its customers, because the suppliers can charge high prices for their limited products. For example, if Zoe's next-door neighbor owned the lemon tree, the neighbor would generate the excess returns, not Zoe. An example in the "real world" is FRP Holdings, a company that has mines in Florida from which tenants like Vulcan Materials, Martin Marietta Materials, and Cemex pay royalties to extract aggregates. FRP's mines earn extraordinary returns on invested capital because the cost of transporting aggregates over long distances is prohibitively high, making the company's properties (literally) uniquely positioned.

Finally, a company can have a cost advantage if it has access to **distribution networks** that are unavailable to its competitors, which enables the company to deliver its products or services to its customers at lower costs. For example, if Snapple decides to introduce a new flavor of lemonade, the company will have access to premium shelf space at retail stores because it has established relationships with key distributors. Conversely, if Zoe tried to broaden her market into retail stores, she most likely would find it extremely challenging and costly to obtain *any* shelf space for her lemonade.

A company will have an **efficiency advantage** if it has economies of scale in some aspect of its business. There are three general sources of scale: **learning curve**, **economies of scale or scope**, and **network effects**.

Any process that becomes more cost-efficient over time from cumulative learning benefits from what is generally referred to as a **learning** or **experience curve**. The increased efficiency results from a company learning how to make its products more efficiently or with less waste, which lowers its manufacturing costs per unit over time.

A second source of scale exists when a company can spread high fixed costs over a large volume of units, which reduces the fixed cost per unit. These advantages are referred to as **economies of scale** or **scope**. For instance, Coca-Cola has *scale* with its marketing budget because the cost of its advertising can be spread over more individual units than its competitors'. A new competitor entering the market would have trouble generating demand for its products because it cannot match Coca-Cola's level of advertising and its operating costs per bottle of soda would be materially higher than Coke's. The same potential scale benefits apply to fixed production cost, research and development, and the cost of operating a company-owned distribution network. These expenses are generally fixed, at least in the short term. Therefore, the company with the largest unit volume has a cost advantage because the fixed cost is spread over a large volume of individual units.

The third potential source of scale comes from **network effects**, which are products or services that deliver more value to the consumer as the number of users increases. These products tend to result in winner-take-most markets because the network effect favors a single vendor. Recent examples of businesses that enjoy advantages based on network effects are Facebook, LinkedIn, Airbnb, and Uber.

It is hard to maintain relative scale in large markets, however. In fact, except for advantages from network effects, scale advantages are often limited to regional geographies or well-defined markets. Scale is rarely static over time and must be maintained for it to remain a competitive advantage. Furthermore, it is hard for any company to maintain large relative scale in a growing market because the growth in demand creates new customers, which provide opportunities for competitors to enter the market, grab market share and reach scale.

The final potential source of competitive advantage is **advantage due to government policy**. In some instances, governments can limit entry into specific markets. This barrier provides existing firms with a competitive advantage, which will exist only for as long as the regulation remains in place. Government policies affecting competition usually involve antitrust, zoning, or environmental regulations; patents; tariffs; quotas; and subsidies. Classic examples of this type of advantage is the U.S. patent system or regulation affecting electric utilities. Advantages due to government regulations can disappear quickly if the government decides to change its policies. And, in the case of a patent, an advantage can literally change in a day as patents expire 17 years after their issue date.

We summarize the four potential sources of competitive advantage in Figure 3.6.

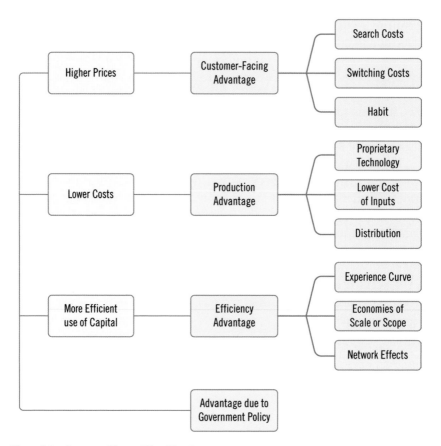

Figure 3.6   Sources of Competitive Advantage

Sustaining Competitive Advantage

We have found that a company's competitive advantage will be sustainable if, and only if, it possesses a true customer-facing advantage coupled with a scale-based advantage. The customer-facing advantage makes it hard for competitors to steal customers, and the scale-based advantage provides the incumbent vendor with lower operating costs. The two advantages reinforce each other and make it extremely challenging for any new company to enter the market successfully.

Now that we have discussed competitive advantage, we can move forward with showing how to value the cash flow a company generates from operating its assets. There are three layers to consider—the value of the assets with no competitive advantage, the value of the assets with a competitive advantage, and the value of incremental growth. We show these factors in Figure 3.7.

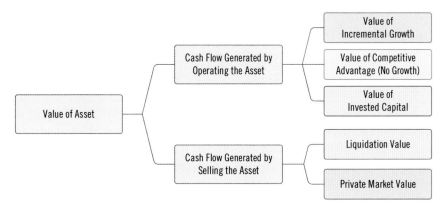

Figure 3.7   Potential Sources of Cash Flow

How Competitive Advantage Affects Valuation?[11]

To determine how competitive advantage affects valuation we start with the definition of the estimated value of an asset:

> The estimated value of an asset equals the sum of the cash flows expected to be produced by that asset, over its useful life, discounted for the time value of money and the uncertainty of receiving those cash flows.

And then add the definition of competitive advantage:

> Competitive advantage is a company's ability to produce and sustain excess returns over time.

To arrive at the definition of the *value* of a company's competitive advantage:

> The estimated value of a company's competitive advantage is the sum of the estimated cash flow solely generated by excess returns, over the period that the company can sustain those excess returns, discounted for the time value of money and the uncertainty of receiving those cash flows.

---

[11] We use a lot of discounted cash flow (DCF) models in this section of the book. Although some readers might feel this approach to be overly academic, we find using a DCF-based analysis effective in explaining the core concepts. Further to the point, we argue in the box 'But I Don't Do That!' (Chapter 2) that all valuation methods are derivatives of the DCF model. Therefore, the analysis in the current chapter translates well to other valuation approaches.

Value of Zoe's Lemonade Stand With No Growth

To determine the value of Zoe's Lemonade Stand's competitive advantage we need to calculate how much of the lemonade stand's cash flows is generated from excess returns.

Scenario 1: Value of Zoe's Lemonade Stand When ROIC Greater Than the Cost of Capital With No Growth   We calculated in Chapter 2 that the lemonade stand's present value, assuming 20% return on invested capital and no growth, equals $1,412, which we replicate in Figure 3.8.

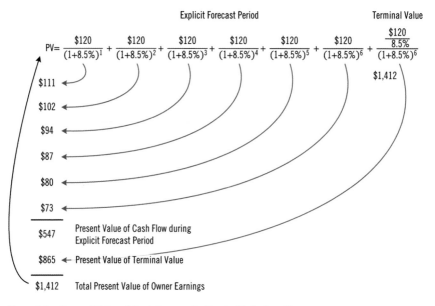

Figure 3.8   Present Value of Zoe's Lemonade Stand with No Growth

Although the approach calculates the lemonade stand's present value correctly, it does not identify the value of the lemonade stand derived from its excess returns, which we need to quantify to see how competitive advantage impacts valuation.

To perform this analysis, we need to split the lemonade stand's earnings into its excess returns in dollars and the cash flow allocated to its capital charge, as we did on page 84:

$$\text{Owner Earnings} = (\text{Excess Returns} + \text{Cost of Capital}) * \text{Invested Capital}$$

$$\text{Owner Earnings} = (\text{Excess Returns} * \text{Invested Capital})$$
$$+ (\text{Cost of Capital} * \text{Invested Capital})$$

$$\text{Owner Earnings} = (20.0\% * \$600) = (11.5\% * \$600) + (8.5\% * \$600)$$

$$\text{Owner Earnings} = \$120 = \$69 + \$51$$

The analysis shows that the lemonade stand's $120 in annual owner earnings are comprised of $69 from its excess returns and $51 to cover its capital charge. We can use arrow charts to show this analysis graphically, with the lemonade stand's overall annual owner earnings on the left and the subcomponents of excess returns ($69 per period) and capital charge ($51 per period) on the right, as shown in Figure 3.9.

Figure 3.9   Owner Earnings Equals Excess Return Plus Capital Charge

We can determine how much of the lemonade stand's present value is derived from the company's excess returns using the following formulas:

$$\text{PV Owner Earnings} = \frac{\$120}{(1+8.5\%)^1} + \frac{\$120}{(1+8.5\%)^2} + \frac{\$120}{(1+8.5\%)^3} + \frac{\$120}{(1+8.5\%)^4}$$

$$+ \frac{\$120}{(1+8.5\%)^5} + \frac{\$120}{(1+8.5\%)^6} + \frac{\dfrac{\$120}{8.5\%}}{(1+8.5\%)^6}$$

Since:

$$\text{Owner Earnings} = \$120 = \$69 + \$51$$

We can repopulate the formula by substituting owner earnings with the excess returns in dollars and the capital charges, as the following calculation shows:

$$PV\ Owner\ Earnings = \frac{\$69+\$51}{\left(1+8.5\%\right)^1} + \frac{\$69+\$51}{\left(1+8.5\%\right)^2} + \frac{\$69+\$51}{\left(1+8.5\%\right)^3} + \frac{\$69+\$51}{\left(1+8.5\%\right)^4}$$

$$+ \frac{\$69+\$51}{\left(1+8.5\%\right)^5} + \frac{\$69+\$51}{\left(1+8.5\%\right)^6} + \frac{\dfrac{\$69+\$51}{8.5\%}}{\left(1+8.5\%\right)^6}$$

First, we calculate the present value of the excess returns in dollars using a standard DCF:

$$PV\ of\ Excess\ Returns = \frac{\$69}{\left(1+8.5\%\right)^1} + \frac{\$69}{\left(1+8.5\%\right)^2} + \frac{\$69}{\left(1+8.5\%\right)^3} + \frac{\$69}{\left(1+8.5\%\right)^4}$$

$$+ \frac{\$69}{\left(1+8.5\%\right)^5} + \frac{\$69}{\left(1+8.5\%\right)^6} + \frac{\dfrac{\$69}{8.5\%}}{\left(1+8.5\%\right)^6}$$

Figure 3.10 shows the discounting of the individual cash flows and terminal value of the excess returns to arrive at the present value of the excess returns in dollars:

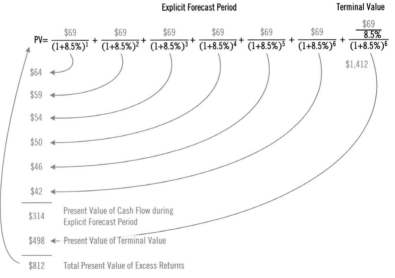

Figure 3.10   Present Value of Excess Return

We can calculate the present value of the capital charges using the same approach:

$$\text{PV of Capital Charges} = \frac{\$51}{\left(1+8.5\%\right)^1} + \frac{\$51}{\left(1+8.5\%\right)^2} + \frac{\$51}{\left(1+8.5\%\right)^3} + \frac{\$51}{\left(1+8.5\%\right)^4}$$

$$+ \frac{\$51}{\left(1+8.5\%\right)^5} + \frac{\$51}{\left(1+8.5\%\right)^6} + \frac{\dfrac{\$51}{8.5\%}}{\left(1+8.5\%\right)^6}$$

Figure 3.11 shows the discounting of the individual capital charges and the terminal value, to arrive their present value.

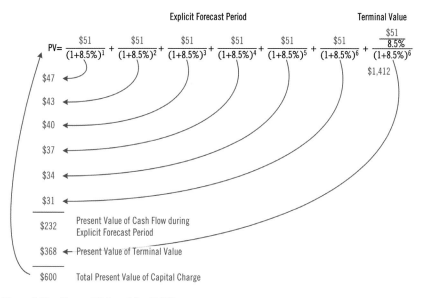

Figure 3.11   Present Value of Capital Charge

The analysis shows that the present value of the excess returns equals $812 and the present value of capital charges equals $600, which, when summed together, equal the lemonade stand's total present value of $1,412, as the following formulas confirm:

$$\text{PV of Zoe's Lemonade Stand} = \text{PV of Excess Returns} + \text{PV of Capital Charges}$$

$$\text{PV of Zoe's Lemonade Stand} = \$812 + \$600$$

$$\text{PV of Zoe's Lemonade Stand} = \$1,412$$

It is important to note that the lemonade stand derives $812 of its value from its excess returns. Since we define **competitive advantage** as a company's ability to generate excess returns, the value of Zoe's Lemonade Stand's competitive advantage is $812. Therefore, since the lemonade stand has a competitive advantage, as evidenced by its excess returns, Zoe is better off by investing in the business than leaving the money in savings.

Scenario 2: Value of Zoe's Lemonade Stand when ROIC Equals the Cost of Capital with No Growth   If we assume that Zoe has *no competitive advantage*, then the lemonade stand's return on invested capital would equal its cost of capital, and the business would have no excess returns, as the following calculation shows:

$$\text{Excess Returns in Percent} = (\text{ROIC} - \text{WACC})$$

$$\text{Excess Returns in Percent} = (8.5\% - 8.5\%) = 0.0\%$$

We can also show that the lemonade stand generates no excess returns when we split its owner earnings into the two subcomponents:

$$\text{Owner Earnings in Dollars} = (\text{ROIC} * \text{Invested Capital})$$

$$\text{Owner Earnings in Dollars} = (\text{Excess Returns} * \text{Invested Capital})$$
$$+ (\text{Cost of Capital} * \text{Invested Capital})$$

$$\text{Owner Earnings in Dollars} = (0.0\% * \$600) + (8.5\% * \$600) = (8.5\% * \$600)$$

$$\text{Owner Earnings in Dollars} = \$0 + \$51 = \$51$$

We show the individual cash flows in Figure 3.12, although there are no excess returns in this case because owner earnings equals the capital charge.

Figure 3.12   Owner Earnings Equals Capital Charge with No Competitive Advantage

To illustrate the point, we can split the lemonade stand's owner earnings into excess returns in dollars and the annual capital charge, as we did with the prior example.

$$\text{Owner Earnings in Dollars} = \$0 + \$51 = \$51$$

And then use the same approach to calculate their present value:

$$\text{PV of Owner Earnings} = \frac{\$0 + \$51}{(1+8.5\%)^1} + \frac{\$0 + \$51}{(1+8.5\%)^2} + \frac{\$0 + \$51}{(1+8.5\%)^3} + \frac{\$0 + \$51}{(1+8.5\%)^4}$$

$$+ \frac{\$0 + \$51}{(1+8.5\%)^5} + \frac{\$0 + \$51}{(1+8.5\%)^6} + \frac{\dfrac{\$0 + \$51}{8.5\%}}{(1+8.5\%)^6}$$

Although the exercise is not necessary because the lemonade stand generates no excess return, we can use the following formula to show that the present value of excess returns equals $0 by calculating the present value of excess returns in dollars:

$$\text{PV of Excess Returns} = \frac{\$0}{(1+8.5\%)^1} + \frac{\$0}{(1+8.5\%)^2} + \frac{\$0}{(1+8.5\%)^3} + \frac{\$0}{(1+8.5\%)^4}$$

$$+ \frac{\$0}{(1+8.5\%)^5} + \frac{\$0}{(1+8.5\%)^6} + \frac{\dfrac{\$0}{8.5\%}}{(1+8.5\%)^6}$$

$$\text{PV of Excess Returns} = \$0$$

We know from the previous example that the present value of the capital charges equals $600.

$$\text{PV of Capital Charges} = \$600$$

We can use the following formula to show that the lemonade's present value equals $600 when it generates no excess returns:

$$\text{PV of Zoe's Lemonade Stand} = \text{PV of Excess Returns} + \text{PV of Capital Charges}$$

$$\text{Total Present Value of Zoe's Lemonade Stand} = \$0 + \$600$$

$$\text{Total Present Value of Zoe's Lemonade Stand} = \$600$$

It is clear that the lemonade stand has no competitive advantage in this example because the business generates no excess returns. As a consequence, the value of the lemonade stand equals the value of its invested capital (which equals the present value of the annual capital charges). Zoe is better off leaving the money in her savings account as the investment in the business would create no excess value.

Scenario 3: Value of Zoe's Lemonade Stand when ROIC is Less Than the Cost of Capital with No Growth   What would be the value of the lemonade stand if its return on invested capital is *less* than its cost of capital? For instance, let's assume that the business generates a return on invested capital of only 6.4%, versus its cost of capital of 8.5%.

In this case, the lemonade stand's excess returns would be *negative* and the business will be *worth less* than the value of its invested capital, as the following analysis demonstrates:

$$\text{Excess Returns in Percent} = \left(\text{ROIC} - \text{WACC}\right)$$

$$\text{Excess Returns in Percent} = \left(6.4\% - 8.5\%\right) = -2.1\%$$

We show the negative excess returns in dollars when we split owner earnings into its two subcomponents, as we did in the two prior examples:

$$\text{Owner Earnings in Dollars} = \left(\text{ROIC} * \text{Invested Capital}\right)$$

$$\text{Owner Earnings in Dollars} = \left(\text{Excess Returns} * \text{Invested Capital}\right)$$
$$+ \left(\text{Cost of Capital} * \text{Invested Capital}\right)$$

$$\text{Owner Earnings in Dollars} = \left(-2.1\% * \$600\right) + \left(8.5\% * \$600\right) = \left(6.4\% * \$600\right)$$

$$\text{Owner Earnings in Dollars} = -\$13 + \$51 = \$38$$

We compare the owner earnings of $38 to the capital charge of $51 in Figure 3.13.

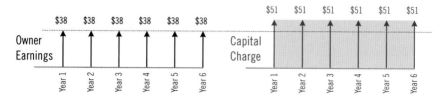

Figure 3.13   Owner Earnings Less than Capital Charge

We show the negative excess returns of $13 in Figure 3.14:

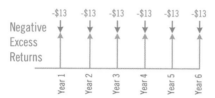

Figure 3.14   Negative Excess Returns Destroys Value

We can further demonstrate that the negative excess returns decrease the value of the lemonade stand using the same analysis we did in the two prior examples:

$$\text{PV of Owner Earnings} = \frac{\$38}{\left(1+8.5\%\right)^1} + \frac{\$38}{\left(1+8.5\%\right)^2} + \frac{\$38}{\left(1+8.5\%\right)^3} + \frac{\$38}{\left(1+8.5\%\right)^4}$$

$$+ \frac{\$38}{\left(1+8.5\%\right)^5} + \frac{\$38}{\left(1+8.5\%\right)^6} + \frac{\dfrac{\$38}{8.5\%}}{\left(1+8.5\%\right)^6}$$

$$\text{PV of Owner Earnings} = \$452$$

Once again, we can split owner earnings into its two subcomponents:

$$\text{Owner Earnings in Dollars} = -\$13 + \$51 = \$38$$

and repopulate the formula like we did in the previous examples:

$$\text{PV of Owner Earnings} = \frac{-\$13+\$51}{(1+8.5\%)^1} + \frac{-\$13+\$51}{(1+8.5\%)^2} + \frac{-\$13+\$51}{(1+8.5\%)^3} + \frac{-\$13+\$51}{(1+8.5\%)^4}$$

$$+ \frac{-\$13+\$51}{(1+8.5\%)^5} + \frac{-\$13+\$51}{(1+8.5\%)^6} + \frac{\dfrac{-\$13+\$51}{8.5\%}}{(1+8.5\%)^6}$$

It is clear that the present value of the excess return will be negative because the annual excess return in dollars is also negative, as we show in the following calculations:

$$\text{PV of Excess Returns} = \frac{-\$13}{(1+8.5\%)^1} + \frac{-\$13}{(1+8.5\%)^2} + \frac{-\$13}{(1+8.5\%)^3} + \frac{-\$13}{(1+8.5\%)^4}$$

$$+ \frac{-\$13}{(1+8.5\%)^5} + \frac{-\$13}{(1+8.5\%)^6} + \frac{\dfrac{-\$13}{8.5\%}}{(1+8.5\%)^6}$$

$$\text{PV of Excess Returns} = -\$148$$

We know from the prior examples the present value of the capital charges:

$$\text{PV of Capital Charges} = \$600$$

We show how the two subcomponents affect the lemonade stand's value in the following equations:

$$\text{PV of Zoe's Lemonade Stand} = \text{PV of Excess Returns} + \text{PV of Capital Charges}$$

$$\text{PV of Zoe's Lemonade Stand} = -\$148 + \$600$$

$$\text{PV of Zoe's Lemonade Stand} = \$452$$

The analysis confirms that the negative excess returns *destroy* value. Zoe is better off holding on to her savings and *not* investing in the lemonade stand because the business would be *worth less* than its invested capital.

Scenario 4: Value of Zoe's Lemonade Stand with ROIC Declining to the Cost of Capital with No Growth   What if Zoe's neighbor Charlotte enters the market? Unless Zoe has a sustainable competitive advantage to keep Charlotte from stealing her customers, the cash flows of Zoe's Lemonade Stand will fall and the excess returns will slowly disappear as the return on invested capital for the business is driven down to its cost of capital. For instance, let's assume that the lemonade stand's return on invested capital is 20% before Charlotte enters the market, but declines to its cost of capital by the end of year 6 because of increased competition. We show that the lemonade stand's owner earnings decline each year in Table 3.10.

Table 3.10   Declining Owner Earnings from Increasing Competitive Pressure

	Year 1	Year 2	Year 3	Year 4	Year 5	Year 6	Terminal Value
Owner earnings	120	106	92	79	65	51	600
PV of owner earnings	111	90	72	57	43	31	368
Total PV of owner earnings 772							

We demonstrate that the competitive pressure from Charlotte's entering the market erodes the lemonade stand's excess returns in Figure 3.15.

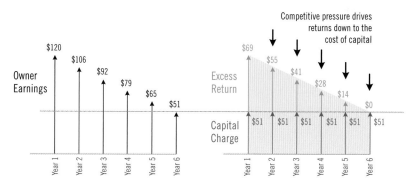

Figure 3.15   Competitive Pressures Drive Excess Returns to Zero

In Table 3.11 we show how we calculate the cash flows in Figure 3.15.

Table 3.11   Sources of Owner Earnings with Competitive Pressures

	Year 1	Year 2	Year 3	Year 4	Year 5	Year 6	Terminal Value
Owner Earnings	120	106	92	79	65	51	600
PV of owner earnings	111	90	72	57	43	31	368
Total PV of Owner Earnings 772							
Excess Returns	69	55	41	28	14	0	0
PV of Excess Returns	64	47	32	20	9	0	0
Total PV of Excess Returns 172							
Capital Charge	51	51	51	51	51	51	600
PV of Capital Charge	47	43	40	37	34	31	368
Total PV of Capital Charge 600							

It is important to emphasize this point a bit further. The lemonade stand's excess returns will be eliminated as its return on invested capital is driven to its cost of capital because of increased competitive pressures. While the business creates additional value during the years it generates excess returns, the value of the lemonade stand eventually will equal only the capital invested in the business after all excess returns have been competed away.

We can calculate the present value of the lemonade stand's owner earnings by discounting its future cash flows:

$$\text{PV of Owner Earnings} = \frac{\$120}{(1+8.5\%)^1} + \frac{\$106}{(1+8.5\%)^2} + \frac{\$92}{(1+8.5\%)^3} + \frac{\$79}{(1+8.5\%)^4}$$

$$+ \frac{\$65}{(1+8.5\%)^5} + \frac{\$51}{(1+8.5\%)^6} + \frac{\dfrac{\$51}{8.5\%}}{(1+8.5\%)^6}$$

$$\text{PV of Owner Earnings} = \$772$$

We can repopulate the formula like we did in the earlier examples by splitting owner earnings into its two subcomponents:

$$PV \text{ of Owner Earnings} = \frac{\$69 + \$51}{(1+8.5\%)^1} + \frac{\$55 + \$51}{(1+8.5\%)^2} + \frac{\$41 + \$51}{(1+8.5\%)^3} + \frac{\$28 + \$51}{(1+8.5\%)^4}$$

$$+ \frac{\$14 + \$51}{(1+8.5\%)^5} + \frac{\$0 + \$51}{(1+8.5\%)^6} + \frac{\dfrac{\$0 + \$51}{8.5\%}}{(1+8.5\%)^6}$$

And can calculate the present value of each subcomponent:

PV of Excess Returns = $172

PV of Capital Charges = $600

We show how the two subcomponents affect the lemonade stand's value in the following equations:

PV of Zoe's Lemonade Stand = PV of Excess Returns + PV of Capital Charges

Present Value of Zoe's Lemonade Stand = $172 + $600

Total Present Value of Zoe's Lemonade Stand = $772

The value of the lemonade stand is greater than the value of its invested capital, and Zoe is better off investing in the business. However, although the business starts off generating excess returns, Zoe cannot maintain them because the lemonade stand does not have a sustainable competitive advantage. While the lemonade stand creates $172 of value over the six-year period, the business creates value only during the period when it generated excess returns.

How Growth Affects Valuation

As we demonstrate in the examples above, a business does not create value for its owners simply by *producing* owner earnings; rather, a business *creates* value only when it generates excess returns (returns above its cost of capital).

We need to be more precise with the terms when we discuss growth, however. Growth in owner earnings creates incremental value only if the growth generates *positive* excess returns. And because essentially all growth requires additional investment, any incremental growth in owner earnings needs to be netted against the capital charge associated with the additional investment necessary to support the growth.

Consequently (and at the risk of being repetitive), the *perceived* value of growth can be misleading because, counterintuitively, **nominal incremental growth in owner earnings does not always increase the** incremental value **of the business,** as we demonstrate in the following examples.

Nominal Growth: The Illusion of Moving Forward

Imagine you are flying to London. You arrive at the airport, go through security, and start walking toward the gate. You look ahead and realize that the distance to your destination is a long walk, so you decide to step onto a moving sidewalk to accelerate your pace. About halfway to the gate, the sidewalk stops abruptly and begins moving in the opposite direction at 8.5 feet per second (fps).

If you stand still, you will end up back where you started. You begin to walk at a modest pace of 3 fps. Although you are *walking forward*, you are actually *moving in reverse* at 5.5 fps because you have not overcome the sidewalk's speed of 8.5 fps in the opposite direction. You pick-up your pace and begin to jog at 8.5 fps. You make no forward progress, however, because the sidewalk is moving in the opposite direction at the same speed that you are jogging. You decide to break into a run and quickly hit a pace of 20 fps. Although you are running at 20 fps, you are moving forward at only 11.5 fps because the sidewalk is moving against you at 8.5 fps. Eventually, you make it to the end of the sidewalk and get off to board your flight.

One can characterize your movement in **nominal** and **real** values. For instance, your nominal speed is the speed at which you walk, be it 3, 8.5, or 20 fps, whereas your real speed is -5.5, 0, or 11.5 fps, which is your nominal speed offset by the sidewalk's movement in the opposite direction, as we show in Table 3.12:

Table 3.12   Nominal and Real Speeds on Moving Sidewalk

	Nominal Speed	Speed of Sidewalk	Real Speed	
Nominal Speed < Sidewalk	3.0	-8.5	-5.5	Going Backward
Nominal Speed = Sidewalk	8.5	-8.5	0.0	Stay in the Same Place
Nominal Speed > Sidewalk	20.0	-8.5	11.5	Forward Progress

We can use the airport analogy to discuss the various components of growth. Since virtually all growth requires incremental investment, the return on incremental invested capital (ROIIC) can be thought of as the nominal speed. The associated capital charge (WACC * incremental invested capital) from the incremental investment can be thought of as the speed of the sidewalk moving in the opposite direction. The difference between the ROIIC and the cost of capital (WACC) can be thought of as the real speed, which is the net forward progress or, in the case of a business, the incremental value created from growth. We substitute these values in Table 3.13:

Table 3.13   Nominal and Real Return on Incremental Investment

	ROIIC	WACC	Incr Excess Returns	
ROIIC < WACC	3.0%	8.5%	-5.5%	Negative Incremental Value
ROIIC = WACC	8.5%	8.5%	0.0%	No Incremental Value
ROIIC > WACC	20.0%	8.5%	11.5%	Increased Incremental Value

As the table shows, the difference between the nominal ROIIC and the WACC is the *real* or *excess return*, which will be positive when the ROIIC is greater than WACC, zero when the ROIIC equals WACC, and negative when the ROIIC is less than WACC. Therefore, growth creates *negative* incremental value if the incremental investment earns only 3%, no incremental value if the investment earns 8.5%, and *positive* incremental value if the investment earns 20%.

Real Growth: Removing the Illusion

As we show earlier in the chapter, the value of Zoe's Lemonade Stand (base business) equals the present value of owner earnings, which is comprised of excess returns and capital charges:

PV of Owner Earnings of Zoe's Lemonade Stand (base business)

= PV of Excess Returns + PV of Capital Charges

We can calculate the nominal incremental growth in owner earnings using the same formula:

Nominal PV of Incremental Growth in Owner Earnings of Zoe's Lemonade Stand

= PV of Incremental Excess Returns + PV of Incremental Capital Charges

To calculate the *total* nominal present value of Zoe's Lemonade Stand, with growth, we simply add the two components—the present value of the base business and the nominal present value of the incremental growth:

Total Nominal PV of Zoe's Lemonade Stand

= PV of Owner Earnings of Zoe's Lemonade Stand (base business)

+ Nominal PV of Incremental Growth

In the next three examples, we calculate growth under three different scenarios, as outlined in Table 3.13—growth when ROIIC equals WACC, growth when ROIIC is less than WACC, and growth when ROIIC is greater than WACC. We show that while the incremental growth in owner earnings increases the lemonade stand's nominal value in each example, it does not always *increase* its real value.

Scenario 5: Real Value of Zoe's Lemonade Stand with Growth When ROIIC Equals the Cost of Capital   Let's suppose that Zoe decides to expand her business by opening an additional, smaller lemonade stand a few blocks from her house and invests 10% more capital each year to support that growth. In this example, the incremental investment in year 1 is $60, which is 10% of $600 invested in the original business. The incremental investment in year 2 is $66, which is 10% of $600 invested in the original business and the $60 incremental investment in year 1. The incremental investment of 10% continues for each of the next four years, as we show in Table 3.14.

As it turns out, the new location has fewer sales, higher operating expenses, and lower profitability than Zoe's original lemonade stand and the return on the incremental invested capital is only 8.5%, which,

Table 3.14   Incremental Capital Charge for Zoe's Lemonade Stands with Invested Capital Growing at 10% Per Annum

	Year 1	Year 2	Year 3	Year 4	Year 5	Year 6	Terminal Value
Incremental Invested Capital for Growth	60	126	199	278	366	463	
Cost of Capital		8.5%	8.5%	8.5%	8.5%	8.5%	
Incremental Capital Charge		5	11	17	24	31	366
PV of Incremental Capital Charge		4	8	12	16	19	225
Total PV of Incremental Capital Charges 284							

as we know, equals the lemonade stand's cost of capital. This case is like the airport sidewalk example when the nominal speed forward was 8.5 fps while the walkway moved 8.5 fps in the opposite direction. You made no forward progress in that example, and we will show that similarly the investment in this example creates no *incremental* value for Zoe's lemonade stand.

We calculate the nominal incremental growth in owner earnings for each year during the six-year forecast period and the total nominal present value of incremental growth in Table 3.15.

Table 3.15   Total Nominal Present Value of Incremental Growth

	Year 1	Year 2	Year 3	Year 4	Year 5	Year 6	Terminal Value
Incremental Invested Capital for Growth	60	126	199	278	366	463	
Nominal ROIIC		8.5%	8.5%	8.5%	8.5%	8.5%	
Nominal Incremental Growth		5	11	17	24	31	366
Nominal PV of Incremental Growth		4	8	12	16	19	225
Total Nominal PV of Incremental Growth 284							

As we explain, the nominal present value of incremental growth is comprised of two components—present value of incremental excess returns and present value of incremental capital charges, which we show in Table 3.16:

Table 3.16   Total Nominal PV of Incremental Growth with Excess Returns and Capital Charges

	Year 1	Year 2	Year 3	Year 4	Year 5	Year 6	Terminal Value
Nominal Incremental Growth in Owner Earnings	0	5	11	17	24	31	366
Nominal PV of Increase in Owner Earnings	0	4	8	12	16	19	225
Nominal PV of Incremental Growth in 284 Owner Earnings							
Incremental Excess Returns	0	0	0	0	0	0	0
PV of Incremental Excess Returns	0	0	0	0	0	0	0
PV of Incremental Excess Returns 0							
Incremental Capital Charge	0	5	11	17	24	31	366
PV of Incremental Capital Charge	0	4	8	12	16	19	225
PV of Incremental Capital Charges 284							

The nominal present value is calculated using the following formula:

Nominal PV of Incremental Growth = PV of Incremental Excess Returns
+ PV of Incremental Capital Charges

Nominal PV of Incremental Growth = $0 + $284 = $284

The calculation shows that the nominal present value of incremental growth equals $284.

To calculate the *total* nominal value of Zoe's Lemonade Stand, we add the nominal present value of incremental growth of $284 to the previously calculated (no growth) value of $1,412, which produces a total value of $1,696:

Nominal PV of Zoe's Lemonade Stand with Incremental Growth
= $1,412 + ($0 + $284) = $1,696

Nominal PV of Zoe's Lemonade Stand with Incremental Growth
= $1,412 + $284 = $1,696

While it *appears* that growth in this example increases the value of Zoe's Lemonade Stand by $284, the calculation ignores the incremental capital charges. To calculate the real present value of incremental growth, we need to subtract the present value of the capital charges to determine if the nominal growth in owner earnings actually produces incremental value, which we can do using the following formula:

Total Real PV of Zoe's Lemonade Stand with Incremental Growth
= Nominal PV of Zoe's Lemonade Stand with Incremental Growth
− PV of Incremental Capital Charges

Total Real PV of Zoe's Lemonade Stand = $1,696 − $284 = $1,412

Since the total value of $1,412 in this example equals the Lemonade Stand's original (no growth) value, the incremental investment creates no value. We illustrate this result in Figure 3.16A, where we show that the nominal incremental growth in owner earnings equals the incremental capital charges.

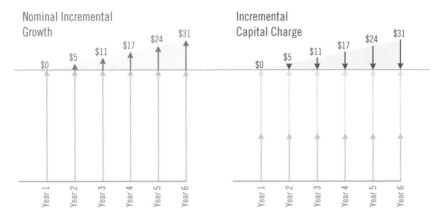

Figure 3.16A   Nominal Incremental Owner Earnings Equals Incremental Capital Charge

Consequently, there is no real incremental value created from the additional investment because there is no incremental excess return, as we show in Figure 3.16B.

Figure 3.16B   No Excess Returns from Growth Creates No Value

The analysis demonstrates that the real present value of Zoe's Lemonade Stand with incremental growth when ROIIC equals WACC is the same as the present value of the lemonade stand before investing in growth. **The example reveals that because the incremental growth generates no incremental value, Zoe is no better off expanding her business.**

Scenario 6: Value of Zoe's Lemonade Stand with Growth when ROIIC is Less Than the Cost of Capital   Instead of opening an additional small lemonade stand a few blocks from her house, Zoe decides to expand her lemonade stand into Paris's neighborhood on the other side of town. In additional to having higher operating expenses, Zoe needs to sell her lemonade at a discount to steal customers from Paris, which constrains the new lemonade stand's financial returns. Consequently, the return on the incremental invested capital is only 3.0%, which is below the lemonade stand's cost of capital.

We calculate the nominal incremental growth in owner earnings from the incremental investments for each year during the six-year forecast period, as shown in Table 3.17.

Table 3.17   Nominal Present Value of Incremental Growth

	Year 1	Year 2	Year 3	Year 4	Year 5	Year 6	Terminal Value
Incremental Invested Capital for Growth	60	126	199	278	366	463	
Nominal Return on Incremental Invested Capital		3.0%	3.0%	3.0%	3.0%	3.0%	
Nominal Incremental Growth		2	4	6	8	11	129
Nominal PV of Incremental Growth		2	3	4	6	7	79
Total Nominal PV of Incremental Growth	100						

The nominal present value can be calculated using the following formula:

$$\text{Nominal PV of Incremental Growth} = \text{PV of Incremental Excess Returns} + \text{PV of Incremental Capital Charges}$$

$$\text{Nominal PV of Incremental Growth} = -\$184 + \$284 = \$100$$

The calculation shows that the nominal present value of incremental growth equals $100.

As we discuss, the nominal present value of incremental growth is comprised of two components—the present value of incremental excess returns and the present value of incremental capital charges, which we show in Table 3.18:

Table 3.18   Nominal Present Value of Incremental Growth with Excess Return and Capital Charges

	Year 1	Year 2	Year 3	Year 4	Year 5	Year 6	Terminal Value
Nominal Incremental Growth	0	2	4	6	8	11	129
Nominal PV of Incremental Growth	0	2	3	4	6	7	79
Nominal PV of Incremental Growth 100							
Incremental Excess Returns	0	−3	−7	−11	−15	−20	−237
PV of Incremental Excess Returns	0	−3	−5	−8	−10	−12	−145
PV of Incremental Excess Returns −$184							
Incremental Capital Charge	0	5	11	17	24	31	366
PV of Incremental Capital Charge	0	4	8	12	16	19	225
PV of Incremental Capital Charges 284							

To calculate the total nominal value of Zoe's Lemonade Stand in this example, we add the nominal present value of incremental growth of $100 to the previously calculated (no growth) value of $1,412, to arrive at a value of $1,512:

Nominal PV of Zoe's Lemonade Stand with Incremental Growth

$$= \$1,412 + \left(-\$184 + \$284\right) = \$1,512$$

Nominal PV of Zoe's Lemonade Stand with Incremental Growth

$$= \$1,412 + \$100 = \$1,512$$

While it *appears* that the incremental growth increases the value of Zoe's Lemonade Stand by $100, the calculation (once again) ignores the incremental capital charges. And since the new lemonade stand produces negative excess returns, the incremental growth in owner earnings destroys value. This situation is like the airport sidewalk example when the nominal speed forward was 3 fps, but the real speed was −5.5 fps because the walkway was moving in the opposite direction at 8.5 fps.

To calculate the real present value of incremental growth, we need to subtract the present value of the capital charges from the nominal growth in owner earnings to see if it produces incremental value, as we show in the following formula:

Total Real PV of Zoe's Lemonade Stand with Incremental Growth

= Nominal PV of Zoe's Lemonade Stand with Incremental Growth

− PV of Incremental Capital Charges

Total Real PV of Zoe's Lemonade Stand = $1,512 − $284 = $1,228

Since the total value of $1,228 in this example is *less* than the lemonade stand's original (no growth) value of $1,412, the incremental investment destroys value and Zoe is worse off making the investment.

The charts in Figure 3.17A show that the incremental growth in the lemonade stand's owner earnings is less than the incremental capital charges from that investment, which confirms that the incremental growth *destroys* value for the lemonade stand because of the negative incremental excess returns, which runs counter to the claim that growth increases value.

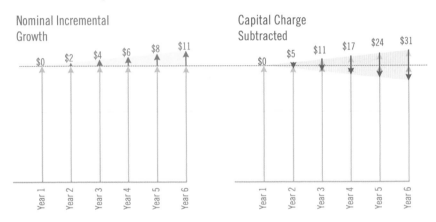

Figure 3.17A   Nominal Incremental Owner Earnings Less Than Incremental Capital Charges

Consequently, there is no real incremental growth from the additional investment in this example because of the negative excess returns it produces, as we show in figure 3.17B.

Figure 3.17B   Negative Excess Returns from Growth Destroy Value

The analysis shows that in this example the real present value of Zoe's Lemonade Stand with growth is worth less than the present value of the lemonade stand without growth, after accounting for the capital charges from the incremental investment. It is important to stress this point. **The lemonade stand destroys value by growing owner earnings because the return on the incremental invested capital is less than the incremental cost of capital**.

Consequently, Zoe is better off *not* expanding her business because the incremental investment would destroy value.

Scenario 7: Value of Zoe's Lemonade Stand with Growth When ROIIC is Greater Than the Cost of Capital

Instead of opening a smaller lemonade stand a few blocks away or expanding into Paris's neighborhood across town, let's assume that Zoe expands her operations in response to increasing demand from her current customers. Because she has no competition, we can assume that the expanded business produces the same level of profitability and that her return on incremental invested capital is 20.0%.

We calculate the increase in owner earnings from the incremental investments for each year during the six-year forecast period, as shown in Table 3.19.

Table 3.19   Increase in Annual Incremental Investment Required to Fund Growth

	Year 1	Year 2	Year 3	Year 4	Year 5	Year 6	Terminal Value
Additional Invested Capital for Growth	60	126	199	278	366	463	
Nominal ROIIC		20.0%	20.0%	20.0%	20.0%	20.0%	
Nominal Incremental Growth		12	25	40	56	73	862
Nominal PV of Incremental Growth		10	20	29	37	45	528
Total Nominal PV of Incremental Growth 669							

As we demonstrate in the examples above, nominal present value of incremental growth is comprised of two components—the present value of incremental excess returns and the present value of incremental capital charges, which we show in Table 3.20:

Table 3.20   Nominal Present Value of Incremental Growth with Excess Return and Capital Charges

		Year 1	Year 2	Year 3	Year 4	Year 5	Year 6	Terminal Value
Nominal Incremental Growth		0	12	25	40	56	73	862
Nominal PV of Incremental Growth		0	10	20	29	37	45	528
Nominal PV of Incremental Growth	669							
Incremental Excess Returns		0	7	14	23	32	42	496
PV of Incremental Excess Returns		0	6	11	16	21	26	304
PV of Incremental Excess Returns	385							
Incremental Capital Charge		0	5	11	17	24	31	366
PV of Incremental Capital Charge		0	4	8	12	16	19	225
PV of Incremental Capital Charges	284							

The nominal present value can be calculated using the following formula:

$$\text{Nominal PV of Incremental Growth} = \text{PV of Incremental Excess Returns} + \text{PV of Incremental Capital Charges}$$

$$\text{Nominal PV of Incremental Growth} = \$385 + \$284 = \$669$$

The calculation shows that the nominal present value of incremental growth equals $669.

To calculate the total nominal value of Zoe's Lemonade Stand with growth, we add the nominal present value of incremental growth of $669 to the lemonade stand's previously calculated (no growth) value of $1,412, to arrive at a value of $2,081:

$$\text{Nominal PV of Zoe's Lemonade Stand with Incremental Growth}$$
$$= \$1,412 + (\$385 + \$284) = \$2,081$$

$$\text{Nominal PV of Zoe's Lemonade Stand with Incremental Growth}$$
$$= \$1,412 + \$669 = \$2,081$$

While it *appears* that the incremental growth increases the value of Zoe's Lemonade Stand by $669, the calculation ignores the incremental capital charges, as we show in the previous examples. To calculate the real present value of incremental growth, we need to subtract the present value of the capital charges from the nominal growth in owner earnings to see if the investment produces incremental value:

Total Real PV of Zoe's Lemonade Stand with Incremental Growth
= Nominal PV of Zoe's Lemonade Stand with Incremental Growth
− PV of Incremental Capital Charges

Total Real PV of Zoe's Lemonade Stand = $2,081 − $284 = $1,796

Since the total value of $1,796 is *greater* than the lemonade stand's original (no growth) value of $1,412, the investment produces incremental value and Zoe is better off by making the investment and expanding her business.

The charts in Figure 3.18A show that the increase in the lemonade stand's owner earnings from growth is significantly higher than the incremental capital charges for that growth, which confirms that the incremental growth *increases* the value of the lemonade stand.

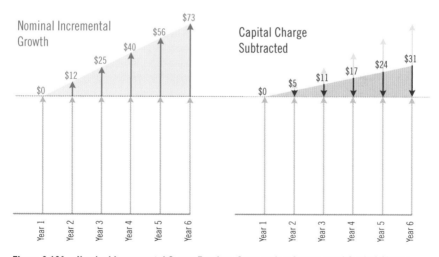

Figure 3.18A   Nominal Incremental Owner Earnings Greater than Incremental Capital Charge

And, as a consequence, because the lemonade stand produces incremental *positive* excess returns in this example, the additional investment generates real incremental growth, as we show in Figure 3.18B.

Figure 3.18B   Positive Excess Returns from Growth Create Value

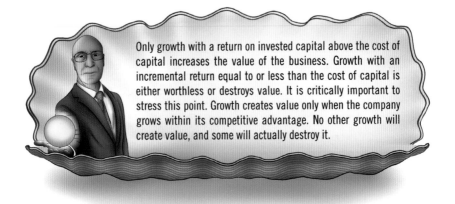

Only growth with a return on invested capital above the cost of capital increases the value of the business. Growth with an incremental return equal to or less than the cost of capital is either worthless or destroys value. It is critically important to stress this point. Growth creates value only when the company grows within its competitive advantage. No other growth will create value, and some will actually destroy it.

Real World Example—McCormick Inc.

Investors can use these tools to analyze companies in the real world. For instance, it is generally straightforward to calculate a business's annual capital charge simply by multiplying the company's weighted average cost of capital (WACC) times its invested capital. Companies like McCormick make it easy to do this analysis because they provide supplemental financial information to investors, as Table 3.21 shows (all amounts are in U.S. dollars):

Table 3.21   McCormick: Calculation of Capital Charge[*]

	2016
Current debt	393
Long-term debt	1,054
Shareholders' equity	1,638
Total capital	**3,085**
Average total capital	3,083
Weighted average cost of capital (WACC)	8.0%
Capital charge	247

* "Other Information—ROIC." McCormick's Investor Relations Website. Accessed February 4, 2017.

In a similar vein, determining a company's cash flow from excess returns can be calculated by multiplying the company's ROIC—WACC spread by the same invested capital. Again, McCormick makes it easy by providing this information, as shown in Table 3.22.

Table 3.22   McCormick: Calculating ROIC

	2016
Net income	472
Interest expense, net of taxes	41
NOPAT	514
Average total capital	3,083
ROIC	**16.7%**

$$\text{Owner Earnings} = (\text{ROIC} * \text{Invested Capital})$$

$$\text{Excess Returns in Dollars in 2016} = (\text{ROIC} * \text{Invested Capital})$$
$$- (\text{Cost of Capital} * \text{Invested Capital})$$

$$\text{Excess Returns in Dollars in 2016} = (16.7\% * \$3,083) - (8.0\% * \$3,083)$$

$$\$267 = \$514 - \$247$$

The calculation shows that the $514 in annual cash flow McCormick generated in 2016 is comprised of two parts: $267 in cash flow from excess returns and cash flow to cover its capital charge of $247. The high percentage of cash flow from excess returns indicates that the company has a strong competitive advantage.

If we assume that McCormick has a *sustainable* competitive advantage, then we can use the perpetuity valuation formula to calculate that the present value of excess returns of $267 per year equals $3,338, as the following calculation demonstrates:

$$\text{Present Value of Excess Returns} = \frac{\text{Excess returns}}{\text{WACC}}$$

$$\text{Present Value of Excess Returns} = \frac{\$267}{8.0\%}$$

$$\text{Present Value of Excess Returns} = \$3,338$$

We can also calculate that the present value of the capital charge of $247 per year equals $3,083:

$$\text{Present Value of Capital Charges} = \frac{\text{Capital Charge}}{\text{WACC}}$$

$$\text{Present Value of Capital Charges} = \frac{\$247}{8.0\%}$$

$$\text{Present Value of Capital Charges} = \$3,083$$

We can use this analysis to link McCormick's sources of cash flow to its valuation. For instance, the present value of the company's annual capital charge equals the company's invested capital and represents McCormick's no-growth, steady-state value, assuming the company has no competitive advantage. It should be easy to see that this value equals McCormick's no-growth, invested capital.

If a company has a sustainable competitive advantage, which allows it to maintain its excess returns in the future, then the present value of the cash flows from its excess returns represents the value of the company derived from its competitive advantage. If we further assume that the company's excess returns will not change in the future, then we can use the perpetuity valuation formula to calculate the present value of the company's cash flow from excess returns, which is the present value of its competitive advantage, as we show for McCormick in the following equations.

$$\text{PV of Competitive Advantage with No Growth} = \frac{\text{Cash Flows from Excess Returns}}{\text{WACC}}$$

$$\text{PV of Competitive Advantage with No Growth} = \frac{\$267}{8.0\%}$$

$$\text{PV of Competitive Advantage with No Growth} = \$3,338$$

Finally, we can calculate investors' estimate of the present value of growth, or the **market implied value of growth**, using the following approach. First, calculate the company's enterprise value, as we do with McCormick in the analysis shown in Table 3.23.

Table 3.23   McCormick: Calculation of Enterprise Value

Price (2/4/17)	$ 95.86
Shares Outstanding	125
Market Value of Equity	11,983
– Cash	118
+ Debt	1,456
= Enterprise Value	13,321

Based on November 2016 balance sheet

Then subtract from the enterprise value the present value of the company's capital charges (the company's invested capital) and the present value of the company's competitive advantage to arrive at the market implied enterprise value of growth, as the analysis in Table 3.24 shows.

Table 3.24   McCormick: Market Implied Value of Growth

Enterprise Value	**13,321**
– Invested Capital (PV of Capital Charges)	3,083
– PV of Competitive Advantage (No Growth)	3,338
Market Implied Enterprise Value of Growth	**6,900**

Then add back cash, subtract debt, and divide by shares outstanding to arrive at per share values, as shown in Table 3.25.

Table 3.25   McCormick: Per Share Sources of Value

	Per Share	Percent of Value
Stock Price (2/4/17)	**$95.86**	100%
− Invested Capital (PV of Capital Charges)	$22.19	23%
− PV of Competitive Advantage (No Growth)	$24.02	25%
= Share Price No Growth	$46.21	48%
Market Implied Equity Value of Growth	**$49.65**	**52%**

McCormick's market implied value of growth equals $49.65 per share, or more than 50% of the share price.

Companies can generate excess returns, over time, only if they have a sustainable competitive advantage, and growth only creates value when the return on the incremental investment is greater than the cost of capital on the incremental investment. Therefore, cash flows from excess returns and any value created from growth are a direct function of a company's competitive advantage. We show in Table 3.26 an impressive 77% of McCormick's market value comes from the present value of its excess returns and its market implied value of growth.

Table 3.26   McCormick: Sources of Value from Competitive Advantage and Growth

	Per Share	Percent of Value
Stock Price (2/4/17)	$95.86	100%
− Invested Capital (PV of Capital Charges)	$22.19	23%
− PV of Competitive Advantage (no growth)	$24.02	25%
= Share Price with No Growth	$46.21	48%
Market Implied Equity Value of Growth	**$49.65**	**52%**

77%

We present this result graphically in Figure 3.19, showing how much of McCormick's market price is attributed to each source of value. This analysis illustrates that it is critically important to understand the source of the company's competitive advantage when trying to calculate its value because, as we see with McCormick, a significant portion of the company's value will be a direct function of its competitive advantage.

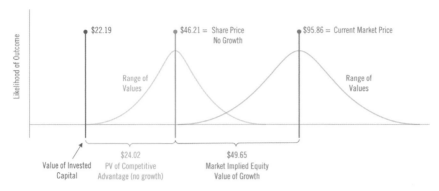

Figure 3.19   McCormick: Ranges for Sources of Value

Gems:

- ◈ A company may decide to cease operations and sell its assets outright, rather than continuing to operate them, generating cash in the process. The value of the business in this case is calculated by estimating how much cash the company would receive from liquidating its assets. This analysis is referred to as a company's **liquidation value**.
- ◈ A company may decide to sell part or all of its operating entities to a financial or strategic buyer. Valuing the company based on its value to a potential buyer is referred to as a company's **Private Market Value**, which represents the price a rational buyer (an industrialist) would be willing to pay to gain control of the company's assets. Professor Roger Murray defined **Private Market Value** as the business's value plus a control premium and a patience factor, minus access to public capital markets.
- ◈ A company generates excess returns when its return on invested capital is greater than its cost of capital for that investment.
- ◈ Having a return on invested capital significantly above its cost of capital does not guarantee that the company has a true competitive advantage. Because the excess returns will attract competitors, the business's strong financial performance will decline quickly if competitors successfully enter the market. Therefore, for the advantage to be a true barrier, it must be **sustainable** over time.

▽ **Competitive advantage** is defined as a company's ability to generate excess returns. A **sustainable competitive advantage** is defined as a company's ability to generate excess returns over an extended period of time in the future, which requires **barriers to entry** to prevent competitors from entering the market and eroding away the excess returns.

▽ There are four main sources of competitive advantage:

▿ **Customer-facing advantages** implies that the customer is willing to stick with the current supplier rather than switch to a new supplier, even though they may offer a similar product at a lower price or a superior product at the same price.

▿ **Production advantages** provide a company with lower manufacturing costs than its competitors'.

▿ **Efficiency advantages** are present if a company has economies of scale in some aspect of its business.

▿ **Advantage due to government policy** effectively limit entry into specific markets.

▽ Valuing competitive advantage:

▿ If the company does not have a competitive advantage, then its ROIC = WACC, it produces no excess returns, and creates no value for its owners.

▿ If the company has a sustainable competitive advantage, then its ROIC > WACC, it produces excess returns, and creates value for its owners.

▿ If the business's ROIC < WACC, then it produces negative excess returns, and destroys value for its owners.

▽ Valuing incremental growth:

▿ If the business's ROIIC = WACC, then growth creates no value because it produces no excess returns and incremental owner earnings equals incremental capital charges.

▿ If the business's ROIIC > WACC, then incremental growth creates value because it produces positive excess returns and incremental owner earnings are greater than incremental capital charges.

▿ If the business's ROIIC < WACC, then growth destroys value because it produces negative excess returns and incremental owner earnings are less than incremental capital charges.

CHAPTER 4

How to Think About a Security's Intrinsic Value

In Chapter 1 we show how to value an asset using a discounted cash flow model and in Chapter 2 we use these tools to value a simple business. In Chapter 3 we show how to evaluate a company's competitive advantage to properly value growth. We finish that discussion by converting the resulting business value to a single point estimate. At the risk of confusing the reader, we will show in this chapter that it is unrealistic to assume that one can derive a single-point estimate of value. Rather, it is better to think of a company's intrinsic value as a **range of values**. However, we need to define intrinsic value before proceeding.

What is "Intrinsic Value"?

One might ask: "Isn't the definition of **intrinsic value** simply the value of the business?" Yes and no. While Benjamin Graham and David Dodd introduce the term intrinsic value in their seminal work *Security Analysis*, first published in 1934, surprisingly, the authors never provide a specific definition.

Rather, they discuss the concept in more general terms. For instance, the first[1] mention of the phrase intrinsic value appears on page 16:

> [In 1922] Wright Aeronautical Corporation stock was selling on the New York Stock Exchange at only $8, although it was paying a $1 dividend, had for some time been earning over $2 a share, and showed more than $8 per share in cash assets in the treasury. In this case analysis would readily have established that the *intrinsic value* of the issue was substantially above the market price [emphasis added].[2]

Why doesn't Graham provide the reader with a clear definition? One could surmise that this decision was intentional as it is likely Graham wanted to force the reader to develop the concept in their

---

[1] Technically this instance is the second time the authors use the phrase in the book. The first time is on page 12 in the Introduction, but the authors use the phrase in a different context comparing fundamental and behavioral factors.

[2] Benjamin Graham and David L. Dodd. *Security Analysis* (New York: The McGraw-Hill Companies, Inc. 1934), 17.

own minds.[3] Therefore, instead of offering a precise definition, Graham discusses intrinsic value more abstractly:

> The essential point is that security analysis does not seek to determine exactly what is the intrinsic value of a given security. It needs only to establish either that the value is adequate—e.g., to protect a bond or to justify a stock purchase—or else that the value is considerably higher or considerably lower than the market price. **For such purposes an indefinite and approximate measure of the intrinsic value may be sufficient.** To use a homely simile, it is quite possible to decide by inspection that a woman is old enough to vote without knowing her age, or that a man is heavier than he should be without knowing his exact weight [emphasis added].[4]

Graham also emphasizes that it is not easy to calculate intrinsic value:

> We must recognize, however, that intrinsic value is an elusive concept. In general terms it is understood to be that value which is justified by the facts, e.g., the assets, earnings, dividends, [and the company's] definite prospects . . . and that, it is a great mistake to imagine that intrinsic value is as definite and as determinable as is the market price.[5]

Like so many things in life, after the more than 80 years since *Security Analysis* was written, nuance has been lost in the retelling. We can infer that Graham *never* intended for intrinsic value to be thought of as a single-point estimate of value. Rather, he thought of it as more of a *concept* of value. In fact, on page 19 of *Security Analysis* he discusses the "flexibility of the concept of intrinsic value" as "a **very hypothetical 'range of approximate value,' which would grow wider as the uncertainty of the picture increased** [emphasis added]."[6]

---

[3] While not giving a specific definition, from reading this passage, one could easily conclude that the intrinsic value of Wright Aeronautical is greater than its $8 trading price. If the earnings of $2 are given even a low P/E multiple of 5, the value of the business would equal $10. When the $8 of excess cash on the balance sheet is added to the result of that calculation, it produces an intrinsic value of $18 per share. While not explicitly defining intrinsic value, the reader is left with a clear, although more abstract, idea of what the phrase means.

[4] Graham and Dodd. *Security Analysis*, 1934.

[5] Ibid.

[6] Ibid.

Seth Klarman, in his book *Margin of Safety*, similarly explains the challenge of finding a precise intrinsic value estimate, although in a slightly different manner:

> Many investors insist on affixing exact values to their investment, seeking precision in an imprecise world, but business value cannot be precisely determined.[7]

Graham's most famous student, Warren Buffett, echoes the same observations in Berkshire's Owner's Manual:

> The calculation of intrinsic value, though, is not so simple. As our definition suggests, intrinsic value is an *estimate rather than a precise figure*, and it is additionally an estimate that must be changed if interest rates move or forecasts of future cash flows are revised. Two people looking at the same set of facts, moreover—and this would apply even to Charlie and me—will almost inevitably come up with at least slightly different intrinsic value figures [emphasis added].[8]

And in Berkshire Hathaway's 2014 letter to shareholders Buffett alludes to the difficulty of arriving at a single number:

> As much as Charlie and I talk about intrinsic business value, we cannot tell you precisely what that number is for Berkshire shares (nor, in fact, for any other stock).[9]

It is clear from these statements that:

1. Graham never intended for intrinsic value to be thought of as a single number; rather it was meant as a concept of value.
2. Business values cannot be precisely determined.[10]
3. Since value cannot be determined precisely it is unrealistic to attempt to derive a **single-point estimate** of intrinsic value. Rather, the goal is to estimate a *range of approximate values*.

---

[7] Seth A. Klarman, *Margin of Safety: Risk-Averse Value Investing Strategies for the Thoughtful Investor* (New York: HarperCollins, 1991).

[8] Warren E. Buffett, "An Owner's Manual: A Message from Warren E. Buffett, Chairman and CEO." Berkshire Hathaway Inc., January 1999.

[9] Berkshire Hathaway Inc., 2014 Annual Report.

[10] We are sure that certain readers will object to the definitiveness of this statement. However, we side with Buffett and Klarman—if they say that business values cannot be determined precisely, then they cannot be determined precisely.

We have two choices at this point. We can either keep the defini-tion of intrinsic value intentionally vague or forge ahead with the goal of getting closer to a working/practical definition. We chose the second opinion. However, before providing a specific definition, we want to review comments by Buffett, Klarman, and Murray.

Buffett provides a succinct definition of intrinsic value in his 1999 *Owner's Manual:*

> Let's start with intrinsic value, an all-important concept that offers the only logical approach to evaluating the relative attractiveness of investments and businesses. Intrinsic value can be defined simply: It is the discounted value of the cash that can be taken out of a busi-ness during its remaining life.[11]

Klarman makes a parallel statement in *Margin of Safety*:

> While a great many methods of business valuation exist, there are only three that I found useful. The first is an analysis of the going-concern value, known as net present value (NPV) analysis. NPV is the discounted value of all future cash flows that a business is expected to generate.[12]

Roger Murray[13] discusses intrinsic value in a similar, although intriguingly different way, during a lecture hosted by Mario Gabelli at the Museum of Television & Radio[14] in New York City in 1993:

---

[11] Buffett, An Owner's Manual.

[12] Seth Klarman, *Margin of Safety.* The other two valuation approaches are liq-uidation value and breakup value, which are also discounted cash flow estimates at their core, as we note in the feature box "But I Don't Do That" in Chapter 2.

[13] Roger E. Murray, after a distinguished career on Wall Street, became an Associate Dean at Columbia Business School in 1956. Upon Graham's retirement in 1956, he assumed responsibility for teaching security analysis at the school and taught the course until 1977. Murray also coauthored the fifth edition of *Security Analysis* with Sidney Cottle and Frank Block, which was published in 1988.

[14] This series of lectures was organized by Mario Gabelli, one of Murray's most successful students. Bruce Greenwald, who had joined Columbia Business School a few years earlier, was enlisted by Dean Meyer Feldberg to attend these lectures. After listening to Murray speak, Greenwald said, "Like generations of investors who preceded me, I was struck by the compelling logic of Graham's approach. As a consequence of those lectures, in 1993, I dragooned Roger Murray into joining me in offering a revised version of the value course." The Value Investing course at Columbia has been the cornerstone to the finance program ever since.

What we are talking about when we use the term intrinsic value is this is our estimate of the economic value of a company . . . intrinsic value is a magnet in a rational world . . . that is constantly pulling market prices towards it. And, if you prefer, you can call it towards intrinsic value or you can call it regression to the mean, which implies, to some extent at least, that the intrinsic value is the true, underlying, central tendency in the valuation of an enterprise . . .

I do not care whether we are talking about a real estate equity or I am talking about a company, the same elements that give that physical asset value in financial terms have to be the same. We are talking about the level at which the asset generates returns and the characteristics of that stream of returns across future periods.

The part of Murray's talk that intrigues us is his metaphor of a magnet pulling the market price toward its intrinsic value, which we discuss in greater detail in Chapter 7.

Buffett's, Murray's, and Klarman's comments are consistent with the definition we provide in the previous chapters:

The estimated value of any asset is the sum of the cash flows expected to be produced by that asset, over its useful life, discounted for the time value of money and the uncertainty of receiving those cash flows.

To arrive at a working/practical definition of intrinsic value that we can use going forward, we simply add the word "intrinsic" to the earlier definition of the value of an asset:

> The estimated *intrinsic* value of any asset is the sum of the cash flows expected to be produced by that asset, over its useful life, discounted for the time value of money and the uncertainty of receiving those cash flows.

- Intrinsic value is more of a conceptual framework than it is a precise calculation.

- Since business value cannot be determined precisely it is unrealistic to attempt to derive a single-point estimate of its intrinsic value.

- Rather than a single-point estimate, intrinsic value should be thought of as "a very hypothetical 'range of approximate value,' which would grow wider as the uncertainty of the picture increased."

Thinking of Intrinsic Value as a Range of Values

Although the definition we provide implies that the asset's intrinsic value is a single-point number, we believe firmly that the goal is to determine a **"range of approximate value."**

As we discuss in Chapter 1, assets with more predictable cash flows are preferable to assets with less predictable ones. Echoing Graham's comment that intrinsic value is "*a very hypothetical 'range of approximate value,' which would grow wider as the uncertainty of the picture increased,*" it would logically follow that a business with less predictable (more uncertain) cash flows will have a wider distribution of estimated intrinsic value than will a business with more predictable cash flows, as shown in Figures 4.1A and 4.1B.[15]

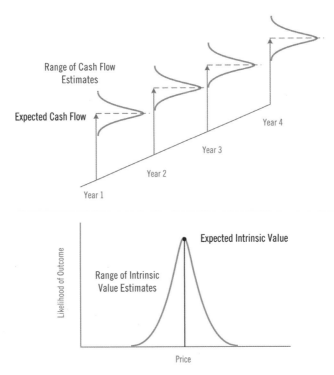

Figure 4.1A   Narrower Distribution of Cash Flows Is More Predictable

To deal with an inherently uncertain future, the analyst needs to consider various possible scenarios when forecasting the company's future cash flows and calculating its intrinsic value. He can produce a range of potential intrinsic values by performing a **sensitivity**

---

[15] Please note that we have presented the top chart in figures 4.1A and 4.1B slightly differently than previous charts in that we have rotated them counterclockwise by 90 degrees so that the y-axis is now the likelihood of outcome, the x-axis is the price in dollars, and the z-axis represents time.

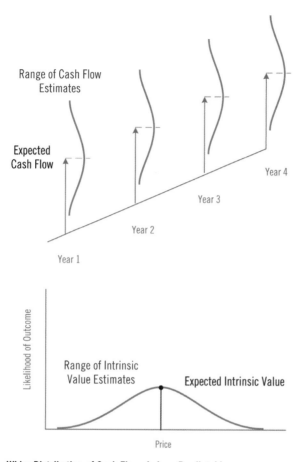

Figure 4.1B   Wider Distribution of Cash Flows Is Less Predictable

analysis in which the assumption about one or more of the future cash flow components varies over time. Each scenario will produce a different discrete present value estimate that the analyst can use to create a **range of possible intrinsic values**.

For instance, we calculate seven different scenarios for Zoe's Lemonade Stand in Chapter 3, and show in that analysis that each scenario produces a different intrinsic value estimate. In

Table 4.1, we show the present value of three of the scenarios and divide by 150 shares outstanding[16] to arrive at a value per share figure.

Table 4.1   Present Value and Value Per Share Estimates for Zoe's Lemonade Stand Under Different Scenarios

	Present Value of Cash Flows	Value Per share
Scenario 5: No Growth with ROIC → WACC	$772	$5.15
Scenario 1: No Growth with ROIC > WACC	$1,412	$9.41
Scenario 7: Growth with ROIIC > WACC	$1,796	$11.98

The intrinsic value for Zoe's Lemonade Stand from Scenario 1 is presented as a single-point estimate in Figure 4.2:

Figure 4.2   Single-Point Estimate for Intrinsic Value of Zoe's Lemonade Stand

We can begin to create a **range** of estimated potential intrinsic values by adding the two-other single-point estimates from Table 4.1, Scenario 5 and Scenario 7 to the initial single-point estimate, as shown in Figure 4.3.

---

[16] We arbitrarily assume that Zoe's Lemonade Stand has 150 shares outstanding.

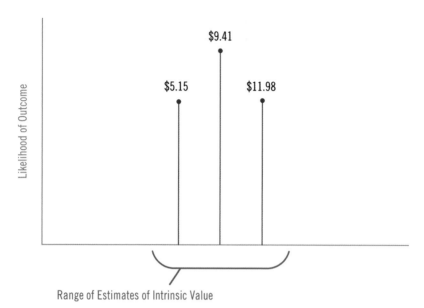

Figure 4.3   Single-Point Estimates for Intrinsic Value of Zoe's Lemonade Stand Under Different Scenarios

The analyst can produce additional possible intrinsic values by running a sensitivity analysis based on other growth scenarios. Different intrinsic values calculated using this method are shown in Table 4.2:[17]

Table 4.2   Intrinsic Value Estimates for Zoe's Lemonade Stand Based on Different Annual Growth Rates

Growth Rate	Present Value of Free Cash Flows	Value Per Share
−20.0%	$605	$4.03
−17.5%	$690	$4.60
−15.0%	$777	$5.18
−12.5%	$858	$5.72
−10.0%	$948	$6.32
−7.5%	$1,048	$6.99
−5.0%	$1,158	$7.72
−2.5%	$1,279	$8.53
0.0%	$1,412	$9.41
2.5%	$1,495	$9.97
5.0%	$1,587	$10.58
7.5%	$1,687	$11.25
10.0%	$1,796	$11.97
12.5%	$1,915	$12.77
15.0%	$2,044	$13.63
17.5%	$2,184	$14.56
20.0%	$2,336	$15.57

[17] Please note, for this example, we simply started with Scenario 1 (no growth, ROIC > WACC) and changed the growth rate in plus or minus 250 basis point increments.

Adding the intrinsic value estimates for each of the different growth scenarios calculated in Table 4.2 to the chart in Figure 4.3 produces an even wider range of possible intrinsic values, as shown in Figure 4.4. As a reminder, the analyst calculates a range of possible intrinsic values because he is uncertain which of the scenarios will prove to be the actual outcome, although it is important to note that he will not know the true value of Zoe's Lemonade Stand until the actual future unfolds.

Figure 4.4   Distribution of Intrinsic Value Estimates for Zoe's Lemonade Stand Assuming Different Annual Growth Rates

The values closest to the central point represent the estimates that the analyst believes have the highest likelihood (probability) of being the company's true intrinsic value, while the estimated values toward each of the tails are the scenarios the analyst believes are less likely to occur. The vertical distance away from the horizontal axis represents the analyst's confidence in each estimate's relative likelihood of unfolding. For instance, the graph shows that the analyst believes the most likely scenario for the lemonade stand results in an intrinsic value estimate of $9.41 per share, which is based on a no growth scenario.

We can use a simple example to illustrate how the range of distributions (and the shape of the distribution curve) can differ. Assume that a company has as its sole asset a $1,000 face value 10-year U.S. Treasury Note, which currently trades at $995.31. The best estimate of the company's intrinsic value is also $995.31, which is the note's current value.

It is relatively easy to estimate the company's current intrinsic value in this example. The only information we need is the price of the Treasury Note[18] since this is the company's only asset. The chart in Figure 4.5 also includes a range of other possible intrinsic values to show that a change in interest rates would impact the value of the Treasury Note and, in turn, the company's intrinsic value. However, the distribution is narrow because it is unlikely that interest rates will change much in a short span of time.

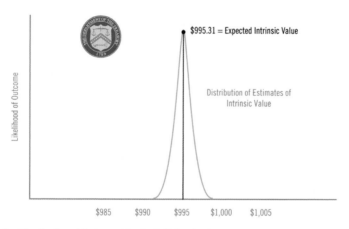

Figure 4.5   Distribution of Estimated Intrinsic Value for Company with Treasury Note as its Single Asset

Although we use a normal distribution to depict the range of possible intrinsic values in figure 4.5, we do not mean to imply that this or any other distribution will be normally distributed. We use the chart for illustrative purposes only.[19]

---

[18] T-note (CUSIP 912828XB1) was auctioned on May 13, 2015, and on August 17, 2015, the bid price was $995.31.

[19] Although we use the phrase *expected* intrinsic value in Figure 4.5, we do not mean to imply that the value is equivalent of the expected value for the distribution. Rather, we mean that the analyst believes this scenario for the value of the Treasury Note to be the one that is the most likely to occur.

We can use Tesla, a company using a new technology to manufacture electric cars, to illustrate the importance of determining the range of instrinsic value. Although Tesla operates in an established industry, the company's outlook is highly **uncertain** because it is a relatively small auto manufacturer, selling cars based on new and completely different technologies. The car's price, features, and reliability will dramatically affect its demand and, in turn, the company's future revenue and cash flow. Not surprisingly, analyst estimates for the company's intrinsic value vary greatly.

The uncertainty in the company's prospects is evident by the wide **range** of price targets (estimates of intrinsic value)[20] for Tesla from the 15 sell side analysts who have published forecasts, as shown in Figure 4.6. The estimates range from a low of $178 per share to a high of $400 per share, with an average estimated one year price target of $293 (which represents the consensus). The stock traded at $245 at the time these estimates were published, in August 2015.

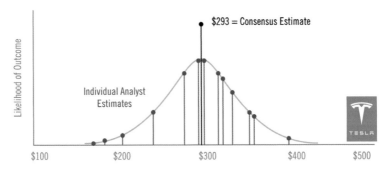

Figure 4.6   Tesla: Individual Analyst Estimated One-Year Price Targets and Average Estimate

The wide range of estimates results from the fact that the **timing**, **duration**, **magnitude**, and **growth** of Tesla's cash flows are highly **uncertain**. The range of estimates shows that the analysts have significantly different views for Tesla's prospects, as they each have

---

[20] For this example we will use estimated one year price targets as a proxy for intrinsic value.

analyzed the available data differently in calculating their estimate of the company's intrinsic value. As Buffett observed, "Two people looking at the same set of facts . . . will almost inevitably come up with at least slightly different intrinsic value figures." The wide distribution also shows that the likelihood that any single estimate will be close to the actual intrinsic value is low and the possibility that the intrinsic value will be significantly higher or lower than the average (consensus) estimate is high.

Instead of comparing Tesla to a fictitious company whose sole asset is a Treasury Note, it is more instructive to compare it to another operating company. We chose McCormick, a company founded over 125 years ago that sells a wide range of kitchen spices. Compared to Tesla, given the nature of its business, McCormick's future cash flows should be significantly more consistent and predictable, as we see in the distribution of estimates in Figure 4.7.

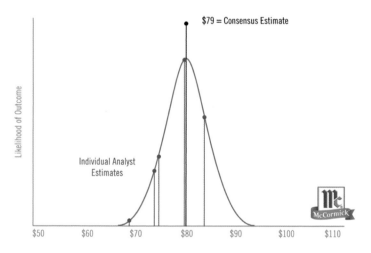

Figure 4.7   McCormick: Individual Analyst Estimated One-Year Price Targets

This difference between the three different distributions becomes evident when they are superimposed, as illustrated in Figure 4.8.

The distribution of analyst price targets for McCormick more closely resembles the distribution for the estimated value for the Treasury Note than it does to the distribution for Tesla, as the chart in Figure 4.8 demonstrates.

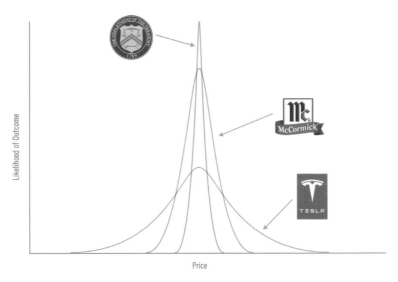

Figure 4.8   Comparing Distributions of Estimated One-Year Price Targets for U.S. Treasury Bill, McCormick, and Tesla

McCormick sells hundreds of different products to millions of customers, which makes the business more stable and its cash flows more predictable than Tesla's. People use spices such as cinnamon and nutmeg on a regular basis, and most people buy more when they run out of a spice. While they *might* buy fewer spices during a recession, demand for the company's products will not change much from year to year and McCormick's operating income should not vary much over time. Consequently, the range of possible estimates for the company's intrinsic value is relatively narrow. As such, the likelihood of McCormick stock increasing dramatically from the price at which it traded in January 2017 of $95 per share to $140 per share in a short period of time is highly unlikely.

On the other hand, unlike McCormick, Tesla could see a significant increase or decrease in its financial performance because of the high degree of unpredictability in demand for the company's electric cars. As a result, the price of Tesla's stock increasing or decreasing by 50% in any given year is not beyond the realm of possibility.

We calculate the sources of value for McCormick at the end of the previous chapter, which we replicate in Table 4.3.

Table 4.3   Calculated Sources of McCormick's Value

	Per Share	Percent of Value
Stock Price (2/4/17)	**$95.86**	100%
– Invested Capital (PV of Capital Charges)	$21.86	23%
– PV of Competitive Advantage (No Growth)	$24.02	25%
= Share Price with No Growth	$45.88	48%
Market Implied Equity Value of Growth	**$49.98**	52%

We superimpose the range of analysts' estimates from Figure 4.7 onto the range of values from Table 4.3 to create the combined graph in Figure 4.9.

Figure 4.9   Sources of McCormick's Value Presented Graphically

This chart shows that the range of analysts' estimates for McCormick's value falls in the value of growth area for the company, which highlights that *all* the analysts expect the company to grow in the future and only differ in their views by the *rate* at which they expect the company to grow, as shown in the chart.

Gems:

- ▽ We can distill the comments from Buffett, Murray, and Klarman into a list of important factors that we need to keep in mind when estimating a company's intrinsic value:
    - ▿ Intrinsic value is more of a conceptual framework than a precise calculation.
    - ▿ Intrinsic value is ultimately the discounted cash flow the asset will produce, as we discuss throughout the book.
    - ▿ The intrinsic value must be justified by facts—assets, earnings, and the company's future prospects.
    - ▿ Intrinsic value is best expressed as *a range of approximate values* rather than a single-point estimate.
    - ▿ The range of possible intrinsic values grows wider as uncertainty increases.
- ▽ Intrinsic value is defined as follows: The *intrinsic value* of an asset is the sum of the cash flows produced by that asset, over its useful life, discounted for the time value of money and the uncertainty of receiving those cash flows.

CHAPTER 5

How to Think About Market Efficiency

A core concept in investing, and a key foundation of the book, is **market efficiency**. The discussion of market efficiency forms the backbone of the book's content and permeates all the other topics we discuss. Unfortunately, market efficiency cannot be taught by simply stating the basic laws on a single page and then showing how those laws work in all possible circumstances (unlike with Euclidean geometry, where the axioms are stated up front and then used to make all sorts of deductions). Instead, we need to explain market efficiency in pieces, starting with the core building blocks and then adding critical facets with increasing complexity as we further the discussion.

We care about market efficiency because, ironically, we need the markets to be efficient to generate alpha. If we can identify a mistake, such as a temporary inefficiency or mispricing, the only way for that mistake to be corrected is if the market is eventually efficient. The market must realize it has made an error and then correct that mistake for investors to be able to outperform. The alternative would be a market where mispricings persist forever. In such a world, no one could reliably outperform.

Market Efficiency Is More of a Concept Than a Law

Richard Feynman is one of our intellectual heroes. Although he displayed no knowledge, or any interest for that matter, in investing, he cared a lot about knowledge in general, learning, and teaching. Feynman was a theoretical physicist known for his work in quantum mechanics, for which he won the 1965 Nobel Prize in Physics. He was a professor, author, safecracker, artist, and avid bongo player. He assisted with the development of the atomic bomb during World War II and was a member of the panel that investigated the space shuttle Challenger disaster. Sometimes called "the Great Explainer," he wrote *The Feynman Lectures on Physics*, often referred to as "the Red Books," which have become among the most popular physics books ever written.

Feynman makes a statement in the Red Books that draws an interesting parallel to the concept of market efficiency:

> Each piece, or part, of the whole of nature is always merely an *approximation* to the complete truth, or the complete truth so far as we know it. In fact, everything we know is only some kind of approximation, because *we know that we do not know all the laws* as yet. Therefore, things must be learned only to be unlearned again or, more likely, to be corrected.
>
> For example, the mass of an object never seems to change: a spinning top has the same weight as a still one. So, a "law" was invented: mass is constant,

independent of speed. That "law" is now found to be incorrect. Mass is found to increase with velocity, but appreciable increases require velocities near that of light. A true law is: if an object moves with a speed of less than one hundred miles a second the mass is constant to within one part in a million. In some such approximate form this is a correct law. So in practice one might think that the new law makes no significant difference. Well, yes and no. For ordinary speeds we can certainly forget it and use the simple constant-mass law as a good approximation. But for high speeds we are wrong, and the higher the speed, the more wrong we are.[1]

Market efficiency is similar to the concept of mass. For instance, as Feynman explains, the constant mass law holds most of the time, except in special circumstances. The same dynamic applies to market efficiency—the rules of the efficient market hypothesis hold *most of the time,* except in special circumstances. We will show when the rules hold, and the circumstances when they do not.

To return to Feynman discussing the laws of mass:

Now, what should we teach first? Should we teach the correct but unfamiliar law with its strange and difficult conceptual ideas, for example the theory of relativity, four-dimensional space-time, and so on? Or should we first teach the simple "constant-mass" law, which is only approximate, but does not involve such difficult ideas? The first is more exciting, more wonderful, and more fun, but the second is easier to get at first, and is a first step to a real understanding of the first idea. This point arises again and again in teaching physics. At different times, we shall have to resolve it in different ways, but at each stage it is worth learning what is now known, how accurate it is, how it fits into everything else, and how it may be changed when we learn more.[2]

We follow Feynman's approach by discussing the aspects of market efficiency that are "easier to get at first" and "the first step to a real understanding." But don't worry, we will get to, as Feynman puts it, "the more exciting, more wonderful and more fun" stuff as well. Just as Feynman taught his concepts step-by-step, we have split the discussion of market efficiency into several parts as well.

---

[1] Richard P. Feynman, Robert B. Leighton, and Matthew L. Sands, *The Feynman Lectures on Physics* (New York: Basic Books, 2010).

[2] Ibid.

First, we present the **efficient market hypothesis**, which establishes the *rules* for market efficiency. Next, we show that the **wisdom of crowds** is the mechanism by which the rules of market efficiency are implemented in the stock market. Third, we demonstrate what happens when human behavior stretches and contorts the market price, putting strains on the rules. Finally, we discuss how an investor can identify, and then take advantage of, mispricings to outperform the market. The road map is as follows:

> Chapter 5, "How to Think About Market Efficiency": the rules of market efficiency.
>
> Chapter 6, "How to Think About the Wisdom of Crowds": the mechanism by which the rules of market efficiency are implemented in the stock market.
>
> Chapter 7, "How to Think About Behavioral Finance": how human behavior can foul up the wisdom of crowds and create errors in market prices.
>
> Chapter 8, "How to Add Value Through Research": how investors can use market distortions to their advantage and gain an "edge" to outperform.

The Holy Grail of Money Management: *Generating Alpha*

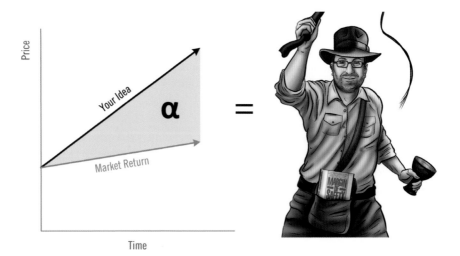

A money manager's sole purpose is to earn an investment return greater than the market, adjusted for risk, which is known in the investment business as "generating **alpha**." If a fund manager cannot beat the market after accounting for fees, an investor would be better off putting his money in a low-cost index fund. The true measure of investment success on Wall Street is not just making a positive return; rather, it is delivering a return *greater* than the overall market or a specific **benchmark**. For most investors, the benchmark to beat is one of the broader market averages such as the S&P 500, Dow Jones Industrial Index, or the Russell Microcap Value Index. The ability to outperform over long periods of time is the holy grail of investing, **and history has shown that very few professional money managers have achieved this goal**.

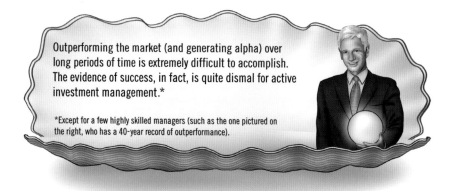

Outperforming the market (and generating alpha) over long periods of time is extremely difficult to accomplish. The evidence of success, in fact, is quite dismal for active investment management.*

*Except for a few highly skilled managers (such as the one pictured on the right, who has a 40-year record of outperformance).

One of the first papers to highlight the difficulty of outperforming the market, titled "Can Stock Market Forecasters Forecast?" was written in 1933 by Alfred Cowles III. He tracked the investment performance of 20 fire insurance companies, 16 financial services firms, and the recommendations from 24 financial publications to see if they outperformed the market. The average performance for the fire insurance companies and financial services firms underperformed the market by –4.72% and –1.43%, respectively, while the results for the group of 24 financial publications—more than 3,300 forecasts in total—were equally disappointing, at –4% per year over a $4\frac{1}{2}$ year period.

More recently, a report issued by Vanguard in March 2015 showed that approximately 85% of managed funds underperformed the stock market over a five-year period. The 2016 year-end edition of S&P Dow Jones Indices SPIVA U.S. Scorecard shows that over a 15-year period ending December 2016, "92.2% of large cap, 95.4% of mid-cap and 93.1% of small cap managers trailed their respective benchmarks."[3] Another report, titled "Does Past Performance Matter?" shows that *not one* of the 703 top performing domestic mutual funds measured (over a five-year period) remained in the top quartile five years later.[4]

SOBERING ADVICE TO STUDENTS:

Paul S. gave a lecture in the spring of 2017 to about 35 of Professor David Smith's undergraduate Financial Honors students at SUNY Albany. Paul asked the students, "By a show of hands, how many of you want to manage money?" Most of the students' hands shot-up. Paul then said, "Let's go over some statistics that you might want to keep in mind as you embark on your career."

"I am guessing you guys are around 21 years old. Well, no one in their right mind is going to give you money to manage until you have had at least 10 years of work experience. So, your track record will start when you are in your early 30s. If you retire in your mid-70s, which no one does, that means you ultimately will have a 40-year performance record. Think about it. How many people do you think have beat the market over the past 40 years by 300 basis points or more? A dozen? Fifty? A hundred? Two hundred? Unfortunately, I don't know the number, but I would think that the list is incredibly short.

Keep in mind that the select few who outperformed over the past 40 years produced their returns in a different environment than you will face in the future. Today, there is all sorts of new technology like satellites counting cars in parking lots, computer programs analyzing credit card "exhaust" and other "big data," computers doing natural language processing, former CIA operatives listening for voice stress on conference calls, the list goes on. And technology isn't static, there is always more and more of it.

What about the people you will be competing with over the next 40 years? For starters, there will probably be more of them. And not only are they going to be smart, hungry, and motivated, but they will also be highly trained. Did a program like this one exist at Albany 20 years ago? No. Are there a lot of similar programs in colleges across the country today? Yes, a lot more. Nowadays, most schools have a student-run investment fund and a class that accompanies it.

[3] Aye M. Soe, CFA, and Ryan Poirer, FRM, "SPIVA U.S. Scorecard" Year-End 2016. S&P Dow Jones Indices, McGraw Hill Financial, Inc.

[4] Aye M. Soe, CFA, "Does Past Performance Matter? The Persistence Scorecard." June 2014. S&P Dow Jones Indices, McGraw Hill Financial, Inc.

What about the number of companies all these people will be analyzing? There were about 7,000 public companies on organized US exchanges in 1995. Today, there are roughly 3,500. As a consequence, there are a greater number of highly trained analysts analyzing half as many public companies as there were just 20 years ago.

Given all these facts: more people with more technology looking at fewer companies, do you think that the market is going to be more efficient or less efficient over the *next* 40 years? Probably more efficient. Probably *a lot* more efficient.

With all these challenges, will the number of individuals outperforming the market go up in the future? Probably not.

I'm not trying to discourage you from pursuing your dreams, but you should do it with your eyes open. Do it because you love analyzing companies, not to make a quick buck. And, if your goal is to outperform the market, keep in mind how difficult it has been in the past and the fact that it will only be more challenging in the future."

Generating Alpha Is a Zero-sum Game

Why is it so difficult to beat the market? For starters, *generating alpha* in the stock market is a **zero-sum game**,[5] meaning that one participant's gains result only from other participants collectively losing an equivalent amount. In the immortal words of Gordon Gekko:

> It's a zero-sum game, somebody wins, somebody loses. Money itself isn't lost or made, it's simply transferred from one perception to another.[6]

A simple example of a zero-sum game is the classic Friday night poker game, where four buddies, each starting with $250, or $1,000 collectively, sit down at a table for a friendly evening of poker. If, at the end of the night, one person has won the entire $1,000, then each of his friends will be $250 poorer. The amount of money that leaves the room, however, is the same amount that entered—$1,000. Poker is a zero-sum game. In this example, one person won, three people lost, and although money was transferred between them, no new money was created.

---

[5] While there is some argument as to whether the stock market is a zero-sum game, it is much clearer to understand that *generating alpha* is in fact a zero-sum game.

[6] *Wall Street,* directed by Oliver Stone (Twentieth Century Fox Film Corporation, 1987).

William Sharpe, who won the 1990 Nobel Prize in Economics for his theories of pricing financial assets, published a paper in the *Financial Analysts' Journal* titled, "The Arithmetic of Active Management," in which he demonstrates that the stock market is also a zero-sum game, like the Friday night poker game.

Sharpe's argument starts with the simple observation that the holdings of all investors in a particular market aggregate to form that market. In other words, *all investors taken together are the market*. Therefore, for every investor who wins, there is at least another investor who loses. In the aggregate, it is impossible for the *collective* of all investors to beat the market.

In fact, active investment management is *worse* than a zero-sum game; it is actually a **negative-sum game** because of transaction costs and the fees active managers charge their clients. Returning to the Friday night poker game, let's assume that the four friends decide to play at their local country club, which charges $100 ($25 per person) to use a table in the card room for the evening. The total available pot is now $900 instead of the original $1,000 when the friends were playing at home, making it a negative-sum game when the fees for using the table are included. If the pot is split evenly at the end of the evening, each player would leave with $225 instead of the $250 they arrived with. The most **alpha** that can be generated by any single player is $675. However, for someone to win, someone else must lose, and **because of fees, the collective always walks away with less money than when the evening started**.

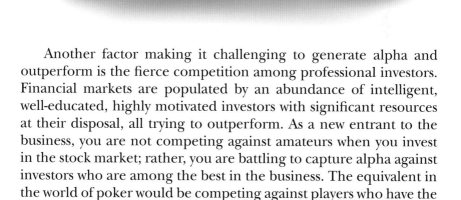

The fact that the stock market is a zero-sum game (actually, it is a negative-sum game) coupled with intense competition from highly motivated, intelligent investors makes it extremely challenging to outperform over long periods of time. The only way to outperform is to systematically and repeatedly identify situations where the market has not priced a security correctly. To know when the market is malfunctioning, however, we need to understand what it looks like when it is functioning properly.

Another factor making it challenging to generate alpha and outperform is the fierce competition among professional investors. Financial markets are populated by an abundance of intelligent, well-educated, highly motivated investors with significant resources at their disposal, all trying to outperform. As a new entrant to the business, you are not competing against amateurs when you invest in the stock market; rather, you are battling to capture alpha against investors who are among the best in the business. The equivalent in the world of poker would be competing against players who have the skills to win the World Series of Poker.

SWIMMING WITH SHARKS IN LAS VEGAS AND WALL STREET

In an article published in *PokerNews* on February 12, 2014, writer Nolan Dalla asked the following question: "Has Poker Become Unbeatable?" Early in the article he makes the statement, "Talk to poker players who have been around for a while, and most will tell you the money isn't as easy as it used to be. The games are getting tougher." The article is rich in commentary about the dynamics in the world of poker at that time, and Dalla presents several arguments why he feels that poker had become a much tougher game to beat, which, we believe, provides important lessons for investors.

Stepping back for a moment, the first serious books on poker strategy were published in the late 1970s fueling an accelerated understanding of the nuances of the game. More sophisticated strategies were introduced by each new generation of poker players turned authors.[7] As would be expected,

---

[7] We have seen the same trend on Wall Street with some of the best money managers writing books, such as Seth Klarman's *Margin of Safety* (1991) and Joel Greenblatt's *You Can Be a Stock Market Genius* (1997) imparting their knowledge to the masses and making the "game" significantly harder to win.

(Continued)

(Continued)

the level of competition among players resolves quickly. Newbies had access to sophisticated strategies and could play endlessly online to hone their card skills and table instincts. Consequently, poker became dramatically more competitive, making it harder to win matches. As Dalla writes in his article:

> Elementary strategies no longer cut it. Everyone has access to **information**. There are books, training sites, online forums and an open exchange of ideas and critical thinking about the game unlike anything that existed in the past. It's no longer that difficult to become very good at this game relatively quickly, especially if you're willing to put in the hours. As a result, the very best players in poker have seen the ranks of their rivals swell to the point where there are now many more sharks at the top of the pyramid. The super-elite class of players who seemed to know most of the secrets, those on the cutting edge of poker thinking a few years ago, have found the information gap between them and the rest of the field ever narrowing, which has resulted in tougher games and lower profit margins.[8]

We find it interesting that Dalla refers to the increased access to information and the growing skill among all players as resulting in "lower profit margins." These observations apply to the stock market as well, although we would modify the statement slightly, believing that greater access to information and increased skill among investors have resulted in "lower outperformance (alpha generation)."

Dalla observes the same type of arms race in poker that we see on Wall Street. First, he states, "[As] more and more poker players are reaching that Holy Grail of poker knowledge, it seems possible that we may arrive at a place where *no player has a discernible edge over any other*, at which point the game basically becomes an *exercise in pure chance*, unless one is convinced psychology alone is exploitable [emphasis added]." We are especially drawn to his comment that "unless one is convinced psychology alone is exploitable," which parallels observations we make in the next chapters about the interaction of efficient market theories and behavioral finance.

Second, Dalla's statement that "the best players figured out the basics to winning and stuck to it, then once everybody else started catching on, profits dried up," draws an important parallel to the rising level of skill among professional investors.

Finally, Dalla observes, "What's happening now … is what I call a 'bunching factor.' The number of top poker players in the world used to fit inside a single room. Now, there are hundreds, if not thousands, of poker players scattered all over who might rightly belong in that super class, at least on their best playing day. Accordingly, these elite players have come up with new and creative ways amongst themselves to see who is best."

On Wall Street, being best equates to consistently outperforming the market. Dalla's comments apply equally to investing, with a slight modification. The elite investors "have come up with new and creative ways amongst themselves to" outperform the market.

Perhaps the article is best summarized by Dalla's observation that "…we should remember that most profit at the poker table comes not from our own brilliance, but rather from the mistakes of others." In any zero-sum game, one makes money when someone else makes a mistake.

---

[8] Nolan Dalla, "Nolan Dalla Asks, Has Poker Become Unbeatable?" PokerNews.com, iBus Media Ltd., June 23, 2015.

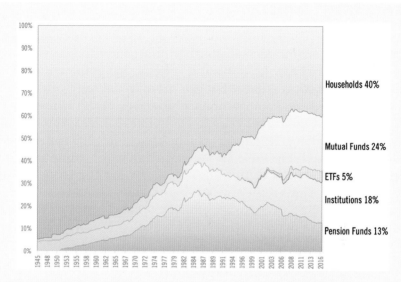

Figure 5.1   Significant Decline in Retail Stock Ownership over the Past 70 Years

However, with all investors now possessing greater skills, each making fewer individual mistakes, the opportunities to exploit less talented investors seem rarer than ever these days. It may have been possible, in the past, for professional investors to take advantage of retail investors, or for more sophisticated investors to prey on less sophisticated ones; that is no longer the case. The mix of investors has shifted over the years decidedly in favor of the professional, while the smaller, less sophisticated investor has been driven almost completely from the market.

Statistics compiled by Haver Analytics,[9] using Federal Reserve Board data, show that the ownership of stocks held by individual (retail) investors has declined sharply, from a high of 95% in 1945 to 40% in 2015 (see Figure 5.1). The results reveal that corporate equities are now primarily owned by institutions, which means that instead of *tens of millions* of individual investors making buy and sell decisions regarding the value of stocks, *tens of thousands* of professional investment managers[10] are making those decisions today.

Dalla's observation of the increasingly competitive poker world and the observation of what has emerged on Wall Street, where only the smart participants survive because the weaker ones have disappeared, is often referred to as the *paradox of skill*.[11] In the investment world, the sharks no longer have enough fish to feed on, so, out of necessity, they are forced to compete against each other to outperform. Unfortunately, there are few patsies left at the poker table or in the investment business.

---

[9] We would like to thank Patrick Sawick at Haver Analytics, who generously provided us with this data.

[10] Ipreo's database lists approximately 23,000 active (as opposed to passive) equity managers in the United States.

[11] Michael Mauboussin wrote an excellent paper on this topic, "Alpha and the Paradox of Skill: Results Reflect Your Skill and the Game You Are Playing," dated July 15, 2013.

Defining Market Efficiency

Market efficiency[12] is the proposition that, at any given moment, a stock price properly incorporates all available information about a company and is the best estimate of its intrinsic value at that point in time. The theory is easy to conceptualize but gets messy in the real world.

In 2013, Eugene Fama, a finance professor at the University of Chicago, shared the Nobel Prize in Economics for his groundbreaking work in **market efficiency**, a term he coined in 1965. Subsequent academic research has fueled a five-decade debate around this concept. Although details of this debate are beyond the scope of this book,[13] we use Fama's theory as a foundation to help us develop a working definition of market efficiency. Fama states in his 1991 paper, "Efficient Capital Markets II":

> I take the market efficiency hypothesis to be the simple statement that security prices fully reflect all available information.[14]

It is important to note that Fama says nothing about valuation in this statement. In fact, he says nothing about what information must be reflected in security prices. He also says nothing about whether the price that reflects all available information represents a logical price!

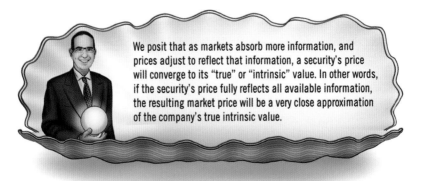

We posit that as markets absorb more information, and prices adjust to reflect that information, a security's price will converge to its "true" or "intrinsic" value. In other words, if the security's price fully reflects all available information, the resulting market price will be a very close approximation of the company's true intrinsic value.

---

[12] Please keep in mind that the discussion of market efficiency throughout the book is restricted to the efficient pricing of **individual securities**, not the stock market as a whole. Therefore, when we refer to "information," it is the set of information for a *particular security*. When we refer to *the crowd, the group*, or *the collective*, we are referring to those investors looking at, opining on, or trading in a *particular security*. While this group is fluid over time (as investors who are new to the situation enter and old investors leave), when looking at a particular slice of time, this group is fixed.

[13] Although we will not take sides in the market efficiency debate in this discussion, we happen to believe that the market is, for all intents and purposes, highly efficient.

[14] E. F. Fama, "Efficient Capital Markets II," *Journal of Finance* 46 (1991): 1575.

We can use Zoe's Lemonade Stand to illustrate this point. In chapter 4, we arrive at a value of $1,412, or $9.41 per share, when we assume a 20% return on invested capital and no growth. Assuming the market for Zoe's Lemonade Stand's common stock fully reflects all available information, the stock would be efficiently priced and equal the intrinsic value:

$$\text{Market Price} = \text{Intrinsic Value} = \$9.41$$

Since the market price equals the intrinsic value in this scenario and no mispricing exists, there is no alpha available to an investor interested in buying the stock. To estimate the intrinsic value of Zoe's Lemonade Stand, we used information about factors such as lemon prices, weather, and the number of glasses sold. If we assume the market has **all available information** concerning these factors, and the security price **fully reflects** this information, then, according to Fama, the result will be an efficient market price for the stock of Zoe's Lemonade Stand.

There are two important issues with Fama's theory that need additional explanation. First, we need to understand what constitutes "all available information," and second, how do we know if that information is "fully reflected" in the stock price?

To define what comprises "all available information," we first need to define **information** and discuss certain words and phrases that we use to avoid confusion.

DISCLAIMER The legality of the use of nonpublic information, material or not, is beyond the scope of this book and therefore will not be discussed. The following discussion is not legal advice, is not to be acted on as such, and may not be accurate or current. Investors should be acutely aware of the ever-changing rules[15] regarding nonpublic information and insider trading.

---

[15] At the risk of overstating this point, there are various rules and regulations issued by the SEC, as well as state and other federal laws that are critical to understand and comply with. These restrictions evolve constantly with new legislation and related court decisions. It is a murky area that is beyond the scope of this book. Nonetheless, Paul S., from his experience of working at the SEC and the compliance department at Goldman Sachs, thought this issue important enough that when he taught his security analysis classes at Columbia Business School he would bring to class as a guest lecturer his dear friend, Jeffrey Plotkin, a former SEC attorney, to discuss various issue regarding insider trading, the work of an analyst and related compliance issues. Despite the warnings contained in these lectures, one of Paul S.'s former students, years after graduation, was convicted of insider trading.

Defining Information

We start with the term **information**, which we define using the definitions found in the U.S. Securities and Exchange Commission's Regulation FD, issued in August 2000.[16]

Pursuant to Regulation FD, "Information is nonpublic if it has not been disseminated in a manner making it available to investors generally."[17] Regarding information originating from a company, a press release over a wire service or a filing made with the SEC (and made available on the SEC website) is generally considered **adequately disseminated**. Other types of information would be considered adequately disseminated if a **sufficient number** of participants have the information.

According to Regulation FD, "Information is material if 'there is a substantial likelihood that a reasonable shareholder would consider it important' in making an investment decision. To fulfill the materiality requirement, there must be a substantial likelihood that a fact 'would have been viewed by the reasonable investor as having significantly altered the "total mix" of information made available.'"[18] In our opinion, a good measure of **materiality** is if the information is reasonably certain to have a *substantial effect on the price* of the company's securities. As we discuss in the footnote below, while we are not legally correct with this statement, we believe it is a good measure for the discussion.[19]

While *non*-material, nonpublic information is *not* specifically defined in Regulation FD, we can infer that this is information that has not been disseminated, but, by itself, would neither influence a reasonable investor's investment decision nor have a substantial effect on the price of the company's securities if made public.

For instance, using these definitions as a guide, if you knew that a company was going to report disappointing earnings or heard from the CEO that his company received a buyout offer before the information

---

[16] FD stands for "full disclosure." For more information, Google "SEC Final Rule: Selective Disclosure and Insider Trading."

[17] SEC Regulation FD, § 17 CFR 243.100-243.103 (2000).

[18] Ibid.

[19] In the 2011 case Matrixx Initiatives, Inc. v. Siracusano, the U.S. Supreme Court rejected the use of a "bright-line" test of statistical significance (if the stock went up in reaction to the news) to determine whether undisclosed information is material (*Matrixx Initiatives, Inc. v. Siracusano*, 131 S.Ct. 1309 (2011)).

was released publicly, you would possess material, nonpublic information.[20] It should be clear in both cases that the information will have a material impact on the stock price once it is released. Conversely, the same CEO telling you that his company is expanding the size of its parking lot at a facility to hire additional employees in response to the higher revenue the company recently reported to shareholders, most likely, is non-material, nonpublic information. The litmus test to see if the information is material or non-material is to ask, "Would the stock price change in response to the news?" Generally, answering yes makes the information material. As Paul S.'s friend Jeff Plotkin would say to the class, "You *know* when you have material, nonpublic information. You get that little tickle in your gut, that *feeling*."

The three different types of information, contained within the overall information set for any given security, are presented in Figure 5.2.

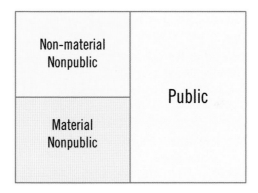

Figure 5.2   Different Types of Information

What Happens When Material Nonpublic Information Is Disseminated?

Adhering to the SEC's definition, material information is information where "there is a substantial likelihood that a reasonable shareholder would consider it important."[21] Material information

---

[20] At the risk of splitting hairs, it is generally accepted (as of the writing of this book in June 2016) that *being in possession* of material, nonpublic information is not illegal per se, although *trading* on it is. Individuals have two basic options if they are in possession of material, nonpublic information: they can either abstain from trading in the security or disclose the information.

[21] SEC Regulation FD, § 17 CFR 243.100-243.103 (2000).

includes, although it is not limited to, earnings releases, winning or losing a substantial customer, acquiring or divesting of a major asset, or some other significant corporate action or development. When a company releases new information, it spreads, or propagates, to all interested parties. Although the information may be only partially disseminated initially, it will spread quickly as investors realize its importance. The new information, however, will not be considered fully disseminated until a sufficient number of market participants are aware of it. This process is rapid in most modern-day situations because most companies employ national news services to distribute important corporate news instantaneously to all interested parties. The information becomes part of the **public information set** once it is fully disseminated, as demonstrated in Figure 5.3.

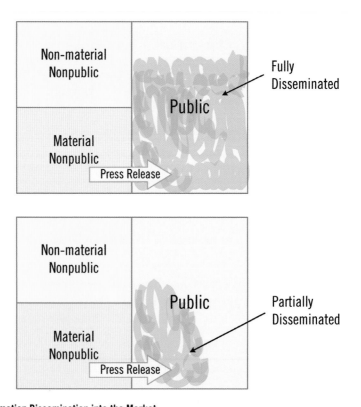

Figure 5.3   Information Dissemination into the Market

Defining "All Available Information"

Now that we have a reasonable, working definition for **information**, we can discuss what constitutes **available information**. All **public** information by definition is available. There is also information that is available to the public, although it is hard or costly to obtain. We refer to this as **quasi-public information**[22] because, although *technically* public, it has many of the same characteristics of non-material, nonpublic information. This type of information includes data gleaned from satellite images, the use of web-scraping software,[23] conducting consumer surveys, Freedom of Information Act (FOIA)[24] requests, court documents, or other similar sources. This information is available for a price, as shown in Figure 5.4.

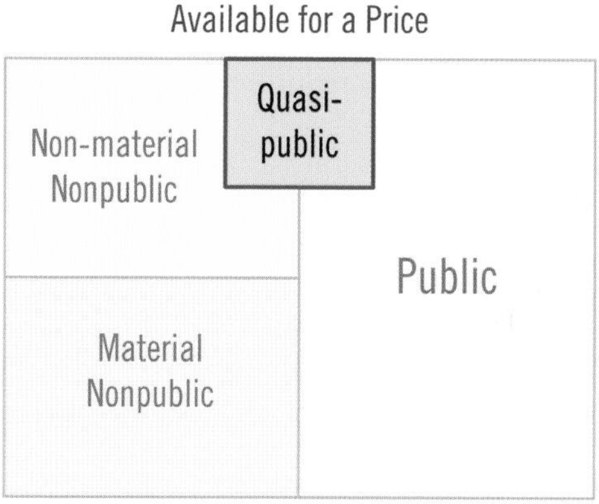

Available for a Price

Figure 5.4   Available for a Price: Quasi-Public Information

There is also a portion of the non-material, nonpublic information that is available to some investors, but it is not available to all of them. The price for that type of information is measured in units

---

[22] This is not an "official" term—we made it up.

[23] An example of web-scraping is having a bot try to make reservations at a certain hotel chain to attempt to determine the hotel's occupancy rate.

[24] The Freedom of Information Act was enacted in 1967 and gives the public the right to request access to records of any federal agency, which is, in turn, required to disclose any information requested, as long as that information would not be harmful to government or private interests. For more information read the excellent 2015 paper by Gargano, Rossi and Wermers, titled "The Freedom of Information Act and the Race Towards Information Acquisition."

of time rather than money. For instance, there are certain investors who have greater access to company management, competitors, customers, suppliers, and other industry experts, because of relationships they have cultivated over time. Examples of this advantage are evident during investment conferences hosted by brokerage firms where only clients of the brokerage firm are allowed to attend management presentations and one-on-one meetings with company management. These clients get access to management while non-clients are excluded from the meetings. Anyone can pay to attend these conferences, although long-standing relationships with management can be hugely beneficial in these discussions because these relationships are based on familiarity and trust, and cannot be bought with money. The price of the information in these situations is time. **While Regulation FD does not allow selective disclosure of material information in any situation, it does not prohibit disclosure of non-material information, which is often obtained in these meetings**. We show available non-material, nonpublic, and quasi-public information in Figure 5.5.

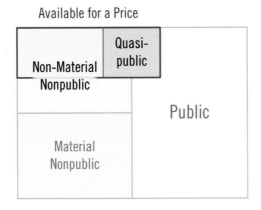

Figure 5.5   Non-Material, Nonpublic Information Also Has a Cost

In Figure 5.6 we show all material, nonpublic information behind bars to emphasize the legal restrictions associated with this type of information (and the consequences if one trades on it). We also show a portion of non-material information behind a chain-link

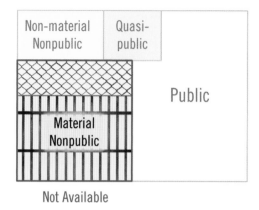

Figure 5.6   Not Available: Material, Nonpublic Information

fence because it is difficult to obtain (although resourceful investors spend considerable money and effort trying to acquire it).[25]

Finally, we show the full set of Fama's **all available information** in Figure 5.7.

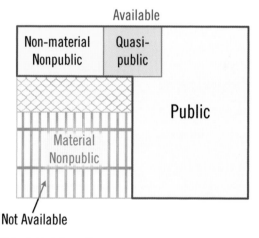

Figure 5.7   Fama's Available Information

Now that we have defined **all available information**, we can turn to the next question: Is the information **fully reflected** in the market price?

_____

[25] It is important to keep in mind that these categories are fluid and change over time. For instance, today's unavailable information becomes available once it is uncovered or released.

The Rules of Market Efficiency

There are three conditions that sufficiently describe a market where **all available information** has been **fully reflected** in the price of a stock:

1. All available information is (or has been) **disseminated** to a sufficient number of investors.
2. The information is **processed** by a sufficient number of investors without any systematic error.
3. The information is expressed and thereby **incorporated** into the market price by a sufficient number of investors trading the security.

While we characterize these tenets as rules, the reality is much subtler. As said by Professor Roger Murray, the efficient market hypothesis can be thought of as "a magnet in a rational world that pulls market price toward . . . intrinsic value." The efficient market hypothesis reflects a process of spontaneous, emergent, unintentional order. To paraphrase Adam Ferguson in *The History of Civil Society*, the rules are a result of human action rather than the result of human design. Unlike the Ten Commandments, no entity, divine or otherwise, gave us a list of rules governing market efficiency, they emerged spontaneously. We lay out the progression of the three rules in Figure 5.8.

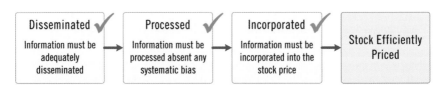

Figure 5.8   Three Rules of Market Efficiency

Notice that each of the preceding market efficiency rules depends upon a **sufficient number** of investors for the rule to be satisfied. Although there is no simple measure as to what constitutes a sufficient number of investors, the following analogy should provide additional insight.

Pharmacology defines a **threshold dose** as the minimum amount of a medication or substance that will produce a desired effect. For example, say you need to stay awake for a few hours to finish studying for an exam. You need to drink just enough coffee to keep you awake, but not so much that you are jittery while you study. A typical cup of coffee contains 95 milligrams of caffeine and there are roughly 16 sips in a cup of coffee, so each sip contains about

6 milligrams of caffeine. You know one sip will not do the job. A pharmacologist would tell you the threshold dose equals the minimum number of sips necessary to keep you awake.

For the purposes of market efficiency, we use the concept of a threshold dose, which equates to the number of investors required to reach the threshold for information to be adequately disseminated, properly processed, and fully incorporated in the stock price. Although it is often impossible to know when this threshold is met, and the number of investors is sufficient to satisfy the rules, we explain in the next chapter how the market gets closer to the threshold level as the number of market participants increases.

The following discussion foreshadows what we cover in the next few chapters as we explore what happens when the tenets do not hold:

Rule 1: Dissemination

For the market to arrive at an efficient price, all available information must be **disseminated** to a sufficient number of market participants. This rule necessitates that investors have the information or are aware that it exists. A stock *may* become mispriced if critical information has not been fully disseminated.

Rule 2: Processing

The market participants need to **process** the information to determine what impact it has on their estimate of the stock's intrinsic value. The rule necessitates that this calculation be done without any widespread **systematic error** among investors. Although investors have processed the information and have calculated their respective estimates as to the stock's intrinsic value, these estimates are not yet reflected in the stock price until they are **incorporated**. A stock *may* become mispriced if there are not a sufficient number of investors processing the information, resulting in some form of neglect, or there are a sufficient number of investors, but they have all been influenced by a similar **bias** resulting in systematic error in in their intrinsic value estimate and that error has become incorporated into the stock price.

Rule 3: Incorporation

These estimates must be **expressed** in the marketplace for the information to be fully reflected and **incorporated** in the stock price. As we discuss more fully later in the book, the only way for an estimate to be **incorporated** is through trading activity. For example, if there is a research report recommending the purchase or sale of the stock, or someone expresses their opinion on a company in another venue such as on TV, a blog, or an investing website, their opinion will only be **incorporated** if other market participants take action and trade on the information. A stock may become mispriced if there are impediments preventing investors from trading the stock and **incorporating** their estimates. If these estimates are not expressed, the information contained in those estimates will not be incorporated into the stock price.

When the Rules of Market Efficiency Operate Flawlessly

We can use the following example to highlight the three market efficiency rules in practice. Before the markets opened on February 23, 2016, MKS Instruments announced its intent to acquire Newport Corporation for $23.00 per share in cash, which was a significant premium to the closing price of Newport's stock the previous day of $15.04 per share. There was no unusual price movement or increased trading volume in Newport's stock leading up to the announcement, which indicates that information about the deal had not leaked to market participants prior to the official release. A surprise takeover clearly surpasses the threshold of **material**, **nonpublic information**, and all investors would naturally expect the information to have a significant effect on the stock price once investors were notified of the deal.

MKS announced the details of the proposed transaction at 7:00 a.m. Eastern Time and Newport's stock **repriced** immediately to reflect the announcement when the stock markets opened for trading at 9:30 a.m., as demonstrated in Figure 5.9.

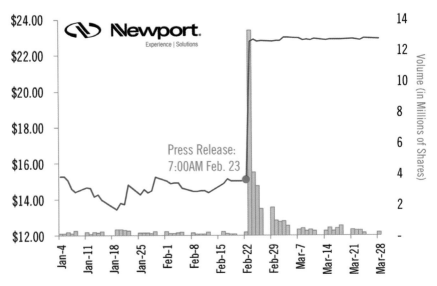

Figure 5.9   Newport Corporation's Stock Reprices Immediately After Takeover Announcement

The press release issued by MKS **adequately disseminated** the new information, satisfying the first rule of market efficiency. A sufficient number of market participants **processed** the new information without any systematic error, satisfying the second rule. The new information was **incorporated** into the stock price almost immediately, as investors exploited the difference between the market price and the value (the takeover price), satisfying the third rule.

The Mechanism That Implements the Rules of Market Efficiency

While we have outlined the *rules* that describe market efficiency, we have not explained the *mechanism* by which those rules are implemented to produce an efficient market price.

The Individual's Process

In practice, individuals purchase a stock because they believe its price will increase in the future, which implies that their estimate of intrinsic value is greater than the market price. By simple correlation, investors must have their own estimate of the stock's intrinsic value to make this determination.

Figure 5.10 illustrates a rudimentary process by which an individual calculates their estimate of a stock's intrinsic value. We expand on this model in more detail in later chapters.

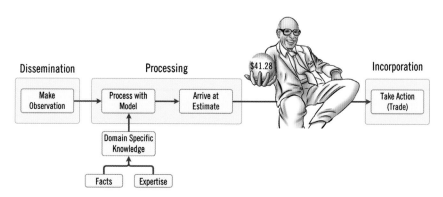

Figure 5.10   An Individual's Process for Estimating Intrinsic Value

As the model in Figure 5.10 shows, the investor begins by observing events about a company, which may include a recent press release, an interview with the company's CEO, a news blog, or any other information about the company's fundamentals. The investor then processes that information with a model[26] in order to generate an estimate of the company's value. The investor takes action based upon whether the current stock price is lower (higher) than his estimate of the stock's intrinsic value. His view will be expressed and incorporated into the stock price when he trades the security.

The Individual Process, Multiplied

The stock market **aggregates** all the individual trades, each representing a different estimate of the stock's intrinsic value, made by thousands, if not hundreds of thousands, of investors all over the world (which we refer to as *the collective* or *the crowd*), into a single market price that represents the consensus estimate of the company's value. When the tenets of the efficient market hypothesis are satisfied, this *collective* produces an efficient stock price, which we represent in Figure 5.11.

This **collective process** is the mechanism governing the three tenets of market efficiency. When this process functions properly, the stock market produces an efficiently priced stock, eliminating any mispricings, which makes it impossible to outperform the market and generate alpha.

This governing mechanism is known as the **wisdom of crowds**. We explain in the next chapter how the theory operates and demonstrate how the crowd implements the rules of market efficiency to produce an efficient stock price.

---

[26] A model is defined as an individual's beliefs, sets of rules, or cause and effect relationships, which govern his decision-making process. A person's model is shaped and influenced by his domain-specific knowledge consisting of facts and expertise, or experiences.

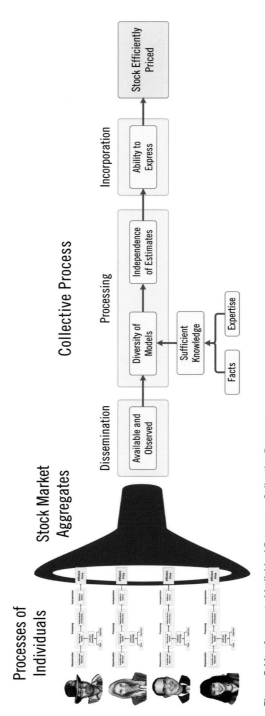

Figure 5.11 Aggregated Individual Process = Collective Process

Gems:

- ♢ The markets need to be efficient to generate alpha. A temporary inefficiency or mispricing will be corrected only if the market is ultimately efficient. The alternative would be a market where a mispricing could persist forever. In such a world, no one could reliably generate alpha and outperform.

- ♢ A portfolio manager's sole purpose is to earn an investment return greater than the market, adjusted for risk. If a manager cannot beat the market after accounting for fees, an investor would be better off putting his money in a low-cost index fund. The true measure of investment success on Wall Street is not just making a positive return; rather, it is delivering a return *greater* than the overall market, or a specific *benchmark*.

- ♢ Outperforming the market over long periods of time is extremely difficult to accomplish. The evidence of success, in fact, is quite dismal for active investment management.

- ♢ The fact that the stock market is a zero-sum game (actually, it is a negative-sum game) coupled with intense competition from highly motivated, intelligent investors makes it extremely challenging for any investor to beat the market. The only way for an investor to outperform is to systematically and repeatedly identify situations where the market has not priced a security correctly.

- ♢ If the security's price fully reflects all available information, it will be efficiently priced and the resulting market price will equal the company's intrinsic value.

- ♢ There are three conditions that must be met for all available information has been reflected in the price of a stock:
  1. All available information is (or has been) **disseminated** to a sufficient number of investors.
  2. The information is **processed** by a sufficient number of investors without any systematic error.
  3. The information is expressed and thereby **incorporated** into the market price.

CHAPTER

6

How to Think About the Wisdom of Crowds

"And the Oscar Goes to . . ."

After taking a security analysis class taught by Paul J. at Columbia Business School in the fall of 1994, Paul S. and 21 of his classmates coaxed Paul J. into teaching an advanced investing course in the spring 1995 semester.

For several years, Paul S.'s friend, Jodi Heller, hosted an annual Academy Awards party where she had guests fill out ballots guessing who would win the Oscar in a small number of popular categories. To make the contest more fun, Jodi had everyone contribute to a betting pool and then awarded a cash prize to the most accurate forecaster.

With the 67th Academy Awards only a few weeks away, Paul S. thought it would be interesting to run a similar contest in Paul J.'s class, not as a test of forecasting abilities, but as a fun diversion. Paul S. suggested using Jodi's contest format.

Coincidentally, Paul J. had recently read an article written by Jack Treynor[1] that discussed a contest Treynor had run in his investment class at USC where he challenged his students to guess the number of beans in a jar he passed around the classroom. According to the article, Treynor ran the experiment twice. The jar had 810 beans in the first experiment. The average (mean) guess for the students was 841 and only 2 of the 46 students' estimates were closer to the true value than the classroom average. The jar held 850 beans in the second experiment. This time the mean estimate was 871 with only one of the student guesses more accurate than the average. Treynor made the following observation in the article:

> Apparently it doesn't take knowledge of beans, jars or packing factors for a group of students to make an accurate estimate of the number of beans in a jar. All it takes is *independence* [emphasis added].[2]

With his interest piqued, Paul J. tried to replicate Treynor's bean jar experiment using the 1995 Academy Awards contest as his bean jar. To facilitate the experiment, Paul J. asked his students to pick their best guess as to who would win the Oscar in each of 12 categories.

In addition to recording each student's guesses, Paul J. tallied the median nominee selected by the students in each category, which he designated as the "group's selection" and deemed the consensus view. After the Oscars had been announced, Paul J. determined the class winner and awarded the prize money. The contest results supported Treynor's experience: *the consensus beat the individuals.*

As Table 6.1 shows, the consensus guessed 9 of 12 winners correctly, which is an impressive 75% accuracy rate. The best student in class *only matched the consensus,* also guessing 9 of 12 correctly, while everyone else in the contest did worse. The

[1] Jack Treynor was an accomplished investment professional, a highly respected finance theorist, and a prolific writer of finance articles. He also served for more than a decade as the editor of the CFA Institute's *Financial Analysts Journal.*

[2] Jack L. Treynor, "Market Efficiency and the Bean Jar Experiment," *Financial Analysts Journal* 43, no. 3 (1987): 50–53.

second-place winner guessed 8 of 12, or 67%, correctly, and the average student (excluding first and second place) got only 5 of 12, or 43%, correct.

Table 6.1   Academy Award Contest Results

	Consensus	Individuals		
		1st Place	2nd Place	Average
Number Correct	9 of 12	9 of 12	8 of 12	5 of 12
Percent Correct	75%	75%	67%	43%

Paul J. ran the contest again in his class the following spring, with more students, the same rules, and similar results. That year's consensus and best student both guessed 8 of 12, or 67%, correctly; second place guessed 7 of 12, or 58%, correctly; and the average participant guessed only 38% correctly.

Paul J. saw a clear connection between Treynor's bean jar experiment, the Academy Awards contest, and how stock markets form consensus views. These early insights fueled Paul J.'s interest in resolving the seeming paradox between the efficient market hypothesis and his personal experience as a sell-side analyst in the stock market.

Paul J. included the Academy Awards contest in his class each spring for the next few years and enlisted Michael Mauboussin (a fellow adjunct professor at Columbia) and Paul Stevens (a colleague of Paul J.'s who taught an investment class at UC Berkeley) to run the same contest in their classes in 1997. The three different classrooms produced similar outcomes, with the consensus easily making the most accurate forecast and beating everyone in the contest. Paul J. wrote a short essay in 1998[3] to present the results of his annual contest, his theory on how a robust consensus is formed from a group of individuals acting independently, and the implications for market efficiency.

Paul J.'s Academy Awards essay spread around Wall Street over the next few years. Jim Surowiecki, a staff writer for *The New Yorker*, referenced Paul J.'s Academy Awards contest in his column "The Financial Page," published in 2001. Surowiecki explained in that

---

[3] Paul J.'s essay was first distributed in draft form in September 1998 and titled "Academy Awards, Sharon Stone and Market Efficiency."

essay how the stock market consensus could be swayed by external commentary from the broader media:

> Watching CNBC those two days provided a lesson in how pointless such minute-by-minute coverage of the stock market is—how it distorts the way the market works and helps turn what should be a *diverse, independent*-thinking crowd of investors into a herd acting upon a single collective thought [emphasis added].[4]

Referencing Paul J.'s contest, Surowiecki observed, "Without fail, the group's picks . . . were more accurate than those of even the most prescient individual," adding that it was "more proof that markets outsmart mavens, yes. But there's something else. Johnson's students made their decisions *independently*." He concluded, "And the collective result of all that *independent* decision making was near-perfect. This is how markets normally work" [emphasis added].

Surowiecki's continued interest in the topic eventually led to his writing *The Wisdom of Crowds,* published in August 2005. Surowiecki coined the term and the title for his book as a play on Charles Mackay's 1841 book *Extraordinary Popular Delusions and the Madness of Crowds.*

While Surowiecki's book brought the wisdom of crowds to the masses, in 1995, more than a decade before Surowiecki's book was published, Scott Page, an economics professor at the University of Michigan, began working on diversity-based models.[5] His research led to his excellent book, *The Difference,* published in February 2007, which in turn, prompted Michael Mauboussin to write a fantastic primer, "Explaining the Wisdom of Crowds, Applying the Logic of Diversity,"[6] published in March 2007.

---

[4] Jim Surowiecki "The Financial Page: Manic Monday (and Other Popular Delusions)," *The New Yorker,* March 26, 2001.

[5] While Page did not specifically write about the Academy Awards, we would be remiss if we did not highlight him in the discussion as he has published more academic research on the wisdom of crowds than anyone else and is *the* authority on the topic.

[6] The article was published in *Mauboussin on Strategy,* Legg Mason Capital Markets, March 20, 2007.

Looking back, after more than 20 years, we are amazed that what started out as a fun, nonsensical contest among a group of students and their professor was part of broader inquiry into crowd behavior that ultimately generated numerous articles, books, and academic studies, resulting in formal models of the wisdom of crowds that have provided further insight into how the stock market operates. These endeavors reinforce the old saying, "A good idea has many fathers."

The Wisdom of Crowds Is Critical to Market Efficiency

As we discuss in the previous chapter, when the mechanism governing the three tenets of market efficiency is functioning properly, a stock will be efficiently priced. Why do we care so much about the wisdom of crowds? **Because the wisdom of crowds serves as the governing mechanism that implements the three tenets of market efficiency**.

We explain later in this chapter that when the wisdom of crowds process is functioning properly:

- Information will be adequately **disseminated**: market participants will observe, extract, and aggregate information.
- Information will be **processed**: market participants will evaluate and make estimates without bias.
- Information will be **expressed**, **aggregated**, and **incorporated** into the stock price through trading absent any material impediments.

And, as a result, prices will **fully reflect all available information**, satisfying Eugene Fama's definition of market efficiency.

How the Wisdom of Crowds Implements the Rules of Market Efficiency

We expand on the basic tenets of market efficiency in this chapter to demonstrate how the wisdom of crowds implements the rules of market efficiency to produce an efficient stock price. This deeper understanding provides tools to identify circumstances when the basic tenets of market efficiency might malfunction, creating mispricings in the process. It can also flag situations where investors can gain an edge to exploit mispricings created by those temporary errors.

The analyst needs to understand the mechanisms by which the wisdom of crowds operates to be able to recognize patterns of inefficiencies and how those inefficiencies are corrected, which, in turn, will allow him to reliably produce alpha and hold the holy grail of investing.

The Three Main Tenets of the Wisdom of Crowds

We disaggregate the three market efficiency tenets into the following six conditions to show how the wisdom of crowds implements the rules. Keep in mind that with each item below, only a **sufficient** or **threshold** number of investors, not all, is required for the condition to hold.

Dissemination
1. Information must be **available** and **observed.**

Processing
2. The group must have an adequate amount of **domain-specific knowledge**, in the form of facts or expertise.
3. The crowd must be **diverse**.
4. Investors must act **independently** of each other.

Incorporation
5. Investors cannot face significant impediments to trading, otherwise estimates of value will not be **expressed**, **aggregated**, and **incorporated** into the stock price.
6. Individuals must have **incentives** to give estimates that they believe are accurate.

When these six conditions are met, the crowd produces an accurate answer and it will be next to impossible for individuals to beat the crowd. We show five of the six[7] conditions of the wisdom of crowds process in Figure 6.1.

---

[7] There are plenty of incentives of Wall Street, so we felt no need to address them directly in our model of the collective process.

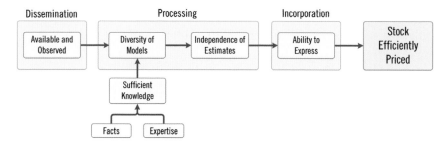

Figure 6.1   Proper Functioning of the Collective Process Produces an Efficient Price

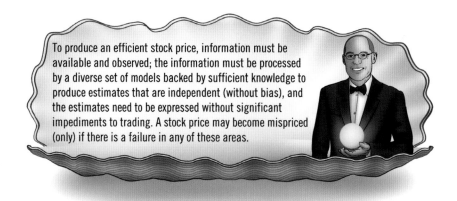

To produce an efficient stock price, information must be available and observed; the information must be processed by a diverse set of models backed by sufficient knowledge to produce estimates that are independent (without bias), and the estimates need to be expressed without significant impediments to trading. A stock price may become mispriced (only) if there is a failure in any of these areas.

An old Japanese proverb summarizes the essence of the wisdom of crowds: "None of us is smarter than all of us." How can the crowd produce an accurate answer when individual members only have partial information or limited knowledge?

Tenet 1—The Dissemination of Information

For the wisdom of crowds to arrive at an accurate estimate, the first condition states that information must be **available** and **observed** by a sufficient number of investors. When available information is overlooked, ignored, or not properly disseminated, investors cannot, or do not, use the information in their model, which may result in mispriced stock, as depicted in Figure 6.2.

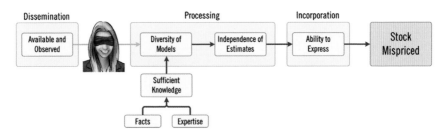

Figure 6.2   Insufficient Dissemination Results in a Mispriced Stock

This first condition satisfies the first rule of the efficient market hypothesis: all available information is (or has been) disseminated to a sufficient number of investors, as shown in Figure 6.3.

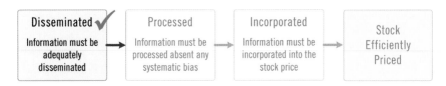

Figure 6.3   First Rule of Market Efficiency Satisfied

Tenet 2—The Processing of Information

For the wisdom of crowds to function properly, a sufficient number of investors must process information without systematic bias, which implies that the crowd is **diverse** and **independent**. The second condition requires that a sufficient number of investors in the group have an adequate level of **domain-specific knowledge** to form the mental model they need to process the information. In other words, if no one in the group has a clue, the wisdom of crowds will not produce an accurate answer.

In his book *The Difference*, Scott Page uses a simple example to make this point. If 10,000 first graders are asked to guess the weight of a Boeing 747, no one would expect their collective estimate to be close to the aircraft's actual weight for the simple reason that the children have absolutely no idea, or reference point from which to guess, how much the 747 weighs. The crowd's guess will not be accurate because none of the children in the crowd has any relevant domain-specific knowledge. In fact, the children might think the 747 is a toy and guess that it weighs only a few pounds!

On the other hand, imagine a group of commercial pilots who fly 747s professionally are asked to guess the plane's weight, instead of the group of first graders. Because the pilots have deep domain-specific knowledge about 747s, we would expect them to have a general idea as to what the plane weighs. Alternatively, think of a group of aeronautical engineers who might not know the weight of a 747 off the top of their head, but have the expertise to estimate its weight accurately. As we show later in this discussion, members of the crowd do not need to have specific knowledge like the pilots or even relevant expertise like the aeronautical engineers for the crowd to produce an accurate estimate.

Even a crowd composed of adults from different walks of life—such as a doctor, a lawyer, and Indian chief; a tinker, tailor, soldier, and spy; a butcher, baker, and candlestick maker—can produce an accurate estimate. While these individuals do not have the expertise that the pilots or the aeronautical engineers possess, they have domain-specific knowledge about the weight of different objects such as a truck or a cargo ship. Using this knowledge, they might be able to arrive at a reasonable guess as to what a 747 weighs. When all of the guesses of this diverse group are averaged, assuming no systematic bias, this "less knowledgeable" crowd will produce a surprisingly accurate estimate of the weight of a 747.

However, while *exact* information is not required, if there is not a sufficient number of individuals in the group with the *requisite* level of domain-specific knowledge, the process will produce a suboptimal answer, like when the first graders attempted to guess how much a 747 weighs, as shown in Figure 6.4.

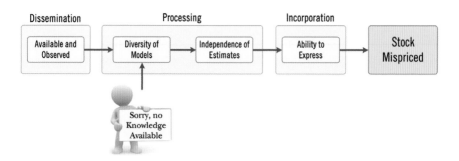

Figure 6.4   Lack of Domain-Specific Knowledge Within the Collective Results in a Mispriced Stock

PRIVATE INFORMATION

An individual's domain-specific knowledge is also called their **private information**. In economics, the theory of **information asymmetry** considers situations when one party has more or better information than the counterparty in a transaction. George Akerlof wrote the seminal paper on the topic, "The Market for Lemons," in 1970, which contributed to his winning the 2001 Nobel Prize in Economic Sciences. Ackerlof presented a market for used cars where sellers have more information than buyers. In Ackerlof's example, a buyer knows the market includes good cars and bad cars (peaches and lemons), but lacks the necessary information to distinguish between the two types of cars available. On the other hand, the seller, having owned the car, knows if they have a peach or a lemon. The informed seller has **private information** that is unavailable to the buyer. In this example, the seller is **informed** because they have superior information (and knows it), while the buyer is **uninformed** because he has no valuable information about the car's quality.

An individual's private information, which includes all their relevant knowledge of facts and experience and represents their **domain-specific knowledge**, forms their information processing model, as shown in Figure 6.5.

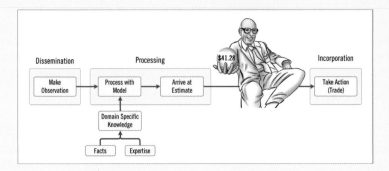

Figure 6.5   Domain-Specific Knowledge Is Comprised of Facts and Expertise That Form an Individual's Processing Model

Every investor possesses their own set of private information, with each investor having different knowledge and experiences, which impacts their determination of a company's intrinsic value. For instance, some investors have only public information, while others have a combination of quasi-public information; non-material, nonpublic information; and material nonpublic information. We show possible information sets for three different market participants: a company's CEO, an informed investor, and an uninformed investor[8] in Figure 6.6.

---

[8] Also known as a "noise trader."

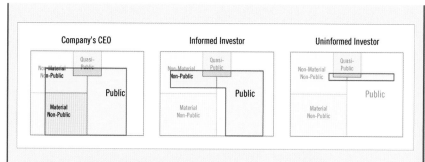

Figure 6.6   Individuals' Private Information

As we discuss in Chapter 8, enterprising investors seek to possess superior private information by combining public and quasi-public information with non-material, nonpublic information to create an **informational advantage**. The investor then applies his analytical process to his superior private information to arrive at *a conclusion* that is material and nonpublic, but *legal*.

The third condition, **diversity**, requires that a sufficient number of individuals in the crowd have different backgrounds, education, experiences, or analytical approaches, and use different models to process their observations. As we just discussed, a person's internal mental model is shaped by their domain-specific knowledge, which includes facts they have gathered and expertise they have acquired.

We represent the different mental models as different car models in Figure 6.7. On Wall Street, the different models can include discounted cash flow analysis, technical analysis, astrology,[9] macro analysis, and fundamental research, as well as other investment approaches.

The crowd's diversity will be lost if everyone has the same facts and expertise, or starts thinking the same way by using the same mental model. And without diversity, individuals within the crowd produce similar answers to each other, the crowd's guess will be only

---

[9] Yes, astrology. Henry Weingarten, director of Astrologers Fund, Inc., has been practicing financial astrology since 1988 and is the author of *Investing by the Stars: Using Astrology in the Financial Markets*.

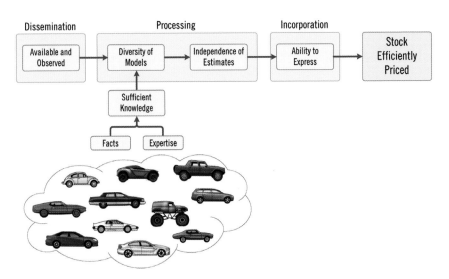

Figure 6.7   Diversity of Models Produces an Efficient Price

a small deviation from the individual estimates, and the crowd's consensus will reflect nothing more than a single view. Consequently, the crowd's answer will lack any of the benefits of diversity and will likely result in a mispriced stock.[10] We represent the lack of diversity as everyone driving the same model car in Figure 6.8.

The fourth condition, **independence**, requires that a sufficient number of individuals in the crowd act autonomously from each other when determining their estimate. Although specific individuals may be influenced by an external factor or a specific set of information, it is important that only a relatively small number of participants are influenced in the same way by the same external stimuli (which could be another person's opinion). **If too many participants are influenced by the same factor, the crowd's consensus view collapses to what is essentially a single view or the view of only a few individuals**, similar to what happens when a crowd loses its

---

[10] Unless, of course, the model everyone is using is the "correct" one. For example, if everyone were trying to estimate the size of a room by using different methods, the models would be diverse. If they were all using an accurate measuring tape, while they are all using the same model or method, it would result in an accurate answer. That caveat aside, there are few "accurate" models for complex situations such as the stock market. Although we are compelled to state this exception, it rarely applies to valuing stocks.

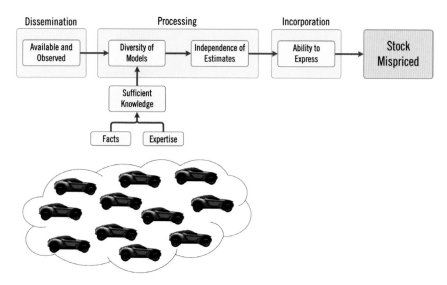

Figure 6.8   Lack of Diversity Results in a Mispriced Stock

diversity, as described previously. If too many members of the crowd become influenced by the views of others and discount or set aside their own information in reaction to an observation, they are said to be caught in an **information cascade**, which we discuss in more detail the following chapter.

If the crowd is influenced **systematically**, it will likely produce an inefficiency in pricing. In the extreme, the collapsing of independence can cause a mania, where everyone believes an overly optimistic view of the situation, or a panic, where the crowd believes a doomsday scenario is likely to unfold. Both examples demonstrate how the lack of independence can feed on itself to produce a significant aberration in a stock's price. Going back to Murray's magnet analogy, we see the effect in Figure 6.9.

Because **diversity** and **independence** are extremely important concepts for understanding the functioning, or potential *malfunctioning*, of the wisdom of crowds and, in turn, market efficiency, we will further emphasize their difference and interrelation with a simple example.[11]

---

[11] We thank Professor Ned Smith of the Kellogg School of Management at Northwestern University for suggesting this example.

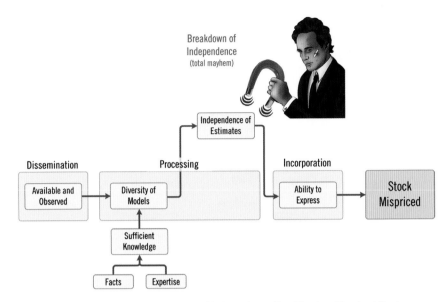

Figure 6.9   Mayhem Causes a Breakdown of Independence Resulting in a Mispriced Stock

Say you wake up one morning, look in the mirror, and see that your nose has turned neon yellow. You make an emergency appointment to see Dr. Ames, an established, well-known ENT specialist at Mount Sinai Hospital on the Upper East Side of Manhattan. She performs a few tests and gives you a diagnosis of malignant neon nose disease, which is not encouraging. The doctor recommends surgery to remove your nose before the infection spreads and your entire body turns neon yellow. She leaves the room and returns 10 minutes later with another doctor in her practice, a young ENT specialist who recently finished his residency, whom she introduces as Dr. Barnes. Dr. Barnes looks at you meekly and says, "I've been briefed by Dr. Ames on your case so I thought I'd take a look at your condition." Dr. Barnes performs a couple of additional tests and declares, "I agree with Dr. Ames, your nose has to go."

You decide that you should get a second opinion before committing to surgery. You make an appointment with Dr. Conner, a world-renowned ENT specialist at Weill Cornell Medical Center, another high-quality medical institution in New York City. Dr. Conner performs a few tests and gives you the same diagnosis as the two doctors at Mount Sinai—malignant neon nose disease—and also recommends surgery. You ask Dr. Conner if she knows either of the two doctors you consulted previously, to which she replies no.

You decide to call your sister Donna, who is a holistic health counselor, and while you don't fully believe in alternative medicine, you ask her what she believes has caused your nose to turn neon yellow. She suggests that you see her good friend William Douglas. Douglas is a doctor of acupuncture and Chinese medicine and is well respected by his peers and patients. You make an appointment to see Dr. Douglas later that day at his office near the NYU Medical Center. Using traditional Chinese medicine diagnostic techniques, such as feeling your pulse and examining your tongue, Dr. Douglas concludes that it is highly unlikely that you have malignant neon nose disease. He hands you a bottle that contains capsules of an exotic Chinese herb, instructs you to take two capsules a day, and tells you that you will be fine in a week. You leave dumbfounded. A week later you wake up, look in the mirror, and see that your nose is back to normal.

While you thought you were getting four separate medical opinions, you really received only two because the doctors you consulted were not diverse and independent. We list each doctor, the different tests they performed, the medical school they attended, the hospital where they work, their diagnosis, and their final recommendation in Figure 6.10 to demonstrate the underlying connection between the three medical doctors.

Dr. Ames's recommendation was surgery. Even though Dr. Barnes performed different tests and, unbeknownst to you, had diagnosed benign neon nose, he ignored his own conclusion and instead relied on Dr. Ames's opinion because of the senior doctor's more extensive experience. Since Dr. Barnes's final recommendation was not **independent**, any **diversity** gained from the additional tests he performed and the fact that he went to a different medical school was lost. Rather than getting two different recommendations, you received just one because of the doctor's *lack of independence.*

The purpose of getting a second opinion is to get a different perspective. To achieve that goal, the new recommendation must be **independent** and **diverse**. You assumed that Dr. Conner's recommendation was independent because he was at a different hospital and had never heard of Doctors Ames and Barnes. Unfortunately, this would be a superficial conclusion. Dr. Conner

Figure 6.10   Doctors' Diagnostic Process

performed the same tests as Dr. Ames and, also unknown to you, went to the same medical school as Dr. Ames. In fact, Dr. Conner had the same classes in the same year as Dr. Ames, and although they never knew each other while in medical school, the two doctors had identical training and were taught the same diagnostic approach. *The domain-specific knowledge that shaped their processing model was identical.* Dr. Ames and Dr. Conner's recommendations were **independent**, but not **diverse**, which is why the two doctors gave the same recommendation. They used the same model and processed the same information in the same way. In effect, the diagnosis and recommendation that you received from Dr. Conner were identical to those from Dr. Ames. Since Dr. Barnes's view was influenced by Dr. Ames's, and Dr. Conner's domain-specific knowledge was identical to Dr. Ames, what you thought were three opinions was just one.

On the other hand, Dr. Douglas went to a school that teaches an unconventional approach to medicine. Dr. Douglas was not swayed by any other doctors' opinions, making his diagnosis both independent and diverse.[12]

Conditions two, three, and four—adequate **domain-specific knowledge**, **diversity**, and **independence**—satisfy the second rule of market efficiency, as seen in Figure 6.11. **The information is processed by a sufficient number of investors without any systematic bias.**

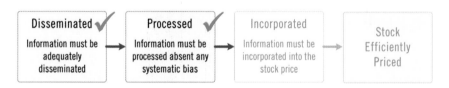

Figure 6.11   Second Rule of Market Efficiency Satisfied

Tenet 3—The Incorporation of Information

Our next two conditions require that estimates and opinions are **expressed**, **aggregated**, and **incorporated** without significant impediments, and that **incentives** exist, to ensure that the processed information is fully incorporated into the stock price.

---

[12] We should point out that while in the example Dr. Douglas's diversity and independence resulted in the right answer, he might have been wrong.

If an investor arrives at an estimate but that estimate is not **incorporated**, the situation will be equivalent to a vote that is not cast. It should be noted that if enough estimates are not **incorporated**, the private information and domain-specific knowledge contained in an individual's estimate will not be **aggregated** with the consensus, which is like the proverbial tree that falls in the woods. If no one is around to hear it, the falling tree does not make a sound. For instance, if someone guessed 12 of 12 correctly in the Academy Awards contest but did not hand in their ballot, their guesses would not be tallied with the results and not **incorporated** into the consensus view. It would be as if they had never guessed. Also, if there is not a critical mass of people expressing their answers, the crowd will not be a crowd and the consensus view will reflect only the opinions of the small group of individuals who expressed their opinion, which often results in a suboptimal answer. In the case of the stock market, that suboptimal answer often results in a mispriced stock. We show in Figure 6.12 what happens when an individual goes through the process of arriving at an estimate, but is not **incorporated** because they are unwilling or unable to express their estimate.[13]

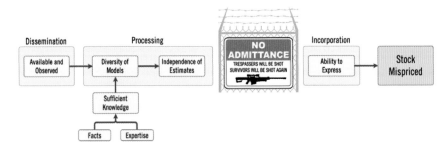

Figure 6.12   Factors Preventing Information from Being Incorporated Results in a Mispriced Stock

The last rule, **incentives**, is important because individuals will match their effort to the reward offered. For instance, if the prize for guessing the correct number of beans in a jar is $10, then individuals will have less of an incentive to invest time and effort to increase the accuracy of their estimate than if the prize is $10,000. For $10,

---

[13] This is known as limits or impediments to arbitrage, which will be discussed in the next chapter.

someone may quickly guess a number because they have only a small incentive to be accurate and win the prize, but for $10,000, the same person will work significantly harder and use much more sophisticated techniques to estimate the correct answer.[14] Interestingly, incentives do not have to be monetary; they can be in the form of professional recognition or an enhanced reputation, which can be thought of as psychic income or bragging rights. Negative incentives, if present, will keep individuals from making wild, off-the-cuff guesses because there will be a penalty for being wrong.

The last two conditions satisfy the third rule of the efficient markets hypothesis: *That information is **incorporated** into the **market price** by a sufficient number of investors through trading.*

When all six conditions of the wisdom of crowds are working properly, the result is a wise crowd, which in the stock market results in an **efficiently priced stock**, one that fully reflects all available information, as shown in Figure 6.13.

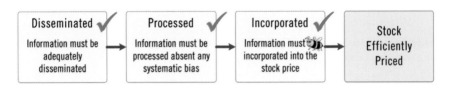

Figure 6.13   Third Rule of Market Efficiency Satisfied

Examples Illustrating How the Wisdom of Crowds Implements the Rules of the Efficient Market Hypothesis

We use several different examples in the remainder of the chapter to explain and highlight the six facets of the wisdom of crowds. We first walk through a simple example of a pen identification contest to show how information from individuals is aggregated, resulting in the crowd being smarter than the individual. Next, we walk through the quintessential wisdom of crowds example—Francis Galton and a 1906 ox-weighing contest—where we discuss the difference between **independence** and **diversity**, and explain why these two conditions are important factors for the crowd to arrive at an accurate answer.

---

[14] For anyone wanting to learn how to accurately estimate beans in a jar, we recommend the excellent article by Edward O. Thorp, published in the November 1965 issue of *Popular Mechanics* titled, "How Many Beans in the Jar?"

We also show what happens to the results when we introduce a **bias**. We then use the Beatles to demonstrate how an accurate answer can emerge from a crowd, even when only a small percentage of the crowd has information relevant to the question asked. Finally, we show how all these factors relate to the stock market.

How the Wisdom of Crowds Aggregates Individual Private Information

We show in the next example how the wisdom of crowds aggregates information to produce accurate answers—answers that are more accurate than any one individual.

Let's pretend that each year the Fountain Pen Hospital in New York City holds a pen identification contest.[15] The goal of the contest is to correctly identify the make and model of 100 different pens from four different manufacturers (25 from each manufacturer). The contestants do not know which four manufacturers the organizers of the contest will choose ahead of time. Teams can have up to four individuals and the winning team gets free pen refills for one year.

When you assemble your team, imagine each member has deep knowledge of one brand of pen. The distributed knowledge is represented in Figure 6.14.

Figure 6.14   Individual Pen Knowledge

When the 100 mystery pens in the contest are unveiled, it turns out that each person on your team has a deep knowledge of one of the four brands picked by the contest organizer.

The combined knowledge allows your team correctly identifies all 100 pens in the contest, while the other team can only identify 50 correctly. Keep in mind that if each member of your group participated alone, they would only know one brand and would only

---

[15] A pen identification contest might seem a bit random but a little-known fact is that Paul J. was an avid pen collector, is incredibly knowledgeable about the subject and possessed one of the largest fountain pen collections in the world.

be able to identify 25 of the 100 pens correctly. However, working together they leverage each other's **domain-specific knowledge** to produce an accurate guess for all the pens in the contest.

The critical point in this example is that none of the members in *your* group had the requisite **domain-specific knowledge** to identify *all* the pens on his own, although when the four teammates combined their expertise, the group could identify all of them. The example shows that two heads (or in this case four) are better than one.

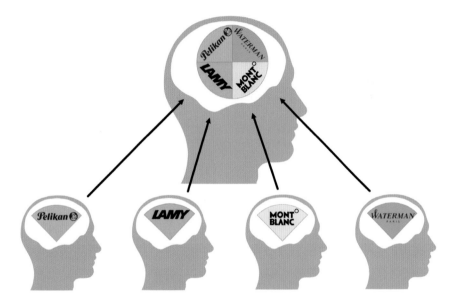

Figure 6.15   The Collective Is More Knowledgeable Than an Individual

The wisdom of crowds aggregation process generates a "correct" answer by transferring (partial) domain-specific knowledge from individuals to the collective. In this example, the knowledge was dispersed among the four individuals (each having only 25% of the total information), although when aggregated, the collective had 100%[16] of the answer.

---

[16] In the pen example, the collective possessed all the information. It should be noted that for the crowd to produce an extremely accurate answer it is not necessary that the collective possess *all* the domain-specific knowledge. All the collective needs to be wise is a group of individuals with a *sufficient* amount of knowledge, as we show in this chapter.

The Quintessential Wisdom of Crowds Example—Francis Galton

The most popular example of the wisdom of crowds is based on an article written by Sir Francis Galton titled *Vox Populi* that appeared in *Nature* magazine's March 7, 1907, issue. Galton, an accomplished English polymath and statistician, published his analysis of an ox-weighing contest held at the 1906 West of England Fat Stock and Poultry Exhibition in Plymouth, England. Each participant in the contest paid 6 pence[17] (US$3.84 adjusted for inflation in 2016 dollars) to enter a guess as to what would be the ox's weight after being slaughtered. The person with the closest guess won a prize. Galton calculated that the average of the 787 guesses was 1,197[18] pounds, *which was only 1 pound off* the actual weight of 1,198 pounds. Even the 86-year-old Galton was surprised by the accuracy of the consensus and the crowd's "ability" to estimate the slaughtered ox's true weight.

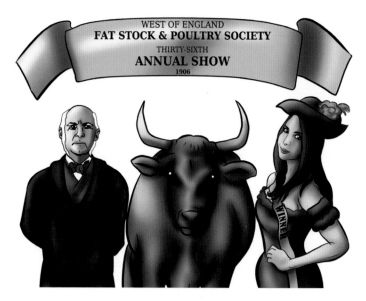

While this story has been repeated ad nauseam in just about every book, article, or paper concerning the wisdom of crowds, we

---

[17] Great Britain was not on a decimal currency system at the time. Its monetary system was based on the £sd, where there were 12 pence in a shilling and 20 shillings in a pound, or 240 pence to the pound.

[18] For those picky readers who are familiar with the story, 1,197 is the correct average for the participants in the contest. It turns out that Galton made an error in his original paper and wrote a letter to the editor, dated March 28, 1907, correcting the mistake. See Kenneth F. Wallis's paper, "Revisiting Francis Galton's Forecasting Competition," in *Statistical Science* 29 (2014): 420–424, for details of the contest results.

felt it important to include it here because the story illustrates certain concepts that are vitally important to the discussion.

Many people *incorrectly* infer from this story that a crowd can generate an accurate guess to just about *any* question asked, even if the individuals in the crowd know little about the situation (however, as we discuss with the first graders guessing the weight of a Boeing 747, there must be sufficient domain-specific knowledge in the crowd for it to arrive at an accurate answer). Scott Page understood the fallacy of that assumption and points out in his book, *The Difference*, that "in 1906 people knew a lot about steers." He goes on to state, "More likely, each had some primitive model of what a steer weighed. These models led to predictions of the steer's weight. The predictions were not naive shots in the dark."[19] Karl Pearson in his biography of Galton said, "The judgments were unbiased by passion . . . The six-penny fee deterred practical joking, and the hope of a prize and the joy of competition prompted each competitor to do his best. The competitors included butchers and farmers, some of whom were highly expert in judging the weight of cattle."[20] It is also logical to infer that people attending an event titled the "West of England Fat Stock and Poultry Exhibition" would probably have a lot more interest in and knowledge about steers than the general population. There would likely be a high level of diversity among attendees at the fair, including a wide range of young and old people, each possessing different levels of knowledge and experience. The fairgoers would be comprised of butchers, cattle ranchers, cattle auctioneers, produce farmers, veterinarians, horse trainers, pig farmers, cooks, and other consumers. This example underscores the importance of domain-specific knowledge and incentives.

It should also be noted that there were 800 tickets sold, although, as Galton wrote in his article, "After weeding thirteen cards out of the collection as being defective or illegible, there remained 787 for discussion." This observation highlights a subtle although important point. If an estimate is made by an individual but is not **incorporated**, it adds nothing to the collective answer—it is as though the guess never existed. This point highlights the importance of an estimate being expressed and included in the aggregation mechanism to be properly incorporated.

---

[19] Scott E. Page, *The Difference: How the Power of Diversity Creates Better Groups, Firms, Schools, and Societies* (Princeton, NJ: Princeton University Press, 2008).

[20] Karl Pearson, *The Life, Letter and Labours of Francis Galton*, vol. 2, *Researches of Middle Life* (Cambridge: Cambridge University Press, 1924).

Using the rudimentary process model in Figure 6.16 to represent how an individual would make a guess in an ox-weighing contest shows that she would first collect data by simply observing the ox. She would process this information to determine how much she believes the ox weighs (drawing from her domain-specific knowledge, which includes facts of what different items weigh)[21] and then express her opinion by writing it on a ticket and handing it in.

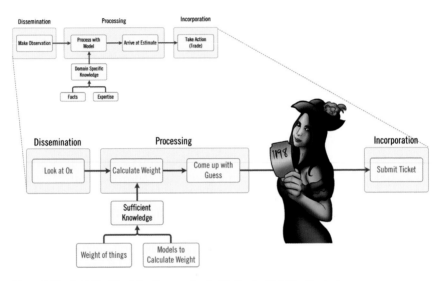

Figure 6.16   Individual Decision Process Applied to the Ox-Weighing Contest

As we mention previously, for the wisdom of crowds to arrive at an accurate answer, the individuals in the crowd must be **diverse** in their approaches and **independent** from each other in their analysis and conclusions. To dive deeper into the importance of diversity and independence, we introduce the potentially intimidating **diversity prediction theorem**, presented in Figure 6.17. The theorem, first introduced by Scott Page in 2007, offers important insight into how crowds produce accurate predictions, such as in the ox-weighing contest.

---

[21] These models don't have to be incredibly complex. For example, someone who knows a lot about steers' weight might say to himself, "The steer looks to be about six feet tall and about five years old so that would mean the weight will be approximately 1,200 pounds." Or, someone who doesn't know a lot about steers might say to himself, "The steer appears to be six feet tall. A man who is six feet tall weighs about 200 pounds and the steer looks about as big as six men, so six men * 200 pounds = 1,200 pounds for the steer."

$$\begin{matrix} \text{Crowd} \\ \text{Error} \end{matrix} = \begin{matrix} \text{Average} \\ \text{Individual Error} \end{matrix} - \text{Diversity}$$

$$(c - \theta)^2 = \frac{1}{n}\sum_{i=1}^{n}(s_i - \theta)^2 - \frac{1}{n}\sum_{i=1}^{n}(s_i - c)^2$$

Figure 6.17   Scott Page's Diversity Prediction Theorem

Where:

c = crowd's prediction

θ = the actual value

s_i = each individual's prediction

The theorem holds that **crowd error** (the accuracy of the crowd's prediction) is a function of **average individual error** (the accuracy of the average individual) and **diversity** (the diversity of the crowd's predictions). Another way to think about this concept is that individual error is offset by diversity, resulting in a low crowd error.

The formula is not nearly as scary as it first appears.[22] The first term, to the left of the equal sign, represents the **crowd's error** and measures the difference between the crowd's prediction and the actual value. In the ox-weighing contest, for example, the crowd's prediction was 1,197 pounds and the actual weight was 1,198 pounds, producing a **crowd error** of only 1 pound.

The second term, just to the right of the equal sign, represents the **average individual error** and measures how far each individual guess is from the true value. In the ox-weighing contest, each person was, on average, approximately 74 pounds away from the true value of 1,198 pounds. This term captures the crowd's **independence**.

The third term represents **diversity** and measures how far each individual's prediction was, on average, from the crowd's prediction. This term captures the differences in **domain-specific knowledge** of individuals within the crowd. Again, these differences include different levels of facts and expertise.

---

[22] Page explains the equation clearly in a video posted online. Google "Scott Page diversity prediction theorem" to find it.

The formula shows that *diversity offsets the average individual error, which reduces the crowd error.* For instance, diversity reduced the average individual error significantly in Galton's experiment, resulting in a crowd's error of only 1 pound, as shown in the following analysis:

$$(c-\theta)^2 = \frac{1}{n}\sum_{i=1}^{n}(s_i-\theta)^2 - \frac{1}{n}\sum_{i=1}^{n}(s_i-c)^2$$

Crowd Error = Average Individual Error − Diversity

$$1\,\text{lb} = \left(74\,\text{lbs} - 73\,\text{lbs}\right)$$

$$1\,\text{lb} = 1\,\text{lb}$$

As the calculation shows, the **crowd's error** was surprisingly low, at just 1 pound, despite a relatively high average individual error of approximately 74 pounds, because the group's individual guesses were **diverse**. We present these results graphically in Figure 6.18, which shows each individual's error, the **average individual error**,

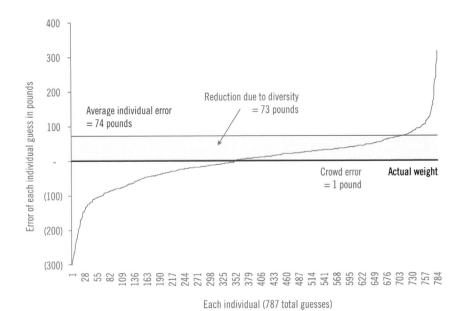

Figure 6.18   Ox-Weighing Contest: Diversity Reduces Error

and the **crowd error**. The gray area in the chart represents the reduction in the average individual error resulting from the crowd's **diversity**.

Challenges like guessing the weight of an ox are difficult for individuals to estimate and, as a result, have a high level of **average individual error**. The crowd's composition plays a critical role in determining the accuracy of the collective estimate in these situations because without **diversity**, the crowd's prediction will reflect the high **average individual error**. In other words, without **diversity**, all individual guesses will be similar and, most likely, wrong. At the risk of being repetitive, the crowd error in the ox-weighing contest would have equaled the individual error of 74 pounds without diversity. However, because the crowd was **diverse**, the large individual errors were offset by their wide range (above and below the actual answer), resulting in a low crowd error.

If, on the other hand, a problem is easy to estimate accurately, then the individual guesses will be close to the actual answer and the **average individual error** will be low. The crowd's **diversity** also will be low, but not a factor in these situations because all the individual guesses will be similar *and* accurate, resulting in a low crowd error.

To demonstrate this point further, let's say that it was easy to estimate the ox's weight and assume that the individual guesses were off from the actual weight by no more than ±1%. The crowd error would be zero, in this case, as it would equal the ox's actual weight of 1,198 pounds. The **average individual error** would be small at just 7 pounds (in contrast to approximately 74 pounds in the actual contest). Diversity reduced the average individual error in the easy-to-estimate scenario by only a small aggregate amount.[23]

$$\text{Crowd Error} = \text{Average Individual Error} - \text{Diversity}$$

$$0 \text{ lbs} = (7 \text{ lbs} - 7 \text{ lbs})$$

$$0 \text{ lbs} = 0 \text{ lbs}$$

We show graphically in Figure 6.19 that there is not much of a difference between the crowd's error and the average individual

---

[23] This statement is somewhat misleading. While it is true that diversity only reduced the average individual error by seven pounds, it also reduced it by 100%.

error in this example when we plot the results using the same scale as we used in Figure 6.18.

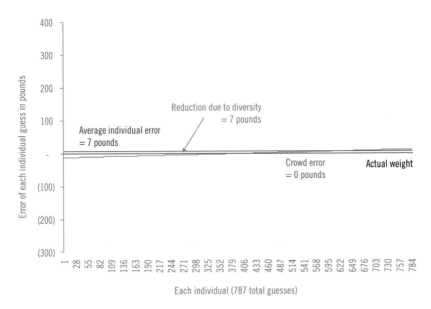

Figure 6.19   Ox-Weighing Contest: Smaller Benefit of Diversity When Estimating is Easy

What happens if we introduce a **bias** and put strain on the second condition, **independence**? Let's pretend that there had been a well-known steer-weighing expert (a "steer seer") at the West of England Fat Stock and Poultry Exhibition who announced to the crowd, "I think that steer weighs 1,400 pounds, so that will be my guess." Although the steer seer's estimate is incorrect, his proclamation would introduce a bias if it influences at least some of the individual guesses, thereby reducing the crowd's independence and increasing its error, as we show in the following example.

Let's assume in this scenario that individuals listen to the steer seer and believe that he may have a more accurate guess than their own. Instead of completely ignoring their original estimate, each individual decides to average their guess with the seer's prediction,[24]

---

[24] For example, if someone originally guessed 1,031 pounds, they will average this estimate with the steer seer's 1,400 pound guess to derive a new guess of 1,216 pounds.

as sort of a hedge. As a result, the crowd's prediction increases to 1,298 pounds. The crowd's error now overestimates the ox's actual weight by approximately 100 pounds, which makes sense since the seer's stated estimate was roughly 200 pounds higher than the correct answer, and the average individual error increases from 74 pounds to 106 pounds.

$$\text{Crowd Error} = \text{Average Individual Error} - \text{Diversity}$$
$$100 \text{ lbs} = (106 \text{ lbs} - 6 \text{ lbs})$$
$$100 \text{ lbs} = 100 \text{ lbs}$$

Diversity narrowed the difference between the average individual error and the crowd error significantly in the original contest. Contrast this result to Figure 6.20, which shows that diversity cannot compensate for the increased individual errors caused by the steer seer's prognostication, which introduced a bias and reduced the crowd's independence.

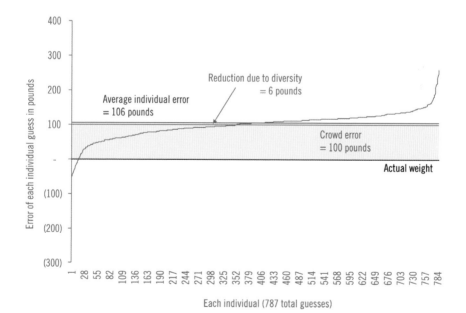

Figure 6.20   Ox-Weighing Contest: Steer Seer Introduces Bias and Misleads the Crowd

The Crowd Arrives at an Accurate Answer Even When Individuals Have Limited Factual Knowledge

The second condition of the three market efficiency tenets states that there must be a sufficient number of individuals in the group who have the requisite level domain-specific knowledge, either in the form of facts or expertise. It probably seems counterintuitive, but it is possible for the crowd to arrive at an accurate answer even if most of the crowd has *no factual* knowledge about the situation. What *is* required is that *some* individuals within the crowd have *some* factual knowledge, even if it is only partial knowledge. As we demonstrate in the pen example, when individuals with only partial information are aggregated together, they can produce accurate answers. Not one person had all the information in that example, yet the crowd produced a highly accurate aggregate answer.

We show in the next example that the crowd can have a majority of clueless individuals, a few individuals with some factual knowledge, no individuals with all the factual knowledge, and still produce an accurate answer. The example also demonstrates that as individuals with more information are added to the crowd, the aggregate answer gets even more accurate.

We borrow an example from Scott Page's book to illustrate this facet of the wisdom of crowds, although we modify the story a bit. Page uses the Monkees, an American rock band from the late 1960s, to illustrate this point in his book, while we use the Beatles. In this example, we ask 800 people, "Who on the following list was <u>not</u> a member of the Beatles?"[25]

A. Ringo Starr
B. Paul McCartney
C. Clarence Walker
D. George Harrison
E. John Lennon

---

[25] Spoiler alert: The non-Beatle is Clarence Walker, although he vigorously claims that he is, in fact, the fifth Beatle and has said so publicly: "I was ripped off by the whole group and the whole group got a behind-kicking coming to them when I see them. I've been looking for them boys since 1963 and that's why they got that around the clock security and them gates around their house 'cause they know that when Clarence Walker find them he is going to take a chunk out of their behinds." You can Google "Clarence fifth Beatle" to see the full interview.

For anyone raised on the Beatles' music,[26] this is an easy, and perhaps trivial, question. In this example, the participants in the survey have different levels of knowledge about the Beatles. A few of them know a lot about the band and can answer the question easily and quickly, some recognize a band member or two but do not know the correct answer, and 75% of the participants have never heard of the band and will basically have to guess the impostor blindly (which we assume they do randomly). Intuitively, it probably seems unlikely that we would get much wisdom from a crowd where most of the people have little or no idea who the Beatles are.

The participants' knowledge of the Beatles breaks down as follows:

- 2.5%, or 20 people, know all four Beatles
- 5.0%, or 40 people, know three of the four Beatles
- 7.5%, or 60 people, know two of the four Beatles
- 10%, or 80 people, know one Beatle
- 75%, or 600 people, have no idea who was in the band

We use this example to show how the correct answer emerges from the crowd and at the same time show how little knowledge is required for the crowd to get the right answer.

Let us assume for the moment that of the first 600 people we surveyed, *not one* of them had heard of the Beatles. Like the first graders

---

[26] Or on the TV show *Saturday Night Live.*

having no clue about the weight of a 747, the participants in the survey cannot determine the correct answer because they simply do not know it. Let us further assume that their pick of the non-Beatle from the five possible choices is *random*. In this case, each of the five possible band members on the list would get the same number of guesses (120) and no consensus would emerge from the first 600 participants, as shown in Figure 6.21.

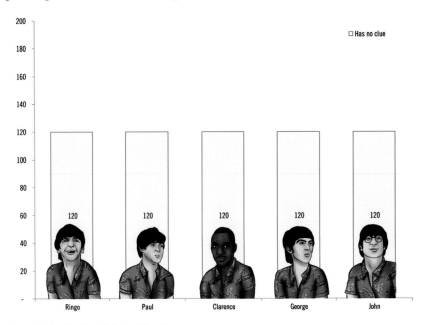

Figure 6.21   Beatles: Tally for First Group

We must emphasize that randomness is critical for the process to work properly. We show with the example of the neon nose and the steer seer that independence is critically important, and any bias will result in an incorrect answer. We assume that since individuals in this group have never heard of the Beatles they will simply pick *randomly*, as if they each rolled a five-sided die.[27] For instance,

---

[27] Surprisingly, a five-sided die does exist. It was invented by Lou Zocchi and granted a U.S. patent (number 6926275) in 2005. Unfortunately, tests have shown that it is not actually a fair die.

the rule could be that if one comes up on the die, they pick Ringo, if two comes up they pick Paul, and so on. The probability of any individual number on the die coming up is 20%; therefore, if the crowd picks randomly, then each band member on the list will receive 120 votes.

FOOLED BY RANDOMNESS, OR WHEN WHAT APPEARS TO BE RANDOM ISN'T REALLY RANDOM

Let's say we poll the same 600 people and get the results presented in Figure 6.22. Are the results random? Actually, they are.

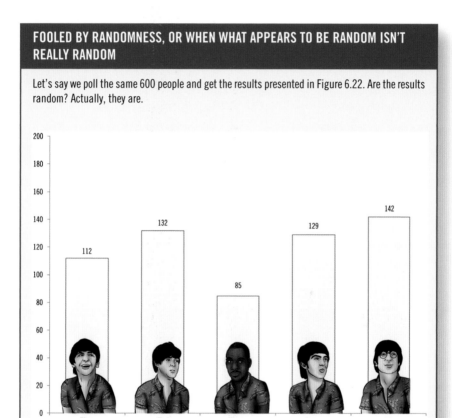

Figure 6.22   Beatles: Random Guesses in the Wild

Although the probability of getting exactly 120 guesses for each band member in any single trial is infinitesimally small, this outcome remains the expected result, as the following discussion shows. We used a random number generator in Excel to perform *10,000* polls of 600 people each. Figure 6.23 shows the results from poll 182 (of 10,000) in which Clarence

(Continued)

(Continued)

randomly received only 85 votes, while John received 142. We show the average votes for 10, 50, 200, and 10,000 trials, along with the minimum and maximum votes from all 10,000 polls, in Table 6.2.

Table 6.2   Beatles: Random Guesses Approach the Average with High Repetition

Number of polls	Ringo	Paul	Clarence	George	John
Average of 10	117	121	120	118	124
Average of 50	121	119	120	119	120
Average of 200	121	120	119	120	120
Average of 10,000	120	120	120	120	120
Minimum votes in any single poll	86	83	85	79	85
Maximum votes in any single poll	166	157	170	155	160

The analysis shows that as the results approach the average random answer of 120 votes for each possible band member as the number of polls increases. However, Clarence getting 85 votes and George getting 142 votes in poll number 182 is still a *random* occurrence. Although these results might seem biased if they occur, it is purely random and you would be fooled if you think otherwise.

Let's assume that the next 80 people we ask coincidentally each know just one of the four Beatles. Because they know one of the band members, they can eliminate that person from the list, leaving four names from which to choose. For example, let's say that the first person we ask knows that Ringo is a Beatle but does not know who the non-Beatle is among the  remaining four names. Let's assume he acts *independently* and picks *randomly* from the remaining four choices (like rolling a four-sided die[28]), and identifies George incorrectly as the non-Beatle, as shown in Figure 6.23.

---

[28] Four-sided dice actually exist and are shown to be fair.

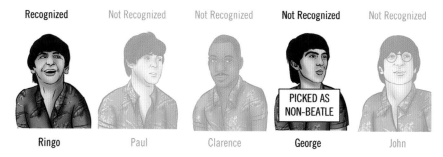

Figure 6.23   Beatles: Random and Wrong

The second person might know Paul is in the band, but none of the other three Beatles, so he picks randomly from the remaining four choices. In this case, let's assume that he correctly chooses Clarence as the non-Beatle, as shown in Figure 6.24.

Figure 6.24   Beatles: Random and Right

Assuming the group is independent, this process would continue for the remaining 78 people in the group who each know one of the actual Beatles. At the end of that round, the 80 people will have identified Clarence most often as the non-Beatle, although by only a slim margin. He will receive 140 of the guesses, or 20.6% of the total, versus the other four names each getting 135 of the guesses, or 19.9% of the total, as shown in Figure 6.25.

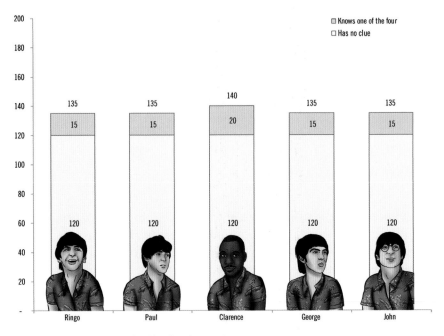

Figure 6.25   Beatles: Tally for First Two Groups

Let's now assume that the next 60 people we ask each know two of the four Beatles, which means that they can eliminate the two band members they know, leaving three names to choose from. Let's say that the first person we ask knows Ringo and Paul are both in the band, but does not know who the impostor is among the remaining three names. He acts independently and picks randomly from the remaining three choices (like rolling a three-sided die[29]), and identifies John incorrectly as the non-Beatle, as shown in Figure 6.26.

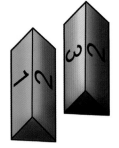

---

[29] Yes, they do exist.

Figure 6.26   Beatles: Random and Wrong

The second person from this group knows Paul and George are both in the band, but he cannot name the non-band member from the remaining three possible choices. He also acts independently and picks randomly from the remaining three names, and incorrectly chooses Ringo as the non-Beatle, as shown in Figure 6.27.

Figure 6.27   Beatles: Random and Wrong

This process would continue for the remaining 58 people in the group. Assuming each participant is also independent, this group will identify Clarence as the non-Beatle by a slightly higher margin than the prior group, receiving 160 of the guesses, or 21.6% of the total, versus the other four possible band members, who each receive 145 guesses, or 19.6% of the total, as shown in Figure 6.28.

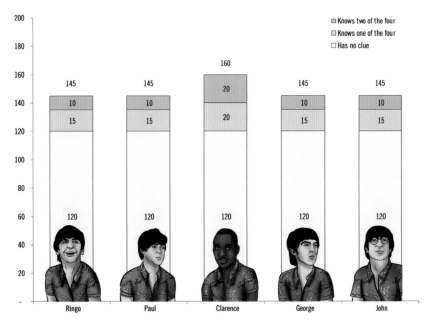

Figure 6.28   Beatles: Tally for First Three Groups

 Let us assume that the next 40 people we ask each know three of the four Beatles, which allows them to eliminate three of the five choices and leaves them with two names to choose from. The first person we ask knows Ringo, George, and Paul are in the band but does not know who the impostor is of the remaining two names. Assuming that person acts independently and picks randomly from the remaining two choices (by flipping a fair coin), he might identify John incorrectly as the non-Beatle, as shown in Figure 6.29.

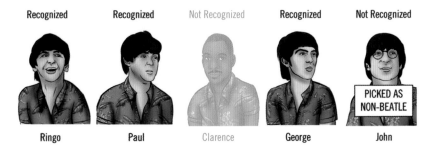

Figure 6.29   Beatles: Random and Wrong

The second person from this group might also know that Ringo, George, and Paul are in the group but does not know who the impostor is of the remaining two possible band members. Assuming this person acts independently and picks randomly from the remaining two choices, he might correctly identify Clarence as the non-Beatle, as shown in Figure 6.30.

Figure 6.30   Beatles: Random and Right

Assuming this group is independent, the process would continue for the remaining 38 people. At the end of the round, this group will have identified Clarence as the non-Beatle by an even higher margin than the prior groups, getting 180 of the guesses, or 23.1% of the total, versus the other four possible band members, who each get 150 guesses, or 19.2% of the total, as shown in Figure 6.31.

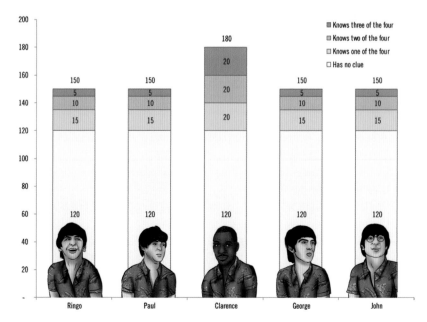

Figure 6.31   Beatles: Tally for First Four Groups

Assuming that the remaining 20 people we ask each know all four Beatles, they will all correctly identify Clarence as the non-Beatle, adding 20 guesses to his total. At the end of this round, Clarence will be identified correctly by the entire group of participants as the non-Beatle, receiving a total of 200, or 25%, of the 800 guesses versus the other four potential band members each getting 150 guesses, or 18.8% of the total, as shown in Figure 6.32.

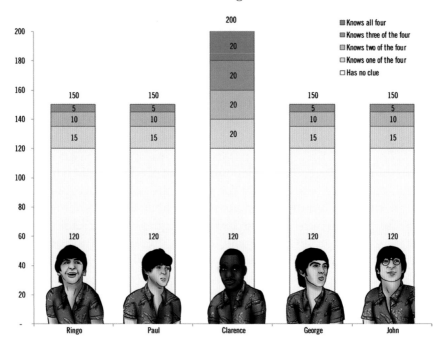

Figure 6.32   Beatles: Tally for All Five Groups

To recap, when asked, the crowd of 800 people voted as follows:

- The 20 highly knowledgeable people who know all the Beatles selected Clarence as the non-Beatle.
- Of the 40 people who know three of the four Beatles, 20 (50%) selected Clarence as the non-Beatle.
- Of the 60 people who know two of the four Beatles, 20 (33%) selected Clarence as the non-Beatle.
- Of the 80 people who know one Beatle, 20 (25%) selected Clarence as the non-Beatle.
- Of the 600 people who do not know any of the actual band members, 120 (20%) selected Clarence as the non-Beatle.

Figure 6.33[30] depicts graphically how the percentage of correct answers *emerges* and the errors decline as we add groups of people with increasing amounts of knowledge to the results. No clear consensus emerges when people have no clue about the correct answer, as the first example shows. Because the individuals guess randomly, each potential band member receives 20% of the guesses. However, as we demonstrate with the subsequent examples, the correct answer emerges quickly as the number of knowledgeable people and their level of knowledge increases, which the charts show clearly.

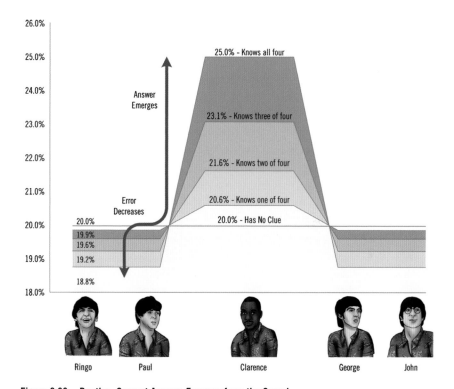

Figure 6.33   Beatles: Correct Answer *Emerges* from the Crowd

As we demonstrate, the crowd correctly identifies Clarence Walker as the non-Beatle even though most the participants (75% of the total) do not know anything about the band. This example shows

---

[30] Figure 6.33 presents the same results as Figure 6.32, but with the results converted to percentages instead of the total number of individual guesses.

that we *do not* need many participants with knowledge for the crowd to arrive at the correct answer. While it may seem incredible, in fact *no one in the crowd needs to have complete knowledge for the crowd to make the correct identification,* as shown in Figure 6.31, where not a single person knows all four Beatles, yet Clarence is still outed by a margin of 180 guesses versus the 150 guesses for each of the other band members. *However, if no one has any knowledge, there is no wisdom to be extracted from the crowd,* as shown in Figure 6.21, where no determination was made. The Beatles experiment demonstrates the fourth condition of the market efficiency tenets, that *there must be a sufficient number of individuals in the group who have the requisite level domain-specific knowledge—in the form of either facts or expertise—*for the crowd to be wise.

How the Crowd Becomes Skewed

We can modify the Beatles story to demonstrate what happens if there is a breakdown in **independence** within the crowd, similar to the example with the steer seer in Galton's ox-guessing contest. To break the independence and induce a **bias**, we show the participants the fake album cover (the lost Beatles, *Aloha from Hawaii* album) before we ask them to pick the non–band member. We then ask the original question, "Which individual from the following list was not a member of the Beatles?"

Although the 20 people who know all four Beatles (and probably know the Beatles never recorded a Hawaiian album) will be amused by the fake cover, they will not be influenced by it and will correctly identify Clarence as the non-Beatle, as they did before.

Let's say that the remaining 780 people we asked are swayed by the fake cover and believe that since Clarence is sitting in the center of the picture, that not only is he a true Beatle, but is also the most prominent member of the band.

Let's assume that when we survey the group of 600 people who have never heard of the Beatles, they all believe Clarence is a real Beatle because of the bias and eliminate him as a choice. If there is no other bias, they will then pick *randomly* from the remaining four choices, although all their picks will be wrong, as shown in Figure 6.34.

Figure 6.34   Beatles: Biased and Wrong

When we poll the group of 80 people who know one of four Beatles, they also eliminate Clarence from consideration because of the bias we introduced, along with the Beatle they know is correct, and choose randomly from the remaining three possible band members. Their pick will also be wrong if there is no other bias, as shown in Figure 6.35.

Figure 6.35   Beatles: Biased and Wrong

The same mistake happens with the 60 people in the group who know two of four and the 40 people in the group who know three of four. They all pick incorrectly.

Figure 6.36 shows that the four real Beatles will be identified as a non-Beatle by 780 people who were influenced by the fake cover, while Clarence, the real non-Beatle, will get only the 20 votes from the small group who know all four of the real band members. Although this example is overly simplistic, it demonstrates how breaking independence by introducing a bias can turn the wise crowd into a dumb one.

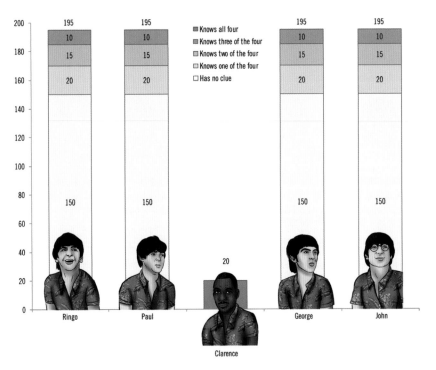

Figure 6.36   Beatles: Biased Answer Produces Wrong Crowd Guess

Similarly, normal human emotions can introduce biases that may pollute diversity and independence in the stock market and gum up the works of the wisdom of crowds. These biases can undermine the efficient market hypothesis, thus creating distortions and potentially mispriced stocks. These distortions are problematic for some but create opportunities for others. We discuss this in much greater detail in the next chapter.

The Wisdom of Crowds Applied to the Stock Market

As we discuss earlier in this chapter, the efficient market hypothesis lays out the rules the markets must follow to ensure an efficient market price, while we show that the wisdom of crowds is the governing mechanism by which those rules are implemented.

To demonstrate the power of the wisdom of crowds applied to the stock market, we present an example that shows how a crowd of individuals predicted Apple's 2015 fourth-quarter earnings more accurately than a group of experienced sell side analysts.

As we state throughout the book, the estimated intrinsic value of any asset is the sum of the cash flows expected to be produced by that asset, over its useful life, discounted for the time value of money and the uncertainty of receiving those cash flows. Since Apple's reported earnings are a reasonable proxy for the company's cash flow, we can use this number in the following example.

The Crowd Is Smarter Than the Experts Most of the Time

To illustrate how the wisdom of crowds arrives at an accurate earnings estimate, we use a unique data set provided by Estimize. com, a company founded by Leigh Drogen, that aggregates quarterly earnings estimates from individuals. The Estimize website attracts a broad spectrum of participants, including Wall Street professionals (analysts and portfolio managers), students, academics, industry professionals, and various other interested parties. Estimize uses an aggregation mechanism similar to Galton's in that they simply tally up the guesses and calculate the average of all the individual estimates.

The average earnings estimate for Apple from the 1,183 individual estimates on the Estimize website for the quarter ending September 2015 was $1.91 per share.[31] By comparison, the Wall Street consensus estimate of 42 sell-side analysts for the same period was $1.88.[32]

---

[31] The numbers in this example might not sum correctly due to rounding.

[32] One could argue that Wall Street analysts deliberately keep their forecasts low so that the company can beat their estimate. While this phenomenon is beyond the scope of the book, we wanted to at least mention a possible alternative reason why the official Wall Street estimate in this case is lower than the consensus estimate.

Apple's reported earnings for the quarter was $1.96. The Estimize prediction of $1.91 was off by only $0.05, while the average of the 42 professional sell side analysts was off by almost twice as much at $0.08 per share. The crowd was clearly more accurate than the experts in this instance. We show the range of estimates for Estimize and for the Wall Street analysts, graphed against the actual results, in Figure 6.37.

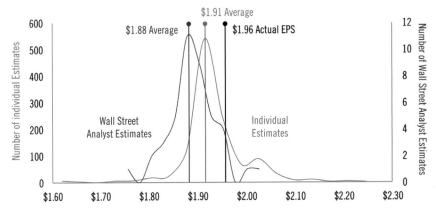

Figure 6.37   Apple: Range of Q4 Earnings Predictions

We should emphasize that this example is not a one-off result. In fact, as we discuss throughout this chapter, the wisdom of crowds process beats experts most of the time, which is supported by academic research showing that the earnings estimates produced by the Estimize collective are more accurate than Wall Street analysts 74% of the time.[33]

The Apple example also demonstrates how **diversity** produces a more accurate result. If we run the Estimize estimates for Apple through Scott Page's diversity prediction theorem, the crowd error equals $0.05, which is the difference between the crowd's prediction of $1.91 and the actual earnings of $1.96. The crowd's average

---

[33] "Frequently Asked Questions." Estimize Inc. Accessed April 04, 2016. Estimize web site.

individual error (which measures how far the average individual is off from the actual earnings) is $0.09, implying that **diversity** (how far away the average individual was from the crowd) improved the crowd estimate by $0.04.

$$Crowd\ Error = Average\ Individual\ Error - Diversity$$

$$Crowd\ Error = \$0.09 - \$0.04$$

$$Crowd\ Error = \$0.05$$

We show these results in Figure 6.38, where we graph each individual's error, the **average individual error**, and the **crowd error**. The gray area represents the reduction in error derived from the crowd's **diversity**.

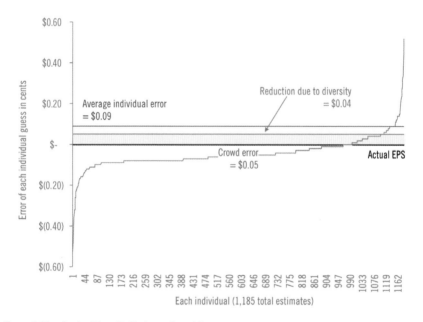

Figure 6.38   Apple: Diversity Reduces Crowd Error

To demonstrate diversity within the crowd, we present details on the estimates submitted on Estimize.com, sorted by the types of individuals making the estimates, in Table 6.3. The individual categories include academics, financial professionals, students, and nonprofessionals, with the remaining participants placed in a category labeled "unknown." Estimize also collected data for the 42 sell-side analysts who published earnings estimates for that quarter. The results (which are sorted by *declining crowd error*) are surprising.

Table 6.3   Apple: Earnings Estimates by Subgroup

	Number of Participants	Crowd Error	Average Individual Error	Diversity	Percent Reduction from Diversity
Sell Side	42	$0.080	$0.094	$0.014	15%
Unknown	77	$0.059	$0.078	$0.019	24%
Student	91	$0.050	$0.083	$0.033	40%
Financial Pro	170	$0.047	$0.104	$0.057	55%
Total Estimize	1,185	$0.045	$0.086	$0.041	48%
Non Pro	813	$0.043	$0.084	$0.041	49%
Academia	34	$0.040	$0.064	$0.041	37%

What is most striking to us is that the Wall Street sell-side analysts produced the highest crowd error at $0.080 ($1.96 actual earnings versus $1.88 average estimate). Their average individual error was $0.094, which means that diversity counteracted the average individual error by only $0.014, or 15%, implying that the group was not particularly diverse. The fact that 42 Wall Street analysts are not that diverse should not be surprising. Analysts have little incentive to be far away from *their* consensus[34] and, because they have much greater access to company management than individual investors, their estimates are probably skewed by management's guidance, which is a form of bias similar to what we discuss in the ox-weighing contest. Also, remember that they are *sell side* analysts, so they are selling

---

[34] This result highlights the fact that Wall Street analysts are often *not independent.* They look at the average Wall Street estimate and, if their estimate is too far off from the Wall Street consensus, they will adjust their estimate to be more "in-line" with other analysts, similar to the steer seer example discussed earlier in the chapter.

more than researching. Finally, because they all receive the same story from the company's management and do not have a lot of time to do additional research, it should not shock anyone that the individual analysts produce estimates similar to each other and, almost by definition, the group is not all that diverse.

The subgroup labeled "financial professionals" is probably the most interesting. This subgroup, which includes professional analysts and portfolio managers, had the highest average individual error at $0.104, which is what we would expect from a complex problem that is difficult to estimate accurately. However, their crowd error was only $0.047, meaning that diversity offset the individual error by $0.057, or 55%, which was the greatest benefit from diversity realized by any of the subgroups. This result might seem counterintuitive at first glance. We would not expect this group to be diverse since we would assume that they would all talk to each other, read the same periodicals, and research reports, and, in turn, produce similar estimates.

It is important to remember that these are professional investors who have taken the time to enter their estimates on Estimize. com, and therefore, are most likely calculating earnings estimates on their own. If they were simply relying on Wall Street research as the primary source for their estimates, they likely would not bother entering them on the website. These analysts are probably independent, competitive, and have incentives to be right. Some of them are likely submitting their estimates for the psychic income of being right; therefore, they will work harder, do more research, and think independently. When we think about this group in that light, their results are not all that surprising.

The Apple example not only shows that the crowd beat the experts, but also shows that when a group is homogeneous and lacks independence, such as the Wall Street analysts, it produces estimates with high individual errors and, because of the group's lack of diversity, also produces a high crowd error. In contrast, a diverse and independent group, such as the financial professionals, has high *individual* errors, but its crowd error will be low because of the group's diversity.

What happens to the consensus results if we introduce a bias and put a strain on the crowd's **independence**?

How the Crowd Can be Fooled

Apple released its fourth-quarter earnings, for the period ending September 30, 2015, on October 27, 2015. Samsung, one of Apple's most fierce competitors, announced earnings guidance for its fiscal third quarter, ending September 30, 2015, on October 7, 2015.

We are now going to create a fake story. Let's assume that Samsung indicated in its release that its revenue for the quarter was going to be materially lower than expected because of slowing smartphone sales and that management expected earnings per share for the September quarter to be 10% less than current consensus estimate.

It is safe to assume that investors in Apple stock monitor news on Samsung to glean insights into the smartphone market (Samsung was the largest producer of smartphones at the time). Let's say that the individuals on Estimize are influenced by the Samsung news, although they reduce their earnings estimate by only 5%, rather than Samsung's 10% shortfall. The crowd's estimate on Estimize would fall from $1.91 to $1.82 as a result. The Samsung news in this example is like the bias we introduced with the steer seer in the 1906 West of England ox-guessing contest.

The average individual error would increase from $0.09 to $0.16, because of the bias, and the crowd would underestimate Apple's quarterly earnings by $0.14 rather than by $0.05 in the original example. Diversity narrowed the difference between the average individual error and the crowd error significantly in the prior Apple example. Contrast this outcome with the biased results, where diversity reduces the individual error by only $0.02, as shown in the following equation:

$$\text{Crowd Error} = \text{Average Individual Error} - \text{Diversity}$$

$$\text{Crowd Error} = \$0.16 - \$0.02$$

$$\text{Crowd Error} = \$0.14$$

Figure 6.39 shows that diversity cannot compensate for the increased individual errors caused when a strong bias is introduced.

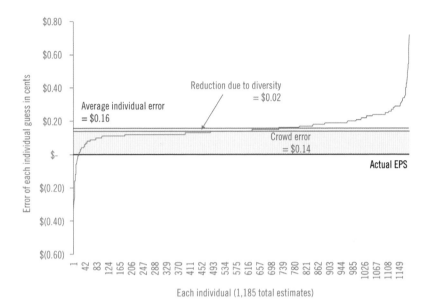

Figure 6.39   Apple: Biased Estimates Affect Diversity

Gems

- ♦ When the wisdom of crowds process is functioning properly:
  - ◊ Information will be adequately **disseminated**. Market participants will observe, extract, and aggregate information
  - ◊ Information will be **processed**. Market participants will evaluate and estimate without bias
  - ◊ Information will be **expressed** and **incorporated** into the stock price through trading
- ♦ An investor seeks to create an informational advantage by combining public and quasi-public information with nonmaterial, nonpublic information. The investor then applies his analytical process to all information he possesses to arrive at a *conclusion* that is material and nonpublic, which, in most cases, is *legal*.
- ♦ To produce an efficient stock price, information must be **available** and **observed**; the information must be **processed** by a diverse set of models backed by **sufficient knowledge** to

produce estimates that are **independent** (without bias); and the estimates need to be **expressed** with no limits on trading. A stock price may become mispriced (only) if there is a failure in any of these areas.

▽ The crowd's **diversity** will be lost if everyone has the same facts and expertise or starts thinking the same way by using the same mental model. And, without diversity, individuals within the crowd produce answers similar to each other, the crowd's guess will be only a small deviation from the individual estimates, and the crowd's consensus will reflect nothing more than a single view. Consequentially, the crowd's answer will lack any of the benefits of diversity and will likely result in an inefficiently priced stock.

▽ If the crowd is influenced systematically, it will produce an inefficiently priced stock. In the extreme, the collapsing of **independence** can cause a mania, where everyone believes an overly optimistic view of the situation, or a panic, where the crowd believes a doomsday scenario is likely to unfold. Both examples demonstrate how the lack of independence can feed on itself to produce a significant mispricing.

▽ If an investor arrives at an estimate, but that estimate is not expressed, the situation will be equivalent to a vote that is not cast. It should be noted that if enough estimates are not **expressed**, the private information and domain-specific knowledge contained in an individual's estimate will not be aggregated with the consensus, which is like the proverbial tree that falls in the woods. If no one is around to hear it, the tree's falling sound will not be noticed.

▽ The wisdom of crowds aggregation process generates a "correct" answer by transferring (partial) domain-specific knowledge from individuals to the collective.

▽ It probably seems counterintuitive, but it is possible for the crowd to arrive at an accurate answer even if most the crowd has **no** *factual* knowledge about the situation. What *is* required is that *some* individuals within the crowd have *some* factual knowledge, even if it is only partial knowledge.

CHAPTER 7

How to Think About Behavioral Finance

While Benjamin Graham is considered the "father of value investing," he had a deep appreciation for the impact human emotions can have on stock prices. For instance, in the first edition of *Security Analysis,* published in 1934, Graham states, "Investment theory should recognize that the merits of an issue reflect themselves in the market price not by any automatic response or mathematical relationship but through the minds and decisions of buyers and sellers." He also understood the importance of feedback loops, stating "the investors' mental attitude not only affects the market price but is strongly affected by it."[1]

The Moody Mr. Market

In *The Intelligent Investor,* first published in 1949, Graham introduces his readers to Mr. Market, an affable fellow who is your equal partner in a private business. According to Graham, "Every day he [Mr. Market] tells you what he thinks your interest is worth and furthermore offers either to buy you out or to sell you an additional interest on that basis. Sometimes his idea of value appears plausible and justified by business developments and prospects as you know them. Often, on the other hand, Mr. Market lets his enthusiasm or his fears run away with him, and the value he proposes seems to you a little short of silly."[2]

---

[1] Benjamin Graham and David L. Dodd, *Security Analysis* (New York: Whittlesey House, McGraw-Hill Book Company, 1934).

[2] Benjamin Graham, *The Intelligent Investor: A Book of Practical Counsel* (New York: HarperBusiness 1973).

Graham used Mr. Market to explain the effect he saw that the human emotions of fear and greed can have on stock prices. When the market is functioning normally, Mr. Market's "idea of value appears plausible and justified by business developments and prospects as you know them." In turn, the price Mr. Market offers to buy or sell will be close to the company's **intrinsic value**. However, there are times where Mr. Market becomes greedy and euphoric, seeing only blue skies ahead, and offers to buy or sell at a price greater than the company's intrinsic value. At other times, Mr. Market will be fearful, anxious, and depressed, seeing only a dismal future, and offers to buy or sell at a price less than the company's intrinsic value. We illustrate Mr. Market's various moods in Figure 7.1.

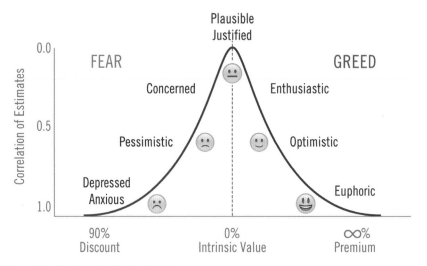

Figure 7.1   Mr. Market's Various Moods

Returning to the definition of the value of an asset:

> The estimated value of any asset is the sum of the cash flows expected to be produced by that asset, over its useful life, discounted for the time value of money and the uncertainty of receiving those cash flows.

We need to emphasize the word *expected* in the definition. *Investors make their decisions based on their **expectations** about the future.* Using this definition, we can say that under most conditions, Mr. Market's *expectations* for the company's future cash flows will be "plausible and justified by business developments and prospects." However, there will be times when Mr. Market's fear or greed unduly influences his *expectations* of future events and alters the value he places on the company. The overreaction drives the market price away from the company's intrinsic value producing a mispricing.

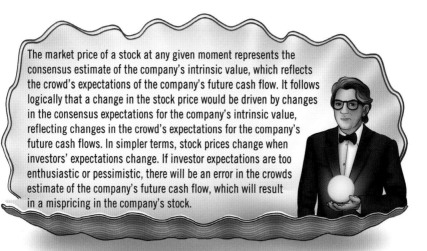

The market price of a stock at any given moment represents the consensus estimate of the company's intrinsic value, which reflects the crowd's expectations of the company's future cash flow. It follows logically that a change in the stock price would be driven by changes in the consensus expectations for the company's intrinsic value, reflecting changes in the crowd's expectations for the company's future cash flows. In simpler terms, stock prices change when investors' expectations change. If investor expectations are too enthusiastic or pessimistic, there will be an error in the crowds estimate of the company's future cash flow, which will result in a mispricing in the company's stock.

Mr. Market's misperception can affect his expectations for one or more of the four components of cash flow (duration, magnitude, timing and growth), the level of **uncertainty** he sees in the business, or a change in the time value of money, as we discuss in Chapter 1, and show in Figure 7.2.

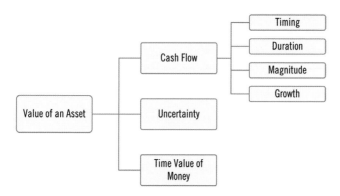

Figure 7.2   Value of an Asset—Primary Components

We can use the valuation of Zoe's Lemonade Stand from Chapter 4 to illustrate this point. As we show in that analysis, we arrive at different per share values when we assume different growth rates for the business, as illustrated in Table 7.1.

Table 7.1   Present Value of Zoe's Lemonade Stand Under Different Growth Assumptions

Growth Rate	Present Value of Free Cash Flows	Value Per Share
0%	$1,412	$9.41
10%	$1,796	$11.97
15%	$2,044	$13.63
20%	$2,336	$15.57

Let's say that the consensus expects Zoe's revenues to grow at 15% per year, and assume that the stock is efficiently priced, thereby trading at $13.63 per share. Unexpectedly, Paris's Lemonade Stand, which operates in the adjacent town, announces that it plans on entering the local market currently served only by Zoe. After the information is **disseminated** and **processed**, the consensus believes Paris will be successful in capturing market share and, in response, reduces its estimate for Zoe's growth to 10% per year. Zoe's stock falls from $13.63 to $11.97 as the market adjusts to fully reflect and **incorporate** the new information.

However, let's say that Mr. Market is in a particularly gloomy mood on the day Paris announces her expansion plans and fears that the increased competition will have a significant impact on Zoe's business, reducing the expected growth rate for Zoe's Lemonade Stand to zero. Because of this pessimism, instead of repricing the stock to reflect a more realistic 10% growth scenario, the market overreacts and reprices the shares to $9.41.

When the Wisdom of Crowds Becomes the Madness of Crowds

As we discuss in the previous chapter, if the market **processes** information absent any **systematic error**, then the stock will be efficiently priced. On the other hand, if we can identify a **systematic bias** in the market, then there is a reasonable likelihood that the consensus has overreacted and produced a pricing error. However, any apparent error in the market price must be linked to either the **dissemination**,

processing, or **incorporation** of information **because a systematic bias that results in an error can only occur if there is a failure in at least one of the following conditions of the wisdom of crowds**:

1. Information is either not **available** or not being **observed** by a sufficient number of investors.
2. There is an insufficient amount of **domain-specific knowledge** within the collective.
3. The crowd lacks **diversity**.
4. There is a breakdown in the crowd's **independence**.
5. Estimates are not being **expressed, aggregated** and **incorporated** into the market price.
6. There is a lack of appropriate **incentives**.

It is important to state up front that behavioral finance can cause mispricings in only three of the six factors just listed: **diversity**, **independence**, and **incorporation**. As we demonstrate with the pen contest, Galton's ox, Beatles, and Apple examples in the prior chapter, the crowd will arrive at an accurate estimate even if information is **available** and **observed** by only a small portion of individuals in the crowd. Interestingly, there are few situations in the stock market where the lack of **domain-specific knowledge** or insufficient **incentives** causes significant mispricings.

Therefore, if Mr. Market has allowed his emotions to get the better of him, the **systematic bias** produces an error if it either reduces the crowd's **diversity**, results in a breakdown in the crowd's **independence**, or produces a limitation in the crowd's ability to **incorporate** its view into the stock price.

While Good for Hunting and Gathering, Evolution Has Left Us Ill-Prepared to Survive on Wall Street

To demonstrate how behavioral finance ultimately impacts Mr. Market, we need to return to the dawn of man. Anthropological data show that anatomically modern *Homo sapiens* originated about 200,000 years ago. However, behaviorally, we reached modernity only about 50,000 years ago. With new agricultural techniques and domesticated animals, our hunter-gatherer ancestors started to settle into what we call civilizations only 10,000 years ago. We have made great strides in developing new communications-related technologies in the last 150 years—electricity, telephones, radios, television, computers, cell phones, and the Internet—all of which have accelerated the amount of information that is available to us and that we must process. To put this technological progress in perspective, our species may be 200,000 years old, but we have lived in an information-rich society, in its modern form, for only 150 of those years. One could argue that the current volume and velocity of information available in the financial markets, and relevant to investment decisions, started only 40 years ago. Simply put, our minds have not had enough time to evolve to a point that we can effectively process the volume of information that we experience daily in order to invest successfully.

Evolutionary biology teaches us that humans have evolved to conserve energy and avoid exertion. Professor Daniel Liberman, an evolutionary biologist at Harvard University, believes that because food was in such short supply for our hunter-gatherer ancestors, only those who conserved physical energy in hard times and expended only the energy necessary to survive had the opportunity to reproduce and flourish. In other words, we are genetically programmed to be lazy. As with our bodies, we are also conditioned to be lazy with our minds, striving to minimize our mental effort, which is also known by its more academic title—**cognitive load**. Here, too, we have evolved to rely on mental shortcuts whenever possible.

Evolutionary psychology teaches us that humans developed conditioned reflexes, which were driven by our need for self-preservation. For example, when our ancestors on the savanna heard a rustling in the bushes, they feared for their lives and ran away, driven by fright, confusion, and stress. Those who weren't afraid and didn't respond quickly enough were eaten.

To survive, humans evolved different **heuristics**—mental "hacks" or shortcuts—to help us navigate our ancestral environment, while conserving as much energy as possible. Unfortunately, the heuristics that allowed humans to survive and flourish thousands of years ago are potentially harmful to our health in modern society and specifically our "financial health" in the stock market.

Human feelings fall into two broad categories. When our needs are satisfied, we have positive feelings—we are happy, excited, peaceful, confident, hopeful, and engaged. On the other hand, when our needs are not being met, we have negative feelings—we are angry, afraid, confused, fatigued, stressed, embarrassed, jealous, sad, and vulnerable.

Behavioral Finance Explains the Errors of Our Hunter-Gatherer Brains

These positive and negative feelings often drive individual behavior and can result in any number of **cognitive biases**, which are defined as mistakes in reasoning, evaluating, remembering, or some other cognitive process. In investing, these biases often express themselves as fear and greed, which can lead individuals to make suboptimal investment decisions.

HEURISTICS AND COGNITIVE BIAS—THE FOUNDATIONS OF BEHAVIORAL FINANCE

Daniel Kahneman and Amos Tversky began working together in 1969 when they were both young psychology professors at the Hebrew University of Jerusalem. While they produced a large body of work over the 14 years that they collaborated, two of their papers, "Judgment Under Uncertainty: Heuristics and Biases,"[3] published in the September 1974, and "Prospect Theory: An Analysis of Decision under Risk,"[4] published in March 1979, by most accounts sparked the behavioral economics revolution.

"Judgment Under Uncertainty" showed that even sophisticated, intelligent individuals were susceptible to erroneous intuitions. Those insights challenged two key assumptions of classical economics concerning the way individuals make decisions, often referred to as the rational-agent model: The first assumption is that individuals are generally rational and their thinking is normally sound; the second assumption is that emotions such as fear, affection, and hatred explain most of the occasions when individuals depart from rationality.

"Judgment Under Uncertainty" contradicted both assumptions. The experiments presented in the article demonstrated that most individuals rely on rules of thumb (heuristics) and unsubstantiated beliefs (biases) when making decisions under uncertainty. The authors described three heuristics that they observed participants in their experiments use when making decisions:

Representativeness is the tendency to judge the probability of an event by how closely it matches other events that the individual can easily recall, while ignoring information such as base rates, sample size, or randomness.

Availability is the tendency to estimate the likelihood of an event by how easy it is to remember similar events occurring in the past.

Anchoring is the tendency to rely too heavily on a single piece of information or salient fact, while ignoring all other, relevant, and potentially critical information.

---

[3] Daniel Kahneman and Amos Tversky, "Judgment Under Uncertainty: Heuristics and Biases," *Science* 185 (September 27, 1974): 1124–1131.

[4] Daniel Kahneman and Amos Tversky, "Prospect Theory: An Analysis of Decision Under Risk," *Econometrica* 47, no. 2 (March 1979): 263–291.

(Continued)

(*Continued*)

The psychologists showed that these heuristics produced systematic and predictable errors. The results of their research radically altered the way many scholars viewed how individuals make decisions.

In Prospect Theory, Kahneman and Tversky presented an alternative to the classic economic theory that utility is a function of the individual's *level* of wealth. Their research showed instead that individual utility is a function of *changes* in the individual's wealth relative to a neutral starting position or reference point. The authors discovered that as a direct consequence, losses produce twice as much pain as gains produce in pleasure. This insight is directly counter to what economists believed at the time. Kahneman and Tversky called this behavior **loss aversion** and demonstrated that individuals will pay a premium to avoid uncertainty, yet become risk-seeking when dealing with potential losses. These behaviors violate the basic assumptions of decision theory and appear to be irrational to proponents of classical economic theory.

These observations became the foundation for behavioral finance, and Kahneman went on to become the first non-economist (and so far, the only one) to win the Nobel Prize for Economics, which was awarded to him in 2002. Tversky would have shared the prize had he not died in 1996.

Behavioral finance has flourished in the 40 years since Kahneman and Tversky first published their research and established its theoretical foundation. It is important to recognize that behavioral finance comprises two distinct, albeit interrelated disciplines: *micro* **behavioral finance**, which deals with decision making and the behavior of individuals, and *macro* **behavioral finance**, which deals with the behavior of the collective.[5] Although actions of the individual can influence the actions of the collective, the relationship is not a direct one, which appears to cause a fair amount of confusion among many people.

Behavioral finance holds that investors may not always act rationally, and investment decisions may be driven more by human emotions than classical economics predicts. This insight leads many people to jump to the conclusion that because men are irrational and markets are made of men (and women),[6] markets are also

_____

[5] Micro and macro behavioral finance are not official terms - we made them up.

[6] Numerous studies have shown that women are actually better investors primarily because they are less emotional than men.

irrational. In turn, many individuals believe that the behaviors of individual market participants (**micro behavioral finance**) can be scaled up to represent the behavior of the collective (**macro behavioral finance**).

Individual Behavior Cannot Explain Crowd Behavior

This belief is an incorrect conclusion, however. Just as we cannot predict the direction of the economy (macroeconomics) by predicting only the behavior of individuals (microeconomics), even though the two disciplines are interrelated, we cannot predict the movements of the stock market by predicting the behavior of individual investors. The primary reason why individual behavior does not aggregate to explain group behavior is that the stock market is a **complex adaptive system**. The most important characteristic of complex adaptive systems is that they exhibit **emergent behavior**, meaning that when individual actions are aggregated, patterns emerge that cannot be predicted from analyzing individual behavior. Simply put, the whole is greater than the sum of the parts. To reiterate, we cannot predict how the collective will behave by analyzing only individual behavior.

Rather than focusing on the *micro* and how individuals behave, Robert Shiller, who shared the Nobel Prize with Eugene Fama in 2013 for his work on behavioral finance, focused on *macro* or collective behavior. In his 1981 paper "Do Stock Prices Move Too Much to Be Justified by Subsequent Changes in Dividends?" Shiller compared the volatility in stock prices to the variations in the underlying company's dividends and found no evidence that investors acted in accordance with the efficient market hypothesis. In other words, Shiller found that stock market swings were significantly greater than could be explained by any rational economic behavior, and he uncovered a consistent pattern of excess volatility. It would logically follow that if investors' behavior is not rational, it must be driven by feelings and emotions. Or, in other words, behavioral finance.

Shiller believes there are too many contradictions to the efficient market hypothesis for it to be considered an accurate theory and "that bubbles or other such contradictions to efficient markets can be understood only with reference to other social sciences such as psychology."[7] He defined a bubble as:

> A situation in which news of price increases spurs investor enthusiasm which spreads by psychological contagion from person to person, in the process amplifying stories that might justify the price increase and bringing in a larger and larger class of investors, who, despite doubts about the real value of the investment, are drawn to it partly through envy of others' successes and partly through a gambler's excitement.[8]

Shiller believes that market movements are influenced substantially by social psychology. Instead of a crowd of rational decision makers, he sees the crowd as "investors who do not pay much attention to fundamental indicators of value"[9] and who are emotionally driven by animal spirits.

It is interesting that Shiller won the Nobel Prize for his work on behavioral finance yet only mentions the work of Kahneman and Tversky twice, and then only briefly, in his 33-page acceptance lecture. Shiller's apparent disregard for micro behavioral finance is consistent with the statement that one cannot predict how the collective will behave by analyzing the individual behaviors within the collective.

In fact, individual behavior *does not matter* unless that behavior *produces a systematic error in the collective*. And, as we discuss at length in the previous chapter, the only way errors are created in the collective is by a reduction in the crowd's diversity or a breakdown in its independence. Individual errors offset each other if the models individuals use are diverse and will not affect the crowd error if the individuals act independently. **Therefore, although individuals can, and will, make errors and may appear to act irrationally, the individual errors will cancel out each other and have no impact on the crowd's error as long as the individual errors are not systematically correlated.**

---

[7] Robert J. Shiller, "Do Stock Prices Move Too Much to Be Justified by Subsequent Changes in Dividends?" *American Economic Review* 71, no. 3, (June 1981).

[8] Ibid.

[9] Ibid.

> While (micro) behavioral finance offers important insights into the potential errors individual investors can (and will) make, those errors will not have a material impact on the collective's (macro) behavioral unless the individual errors within the collective are systematic and correlated. Therefore, although individuals will not always make rational investment decisions, knowledge and understanding of these errors cannot be used to predict how the crowd will behave. Systematic error within the collective will exist only when there is a lack of diversity or breakdown of independence.

Crowd Behavior When Diversity Is Lacking

We define lack of diversity within the collective as when investors think the same way because they use the same, or similar, models to arrive at their estimates of intrinsic value. With a lack of diversity, the crowd's view will reflect nothing more than the view of a select few or a single individual, rather than different views from multiple individuals. Under these circumstances, the crowd produces an answer that often is only a small deviation from the average individual estimate, as we show in the wisdom of the crowd examples in the previous chapter.

On the other hand, a **breakdown of independence** occurs when a diverse group of investors is influenced by the same external stimuli and sets aside its prior estimate or private information when expressing its views. The individuals may be diverse because they use different models to arrive at their estimate of intrinsic value, but they lose their independence when they imitate or adopt the views of other investors. **In other words, diversity is a function of the variety of models used, while independence is compromised if the model outputs are systematically influenced by external stimuli.** Building upon Professor Roger Murray's analogy from Chapter 4, we show the forces introducing error as magnets pulling the consensus away from the correct answer in Figure 7.3.

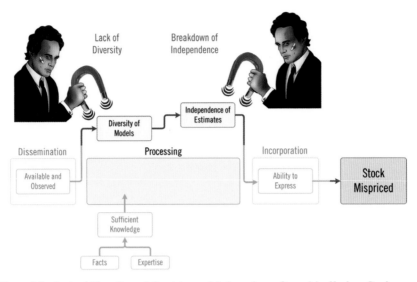

Figure 7.3   Lack of Diversity and Breakdown of Independence Caused by Mayhem Produces a Mispriced Stock

We can demonstrate how diversity decreases and why it results in a mispriced stock using a simple example from Chapter 3. We show in that discussion that cash flow can be generated from either operating an asset or selling an asset. Liquidation value and Private Market Value approaches are used to determine the intrinsic value when selling an asset. Determining the intrinsic value when operating an asset is comprised of three layers: value of invested capital, value of competitive advantage (no growth), and value of incremental growth, as shown in Figure 7.4.

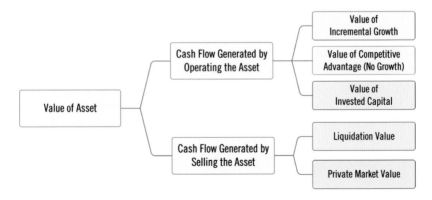

Figure 7.4   Approaches to Determine Intrinsic Value

Each valuation method (or layer) produces a different range or distribution of intrinsic value estimates, as shown in Figure 7.5. We will let each of the five different valuation types represent a different "model" for the discussion and assume 20% of the crowd uses each "model" exclusively to calculate their intrinsic value estimate.[10]

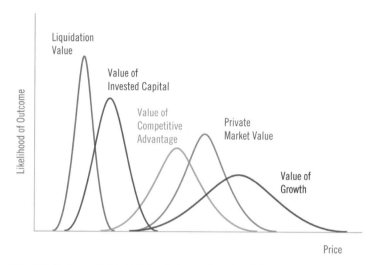

Figure 7.5   Distributions of Intrinsic Value Estimates Based on Different Investor Valuation Models

We derive an estimated liquidation value for Sevcon within a range of $0.50 to $3.00 per share in Chapter 3, with the most likely liquidation value being $1.50, as we show in Figure 7.6. As a reference, the stock was trading at $7.60 at the time of this analysis.

Let's assume that Sevcon announces to the market that it lost an important customer. If, based on this news, Mr. Market becomes fearful, anxious, and depressed, he would likely assign a low value to the company, perhaps nothing more than its liquidation value. If the 80%

---

[10] When determining the intrinsic value by operating an asset, there are three "layers": value of invested capital, value of competitive advantage (no growth), and value of incremental growth. For this example, we pretend that there are three different groups of investors that use each layer as their only model. While this may appear to be a fantasy, it can map to the real world. One can think of "deep value" investors as using only the liquidation method, private equity investors using only PMV, "value" investors using only the value of invested capital, "GARP" (growth at a reasonable price) investors using only the value of competitive advantage, and "growth" investors using the value of growth.

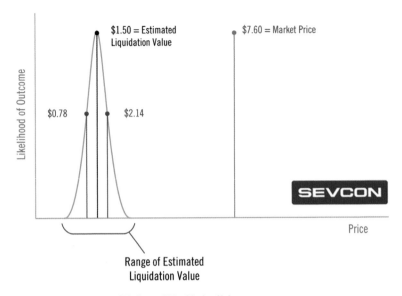

Figure 7.6   Sevcon: Range of Estimated Liquidation Values

of the market participants using one of the other models to value the company begin to think that the lost customer could be the beginning of a trend and all shift to valuing Sevcon using the *same liquidation model*, then a systematic bias will have emerged and the stock would fall from its price of $7.60 to its estimated liquidation value of $1.50. The crowd will have lost its **diversity** as investors are now all using the same model and calculating Sevcon's intrinsic value the same way.

Assume that you had followed the company for a number of years. You thought the stock was fairly valued at $7.60 based on your estimate of Sevcon's **Private Market Value**, which is the model you use in your analysis. You are also aware that Sevcon lost a key customer and incorporate the new information into your valuation model. Your revised estimate of intrinsic value is now $5.45 per share. If you have confidence that your analysis is correct, then Mr. Market's reaction creates a mispricing and an opportunity for you, as shown in Figure 7.7. Although your estimate of the company's intrinsic value dropped from $7.60 per share to $5.45 per share, the market price has declined from $7.60 to its current price of $1.50. Given your estimated value of $5.45, purchasing the stock at $1.50 will seem like a bargain.

However, it is important to note that although the crowd has lost its diversity that alone does not mean that a mispricing exists.

The paragraph above contains an important qualifier, "*If you have confidence that your analysis is correct.*" The implication is that, in *your* opinion, the consensus is wrong. To *you* there appears to be a genuine mispricing and the stock seems "like a bargain." The crowd's bias *may* have created a mispricing, but then again, that is not a foregone conclusion just because of the crowd's lack of diversity.

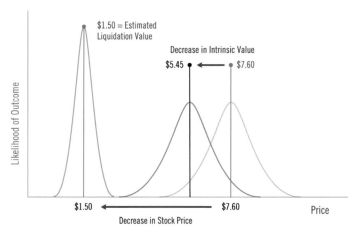

Figure 7.7   Intrinsic Value Estimate Before and After Customer Loss

The extreme price move is also illustrated in Figure 7.8.

Figure 7.8   Mr. Market Overreacts

Although the Sevcon example is overly simplistic, it reflects the fact that the market is comprised of different constituents. In the real world, there are investors who are long-term oriented and others who are focused on the short term. There are investors who focus on technical analysis, quantitative investors, or fundamental analysis. The investors in each of these investment disciplines often think alike and use similar models to generate their estimates of intrinsic value. For example, fundamental investors value companies based on metrics such as price to book or price to cash flow, while investors who practice technical analysis focus on trading metrics such as comparing the stock's 200-day moving average with its 50-day moving average. Growth investors focus on sales or earnings growth and use metrics such as price to sales or earnings momentum. When the shareholder base is diverse and includes investors following different disciplines, most often the collective is wise and the stock will be efficiently priced. If, on the other hand, the shareholder base lacks diversity and is comprised mostly of investors from a single group, the collective is less wise and the stock less efficiently priced. While this statement is an oversimplification, we can use it to make an important point about investor diversity.

There have been many situations in the real world where **crowding** or **herding** among investors exists in an individual stock or market sector, resulting in a lack of diversity among the market participants in that particular area of the market. Because most of the market participants in these situations are using similar models in their analysis, a small, seemingly innocuous event can trigger a stampede, causing Mr. Market to become manic. We want to emphasize that an "appropriate" reaction to an event by an otherwise diversified shareholder base can easily turn into an overreaction to the same event when the shareholder base lacks diversity.

One such incident was the Quant Crisis of 2007. Quantitative investors use computer models to identify patterns in securities prices and then buy or sell thousands of different securities to capture small mispricings. It has been an enormously successful strategy over the years and has made billionaires of investors like James Simons of Renaissance Technologies, Ken Griffin of Citadel, and Cliff Asness of AQR Capital. However, sometimes a successful strategy breaks down and causes pandemonium.

Several large hedge funds and proprietary trading desks on Wall Street began losing billions of dollars over a matter of a few days in early August 2007 and no one knew exactly why. Because the majority of these funds were implementing a similar strategy (*using the same models*) and employing significant amounts of leverage, many of them received margin calls simultaneously when prices started to decline (the securities they held were the collateral for their loans) and were forced to sell at least some of their holdings. Unfortunately, because many of the portfolios were similarly constructed, the margin calls created a ripple effect, and the selling begat more selling, which resulted in a "death spiral" in many of the widely-owned assets.

In his excellent book *The Quants*, Scott Patterson describes events during those days in August that seem more fitting for a John Grisham suspense novel than a Wall Street trading desk. The following are a few excerpts:

> The market moves PDT and other quant funds started to see early that week defied logic. The fine-tuned models, the bell curves and random walks, the calibrated correlations—all the math and science that had propelled the quants to the pinnacle of Wall Street—couldn't capture what was happening. It was utter chaos driven by pure human fear, the kind that can't be captured in a computer model or complex algorithm. *This wasn't supposed to happen!* [emphasis original]
>
> The quants did their best to contain the damage, but they were like firefighters trying to douse a raging inferno with gasoline—the more they tried to fight the flames by selling, the worse the selling became. The downward-driving force of the deleveraging market seemed unstoppable.
>
> It made no sense. A true believer in market efficiency who'd studied under Eugene Fama at Chicago, Rothman expected the market to behave according to the strict quantitative patterns he lived to track. But the market was acting in a way that defied any pattern Rothman—or any other quant—had ever seen. Everything was losing money. Every strategy was falling apart. It was unfathomable, if not outright insane.[11]

---

[11] Scott Patterson, *The Quants: How a New Breed of Math Whizzes Conquered Wall Street and Nearly Destroyed It* (New York: Crown, 2010).

Crowd Behavior When Information Cascades: The Breakdown of Independence

While similar to a lack of **diversity**, a breakdown of **independence** has subtle but important differences. Although members of the crowd might use different models to arrive at their own independent estimates, thus preserving the crowd's diversity, a breakdown of independence occurs when some external influence causes them to alter or set aside their original estimate. This phenomenon is known as an **information cascade**.

This subtlety bears repeating to ensure clarity. When there is a breakdown of **independence**, individuals fixate on some external factor, set their model aside, and follow the crowd.

In Chapter 6, we defined **private information** as an individual's knowledge of facts and experiences that represents their **domain-specific knowledge** and forms their information processing model, which we show in Figure 6.6 and reproduce in figure 7.9:

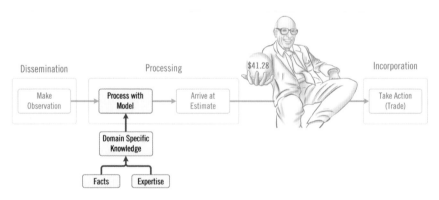

Figure 7.9   Domain-Specific Knowledge Is Comprised of Facts and Expertise That Form an Individual's Processing Model

As we mention throughout the book, each investor has their own unique **private information**, which impacts their estimate of intrinsic value. If the investor arrives at their estimate without any bias, then their estimate is said to be *independent*. Absent a genuine **informational advantage**, however, the investor's **private information** is usually imperfect. Consequentially, the investor might not have a high degree of confidence in the accuracy of their estimate.

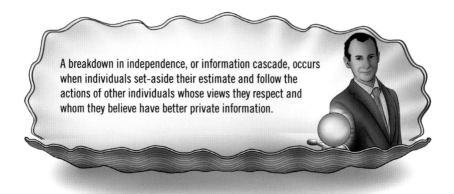

A breakdown in independence, or information cascade, occurs when individuals set-aside their estimate and follow the actions of other individuals whose views they respect and whom they believe have better private information.

The classic example of an information cascade involves choosing where to eat when traveling to a city you don't know well. Imagine you are planning on spending a few days in London on business. You have never been to London before and would like to find a nice restaurant for one of your dinners. Before leaving on your trip, you research options by reviewing the Michelin guide and reading online Yelp reviews. You arrive in London, drop your bags at your hotel, and head out to dinner. As you approach the restaurant you chose through your research, you see that it is empty. When you look at the restaurant next door, however, it is packed and looks like a nice place to eat. At that instant, you change your plans and select the new restaurant for dinner without any additional research or information. What you have done is set aside the **private informa-tion** you obtained from your earlier research *in response to observing the actions of other individuals.* An **information cascade** will unfold if other people decide to eat at the crowded restaurant for the same reasons you did when you made your impromptu decision.

We can illustrate how information cascades occur in the stock market with another simple example. Bob is an investment adviser and manages separate accounts for high-net-worth individuals on a discretionary basis.[12] Bob closely follows Biotech Inc., a company that is developing a drug for neon nose syndrome. The company is cur-rently waiting for the results of the FDA Phase II trials for their drug.

---

[12] Discretionary trading means that Bob's clients have given him a limited power of attorney that grants him authority over the account, which allows him to make buy and sell decisions at his discretion without their consultation.

After talking with several doctors and patients aware of the trial, Bob believes the drug is effective and will get Phase II approval. He purchased Biotech's stock in 20 of his client accounts at an average price of $15.37. A few weeks later the stock price has increased to $17.04.

Judd is a well-known and highly regarded biotech investor. He appears regularly on CNBC and has an impressive investment record. Since Judd is a successful investor, many market participants track his fund's holdings through its 13G filings.[13] Bob notices in a new amended 13G filing with the SEC that Judd's firm no longer holds a position in Biotech Inc., which shocks Bob because he knows Judd's fund previously owned 6.2% of the company's shares.

Bob's heart sinks as he infers that if Judd's fund sold its Biotech Inc. stock, Judd must believe that the company will not get FDA approval for its neon nose drug. If the drug is not approved, Biotech stock could easily fall in half to $8.50, or possibly even lower. Since Bob's accounts own a lot of the stock, he panics and sells the shares for his 20 clients pushing Biotech Inc. stock down from $17.04 to $16.23 in the process. He also notices that there are postings on Twitter also speculating that if Judd's fund sold its Biotech Inc. position, it signals that the company is unlikely to get FDA approval. Reading the negative Tweets further reinforces Bob's decision. By the time the market closes a few hours later, Biotech Inc.'s stock has traded down to $13.78 on seven times the average daily volume.

This series of events is the beginning of an **information cascade**. Bob does not know what **private information** Judd has, although he infers Judd's knowledge from the 13G filing. Bob set aside his private information (his estimate) and imitated (what he thought was) Judd's decision to sell the shares.

Bob's clients, who have been watching the trading in Biotech Inc. stock, receive trade confirmations in the mail prompted by Bob's sales of Biotech Inc. Randi, one of Bob's clients who works at a rival biotech company and is familiar with Biotech Inc.'s neon nose drug, notices Bob sold the stock in her account. Randi hired Bob to manage her money because she thinks he is smart and respects his judgment. She, too, has been following Biotech Inc.'s progress for a while and thought the drug would get FDA approval. She agreed with Bob's original analysis of the company's potential, but now has doubts.

---

[13] A 13G filing is a public filing that is required from certain investors when purchasing more than 5% of a company's shares outstanding.

Randi also invests her money on her own. She notices that Biotech Inc. declined $3.26 on the day to close at $13.78 on significant trading volume. The next morning, she decide to sell short some Biotech stock in her own account the thinking the price will continue to fall further. The information cascade continues. Randi assumes that Bob has good **private information** as expressed by the stock sales in her account. This was "confirmed" by the significant decline in the stock price. Randi thinks that "smart" investors must know something that she does not know about the company's Phase II trial, so she sets aside her private information and imitates Bob and the rest of the traders in the market.[14]

The only way information can be **expressed**, **aggregated**, and **incorporated** into the stock price is through trading. Therefore, although investors have no way of knowing the private information prompting the stock trades, they see the actions of other investors (as evidenced by the decline in Biotech Inc.'s stock price) and infer that the sellers have better private information. It is important to note that the information conveyed by the stock decline might not have been accurate. As every seasoned investor knows, just because someone sells a stock does not mean they have better information. Paul S. remembers one of Chuck Royce's comments after witnessing a large move in a particular stock, "Someone either knows something *or thinks they know something.*"

The price decline in Biotech Inc. stock caused individuals to doubt their independent analysis. Bob and Randi both set aside their private information and imitated other investors. And, as a result, there was a breakdown in the crowd's **independence**.

We also saw that there was a **feedback loop**. As Biotech Inc.'s stock declined in value, the trades reinforced everyone's conviction that someone must know something to justify the lower stock price. Most investors thought that if the stock was falling ahead of the FDA announcement, other investors must have information that indicated that the company would not get approval. However, as it turned out, the market signal was false—it was **noise**. Investor selling pushed the price lower, but the lower price conveyed false information to

---

[14] Investors who think they are trading on information, but in fact are not (like Bob and Randi in the example) are called "**noise traders**." Fischer Black wrote an excellent article on this topic, appropriately called "Noise," in the July 1986 issue of the *Journal of Finance*. Simply Google "Fischer Black Noise" to obtain a copy.

the market participants. The cycle became a positive **feedback loop** based on noise, not better information. **No one really knew anything, although everyone thought that someone must know something**.

If Bob and Randi remained **independent**, they would have ignored the noise and stuck with their original decision, which was based solely on their **private information**. However, because they lacked conviction in their original assessment, they set aside their estimate (private information) and adopted the actions of other investors they thought had better information, which created the **information cascade**.

Biotech Inc. announced a week later that it had passed Phase II FDA trials. The stock closed that day at \$24.55, up sharply from the prior day's closing price, and significantly higher than the prices where Bob and Randi sold their shares. Judd happened to be on CNBC that day and the reporter asked why he had sold Biotech Inc. stock prior to the company's positive announcement. With a look of surprise, Judd exclaimed, "We didn't sell." The reporter referenced the amended 13G filing. Judd responded, "Oh. I see the confusion. No, we didn't sell. My partner and I decided to part ways and we each took half of the assets into our new funds. We did this as an in-kind distribution, so there was no trading involved. Each of our funds now own 3.1% of Biotech Inc., so are we no longer required to file with the SEC since each fund owns less than 5%. We did have to update our filing as the old fund was dissolved and as a result, held no stock. I guess the view from the outside was that we sold our entire position."

For a brief instant, a look of deep thought was apparent on Judd's face. Then he said to the announcer, "You know, that explains a lot. I was wondering why Biotech stock fell so much last week. I didn't even think about our 13G filing as a possible explanation. People must have thought we sold. That's funny. When I saw that the stock was down a lot, my first reaction was fear. We had confidence in our research and thought that the move in the stock was just noise, but it is hard to stick to your guns when the market appears to be telling you that you are wrong. We used the sell-off as an opportunity to add to our position and wound up making a ton of money." Judd sat back and laughed, saying, "**Wow, if I panicked and sold the stock because of the move, I would have been reacting to the noise my filing produced without even knowing it!**"

Is the Crowd's Apparent Madness Irrational?

The lack of diversity and breakdown of independence are both examples of investor **herding** or **crowding**.

It should be noted that herding is not irrational behavior per se. It can be normal and rational for an individual to imitate other people when making a decision if that individual believes the other person has better information.

Back to the example of the restaurant in London. You completed your research and selected a restaurant for dinner. However, as you approach the location you see that the restaurant you chose is empty, while the one next door is packed. As you peer through the window of the packed restaurant you think, "Those people seem normal and they look like me, yet they chose this restaurant over the one I selected originally." **Your instinct is to conclude that they must have better information than you do, and that if you had the same information, you would arrive at the same decision they did.** Maybe the chef left the restaurant you chose but that information was unavailable when you did your research? Or, maybe someone got sick eating at the restaurant a few days prior to your visit and there was a story in the local newspaper that you did not see.

Does it seem irrational to set aside your private information and follow the crowd given the possible scenarios described above? No, it does not. Is it the right choice? Maybe, maybe not. The crowd in the other restaurant could be wrong.

The world of investing is no different. In the example with Biotech Inc. stock, we could have altered the storyline slightly and the 13G filing for Judd's fund could have been an actual sale of stock triggered by new information that Judd received. Bob and Randi made what turned out with hindsight to be the wrong investment decision, but their decision was not irrational.

"Following the leader" is a normal human behavior. Individuals often feel safer in a crowd, a sentiment captured in the classic quote by John Maynard Keynes, "Worldly wisdom teaches that it is better for reputation to fail conventionally than to succeed unconventionally." It is when imitation is taken to an extreme, or when the imitation is based on noise rather than information, that information cascades can cause a breakdown of independence. Again, *this is not irrational behavior.*

Shiller also believes that investors are not behaving irrationally in these situations, as he states in his Nobel lecture:

> My definition puts the epidemic nature, the emotions of investors, and the nature of the news and information media at center of the definition of the bubble. Bubbles are not, in my mind, about craziness of investors. They are rather about how investors are buffeted en masse from one superficially plausible theory about conventional valuation to another.[15]

Shiller asserts that the news and information media influence the crowd **systematically**, and the ensuing herd behavior likely produces an inefficient stock price. In the extreme, the collapsing of diversity or breakdown of independence can cause a mania or bubble, driven by greed, when everyone believes an overly optimistic view of the future, or a panic or crash, driven by fear, when the crowd believes a doomsday scenario is likely to unfold.

How Can Fama and Shiller Both Be Right?

At first glance, it might seem odd that Fama and Shiller jointly won the Nobel Prize despite having radically opposing views on market efficiency. How can Fama and Shiller both be right?

---

[15] Robert J. Shiller, "Prize Lecture: Speculative Asset Prices," December 8, 2013, Stockholm, Sweden.

Daniel Richards, chair of Tufts University's economics department (Fama attended Tufts as an undergraduate), summed up the Swedish Academy's decision perfectly:

> The three-way award combination is brilliant. Fama shows why markets are efficient, Shiller shows why they are not, and Hansen provides econometric tools to show why both are right.[16]

One must assume that the Nobel committee believed the two theories coexist, which is reflected in Professor Per Krusell's remarks during the announcement of the 2013 Nobel Prize winners: "The current understanding of asset prices relies in part on rational investors and their concerns about risk and in part on psychology and behavioral finance."[17]

The committee elaborated further in the Nobel Prize announcement by stating that under the rational investor model:

> Investors rationally calculate what assets are worth. Thus, an asset's value should be based on the payment stream that it is expected to generate in the future. A reasonable assumption is that these payments are discounted: in other words, payments in the distant future carry less weight than more immediate payments.

The committee also stated that another way is to

> Abandon the notion of fully rational investors. Moving beyond this assumption has a new field referred to as 'behavioral finance.' Here, mistaken expectations are at center stage: high asset prices may reflect overestimates of future payment streams. In other words, excessive optimism or other psychological mechanisms may help to explain why asset prices deviate from fundamental values.[18]

These comments imply that the Nobel committee believes assets are priced using a discounted cash flow model, although there will be times when asset prices will deviate from fundamental values driven by human emotions.

---

[16] Philip Primack, "Fama's Market—A Nobel for the Economist Who Explained Why Stock Prices Are So Hard to Predict." *Tufts Magazine*, Winter 2014.

[17] Announcement of the 2013 Sveriges Riksbank Prize in Economic Sciences in Memory of Alfred Nobel, presented by Professor Staffan Normark, Permanent Secretary of the Royal Swedish Academy of Sciences, on October 14, 2013.

[18] The Royal Swedish Academy of Science, "The Prize in Economic Sciences 2013," press release confirming the award of Sveriges Riksbank Prize in Economic Sciences in Memory of Alfred Nobel for 2013 to Eugene F. Fama, Lars Peter Hansen, and Robert J. Shiller, October 14, 2013.

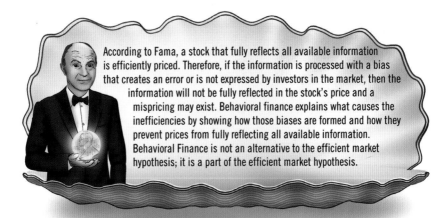

According to Fama, a stock that fully reflects all available information is efficiently priced. Therefore, if the information is processed with a bias that creates an error or is not expressed by investors in the market, then the information will not be fully reflected in the stock's price and a mispricing may exist. Behavioral finance explains what causes the inefficiencies by showing how those biases are formed and how they prevent prices from fully reflecting all available information. Behavioral Finance is not an alternative to the efficient market hypothesis; it is a part of the efficient market hypothesis.

The 2013 Nobel award states clearly that the committee believes that Fama's efficient market hypothesis and Shiller's views on how human behavior produces inefficiencies are complementary and *not* mutually exclusive, as many investors and academics alike seem to believe.

The Magnetism of the Efficient Market Hypothesis

Ben Graham discussed this dichotomy in the *Intelligent Investor* when he stated, "In the short run, the market is a voting machine but in the long run, it is a weighing machine."[19] With this statement, Graham implies that the market *can* be swayed by human emotion, creating a temporary mispricing, although the market tends to settle at the correct price over time.

Roger Murray discussed the same concept in a slightly different way during his 1993 lectures at the Paley Center[20] in New York City when he stated, "It is security analysis,[21] after all, that makes the market efficient, and because all of us have worked so hard at that

---

[19] Graham, *The Intelligent Investor.*

[20] The Museum of Television & Radio was renamed the Paley Center for Media on June 5, 2007.

[21] Murray defines security analysis as the process of calculating the intrinsic value and purchasing a security if it trades at a meaningful discount to that value.

process, we have brought any notion of value, any notion of market pricing together. And you and I cannot possibly improve the market's capacity to estimate the future profitability of an investment." Murray thought of the security analysis process "as a magnet—a drawing together of market prices towards some notion of an underlying value which has some real substance to it." He states further, "If you prefer, you can call it towards intrinsic value or you can call it regression to the mean, which implies, to some extent at least, that the intrinsic value is the true, underlying, central tendency in the valuation of an enterprise, an industry or a class of securities."[22] Murray's implication is that while stock prices can deviate from their intrinsic value in the short run, they are drawn back to that value by market forces over time.

Intrinsic Value Acts as an Electromagnet

Expanding on Murray's magnet analogy, we can think of market efficiency as an electromagnet that draws the stock price toward the true economic or intrinsic value of the underlying business, while thinking of behavioral finance as a different magnet, powered by human emotions, that pulls the stock price away from its intrinsic value.[23]

All one needs to construct an electromagnet is a nail, a battery, and some wire, as shown in Figure 7.10.

Figure 7.10   Homemade Electromagnet

---

[22] Roger F. Murray and Gabelli Asset Management Co., "Lecture #1. Value Versus Price." Roger F. Murray lecture series, Museum of Television & Radio, New York, January 22, 1993.

[23] It is important to note that in the following examples we assume that the market is wrong. As we discuss earlier in this chapter, a systematic bias causes a mispricing only if the consensus view is wrong.

We can demonstrate the magnetic effect market efficiency has on stock prices, and how the efficient market hypothesis and behavioral finance coexist, using a few simple examples. Imagine we place a ferromagnetic emoji ball bearing inside the distribution curve in Figure 7.11 and position an electromagnet at the curve's apex to represent market efficiency's pull. The graphic shows that the electromagnet holds the emoji at the top of the curve, where price equals intrinsic value, representing that the market is functioning without error and there is no mispricing.

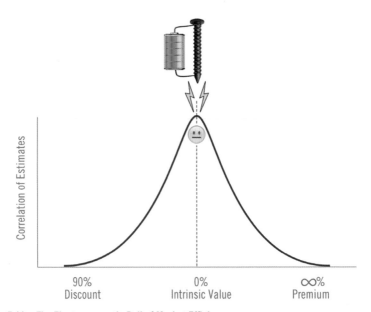

Figure 7.11   The Electromagnetic Pull of Market Efficiency

The Pull of Systematic Error

However, when the wisdom of crowds is not functioning properly because some type of **systematic bias** has created an error, behavioral finance has entered the picture, pulling prices away from their intrinsic value. When investors become overly optimistic or pessimistic, their **independence** and **diversity** declines and the correlation of their estimates increases, which drives the stock to a premium or forces it to a discount to intrinsic value, as shown in Figure 7.12. It helps to visualize biased investor behavior as strong magnets, pulling

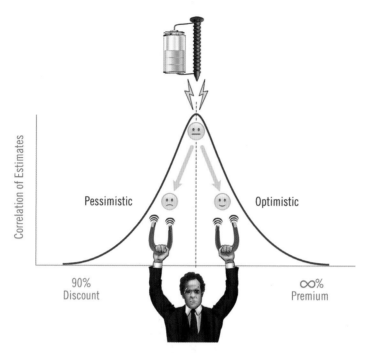

Figure 7.12   Mayhem's Bias Pulls Stock Price Away from Intrinsic Value

the ferromagnetic emoji ball down the curve and away from the electromagnet of intrinsic value.

The pricing error can be corrected in two ways. First, **unbiased** investors could enter the market to exploit the profit opportunity and correct the mispricing, in effect diluting the biased consensus. We can think of these investors entering the market as the equivalent of turning up the power on the electromagnet at the top of the distribution curve (where the price equals intrinsic value). This action overpowers the magnets representing the behavioral bias and pulls the stock back to its intrinsic value, as shown in Figure 7.13. The other way the mispricing could correct is if the bias dissipates or recedes. In the magnet analogy, this action would be equivalent to the behavioral bias magnets losing their strength. Often mispricings are corrected by a combination of the two forces.

Albeit overly simplified, the description illustrates how **the efficient market hypothesis and behavioral finance together influence the movement of stock prices**. A stock will be efficiently priced unless some type of **systematic bias**, driven by human emotions, pulls the

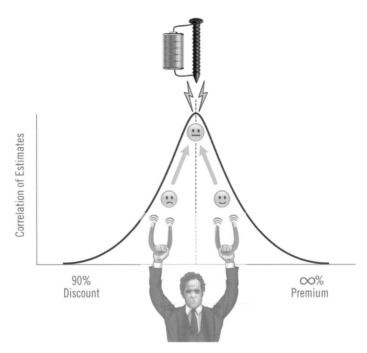

Figure 7.13 Non-Biased Electromagnets Overpower While Bias Weakens and Stock Returns to Its Efficient Price

price away from its true value, as shown in the various charts. Again, even if the consensus is wrong, as we discussed previously, **a systematic bias does not automatically mean that there is a pricing error**.

The Extreme Pull of Excessive Fear and Greed

Mr. Market's overreactions will result in crashes and bubbles when taken to an extreme. Shiller describes the snowball effect of a bubble by stressing that it starts with a price increase, which spurs investor enthusiasm, and spreads like a contagion from person to person, becoming amplified in the process and sucking in more and more investors. This description echoes Graham's observation that, "the investors' mental attitude not only affects the market price but is strongly affected by it."[24]

---

[24] Bejamin Graham and David L. Dodd, *Security Analysis* (New York: Whittlesey House, McGraw-Hill Book Company, 1934).

In a mania or bubble, greed overwhelms fear and investors become overly optimistic. Conversely, in a panic or crash, fear overwhelms greed and investors become overly pessimistic. During these episodes, stock prices move away from their true intrinsic value and valuations expand to large premiums or contract to significant discounts, as the stock prices become detached from the business's underlying fundamentals. Market efficiency is cast aside as the crowd's fear and greed take over. Effectively, the magnetic pull of these emotions temporarily overwhelms the power of the efficient market electromagnet. At that moment, the biased magnets are stronger than the unbiased electromagnet and pull the emoji far away from the company's true intrinsic value, down into the tails of the curve, as shown in Figure 7.14.

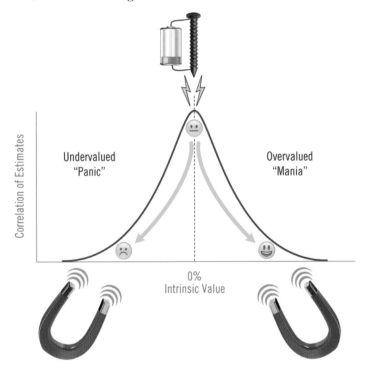

Figure 7.14   Biased Behavioral Magnet Overpowers Unbiased Electromagnet of Market Efficiency

Overwhelmed by fear or greed in these situations, investors begin to think alike, group intelligence becomes groupthink, information cascades and the wisdom of crowds is lost, as the madness of crowds takes over.

In some extreme cases, such as the Internet bubble in 2000 and the 2008 financial crisis, investors get so carried away that their collective emotions overpower the unbiased electromagnet, preventing the emoji from returning to its intrinsic value. The unemotional traders simply do not have enough capital or fortitude to offset the impulsiveness and strength of the emotional crowd, as shown in Figure 7.15.

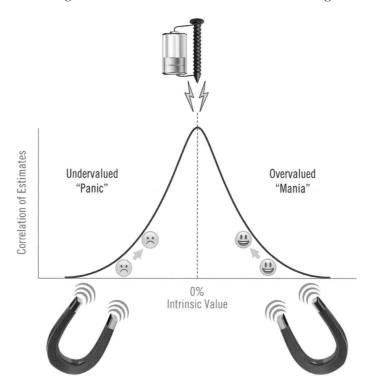

Figure 7.15   Underpowered Unbiased Electromagnet Cannot Correct Extreme Behavior Pull

Bubbles Eventually Burst and Crashes Eventually End

Eventually, some event occurs, the bubble breaks, or the panic ends, and investors are snapped out of their manic state. The force of the biased magnets fades, releasing their grip. Investor independence and the crowd's diversity returns, and stock prices begin to drift (or snap) back toward intrinsic value, as shown in Figure 7.16.

Despite the Nobel Committee's decision to recognize both theories in the same year, blending the theories of behavioral finance with the efficient market hypothesis may still appear to be heresy to many academics and most practitioners. **However, the merged**

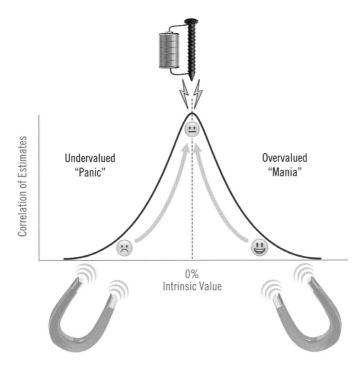

Figure 7.16   Unbiased Electromagnet Ultimately Overpowers the Biased Behavioral Magnets and Stock Returns to an Efficient Price

theory provides us with a more effective mental model to proceed with in the discussion. It is important to note that the overwhelming evidence supports the claim that the efficient market hypothesis is the prevailing force most of the time, although in "normal" market conditions, behavioral finance will skew pricings with some frequency. On the rare occasion, during extreme times of manias and panics, when investor emotions take over and create **systematic errors**, behavioral finance gets the upper hand.

Between "perfect" market efficiency at one extreme and manias and panics on the other, there is a blending of the two forces. The blue area in the middle of Figure 7.17 represents the efficient market hypothesis at its strongest, while the red area on either ends of the curve shows where behavioral factors have the stronger pull. As we discuss earlier, stock prices rarely deviate far from their intrinsic value; however, on some occasions, investor behavior creates a **systematic bias** that takes control, causing the discounts or premiums to intrinsic value to go to an extreme.

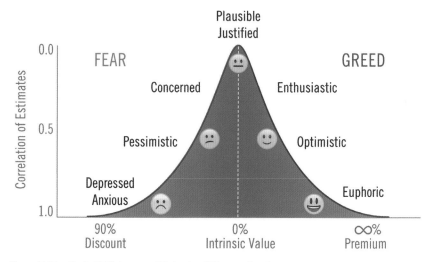

Figure 7.17   Market Efficiency and Behavioral Finance Coexist

Limits to Incorporation: When the Crowd Cannot Act

The third tenet of market efficiency states that for the stock to be efficiently priced, *information must be expressed, aggregated, and incorporated into the market price by a sufficient number of investors,* which only happens when investors trade the stock and affect the market price. Investor opinions must be expressed and aggregated without significant impediments for the market price to **incorporate** the information and satisfy the third tenet.

MAXIMIZING PRIVATE INFORMATION

In August 2016, Paul S. had a conversation with Shane Heitzman, a professor of accounting at USC Marshall School of Business, who wrote an excellent paper titled, "Private Information Arrival, Trading Activity and Stock Prices: Evidence from Nonpublic Merger Negotiations." Paul asked the question, "If I have information and wish to trade on it, I will sit at the bid price and buy stock as sellers come in so I don't move the stock price. If I am trading, but not moving the price, the information that I have isn't being incorporated into the stock price. How does that reconcile?" Shane replied, "You are *maximizing* the value of your private information by not moving the stock price through your activity. The information you have isn't being incorporated into the price." The bottom line is that for the market to be efficient, the information is conveyed to the market by trading activity moving the price. *If the price doesn't move, the information is not incorporated.*

Even if the first two tenets of market efficiency are met—the information is adequately disseminated and then processed absent any systematic error—an inefficiency can result if the estimate is not incorporated into the price through trading.

What impediments might exist that would prevent an investor from trading? The Nobel committee termed these as "institutional constraints and conflicts of interests." These impediments fall into two broad categories, which in both cases prevent an investor from taking or holding a position. The first category is referred to as **liquidity constraints**, which can limit an investor's ability to execute a trade. The second category relates to anticipated or actual **redemptions** from clients that prevent an investor from taking a position in the first place or holding a position long enough for the gap between the market price and their estimate of intrinsic value to close.

When making a buy or sell decision, most investors want to execute the trade immediately. The problem is that buyers *and* sellers are not always in the market at the exact same time, willing to transact the same number of shares, at the same price. A stock is considered **liquid** when these three factors—time, price, and number of available shares—all line up, allowing investors to fill their order without moving the stock price. Conversely, a security is considered **illiquid** if filling the order would cause the stock price to move.

With a liquid stock, such as Apple, where there are a large number of buyers and sellers, the bid/ask spread is usually small as we saw when we looked up the stock price on April 28, 2016.

Last Price	Today's Change	Bid (Size)	Ask (Size)
97.22	-0.60 (-0.61%)	97.21 x200	97.22 x200

Real Time Quote Last Trade as of 9:38 AM ET 4/28/16

Figure 7.18   Apple, Inc.: Price Quote

The quote in Figure 7.18 implies that a trader could buy 200 shares at $97.22 or sell 200 shares at $97.21. The bid/ask spread is only a penny, or 0.01% of the security's price. Apple's daily trading volume averaged roughly 36 million shares at the time of this analysis, which equals about $3.5 billion worth of stock traded each day.

Looking at the market for Associated Capital stock on the same day, the bid/ask spread also does not appear to be large, as seen in Figure 7.19.

	Last Price	Today's Change	Bid (Size)	Ask (Size)
ASSOCIATED CAPITAL GROUP	**30.02**	-0.02 (-0.07%)	**30.02** x1,100	**30.05** x400

Real Time Quote Last Trade as of 3:48 AM ET 4/28/16

Figure 7.19   Associated Capital Group: Price Quote

The quote in Figure 7.19 implies that an investor could buy 400 shares at $30.05 or sell 1,100 shares at $30.02. The bid/ask spread is $0.03, or 0.10% of the security's price. While this amount is 10 times Apple's spread of 0.01%, it is still relatively small. However, the average daily trading volume at the time was approximately 21,000 shares, or only $631,000 worth of stock traded each day.

We use Associated's adjusted book value per share of approximately $40 (at the time of this writing in April 2016) as a proxy of the company's intrinsic value for this discussion. If an investor could buy the stock at the offer price of $30 and have confidence that it is worth $40, he would be purchasing the stock at a 25% discount to his estimate of intrinsic value.

However, Associated's stock is not very liquid, as the daily trading volume suggests. For instance, if an investor manages a $2 billion fund and limits himself to 20 individual positions, he would need to own, on average, $100 million of each stock to have it be considered a full position in his portfolio. However, $100 million of Associated stock is over 3.3 million shares, and the stock trades only 21,000 shares per day an average. Considering there are roughly 250 trading days per year and assuming the fund could buy half the daily trading volume, it would take approximately 315 trading days, or a year and three months, for the investor to accumulate a full position. More important, an investor cannot buy enough stock at the offer price of $30.05 to fill his position, as it is highly unlikely that there would be a seller large enough to match his trades. In reality, it is doubtful the investor could buy that much stock at $35, or even at $40 per share.

Therefore, despite the appearance that the stock is trading at a significant discount to its intrinsic value, the typical manager of a $2 billion fund holding 20 positions would not even bother doing research on Associated because he knows he will not be able to acquire a full position in the stock. On the other hand, if the same manager wanted to buy $100 million of Apple stock, he could probably do so within an hour without moving the stock's price. This example highlights the cost of illiquidity.

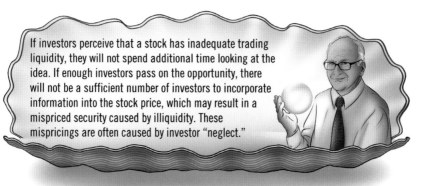

If investors perceive that a stock has inadequate trading liquidity, they will not spend additional time looking at the idea. If enough investors pass on the opportunity, there will not be a sufficient number of investors to incorporate information into the stock price, which may result in a mispriced security caused by illiquidity. These mispricings are often caused by investor "neglect."

The second impediment to incorporation is the ability to take or hold a position. Even if a manager thinks a security is trading at a significant discount and expects the price to eventually converge to its intrinsic value, the path to get there is rarely a straight line.

Most portfolio managers invest other people's money, not just their own. This situation creates a principal/agent problem.[25] The client (the principal) has limited knowledge and understanding about the portfolio manager's (the agent) strategy. If the manager's portfolio begins to lose money, significantly underperforming the market, the client will begin to worry that the manager does not know what he's doing, will not give the manager more money, and will probably begin to consider redeeming his investment in the fund.

---

[25] While not a direct quote, this paragraph borrows heavily from A. Shleifer and R. Vishny, "The Limits of Arbitrage," National Bureau of Economic Research, July 1995.

For example, say a portfolio manager knows, with 100% certainty,[26] that XYZ Corp.'s stock will be worth $26 per share in a year. He purchases the stock at $22 (Figure 7.20), expecting to make an annualized return of 18.2%.

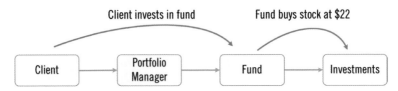

Figure 7.20   Client Invests in Funds

Unfortunately, XYZ stock declines to $17 over the next six months, resulting in an unrealized loss of 22.7%. For simplicity, let's say that the investment is in XYZ Corp, is the portfolio's only position. Assuming that the overall stock market has not changed during the same six months, the portfolio will have underperformed the market considerably during the period, losing 22.7% of its value relative to its benchmark (Figure 7.21).

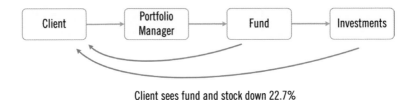

Figure 7.21   Client Sees Fund and Stock Down 22.7%

The manager receives a call from a client who has just reviewed his June quarterly letter reporting the fund's weak six-month performance. The client proceeds to chew out the portfolio manager and calls him an idiot for investing in XYZ. The manager calmly explains that he *knows* XYZ stock will be $26 by year-end, which now is only six months away, and tells the client he should give him more money to invest. The manager points out that if the fund could purchase more stock at the then current price of $17, the expected return on these

---

[26] It is, of course, impossible to know what the price of a stock will be in the future with absolute certainty, although we make that assumption in the example to illustrate the point.

new purchases would be 52.9% over the next six months. Instead, the client panics, gets angry, and demands his money back, threatening to sue if the manager does not comply with his request. To meet the redemption, the portfolio manager is forced to sell, rather than buy, the stock at $17, realizing an actual, rather than a paper, loss of 22.7% (Figure 7.22).

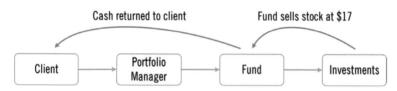

Figure 7.22   Client Redeems Investment

We would say that the client has **weak hands** because he panicked and redeemed his investment when he should have bought more stock. Conversely, an investor with the fortitude and capital base to persevere is said to have **strong hands**. Because this story is a common occurrence in the investment business, fund managers rightfully fear redemptions and often limit the size of their positions, or do not initiate some positions at all, with this concern constantly in mind. Even if the manager has excess cash, he will probably not purchase more stock when it hits $17 despite the very attractive potential return. Rather, the manager will most likely husband the cash in case he receives redemption requests from panicked clients.

If capital is controlled by weak-handed investors, when coupled with the fear of redemptions, investors might not have enough conviction and/or capital to close the gap in these situations, even when security prices deviate significantly from their intrinsic value. To repeat the overquoted John Maynard Keynes: "Markets can remain irrational a lot longer than you and I can remain solvent."

The main takeaway from this discussion is that managers with permanent capital, such as Warren Buffett's Berkshire Hathaway, Mario Gabelli's Associated Capital, Bill Ackman's Pershing Square Holdings, Joel Greenblatt's Gotham Partners, Michael Price's MFP Investors, Carl Icahn's Icahn Enterprises, and Dan Loeb's Third Point Re, to name a few, have a *significant advantage* over other fund managers because they can invest without worrying about their investors pulling the rug out from under them at the worst possible moment. With captive capital, these investors are the **strong hands** in the market.

The Efficient Market Hypothesis Remains "King of the Hill"

To address the question, "Is the market efficient?" we must realize that no model is perfect. Fama reaffirms this insight in his 1998 paper: "Like all models, market efficiency is a faulty description of price formation."[27]

The main question we continue to ponder is, "Are the exceptions to the efficient market hypothesis highlighted by academics, in favor of behavioral finance, large enough that it makes sense to reject the theory completely?" We believe the answer is no. In fact, Richard Thaler, a well-known proponent of behavioral finance, had an interesting response when asked the question, "How can behavioral finance help us consistently beat the stock market?" He responded with an unequivocal, "Two words . . . it can't."

Even if we ignore Thaler's comment, we can ask, "If we discard the market efficiency hypothesis, is there a better model of market behavior to replace it?" We believe that the answer to this question is, as of today,[28] not yet. Fama raises an excellent point in the next sentence from his article, "Following the standard scientific rule, however, market efficiency can only be replaced by a better specific model of price formation." Since no such model yet exists, the efficient market hypothesis remains the king of the hill. Nonetheless, the fact remains that there are anomalies in the market that can, and will, persist.

Although we know that Fama's efficient market hypothesis is less than perfect, we are reminded of Winston Churchill's famous quote about democracy, "No one pretends that democracy is perfect or all-wise. Indeed, it has been said that democracy is the worst form of government except all those other forms that have been tried from time to time."[29] To echo Churchill's democracy quote, although the efficient market hypothesis is not perfect, it remains the best overall description of how the stock market functions.

---

[27] Eugene F. Fama, "Market Efficiency, Long-Term Returns, and Behavioral Finance," *Journal of Financial Economics* 49, no. 3 (1998): 283–306.

[28] When we originally wrote this chapter and this footnote, "today" was May 9, 2016. But now, as we are reviewing page proofs, "today" is July 22, 2017. Over the past year, the authors are even more convinced that there is no foreseeable theory to replace the efficient markets hypothesis.

[29] Speech in the House of Commons, published in 206–07 *The Official Report, House of Commons* (5th Series), vol. 444, November 11, 1947.

Figure 7.23   Fama and Shiller Are Both Right!

Why Do We Care About Market Efficiency?

We care about market efficiency because, ironically, we *need* the markets to be efficient to generate alpha. If we can identify an error, such as a temporary inefficiency or mispricing, the only way for that mistake to be corrected is if the market is *eventually* efficient. The market must realize it has made a mistake and then correct that mistake for investors to generate alpha and outperform. The alternative view would be a market where a mispricing could persist forever. In such a world, no one could reliably outperform.

If we can identify information that has not been properly **disseminated**, a situation where **diversity** or **independence** has been compromised by some type of systematic error, or where there are impediments to **incorporation**, there is potentially a mispricing we can exploit. For this reason, understanding how market efficiency works and, perhaps more important, when the rules become distorted or even break can help investors determine where to look for mispriced securities, how they might be able to get an edge over other investors, and when to exploit those advantages.

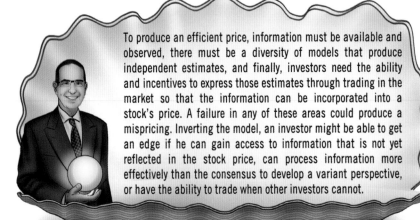

To produce an efficient price, information must be available and observed, there must be a diversity of models that produce independent estimates, and finally, investors need the ability and incentives to express those estimates through trading in the market so that the information can be incorporated into a stock's price. A failure in any of these areas could produce a mispricing. Inverting the model, an investor might be able to get an edge if he can gain access to information that is not yet reflected in the stock price, can process information more effectively than the consensus to develop a variant perspective, or have the ability to trade when other investors cannot.

Gems:

▽ The market price of a stock at any given moment represents the consensus estimate of the company's intrinsic value, which reflects the crowd's **expectations** of the company's future cash flow. A change in the stock price is driven by changes in the consensus **expectations** for the company's intrinsic value, reflecting changes in the crowd's **expectations** for the company's future cash flows. In simpler terms, stock prices change when investors' **expectations** change.

▽ If the market processes information absent any systematic error, then the stock will be priced efficiently. On the other hand, if there is **a systematic bias** in the market resulting in an error, then there is a reasonable likelihood that the consensus has overreacted and produced a mispricing. However, any apparent mispricing must be linked to the dissemination, processing, or incorporation of information because a systematic error can only happen if there is a failure in one of the following conditions of the wisdom of crowds:

- Information is either not **available** or not being **observed** by a sufficient number of investors.
- There is an insufficient amount of **domain-specific knowledge** within the collective.
- The crowd lacks **diversity**.
- There is a breakdown in the crowd's **independence**.
- Estimates are not being **expressed**, **aggregated** and **incorporated** into the market price.
- There is a lack of appropriate **incentives**.

- Although (micro) behavioral finance offers important insights into the potential errors individual investors can (and will) make, those errors will not have an impact on the collective's (macro) behavior unless the individual errors within the collective are systematic and correlated. Therefore, although individuals will not always make unbiased investment decisions, knowledge and understanding of these errors cannot be used to predict how the crowd will behave. Systematic bias within the collective will exist only when there is a lack of diversity or breakdown of independence within the crowd.

- Therefore, behavioral finance can cause mispricings in only three of the six conditions of the wisdom of crowds: **diversity**, **independence**, and **aggregation**.

- Behavioral finance explains what causes market inefficiencies by showing how systematic errors are formed and prevent market prices from fully reflecting all available information. **Behavioral finance is not an alternative to the efficient market hypothesis, it is a part of the efficient market hypothesis**.

- In a mania or bubble, greed overwhelms fear and investors become overly optimistic. Conversely, in a panic or crash, fear overwhelms greed and investors become overly pessimistic. During these episodes, stock prices move away from their true intrinsic value and valuations expand to large premiums or decline to significant discounts, as the stock prices become detached from the company's underlying fundamentals. The efficient market is cast aside as the crowd's fear and greed take over.

▽ If investors perceive that a stock has inadequate trading liquidity, they will not spend additional time looking at the idea, which may result in a mispriced security caused by illiquidity. These mispricings are often caused by investor "neglect."

CHAPTER 8

How to Add Value Through Research

As we explain in the previous three chapters, if the wisdom of crowds is functioning properly, then the stock price will fully reflect all available information and be a close approximation of the company's true intrinsic value. As a result, there will be no mispricing to exploit and no opportunity to outperform with this investment.

Take as an example Dollar General when the stock was trading in mid-2016 at $83 per share. The consensus estimate of the 21 sell-side analysts who followed the stock at the time was a one-year price target of $93, implying a 12% return. If you are researching Dollar General as a potential idea, unless you can identify a mispricing, your estimate of the company's intrinsic value would match consensus expectations, as shown in Figure 8.1.

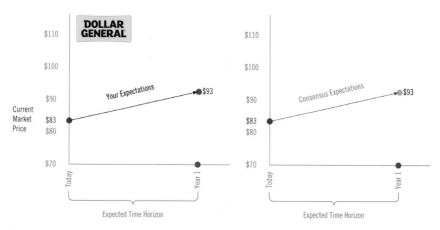

Figure 8.1   Dollar General One-Year Price Targets Without Mispricing

To identify a mispricing in a particular security, however, you must find a situation where there is a breakdown in one or more of the three tenets of market efficiency:

1. **Dissemination**—There is information the market is missing.

2. **Processing**—There is a systematic error in processing (caused by a lack of diversity or breakdown of independence).

3. **Incorporation**—There is something preventing information from being incorporated in the stock price (trading is limited because of liquidity or other institutional constraints or agency issues).

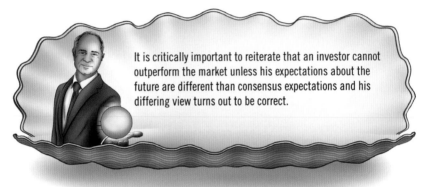

> It is critically important to reiterate that an investor cannot outperform the market unless his expectations about the future are different than consensus expectations and his differing view turns out to be correct.

If you can identify an inefficiency that cauces a mispricing, then your estimate of the company's intrinsic value will be different from the consensus. The "different from the consensus view" is known as a **variant perspective**, as shown in Figure 8.2:

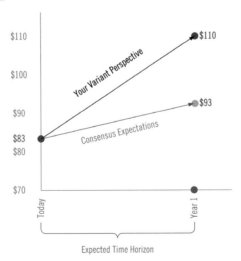

Figure 8.2   Dollar General: Variant Perspective Versus Consensus Expectations

As we state in Chapter 4, the estimated intrinsic value of an asset is the sum of the cash flows expected to be produced by that asset, over its useful life, discounted for the time value of money and the uncertainty of receiving those cash flows. Therefore, to have a true **variant perspective**, you must have a different outlook from the consensus for the company's future cash flow. These diverging expectations must translate into a different estimate of the company's **magnitude**, **duration**, **timing**, or **growth** of cash flows, as we show in Figure 8.3.

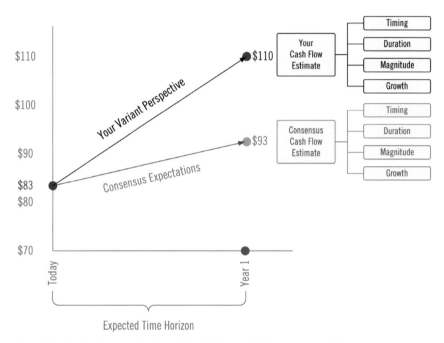

Figure 8.3   Variant Perspective Translates to Divergent Estimate for Cash Flows

Returning to the example of Zoe's Lemonade Stand in Chapter 4, we estimate the lemonade stand's intrinsic value to equal $9.41 per share, assuming no revenue growth, and $11.97 per share, assuming 10% revenue growth.

Let's say that your boss asks you to analyze Zoe's business to determine if it makes sense for him to buy the stock. First, you need to determine **consensus expectations**. You read research reports, speak with the analysts who follow the company, and contact current shareholders to get their viewpoint. You conclude from your research that the **consensus** believes that there will be no growth in future cash flow because the current structure and demographics of the neighborhood will limit the growth in foot traffic in front of Zoe's house. The **consensus view** is that the business is worth $9.41 per share.

You decide to conduct additional research and attempt to gather nonmaterial, nonpublic information and quasi-public information to augment your analysis. As a result of this research, you learn that there is a public hearing scheduled in a few weeks to discuss the re-zoning of a large parcel of land at the end of Zoe's block. In discussions with local politicians and real estate developers, you learn there is a proposal, which has not yet been submitted to the town, to build a park with a large swimming pool on the land. You conclude from your analysis that if the project moves forward, the new park and pool will increase the foot traffic past Zoe's house significantly, which will increase the revenue and cash flow of her lemonade stand substantially. Using this information, you forecast 10% cash flow growth for Zoe's Lemonade Stand, which implies a target price of $11.97. Since you have a view that is different from the consensus and believe you are correct, you have a **variant perspective**, the difference of which is shown in Figure 8.4.

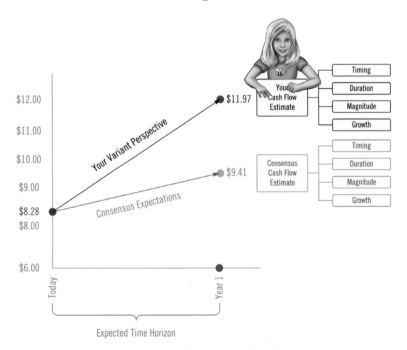

Figure 8.4   Divergent View of Future Cash Flows Produces Variant Perspective

The basis for your variant perspective lies in your estimate for a growth in cash flows that differs from the consensus view, as shown in Figure 8.5.

Figure 8.5   Consensus Expectations and Your Variant Perspective For Future Cash Flows

You need to address two critical questions in your analysis: "If the stock is truly mispriced, what is the market missing?"and "What is causing the inefficiency?" You conclude, from reviewing the different tenets of market efficiency, that there is **information** that has not been adequately disseminated, as shown in Figure 8.6.

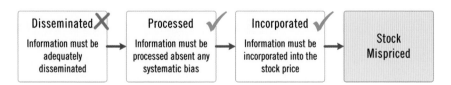

Figure 8.6   Stock Mispriced Due to Information Not Being Fully Disseminated

You believe there is a high probability that the large parcel of land will be developed into a park over the next 12 months. If this information were adequately disseminated, processed without systematic error, and incorporated into the stock price, it would trade at a higher price ($11.97) because the stock would then **fully reflect all available information**, as the process shows in Figure 8.7.

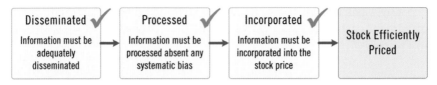

Figure 8.7   Absence of Errors Leads to Efficiently Priced Stock

While this example is simple and makes a lot of assumptions, it illustrates the basic concept of what is necessary for an investor to develop an **investment edge**. We need to more fully develop the concept of **variant perception** before moving forward, which we trace back to a legendary hedge fund manager, Michael Steinhardt.

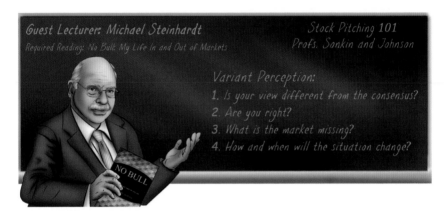

In an interview with Charlie Rose in 2001, Steinhardt explained his concept of variant perception succinctly: "One of the few sure ways to make money in the market is to have a view that is off consensus and have that view turn out to be right." In his 2001 autobiography, *No Bull: My Life In and Out of Markets*, Steinhardt further discusses this concept, which he developed in the deep bear market of the early 1970s:

> During this period, I began to consciously articulate the virtue of using variant perception as an analytic tool. I defined variant perception as holding a well-founded view that was meaningfully different from market consensus. I often said that the only analytic tool that mattered was an intellectually advantaged disparate view. This included knowing more and perceiving the situation better than others did. It was also critical to have a keen understanding of what the market expectations truly were. Thus, the process by which a disparate perception, when correct, became consensus would almost

inevitably lead to meaningful profit. Understanding market expectation was at least as important as, and often different from, fundamental knowledge.[1]

We want to hammer home this point because it is important in
developing an investment edge. There are four critical questions
you need to ask to determine if you truly have a **variant perspective**:

1. *Is your view different from the consensus?* You must have a view
   that is meaningfully different from the market's view.
2. *Are you right?* Your estimate of value must be more accurate
   than the consensus because you either possess better information or have performed superior analysis.
3. *What is the market missing?* You can identify why the current consensus expectations are wrong and whether there is an error
   in **dissemination**, **processing**, or **incorporation** of information.
4. *How and when will the situation change?* You are confident that
   within an identifiable time period, other investors will realize
   that consensus expectations are wrong and reprice the stock
   to correct the mistake and eliminate the inefficiency.

Simply stated, to have a variant perspective, your view needs to
be different *and* correct. Benjamin Graham touched upon this concept in *The Intelligent Investor*, when he wrote, "Have the courage of
your knowledge and experience. If you have formed a conclusion
from the facts and if you know your judgment is sound, act on it—
even though others may hesitate or differ. (You are neither right nor
wrong because the crowd disagrees with you. You are right because
your data and reasoning are right.)"[2]

In the case of Zoe's Lemonade Stand, you have a view that was
different from the consensus, which satisfies the first element of
the **Steinhardt framework**. Based on your research, you believe you
have better information and superior insight, and are confident that
your perspective is correct, which satisfies the second element of the
framework. From your discussions with analysts and shareholders,
you understand why current expectations are wrong—other investors and analysts are unaware of the proposal for a future park and

[1] Michael Steinhardt, *No Bull: My Life In and Out of Markets* (New York: Wiley, 2001).
[2] Benjamin Graham, *The Intelligent Investor: A Book of Practical Counsel* (New York: HarperBusiness, 1973).

pool—which satisfies the third element. Last, you have confidence that when approval of the project is properly disseminated, processed, and incorporated, other investors will recognize their mistake and reprice the stock.

To outperform the market, you need to have a **variant perspective** that provides you an "edge" or advantage to exploit the inefficiency. These advantages fall into three categories, which mirror the market inefficiencies we discuss in Chapter 5:

1. An **informational advantage** is present when you have information other investors do not have and, as a result, has not been adequately disseminated. With an informational advantage the investor can state, "I know this is true."

2. An **analytical advantage** is present when you see things others do not see because there is some type of systematic error (lack of diversity or breakdown in independence) that obscures other investors' views. With an analytical advantage the investor can state, "I think this will happen."

3. A **trading advantage** is present when you can trade or hold the security when investors are unable to take or hold a position.

The entire process, which incorporates elements from the three previous chapters on market efficiency, is shown in Figure 8.8.

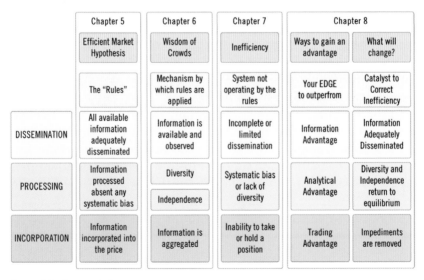

Figure 8.8   Research Process

As Figure 8.8 shows, Chapter 5, states the rules of market efficiency; Chapter 6, explains the mechanism by which those rules are implemented; and Chapter 7, discusses instances where errors might result in inefficiencies. In this chapter, we discuss ways to gain an edge when the rules of market efficiency are strained and how inefficiencies are corrected.

Informational Advantage

A pure **informational advantage** exists when an investor has **material nonpublic** information to which no (or few) other investors have access. The fact that the information is **material** means that it alone would move the stock price, as we discuss in Chapter 5, The investor can say in this situation "I *know* with certainty that this information is true." However, as we previously emphasize, this type of advantage is usually not attainable because of the legalities of trading on material nonpublic information.

Reading an SEC complaint, which the Commission files when charging someone with insider trading, provides a detailed account of how a particular investor can outperform by illegally trading on material nonpublic information.[3] In contrast, there are only a few isolated incidents that offer a window into what it would look like if an investor had a pure information advantage that is *legal*. We should emphasize again that these situations are extremely rare.[4]

---

[3] For example, the following account is a portion of an SEC complaint filed on May 19, 2016: "This case involves repeated and very profitable insider trading by professional sports bettor William 'Billy' Walters based on tips received from his long-time friend, Thomas C. Davis, a director of Dean Foods Company. From 2008 through 2012, Davis tipped Walters with highly-confidential information concerning Dean Foods including sneak previews of at least six of the company's quarterly earnings announcements and advance notice of the spin-off of Dean Foods's profitable subsidiary, The WhiteWave Foods Company . . . . Based on these tips, Walters traded Dean Foods . . . securities and reaped illicit trading profits and avoided losses totaling at least $40 million." To read more, Google "SEC complaint Walters Davis."

[4] For example, if a CEO *unintentionally* makes an off-the-cuff remark that discloses material nonpublic information to an investor or a group of investors. Under Regulation FD, the company needs to make a public disclosure within the next 24 hours or the start of the next day's trading, whichever comes sooner.

One such example occurred on April 28, 2015, when Twitter's first-quarter earnings announcement was posted by mistake on its website at 3:07:56 p.m.—an hour before it was supposed to be officially released. A company called Selerity used its web scraping program to discover the announcement. Without any human involvement, Selerity's software ran the release through several natural language processing algorithms, ascertained the information was genuine, and generated a tweet automatically at 3:07:59 p.m.—a mere three seconds later. Twitter's trading volume jumped significantly, and the stock price drifted lower as investors who saw (and believed) the information realized that Twitter's financial results were worse than expected and that other investors would be disappointed by the news.

By the time trading in the stock was halted by the exchange at 3:29 p.m. it had declined 5%, down $2.56 to $48.67. When the stock resumed trading at 3:48 p.m., after the news had been fully disseminated, it reopened at $40.86, down another $7.81, for an additional loss of 16%. Traders who exploited the inadvertent news release had a clear **informational advantage** over other investors, as demonstrated by the stock's ultimate, and full, reaction to the news, as shown in Figure 8.9.

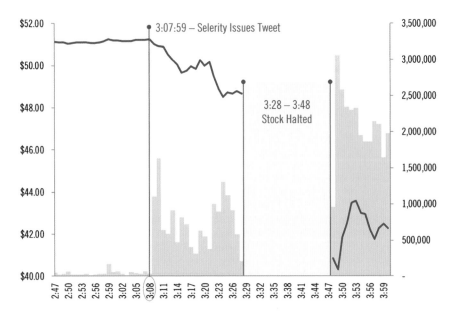

Figure 8.9   Twitter's Stock Performance in Reaction to Its Inadvertent First Quarter Earnings Release

A total of 15.2 million shares traded during the 21 minutes between the Selerity tweet and when trading in the stock was halted. Although several traders exploited the inadvertent news release, it was clear an inefficiency existed because the new information was not adequately disseminated, and therefore not incorporated into the stock price, as shown in Figure 8.10.

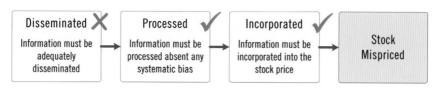

Figure 8.10   Stock Mispriced Due to Information Not Being Fully Disseminated

The materiality of the information was confirmed by the price move when the stock reopened after the news had been broadly disseminated. The investors who had the information contained in the premature release *knew* that the earnings were disappointing when other investors did not. They sold stock before trading was halted because they believed they had a pure **informational advantage**. And it was perfectly legal.

Running this example through the Steinhardt framework confirms that the possession of the information by certain investors gave them a variant perspective:

1. *Was the view different from the consensus?* Yes, investors with the information knew that Twitter had missed analyst consensus estimates for the quarter.

2. *Are you right?* Yes, the advantaged investors knew the information was from a reliable source and accurate.

3. *What is the market missing?* Since the release was not adequately disseminated, the consensus did not have the information of the earnings miss.

4. *When and why will the situation change?* The advantaged investors knew that as soon as the information was adequately disseminated, the stock price would change to **fully reflect** the new information.

Analytical Advantage

Whereas an **informational advantage** is made possible by an inefficiency in the **dissemination** of information, an **analytical advantage**
is made possible by an inefficiency or error in how the market *processes* that information. An investor possesses a *pure* analytical advantage when they see things other investors do not see. An investor
with an analytical advantage can look at the exact same set of public
information as other investors, yet, after analyzing the data, arrives
at an estimated value for the stock that differs from the consensus
and ultimately proves to be correct.

This type of inefficiency is caused by a **systematic error** in the
processing of information from either a lack of diversity or a breakdown in independence, as we discuss in Chapter 6. **Diversity** exists
when individuals in the crowd have different expertise, know different facts, and use different models to arrive at their estimate of
intrinsic value. On the other hand, if the market participants have the
same facts and expertise, use the *same* model, and begin thinking the
same way, then diversity is lost. Without diversity, the crowd produces
an answer that is only a small deviation from the average individual
estimate. In these situations, the crowd's estimate reflects just a single
view rather than multiple views, like the neon nose diagnosis example
in Chapter 6.

In contrast, **independence** is defined as individuals making
guesses autonomously from others in the crowd. If enough of the
participants are influenced and in turn, biased in a systematic way,
the wisdom of crowds collapses to what is essentially a single view or
the view of only a few individuals.

If you possess a true **analytical advantage**, you see the situation differently from other investors because *you* have identified
a **systematic error**. As time passes and events unfold, the other
investors see what you saw and their perception changes to yours.
As your variant nonconsensus view of the stock's true intrinsic
value is proven to be correct, it becomes the new consensus view,
the market corrects, the stock reprices, and your investment
outperforms.

While we discussed in detail the processing errors that result
from a lack of diversity or breakdown in independence in Chapter 6,
we can illustrate this concept with a simple example. The following
story dovetails nicely with Robert Shiller's definition of a bubble,

which he described as "a situation in which news of price increases spurs investor enthusiasm which spreads by psychological contagion from person to person."[5]

Imagine there is an engineered virus that is released by a nefarious radical group, causing a pandemic that renders people colorblind.[6] After being infected, most people see nothing but gray dots when looking at the following image:

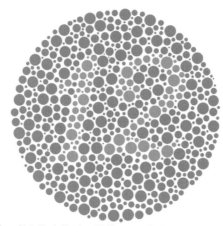

Ishihara Plate No. 1 (Number 12) Nicoguaro. Redrawn with permission.

The virus doesn't infect everyone. Some people are immune, and you are among that group. You look at the same image, and, as plain as day, see the number 12.

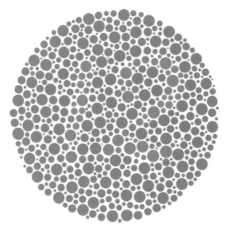

Ishihara Plate No. 1 (Number 12)—Nicoguaro

---

[5] Robert J. Shiller, "Do Stock Prices Move Too Much to Be Justified by Subsequent Changes in Dividends?" *American Economic Review* 71, no. 3, (June 1981).

[6] We loosely based this example on the 2011 movie *Contagion*.

Weeks later, you argue with friends, exclaiming, "Can't you see the number 12? It's right there in front of you." They reply, "I don't know what you are talking about. I'm staring right at the picture and all I see is a bunch of gray dots."

Meanwhile, a team of scientists at the Centers for Disease Control (CDC) frantically works around the clock to find a cure. After a successful vaccine is finally developed, the CDC does everything in its power to produce enough of the antidote, but production is limited and vaccinations are rationed in a lottery based on an individual's birthday, although everyone will receive the medicine over the course of the next 12 months (approximately 1/365 of the population is cured each day). The drug is effective and people's ability to see colors returns immediately after being vaccinated. Your friends look at the image after receiving the vaccine and exclaim, "Hey, I can see the number 12. Now I know what you were talking about!"

The investment world often seems like this fictional story when you have a pure analytical advantage. You see patterns that others don't see, and you often cannot understand why they don't see what seems obvious to you. Assuming you are right, as events unfold over time, other investors eventually begin to see what you originally saw, almost as if they have been cured of some illness, and the stock reprices to reflect your view. Keep in mind that the speed at which investors are "cured" can vary wildly from situation to situation, which is why mispricings can correct in a short period of time or persist for years.[7]

An example similar to this story involves one of Paul S.'s former students, Dan Krueger,[8] who made an investment in Herbalife convertible bonds in 2014.[9] Herbalife is a multilevel marketing company founded in 1980 that sells nutritional products primarily for weight loss. In December 2012, Bill Ackman of Pershing Square, a savvy and successful investor, gave a three-and-a-half-hour, 342-slide presentation

---

[7] This example dovetails with the concept of a 'threshold dose' and the characterization that "a sufficient number of investors are required for the situation to change."

[8] Dan is a partner and portfolio manager at Owl Creek Asset Management (the firm founded by Jeff Altman, who worked for legendary value investor Michael Price at Mutual Shares). Dan is also an adjunct professor at Columbia Business School, where he teaches a class on distressed debt investing.

[9] Convertible bonds are debt securities that are convertible into common stock at a predetermined price. One can think of the security as a "plain vanilla" debt instrument with an embedded call option on the common stock. Instead of getting back his principal upon maturity, the holder has the option to either receive his original principal or convert his investment into a fixed ratio of common stock.

disclosing a huge short position he held in Herbalife's stock. Ackman concluded his remarks by claiming that Herbalife was nothing more than a Ponzi scheme and "a criminal enterprise." After the presentation, the stock promptly fell 42% to $24.24 per share. Ackman said that he thought the stock was "a zero." Eventually, both the U.S. Securities and Exchange Commission (SEC) and U.S. Federal Trade Commission (FTC) opened investigations into Herbalife, most likely prompted by the publicity around Ackman's presentation. In late July 2014, Herbalife posted earnings that missed analyst estimates, and Ackman gave another three-hour presentation. He was so emotional in his delivery that his eyes welled up with tears. The second presentation was extremely persuasive, and the stock fell by 28% that week, while Herbalife's convertible bonds fell by 19% to a price of $78.[10]

The investor base for Herbalife convertible bonds at that time consisted primarily of two distinct groups: convertible arbitrage investors and investment-grade bond investors. Using sophisticated computer models, convertible arbitrage investors buy corporate bonds and sell stock short against their bond position. The investment strategy exploits any mispricing between the bonds and the common stock. Investment grade bond investors, on the other hand, perform fundamental research to identify bonds that offer an attractive return relative to the investor's estimate of the bond's probability of default. Both groups of investors sold bonds during the week after Ackman's second presentation, although for different reasons. The convertible arbitrage investors liquidated their positions because their computer models instructed them to do so when the stock collapsed, while the investment grade bond investors liquidated their positions because they feared the probability that Herbalife might default had increased substantially.

Wall Street bond "experts" looking at the situation at the time calculated that a more "appropriate" value of the bonds was $87 rather than the $78 price quoted for the bonds after the sell-off. While the information from Ackman's presentation was adequately disseminated, the apparent mispricing was caused by investors **processing** the information with a **systematic error** resulting from a pre-existing lack of **diversity** in the two groups holding the Herbalife bonds was exacerbated by a breakdown in **independence**, as shown in Figure 8.11.

---

[10] Bonds are quoted as dollars vs. par value, which is usually $100, although the face amount of bonds is usually $1,000.

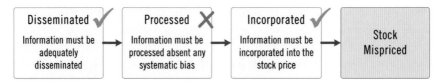

Figure 8.11   Error in Processing Results in Mispriced Stock

The pre-existing investor base lacked **diversity** because it was dominated by the two groups of bond investors, who, within their respective groups, used similar models. The situation was like the herding behavior that occurred during the Quant Crisis in 2007, which we discuss in Chapter 7. While the lack of diversity did not create a mispricing by itself, Ackman's presentation acted as an external force to **skew** the consensus and create a mispricing.

Many of the investment-grade investors believed that Ackman had performed an exhaustive analysis and was correct in his assessment of Herbalife's financial health. These investors set aside their own estimates of intrinsic value in reaction to Ackman's comments and adopted his view, creating an **information cascade**. The result was that investors who might have stepped in to purchase the Herbalife bonds at $87 (where the "experts" felt they should have traded) stood on the sidelines.

Dan, and other investors like him, reached a different conclusion than the consensus view solely based on their analysis of the same public information that all other investors had access to and, as a consequence, developed a **variant perspective**.

Dan made several important observations as he performed his analysis. The decline in the price of the bonds was driven by investors' fear that Ackman was right and the FTC would shut down Herbalife. However, the FTC has jurisdiction over only the company's US operations. The bonds were issued and backed by Herbalife's international subsidiary, which accounted for 80% of the company's revenue. Therefore, even in a worst-case scenario, with the US entity being forced into bankruptcy, the foreign entity would not be directly impacted. Also, the assets and cash flow of the international subsidiary were more than adequate to meet the debt obligation. More to the point, there was no guarantee that the FTC would rule against Herbalife or, if it did, that the US entity would be forced into bankruptcy. Dan bought Herbalife bonds after he concluded that the risk of default was much lower than the price of the bonds implied.

Dan had no special information in this situation. All the information was public, Dan just had better insight. He looked at the same data set that was available to all investors and drew a different conclusion. His **analytical advantage** created a true **variant perspective**. He believed the market view was wrong and had confidence that the default risk of the foreign subsidiary was highly unlikely and, ironically, never really in question despite Ackman's accusations. As the consensus view changed to match Dan's variant perspective, the bonds recovered in price, generating excess returns for Dan's fund.

Reviewing the situation through the Steinhardt framework shows that Dan had developed a variant perspective:

1. *Was the view different from the consensus?* Yes, Dan believed the market was overreacting to the possibility of default.

2. *Are you right?* Yes, Dan could demonstrate that even if the US subsidiary declared bankruptcy, the bonds of the international subsidiary had little default risk.

3. *What is the market missing?* The constituency of convertible arbitrage investors was selling based on their computer models and ignoring the company's fundamentals; the other constituency of investment-grade investors was swayed by Ackman's accusations and overestimated the possibility of default. New investors who might have purchased the bonds were dissuaded from doing so by Ackman's presentation.

4. *When and why will the situation change?* As investors realized that the default risk of the bonds was low, the mispricing would correct and the securities would trade back to their previous value.

As the answers to the four questions show, Dan had developed a view that was different from consensus expectations, as shown in Figure 8.12 A. For Dan, it was a win-win situation. While he expected the Herbalife bonds to trade back to par quickly once investors realized that they had overreacted to Ackman's presentation, which would result in a 28% total return on his investment, he would earn 12.2% annually in the event he had to wait for the bonds to reach maturity, as we show in Figures 8.12 A and B.

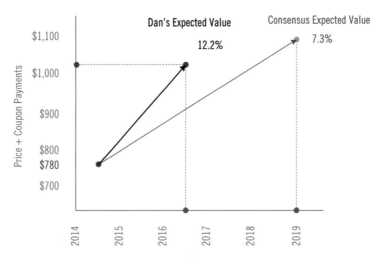

Figure 8.12A   Dan's Expected Return from Herbalife Bond Position

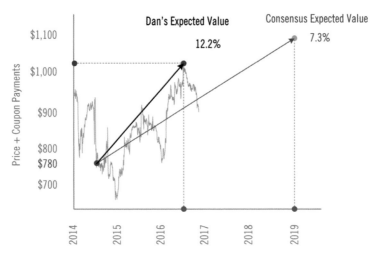

Figure 8.12B   Dan's Actual Return from Herbalife Bond Position

We should emphasize that developing a **variant perspective** solely based on a *pure* analytical advantage is hard to achieve, even for the most experienced investors. It requires a lot of experience and deep **domain-specific knowledge** to pick up on these types of mispricings.

Informational + Analytical Advantage

Because pure **informational advantages** are rare and pure **analytical advantages** require decades of experience, the most common way successful investors identify mispriced securities to outperform the market is by blending the two, combining an informational advantage with an analytical advantage.

This process usually begins with the analyst digesting all publicly available information. An experienced analyst knows where to focus his efforts, which makes this process quick and efficient. If the idea is sufficiently interesting, the analyst will do a deeper dive, which usually entails collecting additional pieces of information, most of which is nonmaterial and nonpublic, or quasi-public. The analyst applies his analytical process to all the information with the **goal of reaching a conclusion that is material, nonpublic**, **but** *legal.* Judge Walter Roe Mansfield of the United States Court of Appeals for the Second Circuit summed up succinctly his views on this approach in 1980, in his decision in *Elkind v. Liggett & Myers, Inc.*:

> A skilled analyst with knowledge of the company and the industry may be able to piece together seemingly inconsequential data with public information into a mosaic[11] to produce a meaningful analytical edge.[12]

It is important to emphasize that the nonmaterial, nonpublic information *alone* would not impact the stock price because the information is nonmaterial, by definition. The information is merely *a piece* in Judge Mansfield's mosaic. When that piece of information is added to the analyst's overall assessment of the opportunity, he begins to see something other investors failed to perceive and the overall picture becomes clearer. The inefficiency in the stock price, and the opportunity for the analyst to develop a **variant perspective**, is caused by the fact that the nonmaterial, nonpublic information has not been **disseminated** and, therefore, has not made its way into the crowd's processing models. The analyst has created an edge by using his analytical expertise to direct

---

[11] As an aside, this is the origin of the term *mosaic theory* in security analysis.
[12] *Elkind v. Liggett & Myers, Inc.*, 635 F.2d 156, Court of Appeals, 2nd Circuit, 1980.

his research process. He has combined nonmaterial, nonpublic information with the fully disseminated public information in a unique way to create a differing view from the consensus. In other words, the analyst has developed a variant perspective based on his informational and analytical edge.

We use a small public company, which we will call Cloverland Timber, as an example to illustrate this point. Although the example is based on a true story, we have taken a little poetic license with the facts and changed the names to protect the innocent (and the guilty).

The company in the example owns and manages approximately 160,000 acres of timberland in northern Wisconsin. At the time the story begins, the family of the founder still controlled approximately 26% of the company's outstanding shares.

In 2013, John Helve of Brownfield Capital became aware of Cloverland and began conducting research. Cloverland's primary asset is its timberlands, which the company harvests to generate cash flow. The company has the timberlands appraised every three years by an independent third party. Management uses the appraisal to value the company's assets and provides the estimates to its shareholders. The most recent appraisal estimated the timberland's value at $140 million, or $865 per acre, which equates to a per share value of $107. At the market price of $78 per share, it appeared to John that the stock was trading at a significant discount to its intrinsic value, although the expected annual return would be dependent on how long would it take for investors to realize the value and close the gap.

John accepted the company's appraised value of the timberland in his initial analysis and assumed a 3% annual growth in the value of the trees,[13] which would result in a per share value of $144 in 10 years. John also calculated that the spread between the stock price and intrinsic value would have to close within the next five years for the stock to generate an annual return above the S&P 500's historical long-term return of approximately 9.7%. From John's vantage point, if the gap closes in less than five years, the stock will outperform the market. If it takes exactly five years for the gap to close, then the stock's annual return will equal the long-term average of the S&P 500. However, if it takes longer than five years for the gap to close, the stock will underperform the market. We show this analysis in Figure 8.13.

---

[13] This assumption was based on how much an average tree typically grows in a year.

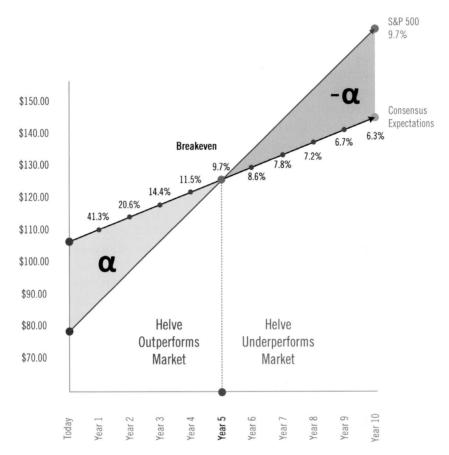

Figure 8.13   Investment Time Horizon and Breakeven Point

John inferred from this analysis that the consensus time horizon *must be* five years or less. Therefore, as part of his analysis, John was on the lookout for any event or corporate development that would cause the gap to close sooner than the implied five-year consensus time horizon.

Consensus expectations became clear to John as he performed his research. Timber is considered to be a unique asset in that trees physically grow larger every year, which increases their financial value. As long as management is prudent and doesn't overcut the trees, there is limited risk to the value of the timberland.

Through his analysis, John noticed certain operating metrics in the financial statements that indicated to him the timberlands were, in fact, being undercut, meaning that management was not harvesting the trees to optimize cash flow and maximize shareholder value.

This strategy could be explained by the fact that the family that controlled Cloverland had significant financial incentives to keep the company's value low to minimize estate taxes.

John surmised that while Cloverland owned attractive assets that were trading at a discount to their intrinsic value, from an average investor's point of view, there was no way to realize the value. There were also other negative factors affecting the situation. Cloverland's stock was not listed on an organized exchange like the NYSE or NASDAQ, and the company was not required to file periodic financial reports with the SEC. In addition, its market capitalization was small and the market for the stock was illiquid.

John recognized that these impediments would discourage investors from buying the stock, and the shareholder list reflected these constraints. The company's shareholder base was comprised primarily of long-term, "deep-value" investors who gravitated toward situations where they could buy assets at a discount, although often without a predetermined catalyst to realize the value. Investors on Wall Street sometimes characterize these situations as "sleeping beauties." These stocks might be "asleep" with little movement for years and years, and then, one day, wake up and reward investors for their patience. However, it is important to note that the group of shareholders in many of these situations lacks diversity because the investors all think the same way.

These factors most likely explain why the stock appeared to trade at a large discount to its intrinsic value, as indicated in Figure 8.13. The mispricing was caused by both a breakdown in **processing** (caused by a lack of **diversity** in the shareholder base) and impediments to **incorporation** (caused by the stock's low liquidity).

However, the mispricing may be a mirage and the investment may be what is referred to as a "value trap." An investor looking at the situation for the first time might buy the stock *thinking* that the value will be realized in less than five years, but if history is an accurate guide, this assumption will be overly optimistic. As Cloverland's shareholders can testify, Cloverland stock has increased by only 2% in the 10 years ending November 2016, while the S&P 500 increased by 58%, producing 56 percentage points of negative underperformance for anyone holding the stock for the prior decade.

John had a **variant perspective** because he believed that a more detailed physical appraisal of the timberland would show that the trees were more valuable than the company's published appraisal. Also, because Cloverland did not file with the SEC, John's fund could accumulate a large position in the company without having to file a notice with the SEC if his fund's ownership exceeded 5%, or even 10%, which is required if an issuer files periodic reports with the SEC.

Normally, forestry experts determine the value of timberland by driving around the property in off-road vehicles and recording statistics such as the species, age, and acreage density of the trees. The experts use that information to estimate the timberland's per-acre value. The process is a low-tech, time-consuming, pen-and-paper process. In Cloverland's case, the company owns 160,000 acres of timberland, spanning 250 square miles, which is an enormous area to survey comprehensively. Rather than analyze each acre, the experts based their appraisal on sampling various sections of the property, which, depending on the size of the sample, can result in highly inaccurate assessments.

In an ideal world, John would conduct his own appraisal and survey each and every acre. However, that wasn't possible for two reasons. First, surveying each acre using traditional methods would be exceedingly time-consuming and prohibitively expensive. Second, the timberlands were private property and it would be highly unlikely that the company would grant John access. Sitting in his office, John thought, "How could I get an accurate estimate with all these constraints?" The answer was technology.

John realized the most cost-effective solution would be to hire a company that specializes in valuing timberland using satellite images. The company he selected starts its analysis by leasing time on a satellite, flying the satellite over the area they want to survey, and taking photographs. The consultants then use computer algorithms to accurately determine the species and size of the trees, and their density per acre. Their methods provide a more accurate value of the timberlands than that used traditionally in the industry, as it eliminates sampling errors.

John was pleasantly surprised by the survey results. The consultants determined that a large percentage of the trees were sugar maple, a hardwood that is much more valuable than softwoods. While Cloverland mentioned in their published survey that there was an "above-average mix of hardwood," the company offered no additional information about their findings. John now had detailed information about the trees. The analysis also confirmed John's suspicions that the trees were undercut, and in fact, the age of the trees was much greater than the average forest. In John's opinion, these factors meant that the value per acre was significantly higher than the appraised value. His newly revised value for the timberlands was

$1,130 per acre, or $142 per share. John's estimate of intrinsic value represented an implied total return of 81% from the market price of $78 per share, with little downside risk.

John was concerned that his fund's accumulation of shares would likely put upward pressure on the stock price, even if he was patient and purchased shares slowly over time. Factoring in the unavoidable price increase caused by his share purchases, John estimated that his fund's average cost would be approximately $85 per share for his entire position. Rerunning his analysis with the higher estimated purchase price and the new intrinsic value estimate of $142 per share, John's expected annual rate of return looked even more appealing because the potential total return was higher and the time frame to match the S&P 500's return was now three years longer, as shown in Figure 8.14:

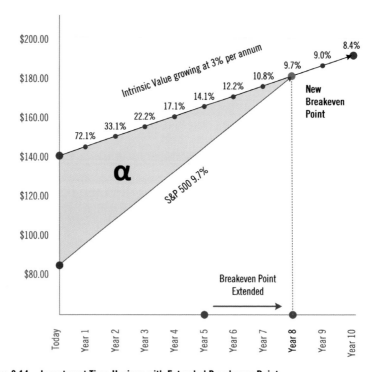

Figure 8.14   Investment Time Horizon with Extended Breakeven Point

The average long-term return for the S&P 500 has been approximately 9.7% since 1926. John assumed in his analysis that the market would generate a similar return in the future. Therefore, he calculated that he had roughly eight years for the stock to reach his estimated future intrinsic value before the investment under-performed the market. The most comforting aspect of the invest-ment was that the return profile was **asymmetrical**. John estimated that there was an opportunity for significant gains with little down-side risk. What about timing? The consensus expectations were that the value was trapped by the large family ownership, a view that was reinforced by the numerous unsuccessful attempts by an activist investor named Ron, who repeatedly tried to get board representation. John felt strongly that he could do a better job of motivating management to unlock value for shareholders. He felt that the best way to realize the true value of the timberlands was to sell the company. He estimated that it might take as long as three years to get the company sold, although there was risk in that he might not be successful. Even if he wasn't successful in forcing a sale of the company, John calculated that there was little downside risk to the investment. Figure 8.15 shows John's **variant perspective**, based on his estimated intrinsic value and expected time horizon, resulting in an implied annual return on the invest-ment of 22.2%.

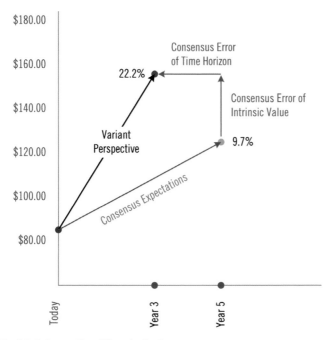

Figure 8.15   John's Perception of Error by the Consensus

John's fund, Brownfield, acquired a significant percentage of Cloverland stock over the next two years, which ultimately matched the family's ownership stake of 26%. Brownfield disclosed this position in the first half of 2016 and was given a board seat shortly thereafter. In late December 2016, Brownfield obtained another board seat and, to avoid a proxy battle, Cloverland's board agreed to engage an investment banker to explore a sale of the company.

John's view differed from the consensus in two important ways. First, he believed the **magnitude** of future cash flows would be higher because the timberlands were worth $1,130 per acre rather than the consensus view of $865. Second, his view on the **time** it would take to realize the value was three years compared to the consensus implied view of five years.

Running this example through the Steinhardt's framework highlights John's investment edge:

1. *Was the view different from the consensus?* Yes. John believed the value per acre to be much higher and the time frame to realize that value much shorter than the consensus view.

2. *Are you right?* Yes. John had the satellite data to back up his estimated value. Although he could not be certain that he could shorten the time frame to realize that value, he was confident that there was little downside risk to his investment.

3. *What is the market missing?* The market did not have the satellite data or know that John was planning to become an activist and ultimately pressure management to sell the company to a third party.

4. *When and why will the situation change?* John believed strongly that he could force management to engage in a "liquidity event" to unlock value for shareholders within three years.

Trading Advantage

Whereas an **informational advantage** is made possible by an inefficiency in the **dissemination** of information and an **analytical advantage** is made possible by an inefficiency in how the market **processes** that information, a **trading advantage** is caused by an inefficiency that prevents the information from being **incorporated** into the stock price because of impediments that limit investors from trading.

If an investor possesses a true **trading advantage**, he can trade a security when other investors are unable or unwilling to take or hold a position. We discuss this limitation at length in Chapter 7, where we identified two main institutional constraints as its cause. The first is liquidity constraints that limit an investor's ability to execute or trade a security. The second is anticipated or actual redemptions from clients that prevent an investor from taking a position in the first place or holding a position long enough for the market to correct the mispricing. We show in Figure 8.16 how an impediment to incorporation can result in a mispricing.

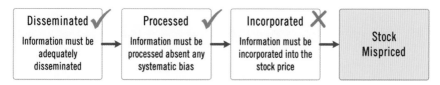

Figure 8.16   Stock Mispricing Caused by Error in Incorporation

To circumvent the liquidity constraint and obtain an advantage, the investor either must be patient while he accumulates a position over time or have a smaller fund or smaller position sizes that enables him to accumulate a full position in a less liquid security.

Captive, loyal, or permanent capital eliminates the fear of redemptions, giving managers with this type of capital a significant advantage over other funds because they can invest without worrying about their investors redeeming their capital at the worst possible moment.

Catalysts

Before we can communicate how to think correctly about **catalysts**, we need to do a bit of a review. First, we need to solidify the understanding of:

- What conditions are necessary for a stock to be efficiently priced.
- What creates an advantage or investment edge.
- What defines a variant perspective.

A stock will be efficiently priced if it *reflects all available information,* which means that:

- Information is adequately **disseminated** with market participants observing, extracting, and aggregating the information.
- Information is **processed** by market participants who evaluate and estimate without systematic error.
- Information is **expressed**, **aggregated**, and **incorporated** into the stock price through trading.

These conditions are shown in Figure 8.17.

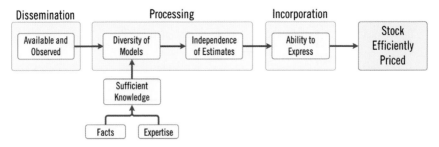

Figure 8.17   **Requirements for an Efficient Stock Price**

We can conclude that the consensus will *fail* to produce an efficiently priced stock *only* if at least one of the following four conditions exists:[14]

1. Information is not **available** and **observed** by a sufficient number of investors.
2. There is a lack of **diversity**.
3. There is a breakdown in **independence**.
4. Estimates are not **expressed**, **aggregated**, and **incorporated** into the market price.

For an investor to obtain an advantage, he needs to develop an **informational advantage** by gathering information the consensus does not have, an **analytical advantage** by seeing something the consensus does not see, or a **trading advantage** where he can trade when other investors cannot or will not trade.

---

[14] Technically there are six conditions that can prevent the wisdom of crowds from functioning correctly. However, because we are hard pressed to identify situations in the stock market where a lack of domain-specific knowledge or incentives creates a mispricing, we focus on the remaining four conditions in this discussion.

To have a **variant perspective**, an investor needs to identify a genuine mispricing or an error made by the market, which means that:

The investor has a view that is different from the consensus: The differing view is reflected by a spread between the stock's price and its intrinsic value. The larger the gap, the greater the potential return and the more the investor's view differs from the consensus.

The investor is right: The investor can demonstrate that they have an informational advantage, analytical advantage, or a trading advantage, and has performed sufficient research to be confident in their claim.

The investor can identify exactly what the market is missing: The investor has identified and understands what is causing the mispricing in the market, which must be an error in the dissemination, processing, or incorporation of information.

The fourth requirement—that *the analyst can estimate with precision when and why the situation will change*—is where **catalysts** enter the discussion. A catalyst is defined as any event that begins to close the gap between the stock price and *your* estimate of intrinsic value, represented by the shaded gray triangle in Figure 8.18.

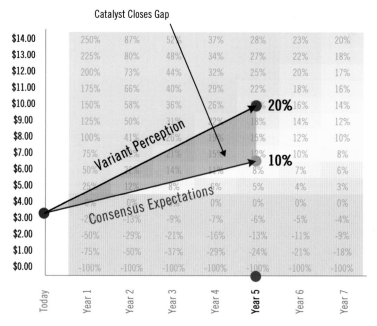

Figure 8.18   Stock Performance Heat Map

> Because stock prices change when consensus expectations change, a catalyst is any event that changes investor expectations and brings them more in line with your variant perspective. This point is important, so we will repeat it. A catalyst is any precipitating event that informs the crowd that the consensus estimate is wrong and causes the consensus view to begin to shift. The catalyst may not close the gap fully, but the event must start the process of closing the gap to qualify as a catalyst. The most important aspect of a catalyst is that it works to correct the market's error by nudging the consensus view toward your variant perspective.

A **catalyst** is an event that increases the dissemination or availability of information, restores the crowd's diversity and/or independence, or alleviates any trading limitations. The catalyst informs the crowd that the consensus view is incorrect and starts the process of having individuals in the crowd begin to adopt your **variant perspective**, similar to how the color blindness vaccine restored individuals' ability to see the number 12 in the example earlier in the chapter. Simply put, the catalyst can be additional information the market does not have, an event that forces investors to observe and process the information without bias, or a change that increases investors' ability to express and incorporate their view by trading the stock. In the end, a catalyst removes the inefficiency in the stock price.

Gems:

- To outperform the market an investor needs a variant perspective that identifies an inefficiency and provides an advantage, or edge, for him to exploit the mispricing. These advantages fall into three categories, which mirror the market inefficiencies:
  1. An **informational advantage** is present when an investor has information other investors do not have and that, as a result, has not been adequately disseminated to a sufficient number of investors.

2. An **analytical advantage** is present when an investor sees things other investors do not see because there is some type of systematic error or lack of diversity that obscures other investors' views.
3. A **trading advantage** is present when an investor can trade or hold the security when other investors are unable to take or hold a position.

▽ With a pure information advantage an investor can say, "I *know* with certainty that this information is true." This type of advantage is usually not attainable, however, because it is illegal to trade on material nonpublic information.

▽ An analytical advantage is made possible by an inefficiency in how the market **processes** information. An investor with an analytical advantage looks at the same set of public information as other investors, yet, arrives at a value for the stock that differs from the consensus and ultimately proves to be correct.

▽ Because pure information advantages are rare and pure analytical advantages require decades of experience, the most common way successful professional investors outperform the market is by blending the two, looking to combine an **information advantage** with an **analytical advantage**.

▽ A trading advantage is made possible by an inefficiency that prevents information from being **incorporated** into the stock because it impedes investors from trading on the information.

▽ A catalyst is any precipitating event that informs the crowd that the consensus estimate is wrong and causes the consensus view to begin to shift. The event may not close the gap fully between the current market price and the stock's correct value, but it must start the process of closing the gap to qualify as a catalyst.

▽ A catalyst increases the availability of information, restores the crowd's diversity and independence, or removes any trading limitations. The catalyst informs the crowd that the consensus view is incorrect and can be additional information the market does not have, an event that forces investors to observe and process the information without bias, or a change that increases investors' ability to express their view by trading the stock.

  ▽ In simple terms, a catalyst removes the inefficiency in the stock price.

CHAPTER

9

How to Assess Risk

The Difference Between Risk and Uncertainty

On Wall Street, **risk** and **uncertainty** are often used interchangeably, although, as we discuss below, they are not the same thing. That fact is apparent if one simply looks at the definition of each term in the Merriam-Webster dictionary:

> **Uncertainty:** Something that is doubtful or unknown

> **Risk:** Possibility of loss or injury

We illustrate the difference with a simple story:

> Your grandmother gives you a lottery ticket as a birthday present.[1] It is impossible to know if the ticket is a winner before the lottery is held. There is **uncertainty** to the outcome, but no **risk** because you have nothing to lose.
>
> Next, assume that you buy a $2 ticket for the same lottery. In this case, there is **uncertainty** AND **risk**. The uncertainty is the same as with the ticket your grandmother gave you, but there is now the possibility of losing the $2 you paid for the ticket. The lottery ticket you purchased has financial risk because of the very real possibility of losing money.

---

[1] This story is not as odd as it may seem. Paul S.'s grandmother, Phyllis, actually included scratch-off lottery tickets in her cards when she gave birthday gifts and Santa puts lottery tickets in the Christmas stockings each year in the Johnson house.

As the example demonstrates, because **uncertainty has no harm associated with it, there is no risk**. **It is only when an investor commits capital to an uncertain outcome that he is exposed to risk**.

Merriam-Webster defines uncertainty as "something that is doubtful or unknown." It is critically important to note that uncertainty is not necessarily bad and in many situations can be good.[2] In general, however, humans crave certainty and hate uncertainty. Certainty makes us feel safe and secure, informed and intelligent, and in control, while uncertainty makes us feel insecure, in doubt, and powerless, and, in turn, often triggers fear. What are we afraid of? **We fear the possibility of loss or injury, which is why most individuals equate uncertainty with risk.**

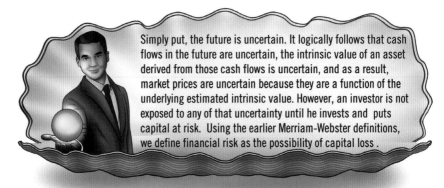

Simply put, the future is uncertain. It logically follows that cash flows in the future are uncertain, the intrinsic value of an asset derived from those cash flows is uncertain, and as a result, market prices are uncertain because they are a function of the underlying estimated intrinsic value. However, an investor is not exposed to any of that uncertainty until he invests and puts capital at risk. Using the earlier Merriam-Webster definitions, we define financial risk as the possibility of capital loss .

Confusing Uncertainty and Risk Causes Mispricings

Confusing uncertainty with risk is a common investor mistake. For instance, most investors will avoid investment opportunities with a high degree of uncertainty, even if the potential return is high and the *actual* risk is low, because they (as human beings) hate uncertainty. Investors often process these opportunities incorrectly because they confuse uncertainty for risk and price the security accordingly. Shrewd investors, on the other hand, view these types of situations as opportunities because the actual risk is mispriced by the consensus.

---

[2] For an excellent explanation of the benefits of uncertainty we recommend reading Nassim Nicholas Taleb's book *Antifragile: Things That Gain from Disorder.*

In an interview in *Graham & Doddsville*, Dan Krueger, a portfolio manager at Owl Creek Asset Management responsible for the Herbalife bond analysis we discuss in the previous chapter, explained his views on the difference between **risk** and **uncertainty** while analyzing Lehman Brothers bonds during the 2008 Financial Crisis:

> Uncertainty, to us as distressed investors, is our friend, because uncertainty is something investors will pay to avoid—sometimes pay a large amount. We love situations like Lehman which we call "high uncertainty, low risk."[3]

Krueger explained further that there was a lot of uncertainty surrounding the Lehman bonds because of the "hundreds of unanswered questions," which he knew "would eventually get answered over the coming months, quarters or years." He added that "occasionally you'll be given an opportunity to buy something at a price where even though you have a hundred unanswered questions, you realize that regardless of what the answers are, you probably cannot lose a lot of money, and most of the time you will make a little or a lot." Exploiting other investors' confusion of risk and uncertainty can be highly profitable and is one of the key reasons we feel the need to distinguish between the two concepts.

BUFFETT TAKES THE PEPSI CHALLENGE

Warren Buffett, Chairman and CEO of Berkshire Hathaway Inc., is one of the grandmasters[4] of exploiting situations where investors have mistakenly priced uncertainty as risk. Buffett uses Berkshire's insurance operations as a vehicle to benefit from these opportunities, which often happen in situations with a high degree of uncertainty. For instance, Berkshire demonstrated its prowess in the summer of 2003, when Pepsi ran a promotion called "Play for a Billion," in which consumers had a chance to win $1 billion at the contest's grand finale. Pepsi, fearing the possibility of losing $1 billion, sought to insure the loss to protect itself from this (very remote) outcome.

The mechanics of the contest were as follows: Pepsi issued 1 billion bottle caps with special codes on them and a total of 4 million people eventually entered the sweepstakes. Of the 4 million entrants, 100 people were chosen randomly to appear on a live gameshow-style television special. Each of the 100 individuals was given a random six-digit number. A person affiliated

(Continued)

[3] "Daniel Krueger: Uncertainty Is Our Friend." *Graham & Doddsville*, Winter 2013, 17–18.

(Continued)

with Pepsi then rolled a 10-sided die to select six numbers, each of which was written on a billiard ball and placed into a bag. A chimp named Kendall drew the balls out of the bag, one at a time, to determine the sequence of the six-digit number. A contestant won $1 billion if their numbers were an exact match to the six-digit number that Kendall generated.

The odds of winning the contest, which is the chance of matching the six-digit number exactly, is one in a million (actually, it is 1 in 999,999 as 1,000,000 is a seven-digit number). The expected loss to Pepsi (if the game was played an infinite number of times) is $1,000, which equals $1,000,000,000/999,999 possible winning numbers.

If anyone won the contest, they had the option to either receive an immediate lump sum payment of $250 million or a tiered payout consisting of an annuity of $5 million a year for 20 years, then $10 million a year for the next 20 years, and finally a $700 million payment in year 41. If the lump sum was chosen, which is usually the case in lottery-type contests, then the real expected loss to Pepsi was $250,000,000/999,999, or $250.

It is rumored that Berkshire charged Pepsi a premium of $10 million to insure against the potential loss. If Pepsi's potential loss of $250 million is divided by the $10 million premium it paid to Berkshire, the implied odds of the potential loss are 1 in 25, while the actual odds of losing were 1 in 1,000. Pepsi clearly mispriced the risk of loss. Although there was the *possibility* of someone winning the $250 million, the *probability* was extremely low. Buffett was delighted to insure the contest because he knew the *probability* was small and the insurance policy was grossly overpriced.

Pepsi faced an uncertain outcome in the contest and the fear of that uncertainty drove the company to equate a *possible* outcome as a *probable* outcome. Effectively, they mistook uncertainty for risk. Pepsi's preference was to lock in a $10 million loss rather than have the possibility of a $250 million loss. Of course, no one won the grand prize of $1 billion.

It is rumored that when asked at the time if he had concerns about the outcome of the Pepsi contest, Buffett stated that his only regret was he wished Pepsi ran the contest more often. Ironically, Berkshire is the largest investor in Coca-Cola and apparently had no problem taking Pepsi's money!

---

[4] It should be noted that Ajit Jain, who currently heads Berkshire's Reinsurance Group, is believed to be the other mastermind behind Berkshire's insurance operations.

How Confusion of Risk and Uncertainty Manifests in the Wisdom of Crowds Framework

When investors confuse uncertainty for risk, that mistake shows up primarily as a **processing error**, which produces a **systematic bias** in the wisdom of crowds framework, as shown in Figure 9.1.

As we discuss in the Sevcon example in Chapter 7, the crowd's **diversity** collapsed when investors panicked in response to Sevcon

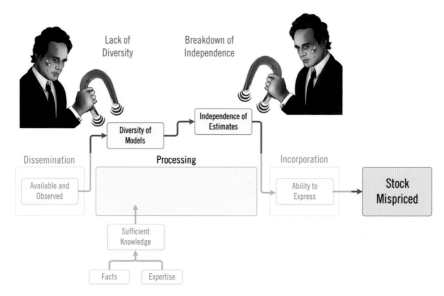

Figure 9.1   Consensus Decision Model Distorted by Error in Processing

losing its biggest customer and all the investors began using the same liquidation model to estimate the company's intrinsic value.

Similarly, as we explain in Chapter 8, Bill Ackman caused a breakdown of **independence** in the consensus view concerning the outlook for Herbalife's bonds because of the high degree of uncertainty his presentation created. Many of the investors misinterpreted the perceived uncertainty as a risk of potential capital loss, which caused a mispricing in the bonds that Dan Krueger and other shrewd investors were able to exploit.

When Uncertainty *Becomes* Risk

When does **uncertainty** become **risk**? As we discuss at the beginning of the chapter, **risk** becomes a factor only when capital is committed, and therefore is *always* a function of the price paid for the investment.

We show Tesla's stock price relative to the consensus estimate for the company's one-year price target and each individual analyst's estimates in Chapter 4, which we replicate in Figure 9.2.

Figure 9.2   Tesla: Analysts' One-Year Price Targets

We removed the individual analyst estimate in Figure 9.3 so that we can present an uncluttered distribution of estimates.

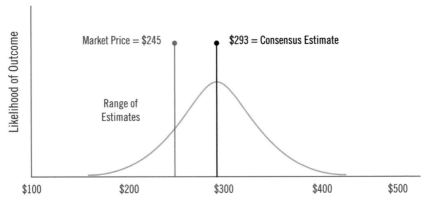

Figure 9.3   Tesla: Consensus Estimate

The difference between the market price of $245 and the consensus one-year price target of $293 is the stock's **expected return**, which equals 19.6% in the example, as shown in Figure 9.4.

Figure 9.4   Tesla: Expected Return Implied by Consensus Price Target

It is straightforward to see from the distribution in Figure 9.5 that the investment will lose money if the *actual* intrinsic value turns out to be less than the price paid for the stock. In Figure 9.5, all possible outcomes less than the market price are depicted by the red-shaded area in the chart and represent the market implied risk of investing in the stock.

Figure 9.5   Tesla: Market Implied Risk of Investing in Stock at $245 per Share

While all possible outcomes *above* the stock price are also uncertain, there is no **risk** because these outcomes will not result in a loss of capital. The **uncertainty** is represented by the sky blue-shaded area in Figure 9.6 and illustrates the difference between risk and uncertainty.

Figure 9.6   Tesla: Outcomes Above Market Price are Uncertain But Not Risky

It should be clear from this discussion that the level of **risk** will change when the market price changes if the range of expected intrinsic values remains the same. To illustrate this point, we start with the initial assumptions presented in Figure 9.7. If the stock price increases from $245 to $278, as shown in Figure 9.8, with no change in the estimated intrinsic value, the expected return declines (falling from 19.6% to 5.4% in the example) and **risk** increases substantially, as we show in Figure 9.9.

Figure 9.7   Tesla: Initial Expected Return versus Market Implied Risk

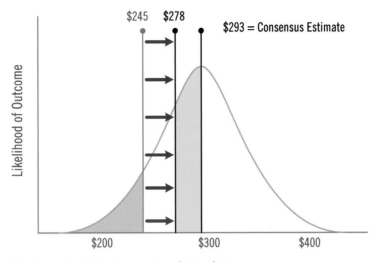

Figure 9.8   Tesla: Stock Price Increase from $245 to $278

Figure 9.9   Tesla: Increase in Price Results in Lower Expected Return and Additional Risk

The reverse is also true. If the market price declines from $278 to $245, without any change in the range of estimated intrinsic values, the potential return increases while the **risk** is reduced, as depicted by the charts in Figures 9.10, 9.11, and 9.12.

Figure 9.10   Tesla: Market Implied Risk with Stock Price of $278

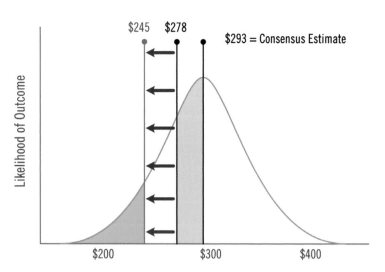

Figure 9.11   Tesla: Stock Price Declines from $278 to $245

Figure 9.12   Tesla: Lower Price Produces Higher Expected Return and Lower Market Implied Risk

We define **risk** as the possibility of a loss of capital, which is equivalent to the possibility of losing money. Therefore, although the future is inherently uncertain, **there is no risk until capital is committed**, as the examples show, and **the level of risk will be a direct function of the price paid relative to all possible outcomes**.

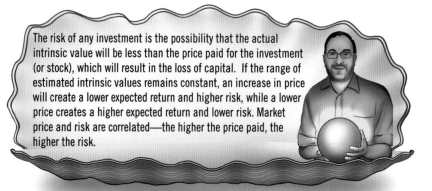

The risk of any investment is the possibility that the actual intrinsic value will be less than the price paid for the investment (or stock), which will result in the loss of capital. If the range of estimated intrinsic values remains constant, an increase in price will create a lower expected return and higher risk, while a lower price creates a higher expected return and lower risk. Market price and risk are correlated—the higher the price paid, the higher the risk.

Margin of Safety Is Really All about Risk

Ben Graham devoted an entire chapter to the discussion of risk in *The Intelligent Investor,* in which he distilled to "the secret of sound investment into three words . . . MARGIN OF SAFETY." Graham's concept of risk is fully captured by his definition of margin of safety, which he describes as:

> A favorable difference between price on the one hand and indicated or appraised value on the other. That difference is the safety margin. It is available for absorbing the effect of miscalculations or worse than average luck. The buyer of bargain issues places particular emphasis on the ability of the investment to withstand adverse developments.[5]

It is straightforward to show that the area between the stock's price and the intrinsic value (Graham's "appraised value"), represents what is generally accepted as the investment's **margin of safety**, as shown in Figure 9.13.

Figure 9.13   **Margin of Safety Equals Expected Return**

Mirroring our previous discussion, Graham adds, "The margin of safety is always dependent on the price paid. It will be large at one price, small at some higher price, nonexistent at some still higher price."[6]

---

[5] Benjamin Graham, *The Intelligent Investor: A Book of Practical Counsel* (New York: HarperBusiness 1973).
[6] Ibid.

A More Certain Business Can Actually Be Riskier

As we discuss in Chapter 4, the distribution of the estimates of intrinsic value will be narrower when the company's cash flows are more predictable. Likewise, the distribution of the estimates of intrinsic value will be wider when the cash flows are less certain. We illustrated this point by comparing analysts' one-year price targets for Tesla with McCormick's, as shown in Figure 9.14.

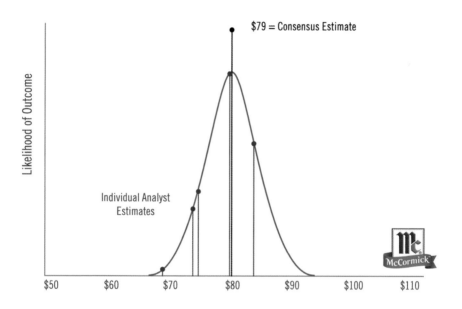

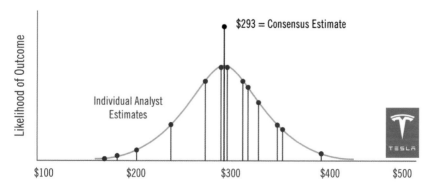

Figure 9.14   McCormick and Tesla Consensus Estimates of One-Year Price Targets

At the time we originally performed this analysis, McCormick's stock price was $85, which was *above* the consensus estimated one-year price target of $79. Ironically, *while McCormick's future cash flows were highly predictable and more certain than Tesla's, if analyst forecasts at that time were correct, then McCormick stock was riskier because it had no margin of safety,* as shown in Figure 9.15.

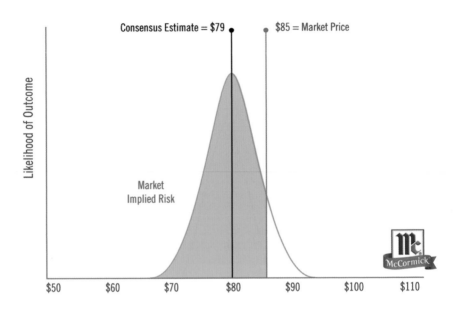

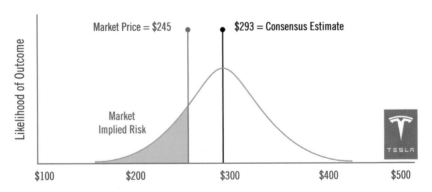

Figure 9.15   Comparing the Risk of McCormick and Tesla

We reiterate that uncertainty and risk are not synonymous. Less uncertainty does not automatically mean less risk. In fact, stocks for companies with more certain cash flows can be riskier than companies with less certain cash flows, because the level of risk is a function of the price paid and whether a margin of safety exists.

Time Matters ... and Matters a Lot ...

In addition to the risk of capital loss, portfolio managers also face the risk of underperforming their benchmark. It continually surprises us that most of the portfolio managers, analysts, and institutional salespeople we have observed in our careers spend almost all their time concerned with estimating the company's **intrinsic value** and little time estimating the investment's **time horizon**. We think this time allocation is a critical mistake because time is a key component in the ultimate return the investment delivers.

Therefore, before discussing the risks from errors in estimating the investment's **time horizon**, we want to make sure the reader fully understands why time is such a critical element in the investment return.

MELTING THEIR WAY TO AN ATTRACTIVE RETURN

A story from *Meltdown*, a reality TV show that aired during 2013 on the National Geographic Channel (sadly, it was canceled after a single season), provides an excellent example of the importance of fully understanding the three elements of any investment and demonstrates that time is an extremely crucial component to the actual return generated.

(Continued)

(*Continued*)

Meltdown is described on Nat Geo's website as being about "three urban treasure hunters [who] battle the market and fierce competition as they seek out precious metals in unorthodox places and melt them down for cash."[7] In the show, the three main characters scour the cities in which they live, looking to buy items containing precious metals, which they extract and take to a smelter to exchange for cash. The hunters' goal is to make an acceptable profit in a short period of time, without losing money.

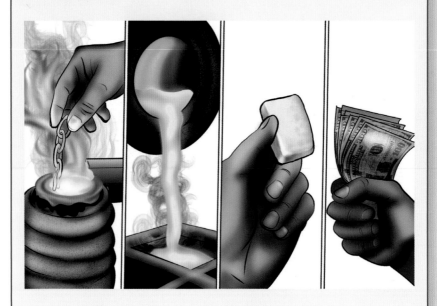

In one episode, "Coffin Up Cash," Diego Calinawan, a tattooed biker and Desert Storm veteran, goes to a funeral parlor in search of gold. He finds an unused coffin with the deceased's initials on the head panel[8] (the family decided to cremate the body at the last minute). The director of the funeral parlor claimed the initials were made of gold but did not know the purity. Before buying the coffin, Diego explains, "Since I have no idea how much gold there actually is, I have to get his price *way* down." After a protracted negotiation with the owner of the funeral parlor, Diego purchased the coffin for $450. He put the coffin in the back of his pickup truck and drove it to his warehouse, where he used a sledge hammer to break-apart the casket to harvest the gold.

---

[7] A Wall Street version of the show could easily be described as "Three recent business school graduates who battle the stock market and fierce competition as they seek out market inefficiencies in unorthodox places with the hopes of beating the market."

[8] For those not well-versed in coffin nomenclature, the head panel is the upper portion of the coffin lid.

Interestingly, there are important similarities in the phrases that repeatedly appear in each of the episodes, such as, "I need to figure out what I can get for it," "I have to get it to the smelter before it closes because time is money," "There has to be enough gold to make this worthwhile," and "I don't know the purity or weight so I have to pay as little as possible so I don't lose money."

There are three common elements that reappear in each situation the characters in the show face:

The price they pay for whatever they are trying to buy—in Diego's case it is the $450 he spent for the coffin.
The cash they receive from the smelter.
The amount of time it takes them to locate an item, purchase it, harvest the gold, and get to the smelter.

We can use the three elements to calculate Diego's **rate of return**, or what he refers to in the show as his payday. The formal way to calculate rate of return is simple [Note: we are using green for value, blue for price, and purple to signify time]:

$$\text{Rate of Return} = \left[\left(\frac{\text{Ending Value}}{\text{Beginning Value}} \right)^{\frac{1}{\text{\# of Years}}} \right] - 1$$

(*Continued*)

(*Continued*)

We can "dumb down" the formula a bit to make it simpler to understand:

$$\text{Rate of Return} = \left[\left(\frac{\text{The Cash Diego Receives}}{\text{Diego's Cash Outlay}}\right)^{\text{How Long It Takes for Diego to Receive the Cash}} - 1\right]$$

After removing the initials from the coffin, Diego took the gold letters to a smelter called KFG, Inc., to have them melted down and exchanged for cash. Simon, the owner of KFG, used a portable X-ray fluorescence analyzer to determine that the gold content was 75%, which yielded 46.7 grams of gold.[9] Diego received $1,510 in the transaction, netting a profit of $1,060 for his efforts. We see that Diego did well in purchasing the coffin when we calculate his rate of return on the transaction, as the following shows:

$$\text{Rate of Return} = \left[\left(\frac{\$1,510}{\$450}\right)^{1\,\text{Day}} - 1\right]$$

$$\text{Rate of Return} = 235\%$$

Diego made 235% on his investment in just one day, which is an impressive return, particularly when annualized.

———————————

[9] 75% gold content is 18k (carats), the other 25% is usually silver and copper. The slug weighed 62.3 grams and contained 46.7 grams of gold.

The return from investing in a stock, or any security for that matter, is determined by three elements: the price you pay, the value you get, and the time it takes for the investment to work out, and is calculated using the following formula.

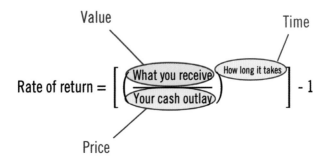

We need to change the labels slightly to account for the fact that we are evaluating a potential investment, one that we have not yet made. Since we do not know for certain what will happen in the future, or how much we will earn from the investment, we relabel what we get as estimated value, while what we pay becomes current market price and time becomes expected time horizon.

$$\text{Expected Rate of Return} = \left[\left(\frac{\text{Estimated Value}}{\text{Current Market Price}} \right)^{\substack{\text{Expected} \\ \text{Time Horizon}}} \right] - 1$$

We use the stock of ZRS Corporation as a simple example to demonstrate how to calculate the expected rate of return for a stock. The company's stock trades at $5.85 per share and we estimate it will be worth $10.25 per share within four years. The expected annualized rate of return is 15.0%, as the following calculation shows.

$$\text{Expected Rate of Return} = \left[\left(\frac{\text{Estimated Value}}{\text{Current Market Price}} \right)^{\substack{\text{Expected} \\ \text{Time Horizon}}} \right] - 1$$

$$\text{Expected Rate of Return} = \left[\left(\frac{\$10.25}{\$5.85} \right)^{\frac{1}{4}} \right] - 1$$

$$\text{Expected Rate of Return} = \left[\left(1.75 \right)^{.25} \right] - 1$$

$$\text{Expected Rate of Return} = 1.15 - 1$$

$$\text{Expected Rate of Return} = 15.0\% \text{ per Annum}$$

Of the three inputs in the expected rate of return formula, the current market price is the only input that is known ahead of time, which is the price you would pay to purchase the stock and can be easily determined by looking at the stock's market price. The other two inputs, the estimated value and expected time horizon, are estimates, which we show graphically in Figure 9.16.

Figure 9.16   Three Components of Investment Return

We use the return formula to calculate an expected rate of return of 15.0% based on the initial market price of $5.85, the estimated ending value of $10.25, and a time horizon of four years. We show the convergence of these three factors, and the expected return, in Figure 9.17.

Figure 9.17   Expected Rate of Return

What if we are wrong? The primary assumption behind every investment is that the current market price will converge to the estimated value within the expected time horizon. However, if the estimated value is wrong or if it takes longer than we expect for the stock to close the gap between price and value, then the *actual* return will be less than what we have forecast.

For instance, if we are right on the expected value of $10.25, but it takes the stock seven years, instead of four years, to reach that price, then the return falls almost in half to 8.3% per year, as shown in Figure 9.18.

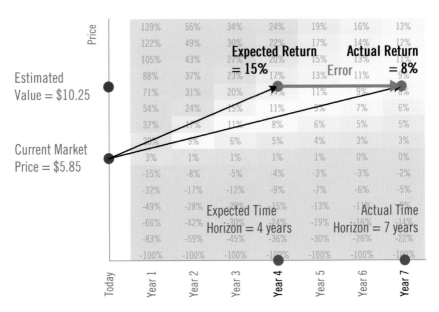

Figure 9.18   Error in Estimating Time Horizon

This example highlights that time is a critical factor in the ultimate return the investment delivers. On the other hand, if we are right in the estimate of the time horizon, but wrong about the expected value for ZRS stock, such that it is worth only $7.00 in four years, then the return falls to 4.6% per year, as shown in Figure 9.19.

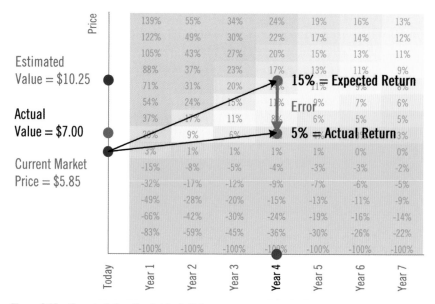

Price							
139%	55%	34%	24%	19%	16%	13%
122%	49%	30%	22%	17%	14%	12%
105%	43%	27%	20%	15%	13%	11%
88%	37%	23%	17%	13%	11%	9%
71%	31%	20%		11%	9%	8%
54%	24%	15%	11%	9%	7%	6%
37%	17%	11%	8%	6%	5%	5%
20%	9%	6%				3%
3%	1%	1%	1%	1%	0%	0%
-15%	-8%	-5%	-4%	-3%	-3%	-2%
-32%	-17%	-12%	-9%	-7%	-6%	-5%
-49%	-28%	-20%	-15%	-13%	-11%	-9%
-66%	-42%	-30%	-24%	-19%	-16%	-14%
-83%	-59%	-45%	-36%	-30%	-26%	-22%
-100%	-100%	-100%	-100%	-100%	-100%	-100%

Estimated
Value = $10.25

Actual
Value = $7.00

Current Market
Price = $5.85

15% = Expected Return
Error
5% = Actual Return

Today   Year 1   Year 2   Year 3   Year 4   Year 5   Year 6   Year 7

Figure 9.19   Error in Estimating Intrinsic Value

Now that we have presented a comprehensive understanding of the components of return and the importance of time as a factor in that return, we can discuss how increased **accuracy** and **precision** in estimating both the intrinsic value and time horizon can reduce risk significantly.

How Increased Accuracy and Precision in Estimating Intrinsic Value Affects Risk

As we discuss in the previous chapter, investors perform research to improve the **accuracy** and **precision** of their estimate of a company's intrinsic value with the goal of producing as tight a range of estimated intrinsic values as possible.

Figure 9.20 shows the difference between **accuracy** and **precision**. The targets were shot at 200 yards with a bolt action Eliseo RTS Tubegun chambered in a 6.5 x 47 Lapua. The center of the black box is the actual target—not the bullseye—as mirage makes it difficult to see the rings of a typical target at 200 yards.[10] At this distance, a group of one-half inch is considered very precise.

---

[10] If you care to learn more about this visual phenomenon there are several good articles and videos. Simply google "how to read mirage."

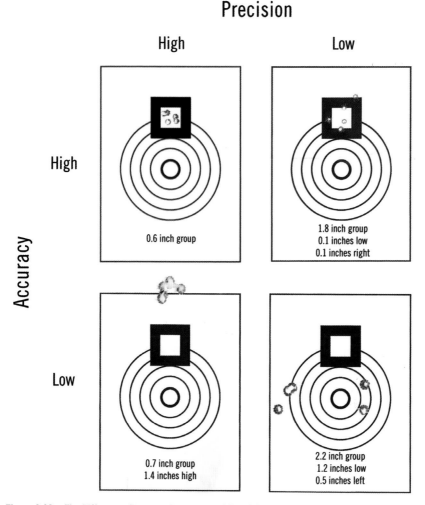

Figure 9.20   The Difference Between Accuracy and Precision

Low accuracy and low precision are obviously not the goal in this exercise. High precision with low accuracy is even worse as you will completely miss the target. High accuracy with low precision is better, although high accuracy and high precision is ideal.

We show in the first example how increased accuracy reduces risk. We start with the initial assumptions that the stock trades at $80, the consensus estimate of the intrinsic value is $85, and the true intrinsic value is $95, as shown in Figure 9.21.

After completing your research, you estimate that the intrinsic value per share is $90. Assuming you are correct, your estimate is

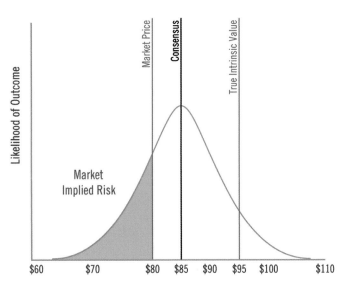

Figure 9.21   Initial Assumptions

more **accurate** than the consensus because it is closer to the true intrinsic value of $95. In Figure 9.22, the green-shaded area shows your increased **accuracy** and the red-shaded area shows the new implied estimate of risk.

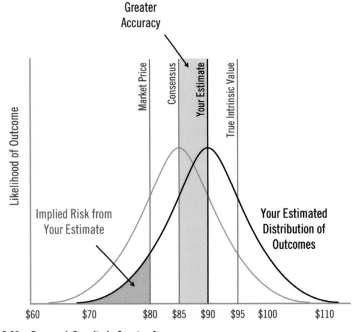

Figure 9.22   Research Results in Greater Accuracy

As a result of the greater **accuracy** in your estimate, the implied level of risk has been reduced, as shown in Figure 9.23.

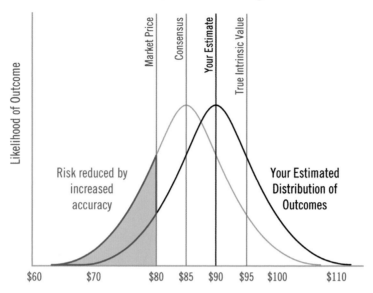

Figure 9.23   Increased Accuracy Reduces Risk

We use the same initial assumptions in the next example to demonstrate how risk is reduced by increasing the **precision** of your estimate of intrinsic value, as shown in Figures 9.24, 9.25, and 9.26.

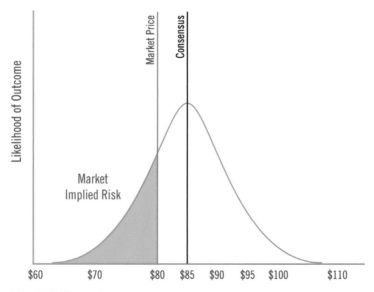

Figure 9.24   Initial Assumptions

After completing your research (assuming you are correct), you arrive at a more *precise* estimate than the consensus, thereby reducing the **uncertainty**, which reduces the implied level of risk of the investment, as shown in Figure 9.25.

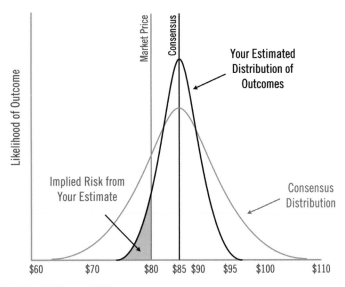

Figure 9.25   Your Estimate of Risk

Figure 9.26 shows how risk is reduced with greater precision:

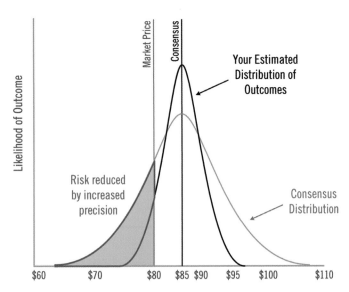

Figure 9.26   Greater Precision Reduces Risk

As we have just demonstrated, increased **accuracy** and increased **precision** individually reduce **risk**. However, risk is reduced even more significantly when both accuracy and precision are combined. We use the same initial assumptions as in the previous two examples to make the point, as shown in Figure 9.27.

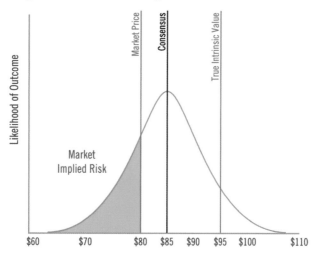

Figure 9.27   Initial Assumptions

Because of your increased accuracy *and* precision there will be an extremely low level of risk (assuming you are correct), as shown in Figure 9.28:

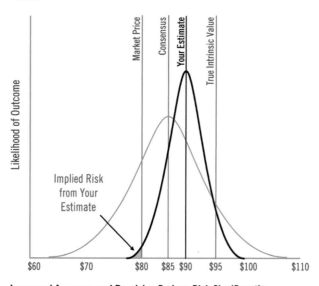

Figure 9.28   Increased Accuracy and Precision Reduce Risk Significantly

Figure 9.29 shows the reduction in risk as the result of increased accuracy and precision.

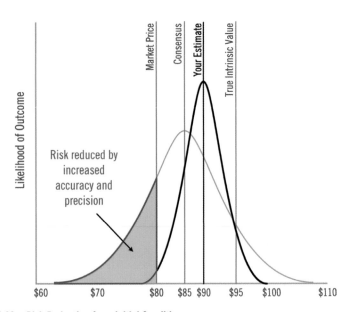

Figure 9.29   Risk Reduction from Initial Condition

How Increased Accuracy and Precision in Estimating Time Horizon Affects Risk

It is not enough for the estimate of intrinsic value to be correct; the investor also must be accurate in his estimate of the amount of time it takes to close the gap between market price and intrinsic value because the actual **time horizon** will determine the realized annual return.

Just as it is important to recognize that there is a **range** of possible outcomes for intrinsic value, it is helpful to think of the expected time horizon as a range of outcomes rather than a single-point estimate, as shown in Figure 9.30.

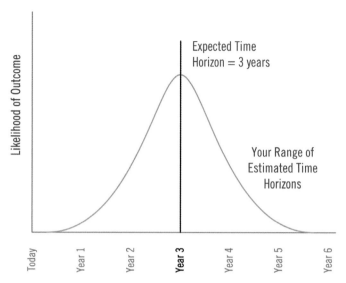

Figure 9.30   Range of Estimated Time Horizon

The red-shaded area in Figure 9.31 shows the implied risk from errors in underestimating the time horizon.

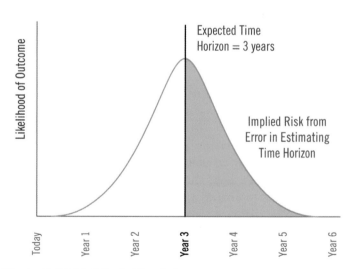

Figure 9.31   Implied Risk in Estimated Time Horizon

Errors in underestimating the time horizon of an investment are a source of risk because any error reduces the realized investment return, as we show in Figure 9.18 and replicate below.

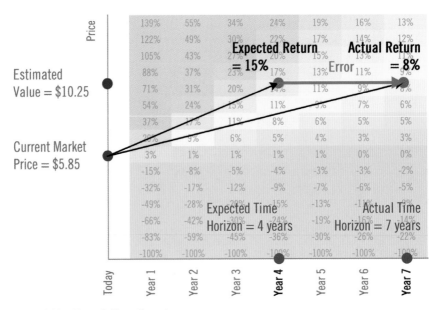

Figure 9.32   Figure 9.18: replicated

Risk and Variant Perception—Skewing the Distribution in the Investor's Favor

For simplicity, many of the figures in this chapter present the range of possible intrinsic values as a **normal distribution** around a single-point estimate. The normal distribution was a useful fiction to highlight the relationship between price and intrinsic value, as well as demonstrate how the price paid determines the level of risk. However, it is important to note that an investor will rarely be able to determine a precise probability for each estimate of intrinsic value, therefore, it will be difficult to *ever* know the actual shape of the distribution of possible values.

Nonetheless, we can use the following example to show how an investor can perform research to skew the distribution of intrinsic value estimates in his favor and reduce the risk of the investment as a result. We begin with a normal distribution in Figure 9.33 to represent the range of possible intrinsic values, a market price of $70, and a consensus estimate of intrinsic value of $75. The area to the left of the market price represents the market implied risk in the investment, as we discuss in previous examples.

Figure 9.33   Market-implied Risk

Now suppose the investor performs extensive research, develops a **variant perspective**, and determines that there is less downside to the investment than implied by the consensus view. His distribution of possible intrinsic values will be **skewed** to the upside, as shown in Figure 9.34:

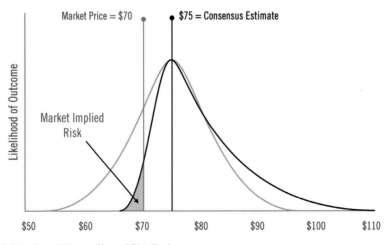

Figure 9.34   Normal Versus Skewed Distribution

Figure 9.35 shows that the skewed distribution significantly reduces the market implied level of risk in the investment.

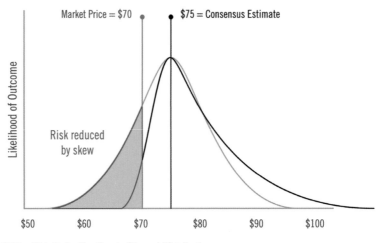

Figure 9.35   Risk Reduction Due to Skewed Distribution

Investments with skewed distributions have **asymmetric returns**. Positively skewed distribution have more upside than downside, which maximizes the upside potential of the investment and minimizes its implied risk, while negatively skewed distributions have more downside than upside. Shrewd, experienced investors are always on the hunt for investment opportunities with positively skewed distributions.

For instance, rather than a normal distribution, the range of *consensus* expectations for Cloverland's intrinsic value, which we discuss in Chapter 8, is negatively skewed, as we show in Figure 9.36. The analysis highlights the relationship between the market price of $85, the estimated intrinsic value of $107, and the implied risk of capital loss as the red shaded area to the left of the price. Because timber is a hard asset, most investors assume that its value will not change much over time and, therefore, there will be minimal upside potential to Cloverland's appraised value of $107, as the chart shows. On the other hand, there are various scenarios that can produce a lower intrinsic value, such as corporate mismanagement, the continued under-cutting of trees, or some type of infestation that destroys the health of a large portion of the timberlands.

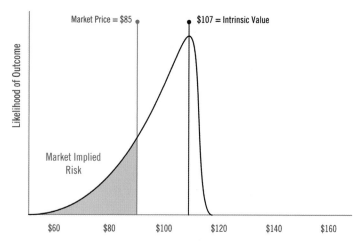

Figure 9.36   Consensus Implied Risk For Cloverland

As we discuss in Chapter 8, John Helve of Brownfield Capital has a **variant perspective** concerning the company and his distribution curve of possible intrinsic values that looks significantly different than the consensus view, as shown in Figure 9.37. Although Helve recognizes that there is the possibility of a loss with his investment, he estimates the probability of that risk as being low, as the chart

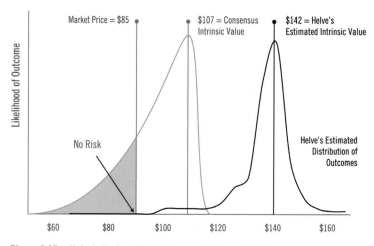

Figure 9.37   Helve's Variant Perspective Results in Lower Risk

shows. If Helve is successful in forcing a sale of the company, which he believes is highly probable, his estimated intrinsic value would equal $142, with only a small probability of it being worth significantly less than this estimate, as the chart shows. It should be noted that because of his **variant perspective**, Helve does not believe there is a scenario where he would lose money, therefore, in his view, there is no risk to the investment.

The Risk of Underperforming

We have limited the discussion of risk so far to the potential of a capital loss (losing money), which we show as negative returns in Figure 9.38.

	Today	Year 1	Year 2	Year 3	Year 4	Year 5	Year 6	Year 7
$14.00		139%	55%	34%	24%	19%	16%	13%
$13.00		122%	49%	30%	22%	17%	14%	12%
$12.00		105%	43%	27%	20%	15%	13%	11%
$11.00		88%	37%	23%	17%	13%	11%	9%
$10.00		71%	31%	20%	14%	11%	9%	8%
$9.00		54%	24%	15%	11%	9%	7%	6%
$8.00		37%	17%	11%	8%	6%	5%	5%
$7.00		20%	9%	6%	5%	4%	3%	3%
$6.00		3%	1%	1%	1%	1%	0%	0%
$5.00		-15%	-8%	-5%	-4%	-3%	-3%	-2%
$4.00		-32%	-17%	-12%	-9%	-7%	-6%	-5%
$3.00		-49%	-28%	-20%	-15%	-13%	-11%	-9%
$2.00		-66%	-42%	-30%	-24%	-19%	-16%	-14%
$1.00		-83%	-59%	-45%	-36%	-30%	-26%	-22%
$0.00		-100%	-100%	-100%	-100%	-100%	-100%	-100%

Figure 9.38   Heat Map: Risk of Capital Loss

However, a return of zero is not the appropriate benchmark to use when evaluating a portfolio manager's investment results for the simple reason that all capital has an **opportunity cost**, as we discuss in Chapter 2. The performance of most professional port-folio managers is benchmarked against an index such as the S&P 500 or Russell 2000. Consequently, underperforming the market is a legitimate concern for most professional portfolio managers because investors have a viable alternative (investing in the index) and will redeem their investment if the manager underperforms the market.

Returning to the Cloverland example, Helve is sensitive to his investment underperforming the market for the reasons just listed. As a result, his variant perspective regarding the estimated **time horizon** is a critical factor in his investment thesis, which we show is significantly different than consensus expectations in Figure 9.39.

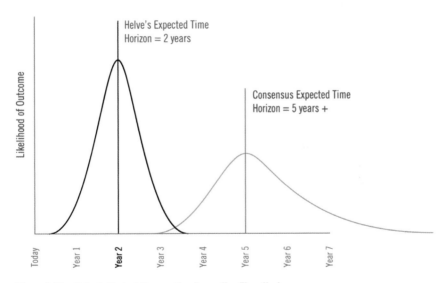

Figure 9.39   Helve's Variant Perspective Regarding Time Horizon

And, as we show in Figure 9.40, Cloverland's stock will outper-form the market if the sale of the company takes place in less than five years, which is Helve's belief, but will underperform if the transac-tion takes longer to occur, which is the consensus view. Helve knows that getting the timing right is critical to his investment because of the ever-present need to outperform the market.

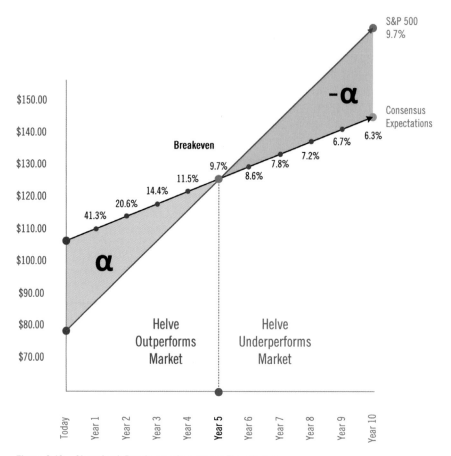

Figure 9.40   Cloverland: Break-even Investment Time Horizon

While most professional portfolio managers are keenly aware that their performance will be benchmarked against the market, others successful investors view the concern as less important. For instance, in 1984, on the television show *Adam Smith's Money World*, Warren Buffett made a statement that over time has morphed into the quote, "There are no-called-strikes in investing," referring to the fact that he believes missed opportunities are not harmful and an investor should not feel undue pressure to invest if they fail to find opportunities that meet their investment criteria. However, as Columbia Professor Bruce Greenwald wryly counters, in professional money management, because there is always the option of investing in an index fund, "they keep running up the score while you wait for the perfect pitch." For this reason, relative performance matters for most professional portfolio managers.[11] This discussion emphasizes that there are two risks to any investment opportunity—the risk of **capital loss** and the **risk of underperformance**, as we show in the heat maps in Figures 9.38 and 9.41.

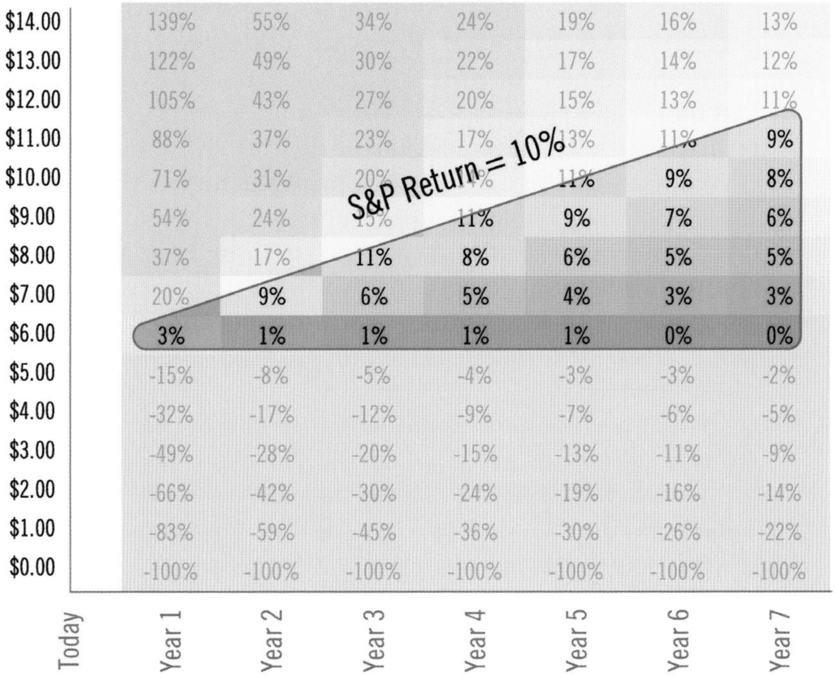

	Year 1	Year 2	Year 3	Year 4	Year 5	Year 6	Year 7
$14.00	139%	55%	34%	24%	19%	16%	13%
$13.00	122%	49%	30%	22%	17%	14%	12%
$12.00	105%	43%	27%	20%	15%	13%	11%
$11.00	88%	37%	23%	17%	13%	11%	9%
$10.00	71%	31%	20%		11%	9%	8%
$9.00	54%	24%	15%	11%	9%	7%	6%
$8.00	37%	17%	11%	8%	6%	5%	5%
$7.00	20%	9%	6%	5%	4%	3%	3%
$6.00	3%	1%	1%	1%	1%	0%	0%
$5.00	-15%	-8%	-5%	-4%	-3%	-3%	-2%
$4.00	-32%	-17%	-12%	-9%	-7%	-6%	-5%
$3.00	-49%	-28%	-20%	-15%	-13%	-11%	-9%
$2.00	-66%	-42%	-30%	-24%	-19%	-16%	-14%
$1.00	-83%	-59%	-45%	-36%	-30%	-26%	-22%
$0.00	-100%	-100%	-100%	-100%	-100%	-100%	-100%

S&P Return = 10%

(x-axis: Today, Year 1, Year 2, Year 3, Year 4, Year 5, Year 6, Year 7)

Figure 9.41   Heat Map: Risk of Underperformance

Gems:

- ◈ **Uncertainty** has no harm associated with it and, therefore, entails no **risk**. It is only when an investor commits capital to an uncertain outcome that he exposes himself to risk.
- ◈ In general, humans crave certainty and hate uncertainty. Certainty makes us feel safe and secure, informed and intelligent, and in control, while uncertainty makes us feel insecure, in

[11] Buffett updated this statement to reflect the realities of professional portfolio management and is quoted in the book *The Tao of Warren Buffett*, as saying, "The stock market is a no-called-strike game. You don't have to swing at everything—you can wait for your pitch. The problem when you're a money manager is that your fans keep yelling, 'Swing, you bum!'" (Mary Buffett, David Clark, and Anna Fields, *The Tao of Warren Buffett* [Tantor Media, 2006]).

doubt, and powerless, and, in turn, often triggers fear. What are we afraid of? We fear the possibility of loss or injury, which is why individuals often equate uncertainty with risk.

▽ The most commonly-recognized risk of any investment is the possibility that the actual **intrinsic value** will be less than the price paid for the investment (or stock), which will result in **permanent loss of capital**. If the intrinsic value remains constant, an increase in price creates a lower expected return and higher risk, while a lower price creates a higher expected return and lower risk. Market price and risk are positively correlated—the higher the price paid, the higher the risk.

▽ Uncertainty and risk are not synonymous. Less uncertainty does not automatically mean less risk. In fact, stocks for companies with more certain cash flows can be riskier than companies with less certain cash flows because the level of risk is a function of the price paid and not the uncertainty in the situation.

▽ Increased **accuracy** and increased **precision** both reduce risk. However, the estimated level of risk is reduced even more significantly when both improvements are combined.

▽ **Time** is a critical factor in the investment's actual realized rate of return and, as a consequence, an additional source of risk. In other words, it is not enough to be correct about a company's true intrinsic value; the investor also must be accurate in his estimate of the amount of time it takes to close the gap between market price and intrinsic value because the actual time horizon will determine the realized annual return.

▽ A return of zero is not the appropriate benchmark to use when evaluating a portfolio manager's investment results for the simple reason that all capital has an opportunity cost. Most professional portfolio managers' performance is benchmarked against an index such as the S&P 500 or Russell 2000 for this very reason, and underperforming the market is a legitimate concern because investors have a viable alternative and will redeem if the manager underperforms the market consistently.

▽ A portfolio manager faces two risks to any investment opportunity—the **risk of capital loss** and the **risk of underperformance**.

THE PERFECT PITCH

As we discuss in the book's introduction, if you don't have a great investment idea, there is nothing to pitch. Part I of the book explained how to:

1. Calculate the range of intrinsic values for a stock.
2. Articulate why the stock is mispriced.
3. Determine whether you have a **variant perspective** and an advantage over other investors.
4. Assess the investment's level of risk.

You now have all the tools you need to vet *the perfect investment*. However, if you have a great idea but cannot communicate it, your pitch will fall on deaf ears.

A pitch is comprised of three main sections: the security you select, the content of your message, and the delivery of that message. To select the proper security, the analyst must know the portfolio manager's selection criteria, which we discuss in Chapter 10. We show that the manager *will not even listen* to an investment pitch unless it satisfies his investment criteria. We then show in Chapter 11 how to organize the content to maximize the impact of the pitch. Finally, we discuss in Chapter 12 the different elements necessary to ensure effective delivery of the message.

The person making the buy or sell decision is the person to whom you are pitching. That person is most often a portfolio manager whose goal is to beat the market, which means he needs to earn an investment return above the market return after fees and adjusting for risk. As a consequence, the portfolio manager's most important concern is performance. To generate good performance, the manager needs to find ideas to put into his portfolio that will beat the market. If a portfolio manager hears a compelling pitch and believes that the idea will outperform the market, he will begin salivating like one of Pavlov's dogs.

The ideal outcome of a stock pitch is that your idea is so captivating in both its **content** and **delivery** that the portfolio manager feels compelled to immediately "clear his desk" and begin working on the idea for fear of missing an opportunity to outperform.

How do you know *what kind of idea* will get him to clear his desk?

CHAPTER 10

How to Select a Security

Because portfolio managers expect analysts to supply them with compelling investment opportunities, the analyst's primary role is to find and present ideas that will outperform the market.

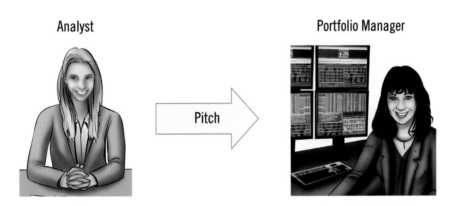

However, since the portfolio manager's success depends on the investment performance she delivers, she will be extremely selective about which ideas she adds to her portfolio and will put any new idea under intense scrutiny to identify its flaws. The analyst must be able to defend her analysis if she is going to survive this gauntlet.

Portfolio managers are also extremely busy. They are inundated with information and new ideas throughout the day and are always short on time. To the portfolio manager, her time is a finite resource and most precious asset. Therefore, the manager will also be extremely selective in allocating her time and, if the analyst is given an opportunity to pitch her idea, the analyst must be quick, concise, and persuasive.

For these reasons, most portfolio managers will have their guard up concerning any new investment idea they are pitched. Imagine that in their mind, they have a highly alert, slightly paranoid, heavily armed sentinel to protect them from bad investment ideas and analysts wasting their time. We can call this guard Dr. No.[1] This layer of protection produces obstacles that the analyst must overcome to get her idea adopted.

Overcome Obstacles

The first task is **security selection**. It is important to find an idea that fits the portfolio manager's **schema,** which is a type of **mental model** comprised of the manager's **investment criteria**. Most portfolio managers have an idea in their mind of the perfect investment (their **schema**), which is the target that the analyst is trying to hit, and experienced managers recognize a good idea by matching its characteristics against this ideal.

---

[1] A portfolio manager usually defaults to "no" when hearing a new investment idea. Chris Flynn, as one of Paul S.'s co-workers at Royce, often said, "Owning a stock is usually painful and something I seek to avoid. I do exhaustive research to find reasons why I *shouldn't* buy a stock. If, in the end, I can't find a good reason *not* to own it, I will reluctantly buy it." Bill Ackman once said that he tries to think of anything and everything that could possibly go wrong and if, at the end of the process, all that is left is nuclear war, he buys the stock.

The Importance of Matching a Portfolio Manager's Schema

Paul S. learned an important lesson about security selection early in his career from his Uncle Arnie that Paul has imparted to his students over the years. When speaking with former students years after graduation, it appears to be the one thing (sometimes the only thing) that many of them seem to remember. That sage advice? *"If your boss asks you for a blue umbrella, don't bring him a red one and then try to explain how it will keep him dry."*

Many rookie analysts make the understandable mistake of finding an idea *that they like* and then try to convince the portfolio manager to adopt it. This approach is generally a bad strategy. It is like trying to pound a square peg into a round hole. A better tactic is to select an idea that the manager will like because it will take a lot less effort convincing her to adopt it.

How should you determine what types of ideas the manager will find attractive? With the precision and persistence of a CIA operative, you will need to study the manager to develop a comprehensive profile of what characteristics they look for in the perfect investment. In other words, you must get inside their head and learn to think like they do.

We discuss in Chapter 5 the process by which an investor calculates their estimate of a stock's intrinsic value, which is replicated in Figure 10.1.

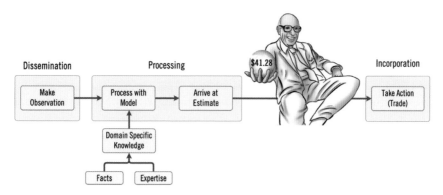

Figure 10.1   An Individual's Process for Estimating Intrinsic Value

As Figure 10.1 shows, an investor makes observations, processes the information with a model that is influenced by his **domain-specific knowledge**, arrives at an estimate based on that analysis, and then takes action based on his conclusion. The investor's domain-specific knowledge is a product of his experience and expertise, and the accumulated facts he has collected. To understand how a portfolio manager thinks, the analyst needs to reverse engineer the manager's decision-making process to determine how he arrives at his estimate. This means the analyst needs to get inside the manager's head to find out how his internal model works. Only then can the analyst figure out what types of investment ideas will grab the manager's attention. Figure 10.2 shows questions to ask when reverse engineering the portfolio manager's investment process.

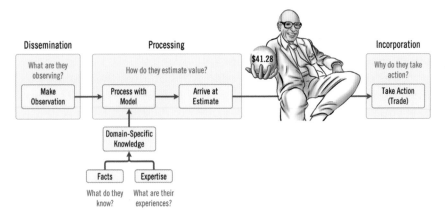

Figure 10.2   Reverse Engineering the Decision-Making Process

Through many years of trial and error, a portfolio manager builds a mental checklist of investment likes and dislikes. As a result, there are opportunities that immediately pique his interest and others that provoke a visceral negative reaction.

In his "mind's eye," the portfolio manager has a vision of what the perfect investment looks like. The criteria he uses to judge potential investment opportunities are best thought of as mental templates of ideal or perfect investments. The manager uses these templates to judge new investment candidates quickly. The criteria in the templates allow the manager to recognize patterns and act as a mental shortcut to reduce the time and energy needed to make an investment decision. In formal terms, these templates are called **schemas**.

A schema is a simple concept. Close your eyes and think of an ice cream sundae. An image will pop into your head of *your* ideal sundae. This mental picture can be either a compilation of the good qualities of sundaes you have eaten over the years rolled into one or a memory of a specific sundae that you thought was perfect. Whenever ordering a sundae you will compare it subconsciously to the sundae in your mind to decide how closely it matches the ideal. For instance, if you are allergic to peanuts, then any sundae with peanuts on it will fall into the "bad sundae" schema template. On the other hand, if you like chocolate sauce and cherries on your sundae, then these likes fall into the "ideal sundae" schema template. We present a schema for a sundae in Figure 10.3.

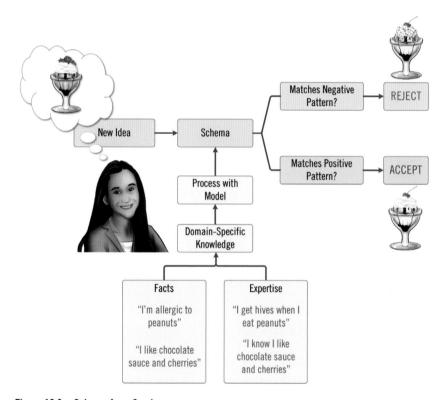

Figure 10.3   Schema for a Sundae

Schemas are not static, however. They evolve over time as individuals are exposed to new facts and additional experiences. The new information is added to, and alters, the old schema. For example, assume you see a commercial on TV for Burger King's bacon sundae.[2] You might not have thought of this combination before, so you do not have that criteria in your sundae schema. You update your

_____
[2] We did not fabricate this story. During the summer of 2012, Burger King offered a bacon sundae with soft vanilla ice cream, topped with hot fudge, caramel, bacon crumbles, and a slice of bacon. Neither author has tried one.

facts to include "bacon can be used as a sundae topping." Your sundae schema is now changed forever as it will always include bacon as a possible sundae topping. Imagine that you go to Burger King to try one, and it's awful. Your **experiences** have altered your "bad sundae" schema by adding a sundae topped with bacon to it. The next time you are offered a bacon sundae, your mind will automatically think, "Sundaes taste lousy with bacon," and you will instantly reject it, as shown in Figure 10.4.

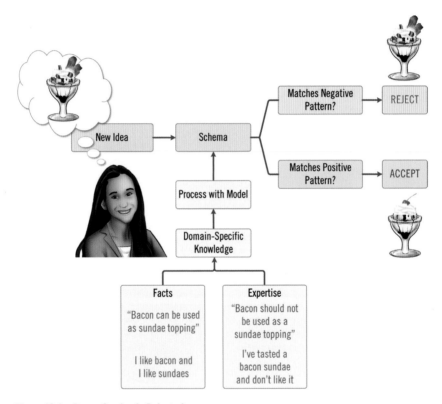

Figure 10.4   Bacon Sundae Is Rejected

This example shows how individuals subconsciously use schemas to identify patterns quickly and make decisions efficiently. Evaluating stocks is no different than evaluating sundaes, and many portfolio managers use schemas to *size up new investment ideas quickly.* For instance, if a new idea matches a portfolio manager's well-established positive pattern, then he will consider it. On the other hand, if the idea does not match a positive pattern, it will be rejected. It is important to note that portfolio managers often have more than one investment schema. For instance, a manager might have a "turnaround" schema, a "new management that will cut costs" schema, a "spinoff" schema, or even a "slow growth, strong cash flow, major stock buyback" schema.

A portfolio manager's schemas change as he is exposed to new facts and different experiences. For example, getting defrauded by a CEO with a mustache might result in the manager creating a new "companies who have CEOs with mustaches are bad investments" schema.[3] There are also schemas within schemas. For example, a portfolio manager might have a few different schemas for CEOs that fit within a larger turnaround schema. Portfolio managers will have schemas of investments that worked out well and schemas for investments that did not. One manager might hate investing in toy companies because they were burned by one before, but love shoe manufacturers because they have made money with those companies in the past. Pitching a toy company stock to the manager will trigger their "toy company" schema and they will most likely shut down your recommendation immediately, although they will be quite receptive to a pitch for a shoe company as it triggers a schema that has previously worked well for them.[4]

A portfolio manager's schema for the ideal investment is a little more complicated than their schema for the ideal sundae. Their investment schema contains two main sets of criteria, one based on the company's **fundamental criteria** and the other on the stock's **valuation criteria**. Fundamental criteria focus on the quality of the business, with factors that include, but are not limited to, the company's industry, competitive position, capital intensity, growth rate, and quality of management. The fundamental criteria address the question, "Is this a good *business*?" The valuation criteria focus on the investment's risk/return profile and address the question, "Is this a good *investment*?"

---

[3] At the 2012 Graham and Dodd breakfast, portfolio manager Meryl Witmer discussed her aversion to companies with mustachioed CEOs.

[4] In terms of being triggered by the mere mention of a toy company, Paul S. remembers a particularly interesting experience when he worked at First Manhattan. The firm's founder and highly-successful fund manager, Sandy Gottesman, said to him once, "I'm going to give you a gun that I want you to keep in your desk. If I ever come to you wanting to buy a toy company, I want you to take the gun out of your desk and shoot me with it."

If the investment idea does not satisfy either the portfolio manager's fundamental or valuation criteria, he will reject it immediately. If the idea satisfies the manager's fundamental criteria but not his valuation criteria, he will listen with some level of interest and may make note to track the stock in the future (putting it on his "shopping list"), although, most likely, will not follow the recommendation to buy the stock. If the opportunity does not fit his fundamental criteria, but the valuation looks compelling, the portfolio manager might take further interest in the idea because of its potential return. If the idea satisfies both the manager's fundamental and valuation criteria, he will clear his desk to move as quickly as possible to exploit the opportunity. We present the four possible scenarios in Figure 10.5.

Figure 10.5   Matrix of Fundamental and Valuation Criteria

The "shopping list" category in Figure 10.5 bears further explanation. Robert Bruce, a legendary value investor, who was handpicked by Warren Buffett to run the investment portfolio at Fireman's Fund in the 1970s, explains that looking for stocks is like shopping for shoes. Bruce says he is always on the lookout for shoes to buy and often window-shops for ones he likes, although he usually waits for them to go on sale before buying them. He stated that he does the same thing with stocks. He is always on the lookout for stocks he wants to own, but only buys them when they go on sale. Because many other portfolio managers window-shop for stocks like Bruce, they will likely be interested in a new idea if the business fits their **fundamental criteria** as long as the stock is not too far from their **valuation criteria**.

In practice, fundamental and valuation assessments are made in parallel, although, for simplicity of explanation, we will discuss them serially. We start with fundamental criteria first and then explain how valuation criteria fit into the investment process.

Identifying a Manager's Fundamental Criteria

To show the different facets of the portfolio manager's fundamental **criteria**, we start with an example of buying a house. When someone goes house hunting, they usually have a good idea of what they are looking for in a new home and often have a picture in their mind's eye of their dream house. The criteria in their dream house **schema** includes all the qualities or factors they desire, which is, essentially, a checklist.

Figure 10.6   Dreaming of the Perfect House and the Perfect Investment

Choosing a Stock Is Like Choosing a House

We illustrate the similarities of buying a home and buying a stock with a short story. Henry is a portfolio manager at the firm where you work as an analyst. Your job is to support the portfolio managers by bringing them ideas that will outperform the market. Simply put, you are trying to find stocks appropriate for them to buy for their portfolio. While you and Henry know each other professionally, you have not worked together closely in the past. One day, you bump into each other in line at the cafeteria, start chatting, and decide to have lunch together.

During the conversation, you discover that Henry is looking to buy a new summer home. You ask what kind of house he is looking for and he mentions several characteristics for his ideal home—five bedrooms, less than $15 million, tennis court, nice neighborhood, modern with a classic design, and priced below market. You tell

Henry, "My good friend Ed Bogen[5] is a real estate agent, and he was just showing me a new exclusive listing that might be perfect for you." You pull up Ed's listing on your phone to show Henry a few pictures of the house. He responds, "Wow, that house looks really nice." You tell him a little about the house: five bedrooms, great neighborhood, on the beach, listed at $12.5 million, with a classic design and modern construction.

The house was presented as a new idea and Henry subconsciously—in the blink of an eye—put the house through his "dream summer house" **schema** to see if it matched his desired criteria. This process is shown in Figure 10.7.

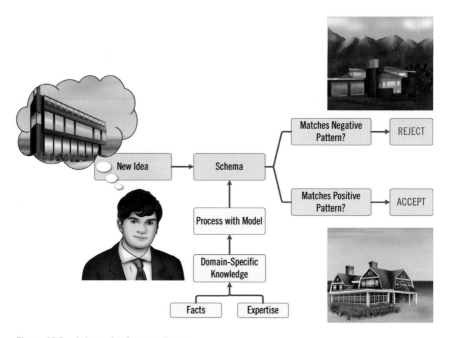

Figure 10.7   Schema for Summer House

Since Henry found the house appealing and it fit his **schema**, at least on the initial pass, he decided to call your friend Ed to schedule an appointment to see the house.

---

[5] Shameless plug (If movies can do product placements, why not books?): Edmund Bogen is a close friend and fraternity brother of Paul S. He is an experienced real estate agent and is happy to help anyone looking for a home in South Florida. Simply Google "Edmund Bogen realtor."

Henry and Ed meet later that week to tour the house. The next morning you walk into Henry's office to ask him what he thought about the house. He responds, "It is a beautiful house, but I passed." You ask, "What didn't you like?" He shrugs his shoulders and says, "I'm not really sure. Ed is a great broker and is very professional. The house he showed me is really nice, but it just didn't *feel* right."

You prod him a bit further. Henry mentions that while the house matches his preferences, is right on the beach, and in a really nice neighborhood, he didn't like it, although he couldn't put his finger on why that was the case. With a slightly puzzled look, he replies, "Maybe it was a little too dark inside."

You return to your office a bit perplexed and think to yourself, "Hmmm. I am a bit surprised. The house seemed to be the perfect match for him. He said that it had all the things he was looking for; I wonder why he didn't like it?"

The following day you bump into Henry in the cafeteria. You start chatting and decide to have lunch together again. During the conversation, you find out that Henry just received an inflow of new capital into his midcap value fund and is looking for new investment ideas. You ask what kind of company he has in mind. Henry tells you his ideal investment—a market cap between $2 billion and $10 billion, undervalued, and a stock that has underperformed the indices in the past year. He generally avoids companies in the financial or biotech industries. He says he likes companies with analyst coverage, that have strong competitive positions and good capital allocation. He also likes companies with a P/E ratio below 20 and a five-year growth rate of more than 7%.

You tell Henry, "I know a company that might be a perfect fit. It's Williams-Sonoma." You pull up Google Finance on your phone and show Henry the company's financials. He responds, "Wow, that stock looks really attractive." You proceed to tell him a little bit about the company: "The market cap is $5.2 billion and the stock has a P/E ratio of 17. The company has generated 5-year growth of approximately 7%, the stock has trailed the index for the past year, and the company has a strong competitive position." You give Henry a copy of your research report on Williams-Sonoma and he promises to read it later that day.

You walk to his office the next morning to ask him what he thought of the idea. Henry responds, "It's a good idea, but I'm going to pass." You then ask him what he didn't like. He shrugs his shoulders and says, "I'm not sure, it looks like a good company, but I don't *feel* that compelled to do any more work on it."

You prod Henry a bit further. He admits that while Williams-Sonoma fits his investment profile based on the company's financials, that the business has high returns on capital, and the stock looks undervalued, the idea is not compelling to him, although he could not put his finger on what he did not like about it. Henry then replied, "Maybe it's that most of their sales are domestic."

You walk back to your office a bit perplexed and think to yourself, "Hmmm. I am surprised. Williams-Sonoma seemed to be the perfect idea for him. He liked the company's financials. The company has a strong competitive positon and consistent revenue growth rate. The stock is cheap and they have had great capital allocation. I wonder why he did not like it."

What Went Wrong?

To figure out where the idea went wrong and why Henry rejected it, we will conduct a review on the recommendation. We will start with the summer house first to see if we can gain insight into how Henry makes decisions and then apply those insights into the stock recommendation.

To start, we need to gather the criteria that Henry gave you for his *dream summer house,* as shown in Figure 10.8.

Figure 10.8   Stated Criteria for Summer House

We can parse the criteria into different categories to diagnose why Henry passed on the house Ed showed him. At first glance, we see that some of his criteria are **quantitative** and some are **qualitative**, as shown in Figure 10.9. That seems like a good place to start the discussion.

Quantitative	Qualitative	
5+ bedrooms	On the beach	Nice neighborhood
3+ car garage	Tennis court	Modern yet classic
Less than $15 million	Priced below market	Inexpensive to maintain

Figure 10.9   Criteria Parsed into Quantitative and Qualitative

The **quantitative** criteria are items that can be **objectively measured**. These items are **numerical** and can be reduced to hard numbers. They are also go/no go–type criteria. If the house doesn't match the numerical criteria, it will be eliminated from further consideration. For example, if the house has two bedrooms, it is clearly not a match and Henry will not spend more time looking at its other attributes. There is no point in suggesting potential houses that do not meet Henry's qualitative criteria because he has been clear in what he is looking for in a new summer home and will reject them outright. The summer house you suggested met all Henry's quantitative criteria, as shown in Figure 10.10, so that is clearly not where the problem lies.

We evaluate the **qualitative** criteria next. We see that the qualitative criteria fall into two broad categories: **objective** and **subjective**. The objective qualitative criteria are binary—*yes or no*–type filters—and the house either matches them or it does not. Three of the six qualitative criteria Henry gave you are objective: The house must have a tennis court, be on the beach, and priced below market for him to be interested. This analysis is similar to the **quantitative criteria** in that it is straightforward to see whether the criteria are met. For example, if the house isn't on the beach, it is clearly not a match for Henry, and he will not spend more time considering the

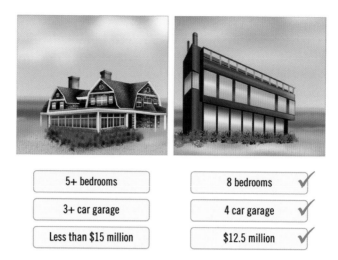

Figure 10.10   Objective Quantitative Criteria Satisfied

house's other features. It should be easy to see that a potential house needs to meet these **qualitative** factors to keep Henry interested. Again, there is no reason not to meet this set of criteria when recommending a summer home because Henry has been specific about what he is looking for.

What about the other three qualitative criteria? We saw that there were hard numbers with the quantitative data. We also saw that it was relatively straightforward to determine whether the house met certain qualitative data, such as being on the beach or priced below market. It is much harder to determine if the house matches the remaining three criteria Henry stated because they are less clear in their meaning. Henry said he wanted the house to be in a nice neighborhood, but how does he define *nice*? He wanted the house to be modern, with a classic design, but what is his idea of *modern*, or *classic*, for that matter? As the saying goes, beauty (or niceness in this case) is in the eye of the beholder. While you might be able to rank *niceness* on a scale of 1 to 10, it will remain a **subjective** measure. One person's 10 can be quite different from another person's 10. We split the qualitative criteria into two subcategories—**objective** and **subjective**—as shown in Figure 10.11.

Figure 10.11   Objective Versus Subjective Criteria

Did the house match Henry's **qualitative** criteria? Obviously not, or he would have continued to be interested in it. The question remains, where did the recommendation go wrong?

As we see in Figure 10.12, it appears that the **subjective qualitative criteria** were the culprit in Henry's rejection of the recommendation. When you had lunch with Henry, you thought you had a good idea of what he wanted when he listed his requirements. However, by a process of elimination, we can determine that for some reason the house didn't meet Henry's **subjective criteria**. Maybe the house wasn't modern enough? Maybe it was too expensive to maintain? Most people would think the house is located in a desirable neighborhood, although it appears that Henry doesn't agree.

Figure 10.12   Subjective Criteria Not Satisfied

The problem is that Henry merely stated his **subjective** criteria, such as nice neighborhood, without fully defining them. While you thought you understood what Henry meant when he said "nice neighborhood" and "inexpensive to maintain," now you are not so sure. Perhaps you should have asked Henry more questions, such as

"How do you define a *nice* neighborhood?" We might conclude that if you had asked those additional questions, you would have been able to better determine if the house was a good match for Henry. However, Henry must be able to explain his subjective criteria for you to fully understand what he is looking for in a summer house. The problem is that when pressed, Henry might not be able to articulate the definition of his criteria, even to himself.[6]

You then remember that when pressed, Henry said, "Maybe it was a little too dark inside?" You think back to the criteria that Henry gave you and realize he didn't mention anything about sunlight. You walk over to Henry's office the next morning and ask if there was anything else he didn't like about the house. He says, "I thought about it as I was driving home last night. The property taxes were a little high, the house didn't have a cobblestone driveway, and I'd like to be closer to town."

You think to yourself, "Hmmm. He didn't mention *any* of those things at lunch. Had I known, I wouldn't have suggested the house." This new insight highlights another type of criteria—Henry's **unstated criteria**. Now that the additional criteria are **stated**, you can add them to your list. Some of the new criteria are **objective** and the rest are **subjective**. You now have a much clearer picture of what Henry is looking for in a summer house.

Figure 10.13   Unstated Criteria Revealed and Included

When you add Henry's unstated criteria to the list, as shown in Figure 10.14, you realize that your recommendation did not match

---

[6] Sit back and try the exercise for yourself. Picture your "dream summer house." What is your definition of a "nice" neighborhood? While typing this comment, Paul S. pondered his definition. Here is his stream of consciousness: "Hmmm. Nice. Nice neighbors. Not too loud. No wild parties. No barking dogs. Not a lot of kids running in the street. Quiet. People on the block taking pride in their houses and keeping their property properly manicured. Minimal crime. People minding their own business." Your definition of a "nice" neighborhood is probably different. It is not easy to articulate these criteria without deliberate thought.

the additional criteria, as we show in Figure 10.14. The new objective criteria are relatively easy to validate, although the subjective criteria remain problematic.

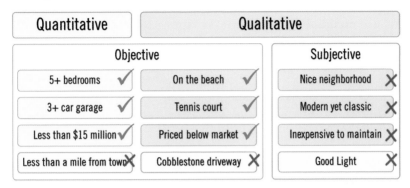

Quantitative		Qualitative	
Objective			**Subjective**
5+ bedrooms ✓	On the beach ✓		Nice neighborhood ✗
3+ car garage ✓	Tennis court ✓		Modern yet classic ✗
Less than $15 million ✓	Priced below market ✓		Inexpensive to maintain ✗
Less than a mile from town ✗	Cobblestone driveway ✗		Good Light ✗

Figure 10.14   Unstated Criteria Were Not Satisfied

While finding Henry a house, and helping your friend Ed earn a fat commission, would be a nice favor to do, it will be much better for your career if you found Henry a new investment idea for his portfolio. Let's evaluate Henry's investment criteria in the same way that we evaluated his summer house criteria to see where your recommendation of Williams-Sonoma fell short. We list the criteria Henry gave you about his ideal investment in Figure 10.15.

Figure 10.15   Portfolio Manager's Stated Investment Criteria

We need to parse Henry's investment criteria into the different categories to diagnose what went wrong with the recommendation, like what we did with the summer house. Similar to the prior example, some of Henry's investment criteria are **quantitative** and some are **qualitative**, as we show in Figure 10.16.

Quantitative	Qualitative	
Market cap $2-$10 billion	Underperformed index	Strong competitive position
5 year growth >7%	No financials or biotech	Good capital allocation
P/E below 20	Analyst coverage	Undervalued

Figure 10.16   Parsed Quantitative and Qualitative Criteria

The **quantitative** criteria are all items that can be **objectively measured**. These criteria can be reduced to hard numbers. They are also go/no go–type criteria. Henry will reject the recommendation from further consideration if it fails to match his quantitative criteria. For example, the company is clearly not a match for Henry's mid-cap fund if its market cap is $500 million. It is critical to point out that any potential investment idea pitched to Henry needs to meet these quantitative factors—there is no reason not to match this set of criteria. Williams-Sonoma met Henry's stated criteria, as shown in Figure 10.17, so that is not where the problem lies.

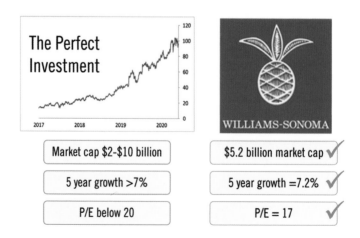

Figure 10.17   Objective Quantitative Criteria Satisfied

Next, we turn to Henry's **qualitative** criteria. We see that these characteristics fall into two broad categories. Some of the criteria are **objective** and **binary**—*yes or no*–type filters. The investment candidate either has that quality or not, which includes three of the six qualitative criteria Henry mentioned such as the company has underperformed the index and the stock has analyst coverage. This vetting process of the objective criteria is similar to the one we performed for the quantitative criteria and is easy to ascertain. For example, if the investment candidate is a financial or biotech company, it is clearly not a match for Henry's fund and he won't spend any more time considering it. There is no excuse for a potential idea not to meet these **qualitative** factors because Henry has been clear in what he is looking for in an investment idea.

The other three qualitative criteria are less clear. Undervalued? Good capital allocation? Strong competitive position? We cannot put a hard number on those factors. Value and quality are in the eye of the beholder because they are **subjective** measures. As a result, we can split the qualitative criteria into two subcategories, **objective** and **subjective**, as shown in Figure 10.18.

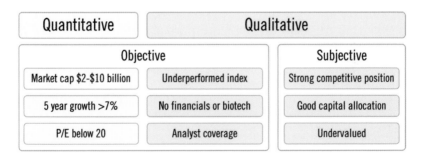

Figure 10.18   Objective versus Subjective Criteria

Did William-Sonoma match Henry's subjective criteria? Obviously not or he would have continued doing work on it. Where did we go wrong with the recommendation? Once again, the **subjective qualitative criteria** appears to be the culprit in Henry's rejecting the idea, as shown in Figure 10.19. We thought we had a good idea of what Henry wanted when he listed his investment requirements during lunch. He told us what we thought was exactly the kind of company he was looking for. However, by process of elimination, we found that for some reason Williams-Sonoma did not meet Henry's **subjective** criteria. Maybe management's capital allocation decisions or the company's competitive position were not good enough, at least in Henry's mind? Maybe the stock was not undervalued, at least by Henry's standards? It seems like most portfolio managers would think Williams-Sonoma is an attractive investment idea, although apparently, Henry didn't agree. But why not?

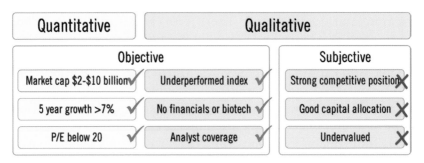

Figure 10.19   Subjective Criteria Were Not Satisfied

Now that we look through the parsed criteria, we realize that maybe you should have asked Henry more questions. How does he define *undervalued* and *good capital allocation*? Which other companies does he think are *undervalued*? You might conclude that if you had asked more questions, you would have been able to better determine if Williams-Sonoma would be a good fit for Henry's portfolio.

The problem is that Henry merely *stated* his **subjective** criteria, such as "good competitive position," without fully defining them. While you thought you understood what Henry meant when he first said "good capital allocation," now you are not so sure. Henry must be able to explain his criteria for you to fully understand what he is looking for in an investment idea. However, when pressed, he might not be able to articulate his subjective criteria, even to himself. The challenge for you is that Henry will expect you to understand exactly what he means when he states his subjective criteria. And, unlike **objective criteria**, which are unambiguous, each person's definition of their subjective criteria will be different.[7]

What about any of Henry's **unstated criteria**? When you discussed the investment idea with Henry, he revealed additional, albeit, unstated criteria, when he said, "And, as I thought more about Williams-Sonoma, I was concerned that most of their sales are domestic; I'm looking for a company that is more global with at least 50% of their sales from outside the US. I like firms trading at a lower valuation than the industry, and the company's management doesn't own much stock."

Some of the new criteria are **objective** and some are **subjective**, as we show in Figure 10.20. You now have a better sense of what Henry wants in a stock and will have a better idea of what kinds of companies to recommend to him in the future.

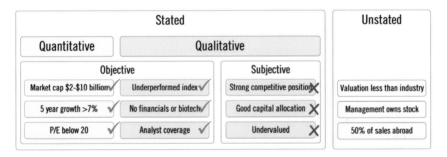

Figure 10.20   Unstated Criteria Revealed and Included

When we add Henry's unstated criteria to the current list, as shown in Figure 10.21, you realize that your recommendation did not meet the additional criteria.

---

[7] Sit back and try the exercise for yourself. Think about "good capital allocation." What is your definition? While typing his response, Paul S. is thinking, "Hmmm. If the company can reinvest in the business at a high return on invested capital, that should be the first use of the capital. If there is excess cash in the business, the company should not let it build up on the balance sheet and should return it to shareholders in the most tax-efficient way, by stock repurchases." Paul does not like dividends. To him, good capital allocation is not about optimizing the capital structure by taking on debt because he doesn't like companies with debt. Your definition of "good capital allocation" is probably different. It is not easy to articulate these criteria without deliberate thought.

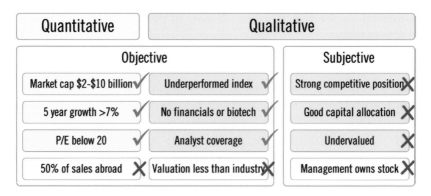

Figure 10.21   Unstated Criteria Were Not Satisfied

It is clear that the subjective criteria continue to remain problematic. You originally thought you understood what Henry wanted when he listed his investment criteria, although, with hindsight, you realize you didn't. Henry passed on your recommendation because it failed to match all his fundamental criteria.

Henry's **objective criteria** are *explicit*—he *stated* them clearly and his metrics were unambiguous. There was little room for confusion or doubt. On the other hand, his **subjective criteria** were open to interpretation. While Henry thought he was clear when he stated he wanted a company with a "strong competitive position," the definition was not articulated well, making it almost impossible for you to match the criteria. To make matters worse, Henry also has a list of **unstated** investment criteria, some of which were also **subjective.** It is not that Henry is intentionally trying to make your life difficult by not stating these additional criteria; it is that he might have forgotten that these criteria were important or they might be subconscious and not easy for Henry to articulate.

Identifying a Manager's Valuation Criteria

If we parse Henry's investment criteria even further, as shown in Figure 10.22, we see that some of the criteria relate to the **fundamentals** of the business while others relate to the stock's **valuation.** Criteria like "P/E below 20" are **quantitative** and **objective,** and are easy to understand. While **qualitative**, the requirement "valuation less than the industry," is also straightforward to match—the stock either matches this criterion or does not. However, criterion like "undervalued" is **subjective** and often open to interpretation. Does this requirement mean the company has a dominant market position in the industry or the strongest product offering in the market? While the criterion is *stated*, it is **subjective**, therefore, its definition is unclear and significantly harder to satisfy.

Figure 10.22   Fundamental and Valuation Investment Criteria

Other Barriers to Adoption

As we discuss at the beginning of the chapter, because the portfolio manager's success depends on the investment performance she delivers, she[8] will be extremely selective about which ideas she puts in her portfolio. Consequentially, most portfolio managers put all new ideas under an intense microscope to identify any flaws. To survive this intense scrutiny, the analyst must be right with his analysis.

There are actually *two* sets of obstacles that the analyst must overcome. The first obstacle is getting past Dr. No, which the analyst must do just to get the portfolio manager to *listen* to his pitch. There is, however, a second, much more challenging obstacle that the analyst must overcome to get the manager to *adopt* his idea.

The analyst circumvents the first obstacle by matching the portfolio manager's **objective criteria**. If satisfied, the manager will listen

[8] To avoid any confusion, we return to using 'she' because the portfolio manager at the beginning of the chapter is a woman.

to the analyst's pitch. However, the second obstacle is a more formidable barrier and guarded accordingly.[9] The analyst will not convince the portfolio manager to adopt the idea unless it satisfies the manager's subjective criteria.

There is no excuse for the analyst not to meet the portfolio manager's **objective** criteria since they are usually stated clearly, well defined, and unambiguous. On the other hand, satisfying the portfolio manager's **subjective criteria** is a much harder challenge to overcome.

It is important to note that getting a portfolio manager to listen to a new idea is much easier than getting her to adopt it. There is no risk in listening to the pitch, other than lost time, which is not insignificant. However, there *is* significant risk to the portfolio manager once she commits capital, which is the possibility of losing money or underperforming the market, as we discuss in Chapter 9. Therefore, for the portfolio manager to take action on your idea it must satisfy *both* sets of criteria, as shown in Figure 10.23.

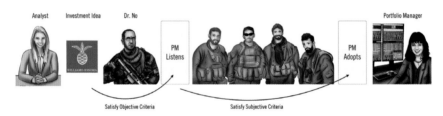

Figure 10.23   Idea Adoption Requires Overcoming Objective and Subjective Obstacles

If you consistently fail to match the portfolio manager's **objective criteria**, you will eventually lose your job, as it demonstrates that you do not seem to grasp the manager's most basic investment criteria (simply put, not matching unambiguous stated criteria is inexcusable). Your failure to match **subjective criteria** will result in a low adoption rate for your ideas. You may keep your job, but you will never get promoted and rarely receive a bonus, and will likely become increasingly frustrated in your job.

---

[9] The Navy SEALS in the drawing used to represent the second obstacle in the portfolio manager's mind are from Operation Red Wings.

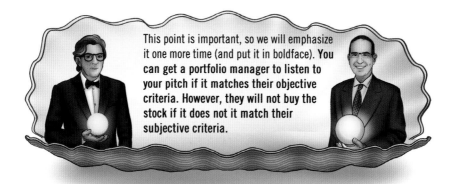

This point is important, so we will emphasize it one more time (and put it in boldface). **You can get a portfolio manager to listen to your pitch if it matches their objective criteria. However, they will not buy the stock if it does not it match their subjective criteria.**

Overcome Barriers by Learning How to Read a Portfolio Manager's Mind

The two most problematic areas in understanding what stocks a portfolio manager will find appealing are her **subjective** and **unstated** criteria. How is it possible for an analyst to read a portfolio manager's mind? You must learn to think how she thinks. How can this be accomplished?

The analyst should ask a lot of questions to learn what the manager's criteria include. The analyst also should read the portfolio manager's letters to investors; review any interviews they have given in *Barron's*, on Bloomberg, or in other industry news sources; and listen or watch any presentations they have delivered.

Analysts can also review the manager's holdings to see which companies she is invested in currently. Managers with more than $100 in equity assets or who own more than 5% of a company's stock are required to make periodic filings with the SEC disclosing their holdings. These filings include 13D filings, 13G filings, and 13F filings[10]. An ambitious analyst might even do additional research on specific positions to see if he can determine the criteria used to make these decisions.

---

[10] Most people think that 13Fs are required to be filed by any advisor who manages over $100 million of securities. That is not accurate. For clarification, 13F filings are required to be filed by 'institutional investment managers' who ". . . exercise investment discretion over $100 million or more . . ." of 13F securities. There is quarterly publication issued by the SEC called, *The Official List of Section 13(f) Securities*, which lists securities that qualify to be included in the $100 million figure. For more information, search the SEC website for "13f filing requirements."

These information sources focus on current investments in the portfolio, while prior filings can provide information pertaining to past investments. However, because the analyst is trying to determine not only the portfolio manager's **objective criteria** but also her **subjective criteria**, having a view into investment ideas that did *not* get adopted would offer additional valuable insight.

This concept is referred to as *negative space* in the art world. The art critic needs to analyze not only what *is there*, but also what *is not there*, to fully grasp all the information the image conveys. The critic sees aspects of the image he would have otherwise missed by doing this analysis. This insight is illustrated by Rubin's vase, which is presented in Figure 10.24. The vase is clear in the image on the left, while two faces are revealed when focusing on the negative space in the image on the right.

John Smithson 2007

Figure 10.24   Negative Space and Rubin's Vase

Because most portfolio managers perform research only on companies that meet their **objective criteria**, rejected ideas provide additional insight because they somehow failed to match the managers' **subjective criteria**. Unfortunately, none of the information previously discussed, such as the SEC filings or news media interviews, reveals the investment ideas that the portfolio manager researched, but decided *not* to pursue. It will be nearly impossible to have access to such information from outside the organization. The analyst will have insight into rejected ideas only if he works closely with the portfolio manager.

Another important exercise when researching a portfolio manager is to build a checklist of criteria that the manager uses to make her investment decisions and to listen attentively to all questions she asks during the research process. These questions often provide insight into the manager's **subjective criteria**. The following list are questions an analyst can ask to gain insight into a manager's criteria:

- Does the manager have a target range or minimum hurdle for the expected investment return?
- What are the manager's market cap constraints? Large, small, mid, nano-cap, or mega-cap?
- What are the growth characteristics the manager looking for? Is slow growth okay, or does the manager insist on high growth?
- What is the manager's preferred valuation metrics? Do they look at EBITDA multiples, P/E multiples, or earnings power value? Are they in search of deep value, value, growth at a reasonable price, or pure growth?
- Are there specific industries the manager focuses on or avoids?
- What geography does the manager prefer? Domestic or international? Developed countries or emerging markets?
- Does the manager insist that a company have a strong competitive position or be an industry leader?
- Is the manager receptive to contrarian investment ideas and turnarounds?
- Does the manager have a preference regarding management? Any requirements regarding corporate governance? How important is the management's ability to allocate capital?
- Is the composition of the company's shareholder base a factor? Does the manager like to be the "only footprints in the parking lot" (meaning very few investors looking at the company), or do they feel more comfortable if there are other well-known investors who hold positions?
- Is there a limit on a company's financial leverage?
- Does the manager look for the possibility of financial engineering or other types of restructuring? Do they gravitate toward companies that are takeover or activist targets? Companies where there is the need for a spinoff or divestitures?
- What is the manager's typical time horizon? Weeks, months, years, or forever?
- What are the characteristics such as concentration and turnover in the manager's portfolio?

Other Communication Pitfalls

Other potential opportunities for miscommunication occur when a portfolio manager has conflicting criteria in his mind for what he looks for in an investment idea. The conflicting requirements will make it nearly impossible for a single idea to match *all* his criteria, objective or subjective. Making the situation more challenging, it is likely the portfolio manager will be unable to articulate all the criteria he has in mind simply because his list of criteria is long. Furthermore, his criteria may change depending on what part of the criteria appears most important to him at that moment.

Another potential area for miscommunication arises when the portfolio manager is vague with his criteria. There are subtle differences between unstated criteria and vague criteria. For instance, the manager may have a good idea in mind of what he is looking for in a new investment, but fails to communicate even the **objective criteria** all that well. This problem is not uncommon. Portfolio managers are inundated with information, and although the analyst may have asked specifically what criteria the manager is looking for in an investment, the manager may not have the time or the interest to make the criteria as explicit as the analyst needs to be effective in selecting appropriate investment ideas. And, sometimes, the portfolio manager may avoid the discussion intentionally because he does not want to be pinned down.

And, of course, the problem may not be the portfolio manager's miscommunication. Instead, he may be explicit in stating his criteria, yet the analyst either hears something completely different or interprets the criteria incorrectly.

Improving Communication Is Crucial to Increase Productivity Within an Organization

As we have tried to emphasize throughout this chapter, the analyst needs to make sure he fully understand all the portfolio manager's **objective criteria** and must carefully research and study the manager to better understand his **subjective criteria**. Nailing the subjective criteria requires observation and communication, and a lot of it.

The portfolio manager has several responsibilities in helping the analyst be effective in his efforts to find appropriate investment ideas. For starters, the portfolio manager cannot expect the analyst to be a mind reader. The manager needs to make sure the analyst understands all his **objective criteria** and be aware that his **subjective criteria** may not be obvious even to himself, much less anyone else. The manager should try to communicate as many details about his full investment criteria as possible and offer direct feedback when a new investment idea fails to match his requirements.

Whether pitching a stock for a job interview, a class, a stock pitching competition, or to a portfolio manager in your organization, the analyst will be challenged to understand the portfolio manager's **schema** and match the manager's investment criteria. It is impossible for the analyst to read the portfolio manager's mind, and vice versa. This disconnect results in wasted time and mutual frustration. The fix is better communication, which leads to greater idea adoption and, ultimately, greater organizational productivity.

BACK TO REALITY

Keep in mind that a portfolio manager's subjective criteria are usually refined over decades of investing and, depending on the situation, can have multiple layers of importance. Much of the subjective criteria for experienced portfolio managers is so ingrained that it has become almost second nature. There is no explicit checklist in their mind that the idea must meet; rather there is a feeling they get when they hear a good idea. Consequentially, most seasoned portfolio managers are unable to fully articulate all their subjective criteria. Don't take our word for it. An interview with legendary investor Leon Cooperman highlights this phenomenon perfectly:[11]

> We try to find some set of statistics that motivate us to act. The analogy I have always used is that when you go into the beer section of the supermarket, you see 25 different brands of beer. There's something that makes you reach for one particular brew. In the parlance of the stock market, there's some combination of return-on-equity, growth rate, P/E ratio, dividend yield, and asset value that makes you act.[12]

We also use Cooperman's comment to illustrate how difficult it can be to discern what a manager is looking for by simply reading an interview, which highlights the importance of performing additional research on any portfolio manager you plan on pitching.

---

[11] Cooperman was the son of Jewish Polish immigrants and grew up in the South Bronx of New York City. He was the first of his family to attend college. He eventually went to Columbia Business School and, upon graduation, got a job at Goldman Sachs, where he ultimately became chairman of Goldman Sachs Asset Management. He started his investment partnership Omega Advisors in 1991 and, at the time of this writing in March 2017, has over $6.1 billion under management. Forbes lists Cooperman's net worth at $3.2 billion.

[12] "Lee Cooperman—Buying Straw Hats in the Winter," *Graham & Doddsville*, Fall 2011, 5.

Gems:
- ⬦ Portfolio managers use schemas to evaluate new investment ideas quickly. Any idea you pitch must match one of the manager's schema.
- ⬦ The portfolio manager's schema contains two main sets of criteria: fundamental criteria, which are focused on the quality of the business, and valuation criteria, which are focused on the risk/return profile of the stock.
- ⬦ The portfolio manager's criteria are further segmented into objective and subjective criteria. There is absolutely no excuse for the analyst not meeting the portfolio manager's objective criteria because they are usually stated explicitly.

▽ Assuming all the portfolio manager's objective criteria are met, most pitches fail because they do not satisfy the manager's subjective criteria, often because it is difficult for the manager to articulate these criteria fully.

▽ The portfolio manager will listen to a pitch if the idea satisfies all her objective criteria, but will not adopt the idea unless it satisfies her stated and unstated subjective criteria.

CHAPTER

11

How to Organize the Content of the Message

Your interview is tomorrow morning. Bright and early. You have done a lot of work and think you have a stock you will feel confident pitching. You have researched the portfolio manager you are meeting and built a dossier that a seasoned CIA operative would envy. You are confident you have his **objective criteria** nailed down and have a reasonably good understanding of his **subjective criteria**. You have done a lot of independent research and have developed a **variant perspective**, combining what you think is an informational and analytical advantage. Finally, you are confident that you have identified a genuine mispricing in the market and know what will correct it. You are as prepared as you could be for the interview.

When you meet the portfolio manager, how much time will you have? Probably not a lot. Maybe a few minutes before he gets bored and starts looking at his watch. Given this time constraint, how do you distill all that research into a persuasive pitch?

How to Capture and Keep a Portfolio Manager's Attention

When determining what elements to include in your pitch, imagine that your house is on fire and you have only 30 seconds to evacuate. What three items would you take? Similarly, you need to think about the three most essential points you want to convey to the portfolio manager in your pitch.

Pitching a stock to a portfolio manager is not like pitching a stock in class or at a stock pitch competition, where you can drone on for 20 minutes, testing your audience's patience as you drag them through your 30-page PowerPoint presentation. You cannot simply throw disembodied facts at the portfolio manager, hoping he will somehow make sense of them. The portfolio manager does not have the time, inclination, or patience to listen to what you have to say, put all the pieces together in a form that makes sense to him, and then weigh the validity of your investment idea. You are simply asking him to do too much work.

Building upon Judge Mansfield's **mosaic theory** that we discuss in Chapter 8, we use an analogy of a puzzle. If you have done sufficient research, while a few pieces might be missing, you feel that you know what the completed puzzle will look like. You may have convinced yourself that the picture is clear, but now you must convince someone else. Most stock pitches fail because the analyst essentially tosses a jumble of pieces onto the table and says to the portfolio manager, "Here, you go figure it out."

Imperial Airship by James Ng, redrawn with permission.

Even when more experienced analysts think they have provided the portfolio manager with enough information for him to see the complete picture and make an investment decision, the pitch often falls flat because they provide a picture with too many pieces missing. The portfolio manager needs to see *the full picture* to understand, comprehend, and adopt your idea.

Imperial Airship by James Ng, redrawn with permission.

To pitch an investment idea successfully, you need to show the portfolio manager as much of the picture as possible.

Imperial Airship by James Ng, redrawn with permission.

How should you use the limited time you have to paint a picture that the portfolio manager can understand? What do you say when the portfolio manager asks, "So whatta you got for me, sport? Why are you here?"

A typical pitch looks like the scene from the movie *Wall Street*,[1] when a young Bud Fox finagles his way into Gordon Gekko's office

---

[1] We encourage the reader to watch the movie clip before reading the following section. To see the clip, Google "Wall Street Bud Fox meets Gordon Gekko."

and, after sitting for hours in the waiting area, finally gets a few moments of Gekko's time. Gekko says to Fox, "So what's on your mind, kemosabe? Why am I listening to you?" In the movie, Fox pitches his first idea: "Chart breakout on this one here. White-wood-Young Industries. Low P/E, explosive earnings, 30% discount to book value, great cash flow, strong management and a couple of 5% holders." Gekko shuts him down, "It's a dog. What else you got, sport?"

Unfazed, Fox immediately jumps to his second idea, "Terafly ... Analysts don't like it, I do. The breakup value is twice the market price. The deal finances itself, sell off two divisions, keep—" Fox is shot down again as Gekko interrupts him midsentence saying, "Not bad for a quant, but a dog with different fleas." Fox gives his third idea:

Fox: Bluestar Airlines.
Gekko: Rings a bell somewhere. So what?
Fox: A comer, 80 medium-body jets, 300 pilots, flies northeast, Canada, some Florida and Caribbean routes ... great slots in major cities—
Gekko: Don't like airlines; lousy unions.
Fox: There was a crash last year. They just got a favorable ruling on a lawsuit. Even the plaintiffs don't know.
Gekko: How do you know?
Fox: I know ... the decision will clear the way for new planes and route contracts. There's only a small float out there, so you should grab it. Good for a five-point pop.
Gekko: Interesting. You got a card? [then a long pause] I look at a hundred ideas a day. I choose one.[2]

This exchange is actually a common scenario in the investment business. The portfolio manager is busy and distracted, and you— the analyst—have only a small window of time to capture his interest. We have found that it is most effective to think about your pitch as comprising three distinctively different elements—a **30-second hook**, a **two-minute drill**, and the ability to sustain five to 10 minutes

---

[2] *Wall Street.* Directed by Oliver Stone. Twentieth Century Fox Film Corporation, 1987.

of **Q&A**. Keep in mind that this structure is just a guide; not every portfolio manager operates this way. Oftentimes an impatient portfolio manager will interrupt the analyst and pepper him with questions only a few sentences into the pitch.

The first element—the **30-second hook**[3]—must be simple, succinct, and extremely compelling to quickly capture the portfolio manager's attention. Like Pavlov's dogs salivating when the bell rings, your hook should trigger *greed* in the portfolio manager's mind. If your hook is persuasive, the portfolio manager will subconsciously shift his weight forward in his seat as he leans toward you. *Now*, you have his attention, and he wants to hear more.

The goal of the hook is to motivate the portfolio manager to listen to your **two-minute drill**, which will present the crux of your pitch. The two-minute drill tells a story and lays out your main arguments. It should reinforce the attractiveness of the investment and draw your audience further into your pitch. The goal is to persuade the portfolio manager that the idea has merit, and if you pass the two-minute drill, you can expect to get a deluge of questions.

LEFT IN THE COLD WITH A WARM FEELING OF ACCOMPLISHMENT

The origin of the 30-second hook and two-minute drill was purely by accident. In his first job after business school, Paul S. worked for the legendary investor Chuck Royce. Royce was extremely busy, and it can sometimes be difficult for a junior analyst like Paul to get his attention. One afternoon, Royce was stretched out with his feet up[4] on the trading desk, a sheaf of papers in his lap, and a red felt-tipped pen in his hand, as he gave orders to his trader, Ken. Paul walked up and waited until Royce sensed his presence. Royce peered over his reading glasses with a look on his face of "Why are you bothering me, kid? I'm busy."

Paul quickly outlined the idea he was working on, Mity-Lite, a manufacturer of folding tables. Royce took his feet off the desk, sat up straight, turned his chair toward Paul, and without saying a word, reached his hand out for the annual report Paul was holding. Royce started reading the chairman's letter, using his red felt-tipped pen to underline certain sentences. After flipping to the back of the report to review the financials, Royce uttered, "Hmmm, tell me more." Paul spoke for a couple of minutes telling the story. Espie, Royce's assistant, interrupted the pitch

---

[3] Why 30 seconds? This was taken from Milo Frank's excellent book, *How to Get Your Point Across in 30 Seconds or Less*, which Paul S. highly recommends. Frank was an agent at William Morris in the 1940s and 1950s, and represented actors including Humphrey Bogart and Marilyn Monroe. He later went on to head talent and casting for CBS Television and then on to a career as a communications consultant. The book, which he published in 1990, was a summary of his experience.

when she handed Royce his overcoat and said, "Chuck, you have to leave for your two o'clock appointment." Royce asked Paul questions as he got up, put on his coat, and started walking toward the door.

The Q&A continued as they waited for the elevator. The door opened, Royce got in the elevator, and Paul followed him in. The back-and-forth continued as Royce left the building and walked across Sixth Avenue to his garage to get his car, which was waiting by the entrance on 58th Street. Before closing his car door and driving off, Royce said to Paul, "Give Kenny an order to buy 100,000 shares." Paul shivered but smiled as he walked across Sixth Avenue back to the office. It was snowing pretty hard and there were already six inches of snow on the ground. Although only in shirtsleeves, Paul did not seem to notice the inclement weather.

This story captures the anatomy of a pitch. A 30-second hook to capture your audience's attention and whet their appetite for the two-minute drill. The two-minute drill to get them more interested in the idea and prompt them to ask questions to vet your research. The questions allow the portfolio manager to ascertain if your idea matches their criteria of what they believe is the perfect investment. Paul gave his hook, which piqued Royce's attention and allowed Paul to deliver his two-minute drill. Then Royce peppered Paul with questions as they left the building and crossed the street. Royce liked the idea and bought the stock. Years later, Royce would eventually acquire over 10% of Mity-Lite's stock.

---

[4] Royce's shoes often had holes in the bottom and it was widely thought he put his feet up so people would notice the holes. To a value investor, holes in one's shoes is a badge of honor.

Returning to the movie—why did Gekko pass on Whitewood-Young and Terafly, but became intrigued by Bluestar? As we discuss in the previous chapter, when a portfolio manager hears a new idea, he will listen if the idea matches his **objective criteria**. However, he will only adopt the idea if it satisfies his **subjective criteria**.

Gekko clearly knew both Whitewood-Young and Terafly well, and had a pre-existing opinion for each company, thinking both were "dogs with fleas." Bluestar was different. Gekko did not know the company, which became obvious when he said, "Rings a bell somewhere." Then he dismissed the idea out of hand, indicating that it did not fit his criteria when he said, "Don't like airlines; lousy unions." However, when Fox mentions a favorable ruling on a lawsuit that "even the plaintiffs don't know," the hook was set and Gekko's attention was captured.

Let's dissect the situation with Bluestar a little further. Greed was the primary motivator when Gekko called later that afternoon to instruct Fox to "buy me twenty thousand shares of Bluestar. No more than 15 ⅛, ⅜ tops, and don't screw it up, sport." To Gekko, the return was very compelling. A "five-point pop" implied a potential return of more than 30% over a very short time horizon. Gekko's greed overwhelmed any concern he had about the unions. The news was imminent, so Gekko felt that the downside was limited because a few days of market risk should not be a big factor. Gekko liked the idea because he knew he had an **informational advantage**. While highly illegal, he had information that had not been **disseminated** to the market, which resulted in a **mispricing**, as we show in Figure 11.1. Last, Fox had identified a **catalyst**—the soon-to-be-issued press release—that he knew would send the stock higher.

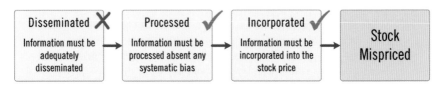

Figure 11.1   Lack of Dissemination Results in Mispriced Stock

When we run Fox's Bluestar idea through the Steinhardt framework, we see that all the boxes are checked:

Is your view different from the consensus? Yes. The consensus is neutral to negative concerning the outcome of the litigation.

Are you right? Yes. Fox has material nonpublic information concerning the favorable outcome of the litigation.

What is the market missing? The market does not know the outcome of the litigation.

When and why will the consensus view change? The consensus view will change when the news of the positive outcome is released.

Ideally, your hook will contain all these factors, although we recognize there is an awful lot of information to squeeze into 30 seconds. If you were to pitch Cloverland, which we discuss in Chapter 8, to Gekko, it might sound like the Bluestar exchange, albeit without the illegal component:

You: Cloverland Timber.

Gekko: Rings a bell somewhere. So what?

You: Owns 160,000 acres of timberland in Wisconsin. It is a microcap that trades on the Pink Sheets with a sleepy investor base and no one paying attention.

Gekko: Don't like microcaps; roach motels—you can get in, but can't get out.

You: Last year an activist—John Helve of Brownfield Capital—flew a satellite over the land and hired a consultant to do an appraisal. Brownfield bought 26% of the stock and got a board seat a few months ago. Market price is $90 a share, but it's worth at least $140. The activist isn't going to just stand by and watch the trees grow; they'll push for a sale.

Gekko: How do you know?

You: I met John a few years ago at a dinner and we've since become friends. His fund, Brownfield, has a good track record. While he didn't give me exact numbers, he said the trees are older, with a higher percentage of hardwood than the market has been told by the company, which means the timberland is a lot more valuable than investors realize. If the activist is successful, you could make 50% on your money in 18 months. Even if the activist isn't successful, given that timber is a hard asset, there is little downside risk.

Gekko: Interesting. You got a card? [then a long pause] I look at a hundred ideas a day. I choose one.

When we run the Cloverland opportunity through the Steinhardt framework, we see that all the boxes are checked:

Is your view different from the consensus? Yes. The consensus thinks the stock is worth $107 per share; you think it's worth $140.

Are you right? Yes. You know your valuation is accurate based on the satellite appraisal of the value of the timberland.

What is the market missing? The market does not know the true value of the timberland. Also, the market appears to be unaware of the activist or does not think he will be successful.

When and why will the situation change? The situation will change when the activist persuades the board to put the company up for sale.

As we identified in Fox's pitch of Bluestar, Gekko's first reaction to the Cloverland pitch was greed. Gekko saw an opportunity to make money. Most portfolio managers are motivated by greed and the opportunity will capture their attention if the implied return is compelling. However, fear often kicks in at the point the manager's thinking shifts from "How much can I make?" to "How much can I lose?"

A manager's fear is measured by his perception of **uncertainty**, which includes both the uncertainty of the investment outcome and his uncertainty in your analytical abilities. The manager's fear will be mitigated if he believes the downside is limited and if he has confidence in your analytical prowess.

If there is sufficient return and low perceived risk, most seasoned portfolio managers will then ask the question, "Why me o'lord?" reflecting their concern that the opportunity looks too good to be true. This only half-rhetorical question is the third potential hurdle you must overcome to convince the manager to adopt the idea. To neutralize this objection, you must demonstrate that a genuine mispricing exists by proving that at least one of the market efficiency tenets has been compromised, as we discuss in Chapter 5.

Once this worry is put to rest, the portfolio manager will most likely raise one final concern: "How will the consensus realize the mispricing exists and, in turn, correct it?" In other words, "What will be the catalyst that closes the gap between the market price and intrinsic value?" Seth Hamot, a well-respected hedge fund manager, posed this question a bit more colorfully by saying, "Now that I have gone through all this brain damage, untangled this rat's nest of a situation and figured it out, how is the next guy going to figure out how to untie the knot so I can make some money?"[5]

We recap the portfolio manager's list of potential concerns in Figure 11.2 and show how the analyst can deliver the *perfect pitch* by anticipating what the manager will think and using the **Steinhardt framework** to structure his presentation.

---

[5] Seth Hamot is a partner at Roark, Rearden, and Hamot Capital Management, a money manager based in Boston. As he often says, the first two named partners of his firm are a lot smarter than he is.

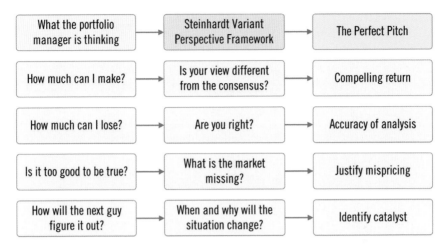

What the portfolio manager is thinking	→	Steinhardt Variant Perspective Framework	→	The Perfect Pitch
How much can I make?	→	Is your view different from the consensus?	→	Compelling return
How much can I lose?	→	Are you right?	→	Accuracy of analysis
Is it too good to be true?	→	What is the market missing?	→	Justify mispricing
How will the next guy figure it out?	→	When and why will the situation change?	→	Identify catalyst

Figure 11.2   Questions to Achieve the Perfect Pitch

We show that the analyst successfully economized his time with no wasted words when we dissect the Cloverland pitch and parse the statements that were made into the different categories listed in Figure 11.2. The review illustrates that the pitch made four specific arguments to address the portfolio manager's four primary questions, which are as follows:

1. The intrinsic value is $140 per share.
2. The activist will be successful.
3. The thesis is not priced into the stock.
4. There is little downside even if the activist is unsuccessful.

We list the different phrases from the hook and place them in the appropriate category in Figure 11.3. By using the Steinhardt framework as a guide, the chart shows that the analyst answered the portfolio manager's basic concerns in a concise fashion, which resulted in the perfect pitch.

After listening to literally thousands of stock pitches, we firmly believe that the most common mistake most inexperienced *and* experienced analysts make is **presenting arguments without fully understanding how they arrived at their conclusion**. This shortcoming results in a weak pitch that is hard to defend and quickly crumbles when challenged. To be successful, you need to answer the *why* questions. *Why* do you believe the intrinsic value is $140 per share? *Why* will the activist be successful? *Why* isn't the investment thesis priced into the stock? *Why* is there little downside to the stock?

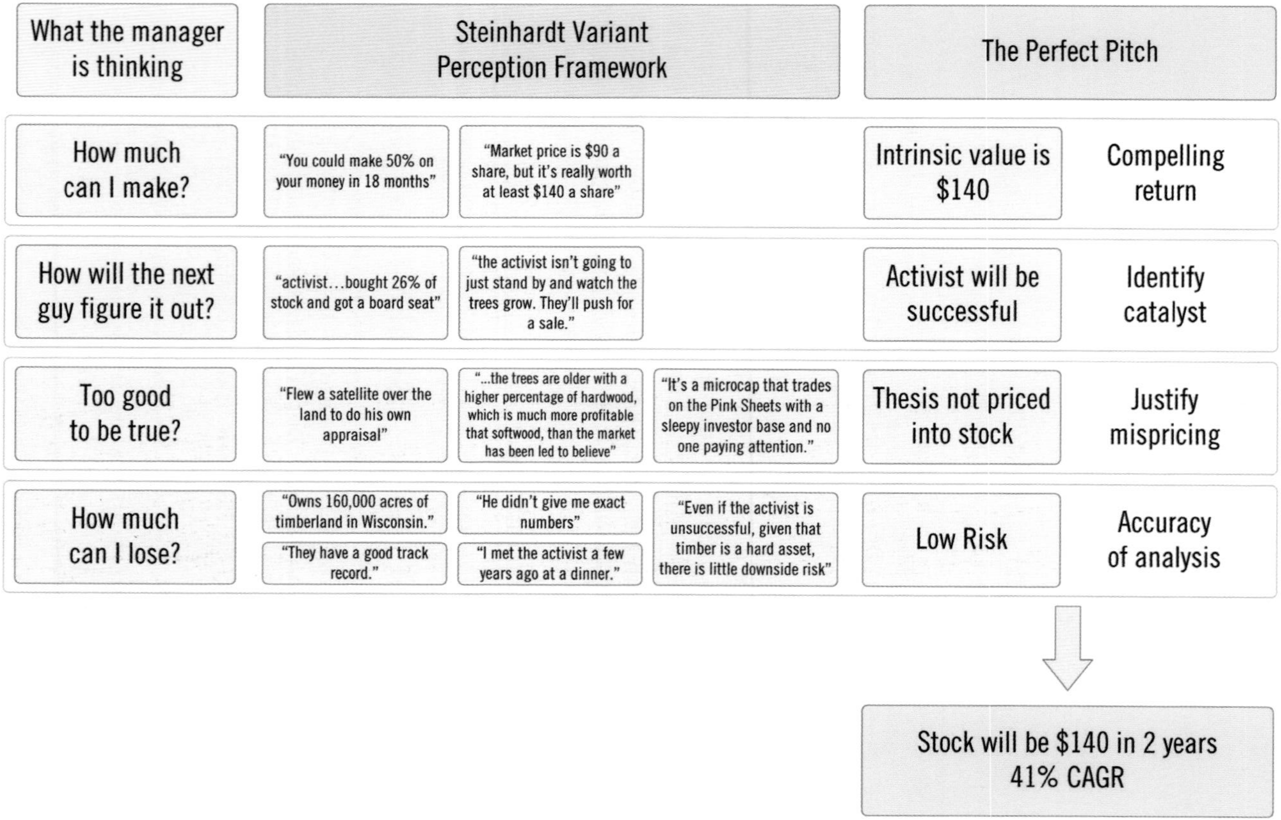
What the manager is thinking
Steinhardt Variant Perception Framework
The Perfect Pitch
How much can I make?
"You could make 50% on your money in 18 months"
"Market price is $90 a share, but it's really worth at least $140 a share"
Intrinsic value is $140
Compelling return
How will the next guy figure it out?
"activist…bought 26% of stock and got a board seat"
"the activist isn't going to just stand by and watch the trees grow. They'll push for a sale."
Activist will be successful
Identify catalyst
Too good to be true?
"Flew a satellite over the land to do his own appraisal"
"…the trees are older with a higher percentage of hardwood, which is much more profitable that softwood, than the market has been led to believe"
"It's a microcap that trades on the Pink Sheets with a sleepy investor base and no one paying attention."
Thesis not priced into stock
Justify mispricing
How much can I lose?
"Owns 160,000 acres of timberland in Wisconsin."
"They have a good track record."
"He didn't give me exact numbers"
"I met the activist a few years ago at a dinner."
"Even if the activist is unsuccessful, given that timber is a hard asset, there is little downside risk"
Low Risk
Accuracy of analysis
Stock will be $140 in 2 years
41% CAGR

Figure 11.3 The Perfect Pitch for Cloverland

Even if you address the portfolio manager's four main concerns with four strong arguments, you cannot stop there. You need to have complete command of the **evidence** that supports your arguments, including the assumptions you are making. You will also need to anticipate and prepare for any possible counterarguments.

Constructing a Formidable Argument Using the Toulmin Model

It is critically important to instill a mental discipline when developing arguments so that you understand what information you need to defend them. To accomplish this goal, you will need some type of systematic framework or checklist with which to scrutinize your arguments. You need someone to look over your shoulder, asking tough questions as you craft your pitch, and acting as your conscience, picking apart your argument and second-guessing all your assumptions. That someone is Stephen Toulmin and the systematic framework is the **Toulmin model of argumentation**.

Stephen Toulmin, a British philosopher, focused his research on moral reasoning. In his seminal work, *The Uses of Argument*, published in 1958, Toulmin outlined six interconnected components for analyzing an argument, referred to as the Toulmin model of argumentation. The Toulmin model can be used to structure and "stress test" the arguments in your pitch, and in the process produce arguments that are more reliable, credible, efficient, and less susceptible to counterarguments. The result will be a much more effective pitch.

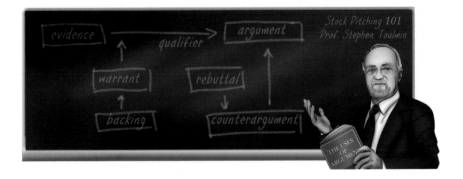

The Argument

One of the arguments you made in the Cloverland pitch was "The activist will be successful in forcing a sale of the company." An argument is a statement you want to convince your audience is true. During the pitch, your statement will likely be challenged by a simple question such as the one Gekko might ask, "How do you know?" When responding, you must have adequate evidence to support your argument.

For instance, you might present the following evidence to prove that John Helve will be successful in forcing a sale of the company in the Cloverland example:

1. Brownfield was successful in their last activist campaign.
2. Cloverland stock has underperformed the S&P 500.
3. Brownfield has a significant position in Cloverland.
4. Brownfield has received one board seat and John Helve is already a board member.

The Evidence

Evidence, often called data points, usually includes facts, statistics, personal observations or expertise, physical proof, expert opinions, or reports and will have different levels of quality across several dimensions, as outlined in Figure 11.4.

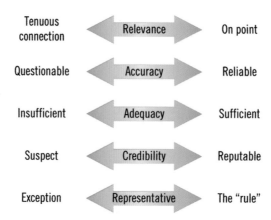

Figure 11.4   The Dimensions of Evidence Quality

The more convincing the evidence, the stronger the argument, which should be obvious. The characteristics listed in Figure 11.4 provide an important guideline as to the relevance of your **evidence** and can provide a measure of its quality.

For example, one of the data points in the argument "Helve will be successful" was that "Brownfield was successful in their last activist campaign." We can screen that piece of evidence through the five characteristics to determine how good it is:

Relevance:	Whether they were successful in their last campaign is relevant to their success with this campaign.
Accuracy:	Depending on how you define *successful*, the data is verifiable, so its accuracy can be determined.
Adequacy:	Taken alone, this piece of evidence is not sufficient to prove that they will be successful with this particular campaign.
Credibility:	The data comes from a reliable source.
Representative:	The data might not be representative since the last campaign had a completely different set of circumstances.

We might conclude that taken alone, the data point is not sufficient to prove the argument that Helve and Brownfield will be successful with Cloverland. However, this statement is only one of four data points we are using to prove the argument and, when added to the other three data points, will make the argument much stronger—which is why it is advisable to have more than one data point supporting your argument.

The Warrant

Questions about evidence are not the only way your audience may challenge your arguments. They might ask you, "How did you arrive at this conclusion?" or "Why do you think that?" These questions are not intended to challenge the validity of the evidence; rather, they ask how you made the leap from the **evidence** to the **argument**. Supplying further facts will not answer this question. Instead, you will need to demonstrate that the argument follows from the evidence in a logical manner. Toulmin calls this bridge a **warrant**, which answers the question, "Why does that evidence mean your argument is true?"

The Fourth Amendment to the U.S. Constitution protects individuals against unreasonable searches and seizures. Only if there is probable cause will a judge issue a search warrant. Imagine there is a jewel heist. Police have collected fingerprint evidence from the crime scene that points to Julie Zlato as the perpetrator. The police suspect Ms. Zlato is hiding the jewels in her home, but they cannot just barge in and rummage around her house looking for the jewels. To enter her house, the police need a search warrant. However, they will need to establish probable cause with the judge, linking the evidence to the accusation, for the judge to grant the warrant.

Toulmin's warrant is conceptually similar to a search warrant as there needs to be a logical connection between the evidence (the fingerprints at the crime scene) and the argument (Zlato is the perpetrator), which is similar to probable cause in the robbery. Toulmin's warrant answers the question, "How did you arrive at this conclusion?"

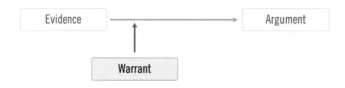

If we put the Cloverland argument through the Toulmin framework, we see that the **warrant** has four facets:

1. Helve was successful in his last activist campaign, so he will be successful in this campaign.
2. Since the stock has underperformed the S&P 500, the shareholder base is disgruntled and will likely vote with Brownfield if they launch a proxy fight.
3. Brownfield has amassed a large position in Cloverland and has significant leverage with the board.
4. Helve is already on the board, so he can better influence management.

The portfolio manager can challenge the warrants by making statements such as, "Just because Brownfield was successful in its last campaign does not mean they will be successful in this one" or "Just because the stock has underperformed the S&P 500 does not mean that Brownfield will get shareholder support." The portfolio manager uses these questions to challenge the **warrant**, which is the *cause-and-effect relationship between the evidence and the argument.*

We firmly believe that most pitches fail because the analyst takes the warrant for granted. While it may not be necessary to state explicitly a warrant when making an argument, it is critical to understand the link between the evidence and the argument, and to be prepared to defend the warrant if it is challenged.

The Backing for the Warrant

You will need what Toulmin calls **backing** to defend or support your **warrant**.

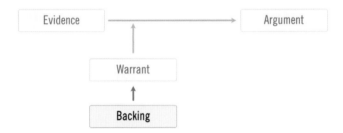

The **backing** supports the **warrant** by outlining the reasons why the warrant is valid. It is the evidence that supports the warrant. For example, if you were defending the warrant "Since the stock has underperformed the S&P 500, the shareholder base is disgruntled and will likely vote with Brownfield if they launch a proxy fight," the backing might be that something like:

1. You spoke with investors representing 30% of the shareholder base and they said that they would likely vote for Brownfield in the event of a proxy fight; or,
2. Brownfield has won 75% of its proxy fights in situations where the target company's stock underperformed the S&P 500 for the previous five years.

The Qualifier

It's important to keep in mind that no argument is foolproof. The world is uncertain and unexpected events can and will happen. For instance, Cloverland's directors could vote to increase the size of the board (diluting Brownfield's influence) or the forest might become infested with mountain pine beetles, which has the potential to kill a large percentage of Cloverland's trees and reduce the company's estimated intrinsic value. To account for these uncertain events, a **qualifier** acknowledges the limitations of the argument and indicates the level of confidence in the argument by using words such as *unlikely*, *possibly*, *likely*, and *probably*.

A **qualifier** in the Cloverland situation might be, "Helve will *probably* be successful, although there is a *possibility* that Cloverland could expand the size of its board." Or, "Brownfield's large position will *probably* give them sufficient leverage to be successful, although it is *possible* that the board will dig in their heels and drag out the process."

The Rebuttal and Counterarguments

The last element of the Toulmin model is the **rebuttal**, which addresses potential **counterarguments**.

Cicero states in his book *De Inventione, I,*

> "Every argument is refuted in one of these ways: either one or more of its assumptions are not granted, or if the assumptions are granted it is denied that a conclusion follows from them, or the form of argument is shown to be fallacious, or a strong argument is met by one equally strong or stronger."[6]

The Toulmin model mirrors Cicero's observation. For instance, a counterargument to the Cloverland example might be, "While Brownfield owns a lot of Cloverland stock, it is not a large position for their fund; therefore, they may not be aggressive in the situation if their attention gets diverted." The **rebuttal** acknowledges limitations or exceptions to the argument and mitigates the **counterargument**. It acknowledges situations where the argument might not hold, such as, "The position for Brownfield is not a large one. They might not focus on Cloverland if they find another situation that diverts their attention. However, they most likely will not lose focus because they don't want their reputation tarnished."

The Stress-Tested Argument

Although using the Toulmin model may seem like overkill for an investment recommendation, it is an excellent tool for stress-testing your pitch and making sure your argument can withstand attack. The model provides you with an X-ray view inside your argument to see its entire anatomy and identify areas where the argument might be vulnerable, before being grilled by an intimidating portfolio manager.

If we decided to redo the Cloverland pitch we gave Gekko's office, the hook might sound like the following:

> Based on a rigorous analysis of a wide range of information that I will discuss later, I have concluded that John Helve's firm, Brownfield Capital, will be successful in forcing a sale of Cloverland Timber, which would then close in 9 to 12 months. The stock, which is currently trading at $90, is worth $140, a 56% potential return. Given the sleepy nature of the shareholder base and the stock's

---

[6] Marco Tulio Cicero and H. M. Hubbell, *Cicero, De inventione: De optimo genere oratorum: Topica* (Cambridge: Harvard University Press, 1960).

limited trading liquidity the stock appears to be mispriced as the market is not properly incorporating the true value of the timber or the actions of the activist investor into the stock price. Even if the activist is not successful, there is little downside because timber is a hard asset.

With this hook, you have covered the four main elements of your investment thesis and address the **four key questions** the portfolio manager will have:

1. *How much can I make?* The stock is worth $140 per share.
2. *How will the next guy figure it out?* The activist will be successful.
3. *Is it too good to be true?* The thesis is not priced into the stock.
4. *How much can I lose?* Even if the activist is not successful, there is little downside.

If the portfolio manager is intrigued by your **hook**, he then will allow you to proceed to your **two-minute drill**. Ideally, you will use the two-minute drill to delve further into the evidence to support the arguments from your hook. If we use the Toulmin model as a framework to develop the two-minute drill, the portion of the presentation discussing the valuation might be similar to the following:

I believe that Cloverland stock is worth $140 per share, implying a value of $1,130 per acre. My valuation is based on the results of a survey performed by consultants hired by Helve's firm that specialize in appraising timberland. The consultants flew a satellite over the forest to take photographs and then, using sophisticated computer modeling, estimated the value per acre based on density, age, and species of the trees. While the average age to harvest a tree is 40 years, the trees on Cloverland's property are closer to 70 years old. Older trees are much more valuable because of their greater volume of wood. The survey also showed a high percent of sugar maple, which is a hard wood and much more valuable than soft wood. Sugar maple is also more resistant to the mountain beetle, which should help prevent any unforeseen damage from an unexpected infestation. While valuation based on appraisals from satellite flyovers is a new technology, and like any valuation method is prone to error, this type of analysis has proven over time to be more accurate than traditional valuation methods from on-the-ground surveys.

If we dissect one portion of the two-minute drill, we see that the analyst has included all the points from the Toulmin model:

Argument:	"I believe that Cloverland stock is worth $140 per share, implying a value of $1,130 per acre."
Qualifier:	"While valuation based on appraisals from satellite flyovers is a new technology, and like any valuation method is prone to error."
Evidence:	"My valuation is based on the results of a survey performed by a consulting firm hired by the activist that specializes in appraising timberland."
Warrant:	"The consultants flew a satellite over the forest to take photographs and then, using sophisticated computer modeling, estimated the value per acre based on density, age, and species of the trees."
Backing:	"While the average age to harvest a tree is 40 years, the trees on Cloverland's property are closer to 70 years old. Older trees are much more valuable because of their greater volume of wood. The survey also showed a high percent of sugar maple, which is a hard wood and much more valuable than soft wood. Sugar maple is also more resistant to the mountain beetle."
Rebuttal:	"This type of analysis has proven over time to be more accurate than traditional valuation methods from on-the-ground surveys."

The argument must consider the counterarguments that the portfolio manager is likely to make and you must be prepared to confront them head-on. To quote Aristotle, "In deliberative oratory . . . one must begin by giving one's own proofs and then meet those of the opposition by dissolving them and tearing them up before they are made."[7] For instance, an obvious counterargument might question the validity of a valuation method based on satellite photography, which is addressed in the rebuttal.

---

[7] Aristotle, *The Art of Rhetoric* (London: HarperPress, 2012).

If the portfolio manager remains interested in the idea after your **two-minute drill**, you will likely get follow-up questions, which you need to anticipate in advance and be prepared to address. You are expected to know more about your argument than anyone else and need to be an expert on the facts. For instance, questions the manager might ask regarding the valuation portion of your argument are:

- How accurate has this method of valuation been over time? Is the estimated value usually understated or overstated? How can the consultants tell the age and species of a tree from satellite photos? Have their results been accurate in the past?
- Tell me more about the background of the consultants. How long have they been in business? What is their reputation? Do they have a blue-chip client base?
- How much more valuable is sugar maple than typical softwoods? How much of the increased valuation is based on this factor?
- Can any additional value be realized from mineral rights or real estate development?

Paul S. always said in his class, "If you don't know the answer to the question the portfolio manager asks, what is the correct response?" He would then pause to see if any of the students would respond. No one ever did. Then he continued, "The right answer is, *I don't know but I'll find out.* And then you write down the question. You are not writing it down so that *you* remember it, you are writing it down so the portfolio manager sees you writing it down. Don't try to fake your way through the answer. An experienced portfolio manager will sense BS like a shark senses blood in the water and you will not survive."

WORDSMITHING

Your choice of words will be extremely important. Stay away from claims that convey little information. For instance, analysts often use phrases such as "dominant market share" in a pitch, which is like empty calories as there is no nutritional value in the comment. Does the company have a 12% or 90% share of the market? Is the company's market position stable over time? If the company doesn't have a competitive advantage, does its market share even matter? Perhaps most important, is the information already reflected in the stock price?

Also, be careful not to overuse qualifiers, which are also known as *weasel words* or *weasel phrases*, such as *may, might, could, should, appears, possibly, I believe, I feel, it is widely believed, it is often said, many are of the opinion*, and so on, because the words allow the presenter to weasel out of their argument when challenged. Paul S. and Paul J. would bring a galvanized bucket with large nuts (the kind that screw onto a bolt[8]) to class when students gave pitches and every time a student would use a weasel word or phrase, the professor would drop a nut in the bucket, making an obnoxious noise that startled everyone. Over time, the students got the point.

---

[8] As opposed to the kind you eat, although unshelled walnuts or Brazil nuts might have worked just as well.

Once you finish the process of properly organizing the content, you will have what amounts to a script or words on paper. However, the message has two components: the content and the delivery of that content. You now have the content, but the delivery matters too, as we show in the next chapter.

Gems:

- ◈ When determining which elements to include in your pitch, imagine that your house is on fire and you have only 30 seconds to evacuate. What three items would you take? Similarly, you need to think what are the three most important points to include in your pitch.
- ◈ The pitch should be structured into a **30-second hook**, **two-minute drill**, and **Q&A**. The analyst uses the hook to tantalize the portfolio manager with the idea and motivate him to listen to the two-minute drill, which the analyst can use to present the crux of his pitch. The two-minute drill tells a story, lays out the main arguments to the pitch and reinforces the attractiveness of the investment. The goal of the two-minute drill is to draw the manager further into the idea and show that it has merit. If the analyst passes the two-minute drill, he can expect to get a deluge of questions from the portfolio manager.
- ◈ To deliver the perfect pitch, the analyst must address the four questions in the portfolio manager's mind, anticipate what the manager will think, and use the Steinhardt framework to structure his presentation.

▽ We firmly believe that most pitches fail because the analyst takes the **warrants** to his arguments for granted. While it may not be necessary to state a warrant when making an argument, it is critical to understand the link between the evidence and the argument, even if it is unspoken, and be prepared to defend the warrant if **the argument** is challenged.

▽ Word choice is extremely important. Try not to use phrases that convey little information and avoid using weasel words in your presentation.

CHAPTER 12

How to Deliver the Message

In the previous two chapters, we discuss how to overcome obstacles of stock selection by matching the portfolio manager's **schema** (Chapter 10) and how to overcome obstacles regarding the content of the pitch by answering the portfolio manager's four key investment questions (Chapter 11). We discuss in this chapter how to overcome obstacles when delivering the message, as shown in Figure 12.1, with **the goal of being efficient in your delivery and minimizing any extraneous factors that detract from the content of your message.**

Figure 12.1   Obstacles to Getting the Idea Adopted

There is a middle ground that bridges the gap between content and delivery. The goal is to capture the portfolio manager's attention. You start with a 30-second hook and, if successful, the manager allows you to proceed with your two-minute drill, which hopefully results in five to ten minutes of the manager showering you with follow-up questions. These three elements—the 30-second hook, the two-minute drill and Q&A—comprise the pitch. Think of these distinct components as three modules that can be used in either written or spoken form.

The 30-Second Hook

For instance, you can use the 30-second hook as a stand-alone module in several different circumstances. In written form, you can use the content from the 30-second hook for the first few sentences of a research report; as the investment summary in a posting on a website such as SumZero, Value Investors Club, or Seeking Alpha; or as part of an e-mail or cover letter you send to a portfolio manager. In spoken form, you can use the 30-second hook if you run into a portfolio manager in the office hallway, on the street, or at an investment conference. The 30-second hook can also be used on a job interview, on the phone with a client, as the introduction in a stock pitch competition, or at an idea dinner.

For instance, the 30-second pitch for Cloverland in the previous chapter is:

> Cloverland Timber owns 160,000 acres of forest in Wisconsin and has a market cap of $156 million. Based on a rigorous analysis of a wide range of information that I will discuss later, I have concluded that Brownfield Capital will be successful in forcing a sale of Cloverland Timber, which would then close in 9 to 12 months. The stock, which is currently trading at $90, is worth $140, a 56% potential return. Given the sleepy nature of the shareholder base and the stock's illiquidity, the stock appears to be mispriced as the market is not properly incorporating the true value of the timber or the actions of the activist investor into the stock price. Even if Helve is not successful, there is little downside risk because timber is a hard asset.[1]

---

[1] This paragraph actually took Paul S. 40 seconds to read out loud.

The Two-Minute Drill

The two-minute drill can also be written or spoken. In written form, you can use the content from your two-minute drill as the introduction or executive summary to any research report you write. In the spoken form, you can use the two-minute drill in any face-to-face meeting with a portfolio manager, such as the ones we discuss in the previous chapter. You should always be prepared to roll into the two-minute drill when having a conversation with a portfolio manager, no matter the situation, once you get past the 30-second hook.

However, even when delivering the two-minute drill verbally, we suggest that you offer the portfolio manager supplemental written material for him to reference during your pitch and refer to after your meeting. It is important to remember that portfolio managers hear numerous pitches every day and you want him to remember yours. As Gekko said to Fox, "I hear a hundred ideas a day. I pick one."

HARSH REALITY

Paul S. once told a CEO during a one-on-one meeting at a sell-side investment conference:

> You are making it too hard for me to analyze your company. Your slide deck is all over the place and I have ADD. It's just too frustrating to decipher it. I'm going to sit through eight presentations today, and by 5:00 p.m. they will all start blurring together in my mind. When I get to my office tomorrow morning, I'm going to take the stack of slide decks out of my bag and look through them, tossing the four that weren't interesting in the trash. I'm going to look through the remaining four and remember that I liked your company and then look through my notes to remember why. I take notes so I'll remember stuff, but when I look at them, I won't be able to read my own handwriting. I will have been out of the office for two days attending the conference and will need to dig out from being away. Then the market opens and the phone starts ringing and I'll move the stack of remaining presentations aside as I get sidetracked with something else. Then, six months later, as I'm cleaning the piles of paper on my desk because they are so high they are starting to fall over, I'll see your presentation, flip through it quickly, and think to myself, "Why did I save this?" before tossing it in the trash.

(Continued)

> (*Continued*)
>
> You need to make it easy for me. Heed the words of Robert Herjavec on *Shark Tank* who says, "It's not my job to listen, its's your job to engage me." You need to lay out the investment case succinctly in the slides so when I get to my office tomorrow morning its right there in front of me. You must serve the story to me on a silver platter . . . wrapped with a big red bow. You have to realize that I'm not unique; this happens with most portfolio managers I know.
>
> While this exchange was with the CEO of a public company, the same lessons hold true for an analyst pitching a stock. In other words, make it easy on the portfolio manager to remember you and your idea.

Make It Easy for Them

To make the portfolio manager's job even easier, you should provide him with supplemental information to your pitch that we call a pitch pack.[2] The pitch pack includes your slide presentation, any reports you have written, and the company's financial documents, such as its annual report, most recent 10Q, and latest earnings release. Portfolio managers might want to flip through the material during the meeting and afterward appreciate having this material at their fingertips so that they don't have to hunt around for basic information on the company. You need to make it easy for them. You want to serve it up on a silver platter wrapped with a big red bow.

If you mail your report ahead of the meeting, include the 30-second hook in your cover letter, and send with it the company's annual report, most recent 10Q, and latest earnings release. Then give the entire pitch pack to the portfolio manager again when you go to the meeting. Do not expect that they will have saved it and bring it with them when they meet you. It is most likely lost in one of those tall piles of paper on their desk.

Most students create incredibly busy slides, either to prove they have completed exhaustive research or because they do not

---

[2] We agree that *pitch pack* sounds a little cheesy, but we could not think of anything better to call it. Maybe *sheaf of materials? leave behinds? supplemental documentation?* or *additional due diligence information?* Please e-mail us at info@pitchtheperfectinvestment .com if you think of a better name.

know what is the most relevant information to present. The overly dense slides often leave the portfolio manager more confused than informed. Not only do the slides overwhelm the manager, who is forced to spend time trying to decipher the information, but the slides themselves are usually hard to read, often because the analyst uses a small font to pack as much information as possible onto the slide. The slides in Figure 12.2 are typical.[3] You do not know where to look first when the slide flashes on the screen, and your eyes bounce around until you focus on one area of the slide, hoping to absorb at least some of the information before the speaker moves on to the next slide. Making matters worse, few people can multitask

Market Underestimates Improved Pricing Environment

Overly Conservative Pricing Guidance

- Management's revenue and EPS guidance assumes no pricing growth
- Sell-side analyst consensus estimates assume a 1% increase in pricing

"On pricing, it's very conservative assumptions where we really don't try to assume any price increases in our models."
– Hertz CEO in April 2013

Impact of Pricing on Valuation

- 1% increase in U.S. RPD results in a 6% increase in share price

Sensitivity to U.S. RPD Growth Y/Y

	0.0%	1.0%	2.0%	3.0%	4.0%	5.0%
2014e EBITDA	$2,610	$2,734	$2,859	$2,985	$3,112	$3,239
2014e EPS	$2.44	$2.62	$2.79	$2.96	$3.14	$3.31
Price Target	$30.80	$32.88	$34.97	$37.08	$39.20	$41.34
PT % Increase		6.8%	6.4%	6.0%	5.7%	5.4%

Strong Pricing Environment w/ Price Signaling

"One of the headlines I'd like to make is we don't want to gain share by reducing price. We want to gain share by increasing value, and that's how we're doing it."
– Hertz CEO in April 2013

"We're seeing our competitors move for profitability, rather than share, and that has a positive impact on all of us."
– Avis CFO in February 2013

"We've been very aggressive in initiating price increases over the last 4 months or so and I think that's had a positive impact. And we've seen a fairly good matching of increases by both Hertz and the Enterprise."
– Avis CFO in March 2013

"We made a strategic decision to minimize our participation with less profitable commercial accounts."
– Hertz CEO in February 2013

Hertz 5

Figure 12.2   Typical Overcrowded Slides

---

[3] We should note that the slides in Figure 12.2 were both from presentations that won the $100,000 first prize in the Pershing Square Challenge—one from 2014, the other from 2016. While they were both winning ideas, the slides were busy and very difficult to read.

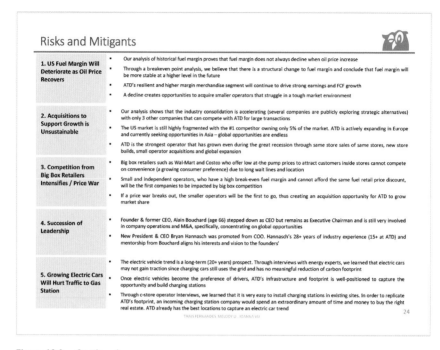

Figure 12.2   *Continued*

effectively, therefore, if the portfolio manager is trying to read the slide while you are talking, he is either comprehending what is on the slide or listening to you, but not both.[4]

Because clearly articulated investment ideas are usually easy to explain, the student projects a lack of confidence in their analysis when they overpopulate their presentation with facts and figures. Although a stock pitch is *not* a TED Talk, much can be learned from

---

[4] On April 21, 2017, Paul S. participated as a judge in the tenth annual Pershing Square Challenge. Judges were emailed the slide decks for the five finalists before the competition and given a two-inch-thick binder of slides to refer to during the presentation. The contest format was a 10-minute presentation followed by 10 minutes of Q&A. One of the presentations was 71 pages long including 7 appendices. Each slide was packed with information in font sizes ranging from 6 to 10 point. When looking at an individual slide, Paul found his eyes bouncing around like a pinball trying to find something to grasp onto to make sense of the overwhelming amount of data presented. While trying to glean information from the slides, his attention was diverted from what the speaker was saying. The situation *typifies* information overload taken to an extreme and in Paul's opinion none of the slides were useful in helping him arrive at an investment decision. Paul kept thinking: *less is more, less is more, less is more.*

the simplicity of the presentations used in that forum, where the slides are uncomplicated and easy to read.

Topography of a Simple Slide Deck

What should your slide deck include? It should be brief! In the immortal words of Judd Kahn, "Less is more."

Slide 1: Company Overview

It is important for the portfolio manager to be able to put the company in context and understand what the company does. That is easy with Cloverland, as it is a timber company and everyone knows what a forest looks like. What about IEH Corporation? You could say that the company "is the only independent US producer of hyperboloid connectors, which are used in military, automotive, and industrial markets." However, it is likely that the portfolio manager has no idea what a hyperboloid connector is, what it looks like, or where it is used. Instead, you can show the portfolio manager a picture of a hyperboloid connector, like the one in Figure 12.3, and he will most likely understand instantly what it is.

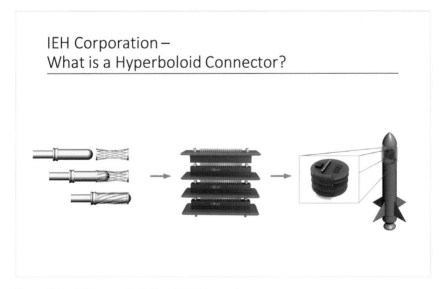

Figure 12.3   IEH Corporation's Hyperboloid Connector

Although a picture is worth a thousand words, we are shocked how often analysts launch into their pitch without explaining what the company does, and the few who do rarely use pictures.

Slide 2: Summary Data

Figure 12.4 shows a simple, uncluttered slide containing summary data for a company. This slide should list only bare-bones information, including:

- Stock chart and basic statistics such as the stock's ticker, current price, 52-week range, and shares outstanding
- Valuation metrics: Enterprise value, market capitalization, and corresponding valuation multiples such as P/E, price to EBITDA, caprate, and current dividend yield, if appropriate
- Income and cash flow metrics: Five years of annual revenues, gross profit margins, operating profit margins, EPS, EBITDA, and free cash flow
- Balance sheet metrics: Total assets, total debt, and shareholder's equity
- Profitability metrics: Five-year history of the company's return on invested capital

Key Statistics

Key Stats	
Ticker	ATD.B
Price (CAD / USD)	57.97 / 45.21
Shares Outstanding (M)	569.2
Market Cap ($M)	25,736
Net Debt	1,777
Enterprise Value ($M)	27,513
ROE 5Y Avg	21.4%
ROIC 5Y Avg	12.8%
ROCE 5Y Avg	17.7%
Dividend Yield	0.47%

Key Financials						
($USD millions) FYE April	2014	2015	LTM	2016E	2017E	2018E
Total Revenue	37,962	34,530	34,033	34,914	38,155	39,029
% Growth	6.8%	-9.0%		1.1%	9.3%	2.3%
Total Gross Profit	4,988	5,268	5,862	6,011	6,539	6,772
% Growth	8.3%	5.6%		14.1%	8.8%	3.6%
Gross Profit Margin	13.1%	15.3%	17.2%	17.2%	17.1%	17.4%
EBITDA	1,568	1,891	2,122	2,282	2,771	3,030
% Growth	14.4%	20.6%		20.7%	21.4%	9.3%
EBITDA Margin	4.1%	5.5%	6.2%	6.5%	7.3%	7.8%
EPS	$1.43	$1.64	$1.97	$2.20	$2.60	$2.99
% Growth	39.8%	14.8%		33.8%	18.4%	15.1%
Concensus EPS				$2.12	$2.33	$2.61
Recurring FCF Yield	3.9%	5.0%	5.4%	6.0%	6.3%	7.3%
P / E	31.6x	27.6x	22.9x	20.6x	17.4x	15.1x
EV / EBITDA	17.7x	14.9x	13.0x	11.9x	10.1x	8.7x
EV / EBITDA - M. Capex	24.1x	19.2x	17.0x	15.2x	12.4x	10.5x
Net Debt / EBITDA	1.3x	1.3x	0.8x	0.6x	0.8x	0.2x

Figure 12.4   Typical Summary Data Slide

That's it! The student should include the rest of the company's financial information in an appendix.

Slide 3: Your Variant Perceptive

Slide 3 in Figure 12.5 presents the four main arguments, as we outline in Chapter 11, that address the portfolio manager's four key questions: How much can I make? How will the next guy figure it out? Is this too good to be true? and How much can I lose?

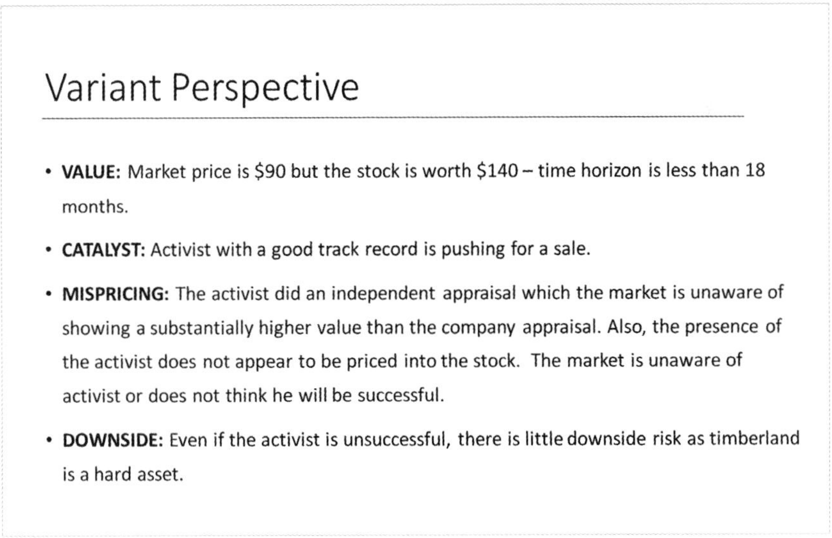

Variant Perspective

- **VALUE:** Market price is $90 but the stock is worth $140 – time horizon is less than 18 months.

- **CATALYST:** Activist with a good track record is pushing for a sale.

- **MISPRICING:** The activist did an independent appraisal which the market is unaware of showing a substantially higher value than the company appraisal. Also, the presence of the activist does not appear to be priced into the stock. The market is unaware of activist or does not think he will be successful.

- **DOWNSIDE:** Even if the activist is unsuccessful, there is little downside risk as timberland is a hard asset.

Figure 12.5   Variant Perspective for Cloverland

The next four slides should each delve further into the four specific arguments shown on the slide in Figure 12.5. The eighth and final slide should contain only the analyst's contact information.

How to Handle Q&A?

While Paul S. graduated from Columbia Business School in 1995, he went back to the school three nights a week for the next year, one night to be the teaching assistant in Paul J.'s class on securities analysis, another to be the grader for Bruce Greenwald's Seminar on Value Investing, and the third to audit Pat Duff's advanced security analysis class, which focused on primary research.

In Duff's class, students were assigned an industry and had to pitch ideas to guest portfolio managers. Paul noticed that the portfolio managers all had similar questions, most of which punched holes in the student's presentation and exposed gaps in the student's analysis. Repeatedly, the guest portfolio managers raised elements of the four key investment questions—How much can I make? How much can I lose? What is the market missing? How will the next guy figure it out?

To anticipate possible questions, it is important to identify any weaknesses in your arguments and which part of the argument is most likely to be attacked during the Q&A period: the evidence, warrant, or backing.

The portfolio manager will probe your arguments during the Q&A period with the goal of exposing weaknesses in your arguments to prove them wrong. The more convincing you are with your responses, the more confident the portfolio manager will be that you are presenting a well-researched idea. While your recommendation should already be a close match to one of the manager's **schema**, he will ask probing questions trying to further match your research and analysis to his investment criteria. This exchange is especially important because the portfolio manager's questions often reveal his **subjective criteria** by exposing the issues he feels are most important in the analysis.

The analyst should have additional slides prepared to offer as further evidence when presenting rebuttals to counterarguments. As a simple trick, it is often best to assemble your presentation with a binder clip, rather than being stapled, so that you can pull out the relevant pages when responding to a portfolio manager's question.

The most common mistake we see young analysts make in pitching a stock is to arrive for their meeting with a 30-slide PowerPoint presentation, expecting the portfolio manager to sit patiently while they drone on with their pitch. We can think of no time in the history of stock pitching when this has happened (unless the manager falls asleep). In fact, most portfolio managers interrupt on the second or third slide, which forces the analyst to jump to a later slide to address the question, only to be interrupted again, forcing the conversation to a different slide. And so on throughout the rest of the meeting. Although the portfolio manager is slowly piecing the story together in his mind and answering the four investment questions he wants addressed, the analyst usually becomes increasingly frustrated because his pitch was interrupted and he never got to return to the first few slides to resume his original plan for the meeting.

The analyst should never forget his prime directive, which is to present ideas that the portfolio manager finds attractive. The analyst serves at the pleasure of the portfolio manager and, therefore, should let the manager drive the conversation. To adopt the idea, the manager needs to have confidence in the analyst's recommendation. Each portfolio manager has his own way of vetting an idea, and the analyst should conform to the portfolio manager's process, not the other way around.

Paul J. had a recent experience with a young analyst who asked for a meeting to practice his pitch before giving it to a portfolio manager the following week. The student launched into his 20-slide presentation with impressive enthusiasm, only to have Paul interrupt in the middle of the second slide with a question. The student looked stunned, caught his breath, and told Paul, "You can't interrupt; I am not done telling the story." To which Paul responded, "I think your presentation just ended." Paul then informed the student that the portfolio manager decides how the pitch will unfold and how he will consume the information. The fix? Stick to the format we have suggested, with five primary slides answering the manager's four key investment questions, and a longer appendix with all the backup material necessary to support your arguments and address the manager's questions. And be flexible.

We have also found that some portfolio managers act combative during presentations, partially out of impatience and partially to see how the analyst will respond. Most young analysts get flustered in these moments, which often fuels the portfolio manager's desire to get even more aggressive. We recommend that the best way to disarm aggressive portfolio managers is to stick with the facts as much as possible and leave the eventual debate centered on any conjecture in your analysis, which is where the potential disagreement should focus.

Stock Pitching Contests

Both authors continue to be amazed at how poor the pitches are in stock picking contests. Although the participants are eager, bright, attractive, and clearly hard-working, the presentations are generally confusing and poorly organized, and remind us of the puzzle problem we laid out at the beginning of Chapter 11.

Imperial Airship by James Ng, redrawn with permission.

Most contests allow students 10 minutes to present their recommendation. Rather than think of the pitch in the way we have structured it, most students elect to present a fire hose of information with the hope that demonstrating how much work they did will help them win the contest. We think this strategy is ineffective because it leaves the judges with the unenviable task of putting the random pieces together to finish the puzzle. And, as Paul S. often comments, the inevitable winner is the best of the worst.

You can think of the three components of the pitch—the 30-second hook, the two-minute drill, and the Q&A—as modules that can be tailored to fit the allotted time. For example, if the format of the contest is a 10-minute presentation followed by five minutes of Q&A, you can adjust the modules to fit the time frame.

For instance, you can use the 30-second hook as an introduction to your pitch and then spend a little time discussing what the company does to give the judges context. This part of your presentation should take no more than a couple of minutes and cover only a few slides. You should use the next four to five minutes for an extended two-minute drill, adding additional evidence, warrants, and backing to the original argument. You should use the remaining four minutes to address any anticipated counterarguments.

There is a total of eight slides in the earlier example. With an extended two-minute drill and discussion of counterarguments, the total number of slides[5] in your presentation should not exceed 15.

Delivering the Message—You Are the Envelope

Think of a letter.[6] The letter's content is the message—the actual words on paper. You cannot simply write a letter and drop it in a mailbox hoping that it will reach its destination. The letter must be put into an envelope. It is the envelope that *delivers* the message. When making a pitch, *you are the envelope.*

Imagine you have an interview with a portfolio manager, and he asks you to send a write-up of your investment idea to him before you meet. What envelope will you choose to send him the report? Each envelope shown here is an option. Each would contain the same content, the investment report you wrote. However, it is important to understand how the manager will *perceive* each envelope as he flips through the stack of mail on his desk.

---

[5] Paul S. believes that pitch contests should limit a student to 10 slides and the font on the slides to no smaller than 20 point. As with the items one would take when their house is on fire and they have only had 30 seconds to react, the limitations would force the analyst to include only the most critical points in their presentation.

[6] For those young readers who don't know what a letter is, imagine you write an e-mail and then print it out. That's a letter—an e-mail printed on paper.

It should be obvious that the portfolio manager will form an initial impression the instant he sees each envelope, even before opening them. The FedEx envelope conveys urgency and importance. The second envelope looks businesslike. The third looks like an invitation, the fourth looks like junk mail, and the fifth is an absolute mess.

The portfolio manager will likely open the FedEx envelope first. Subconsciously, he is thinking, "When someone spends $30 and takes the time and trouble to send something FedEx, it is usually important; therefore, I should open it first." Conversely, the portfolio manager might not even bother looking at the last two envelopes because he is thinking, "This is junk mail; I'm not going to waste my time." Or "This envelope is filthy; I don't even want to touch it." If the contents of the envelopes are identical—each contains the same investment report—then why should it matter what the envelope looks like? Isn't the actual content more important than the envelope it is delivered in?

Each envelope conveys information that will cause the portfolio manager to have a different **initial impression**, which can be positive or negative. The sender wants the envelope to *enhance* the content, not detract from it. Similarly, the delivery of your pitch will affect its content and be directly influenced by many factors, such as how you look, how you sound, and your body language. Like we say, one cannot simply drop the content into a mailbox and hope it reaches its destination. We will show why the way the content is delivered is a critically important part of the pitching process.

Depending on the circumstances,[7] the portfolio manager will begin to form an impression of you even before you meet, most likely from reviewing your resume and reading any research reports you might have sent to him before the meeting.

Nonverbal Signals

The portfolio manager's initial instinct when he enters the conference room to meet you for the first time is to look at your face and establish eye contact. He then shifts his attention to observe your physical appearance and the clothing you are wearing. This process

---

[7] We should emphasize that this chapter is written from the standpoint that you have *not* met the person to whom you are pitching. Obviously, if you have interacted with the person before (or perhaps work with them directly), they will already have made a first impression.

is subconscious and takes milliseconds. However, the portfolio manager is generally unaware that he is making these instant judgments. And, because you have yet to utter a single word, all the information you are conveying is **nonverbal** and becomes the foundation of his initial impression of you.

As the phrase implies, **nonverbal communication** is communication between people that does not involve spoken words. It includes body language, facial expressions, and posture. It also includes the tone, pitch, speed at which you speak, and other qualities in the way you express yourself. It is not *what* is being said, but *how* it is being said. Nonverbal communication comprises everything in the pitch *except* for the actual message itself (the content), which is why we believe it is important to separate the delivery of the pitch from its content.

Academic studies show that a high percent of the information conveyed when individuals communicate is **nonverbal**. Alfred Mehrabian, a professor at UCLA, performed several experiments in the late 1960s, where he concluded that communication was 7% words, 38% inflection and tone, and 55% body language. These observations have morphed into the widespread, and commonly repeated, belief that more than 90% of communication is nonverbal, which is known as the 7-38-55 rule.

Like many other widely accepted "truths," this one is clearly wrong. One cannot visit a foreign country and understand 90% of the message being communicated based on just body language, voice inflection, and tone. You will need to understand the language being spoken and not just for 7% of the communications. Nonetheless, Mehrabian's research highlights the importance of inflection, tone, and body language when communicating.

For example, when choosing a doctor, you want one who is capable and credible. You might care about her years of experience, her hospital affiliation, and the medical school she attended. You might get a recommendation from a friend or search the Internet to see if any patient reviews have been posted online. Then, when you meet the doctor in person, you form a first impression. Most people want their doctor to "look the part." You expect her to enter the room in a white lab coat with a stethoscope around her neck, looking like a stereotypical doctor. You want the office to look organized, clean, and uncluttered. When the doctor talks to you, you expect confidence in her voice, good eye contact, and a calm demeanor. These traits make you feel more **comfortable** and **confident** in her ability to treat you. It is clear from experience that most people form an initial impression of a doctor, or any professional, the instant they enter the room. A portfolio manager forms a judgment of you the same way.

Academic studies also show that most of the nonverbal information that is conveyed when individuals interact is **subconscious** to both parties and that first impressions are made in a fraction of a second. Unfortunately, first impressions are difficult to change, hence the cliché, "You never get a second chance to make a first impression." Sadly, most people are unaware that they are forming these subconscious judgments so quickly and with such limited verbal information exchanged. Understanding the way these judgments are formed should help you to make the right first impression.

Interestingly, several academic studies show that initial impressions of individuals in certain roles can be surprisingly accurate, even when based on only brief observations. For example, Nalini Ambady and Robert Rosenthal, both psychologists at Harvard, conducted a study in 1993 on teacher effectiveness as measured by end-of-semester student ratings. The psychologists showed college students three 10-second video clips of 13 different college teachers without sound. The students were asked to judge the teachers based solely on nonverbal communication, rating the teachers on criteria such as physical attractiveness, attentiveness, competency, confidence, likability, warmth, and honesty. Body language such as fidgeting, frowning, sitting, gazing down, and nodding was also recorded.

The results were surprising. Teachers who were rated higher in their end-of-semester reviews were judged in the study to be more attractive, attentive, confident, likable, and competent. The teachers who frowned or fidgeted received significantly lower student ratings.[8]

Portfolio managers are no different. They are not judging teachers, *they are judging you.* Solely based on nonverbal information, the portfolio manager will assemble subconsciously a list of positive and negative traits in his mind as he enters the room and observes you for the first time. He will make an initial determination of you in a fraction of a second based on your appearance, which will influence how interacts with you during the meeting, *and he will be completely unaware he is doing it.*

---

[8] N. Ambady and R. Rosenthal, "Half a Minute: Predicting Teacher Evaluations from Thin Slices of Nonverbal Behavior and Physical Attractiveness," *Journal of Personality and Social Psychology* 64, no. 3 (1993): 431–441.

Are You Capable and Credible?

As we discuss in the prior chapter, the portfolio manager tries to answer four questions in every pitch he hears:

1. *How much can I make?*
2. *How much can I lose?*
3. *Is the idea too good to be true?*
4. *How will the next guy figure it out?*

As you proceed through your pitch, there is a subconscious dialogue unfolding in the portfolio manager's mind as he weighs your statements against those questions, with his sole desire of answering a single question: **Do I believe him?**

In trying to answer the first question, **How much can I make?** the portfolio manager asks himself, "Is this opportunity analyzable and is the analyst right in their estimate of the stock's intrinsic value and the time horizon to reach that value?"

While trying to answer the second question, **How much can I lose?** the portfolio manager worries to himself: "Has the analyst identified all of the risks and has he underweighted or overweighted the probability of any of them occurring?"

When considering if the opportunity is **too good to be true**, he tries to answer the question: "How can I be sure that the information is not already priced into the stock?"

Finally, he seeks an answer to his final question, **How will the next guy figure it out?** by asking: "Has the analyst correctly identified a catalyst that will close the gap and eliminate the mispricing?"

Underlying *these* nagging questions are *even more questions*: Did the analyst miss anything? Is the analyst right in his conclusion? Can I trust his judgment? Can I trust his research? These additional questions circle back to the original question raised in the portfolio manager's mind: **Do I believe him?** We add this additional layer to the process we developed in the prior chapter, as illustrated in Figure 12.6.

For the portfolio manager to believe you, he needs to feel comfortable that you are trustworthy, used good judgment in your analysis, didn't miss anything in your research, and are correct in your recommendation. He is trying to determine if you are **capable** and **credible**. If the portfolio manager has a history of interacting with you, then he probably knows your strengths, weaknesses, limitations, and biases as well as how often you are right or wrong in your recommendations in the past, and how thorough you are in your research.

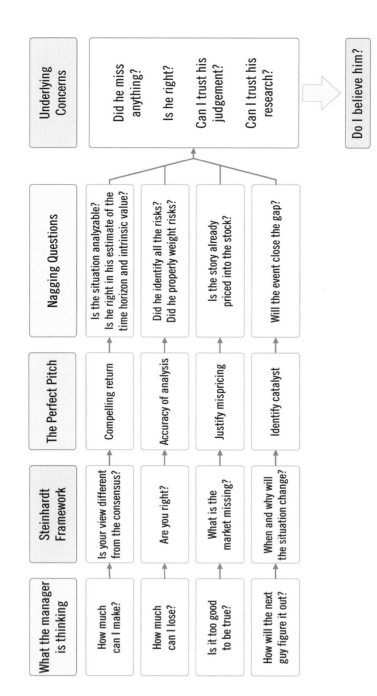

Figure 12.6 Portfolio Manager: "Do I Believe Him?"

On the other hand, how can the portfolio manager decide if you are capable or credible if he doesn't know you or your track record? In the moment that he first lays eyes on you, with nothing else to go on, the manager will rely on what he *perceives* to be your capability and credibility.

Why are capability and credibility important? **Capability** is the portfolio manager's belief that you have the ability to answer the four questions he needs to answer before he will adopt *any* new idea. His assessment of your capability will include his perception of your intelligence, competence, acumen, prowess, talent, creativity, focus, energy, persistence, and resourcefulness. Who would believe an analyst who did not have these qualities?

The portfolio manager initially will assess your **credibility** based on his perception of your honesty, seriousness, integrity, confidence, thoroughness, reliability, and dependability. For example, **confirmation bias** is a common cognitive bias whereby individuals discount information that challenges their beliefs and overweight information that supports it. The manager needs to be confident that you did not fall into this common mental trap in your analysis. He needs to feel that you are confident enough to admit when you do not know something, instead of glossing over or covering up deficiencies in your research.

The Portfolio Manager's Subconscious Biased Schema

Capability and credibility are enhanced or eroded by another underlying factor: **likability**. An analyst's likability will be influenced by factors such as physical attractiveness, charisma, disposition, polish, warmth, cooperativeness, respectfulness, cleanness, temperament, and enthusiasm. Likability will not add to or subtract from the *quality* of the idea or the underlying arguments, but it will *affect the receptivity* of those arguments and augment or retard the effectiveness of the arguments. If the portfolio manager likes you, he will *perceive* you as being more capable and credible, and be *more receptive* to your arguments. Conversely, if the portfolio manager does not like you, he will be more skeptical of your arguments and *less receptive* to any idea you pitch.

As unbelievable (and perhaps unfair) as this might sound, the portfolio manager has already (subconsciously) formed a first impression of your **capability**, **credibility**, and **likability** before you even say hello and shake his hand. You might ask, "How can the portfolio manager possibly make an assessment from just looking at me?" It's simple, he uses a **schema**.

As we discuss in Chapter 10, humans use schemas all the time to evaluate pretty much everything, including, but not limited to, teachers, doctors, policemen, politicians, CEOs, and even potential mates. Our schemas are like an internal radar system that we use to classify individuals, size them up, and form **judgments** about them, all very quickly and completely subconsciously. Portfolio managers are no different from the rest of us, and they use schemas to evaluate all new analysts they meet. Their **mental checklist** is formed from prior interactions with other new analysts, including both positive and negative experiences. And, just as we needed to figure out the manager's schema to find an ideal stock for his fund, we need to understand what happens when he applies his schema and selection process to *you*.

The portfolio manager's schema for assessing new analysts is structured similarly to the schema they use to evaluate new investment ideas we discuss in Chapter 10, with new idea substituted with new analyst, as shown in Figure 12.7.

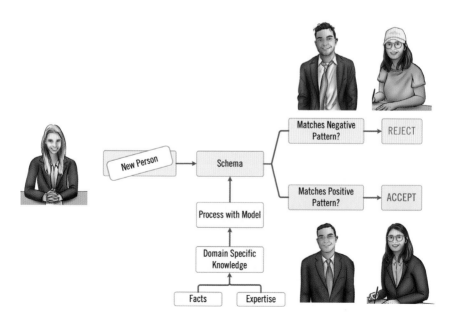

Figure 12.7   Portfolio Manager's "New Analyst" Schema

The harsh reality is that many people have subconscious **biases**, **prejudices**, and **stereotypes** with respect to age, race, height, weight, and gender, that frequently play a role in the **schema** they use to evaluate other people. These biases are often hardwired into their mind and create barriers to effective communication.

It is important to recognize that portfolio managers have cognitive biases and hold stereotypes that will *influence their impression of you.* A bigger problem is that most portfolio managers **are completely unaware that they have these biases and that their prejudices are influencing their actions and feelings**. Whether their impressions are accurate is irrelevant because they still present a potential barrier to your message being heard.

These **biases** come in two basic forms—specific to you, and general to all analysts. The personal prejudice might be justified, at least partially, if it is based on a previous experience the portfolio manager had with you. For instance, the manager may not trust you or your analysis because he feels you did substandard research on a prior assignment. Whatever the cause, this perception creates a significant **barrier** because the portfolio manager is skeptical of your idea before you even get to pitch. The fix? You will need to work hard to rebuild your **credibility** with the manager, and the most effective way to change his impression will be with the quality of your work on future projects.

The most important general **prejudices** concern the analyst's age, experience, and pedigree, which are often intertwined. For instance, it is impossible for you to have 10 years of investment experience if you are only 22 years old, unless, of course, you were a child prodigy and started your investing career at the age of 12. Age bias can be a significant barrier to overcome. Why does age matter? Because age is often equated with experience, and in the investment business, experience matters.

How Nonverbal Signals Form the Portfolio Manager's Initial Impression

We state that a portfolio manager instantly forms an impression of your **credibility**, **capability**, and **likability**, but it is important for you to understand *what subconsciously triggers these feelings.* As we mention earlier in this discussion, most people focus on the eyes and face when they meet someone new and then on their physical presence, posture, and clothing.

For example, Alexander Todorov, a professor of psychology at Princeton University, has conducted several fascinating studies showing that facial features such as curvature of the mouth, distance between the eyes, and fullness of lips are important in forming first impressions and affect how individuals perceive intelligence and trustworthiness in people they meet. Todorov concludes in one study that "faces perceived as distinguished, intelligent, and determined were older, had thin lips, and had wrinkles at the eye corners."[9] Apparently, wrinkles are not necessarily a bad thing! We do not discuss these physical attributes in detail because individuals cannot change them, although we mention it to increase awareness that these biases exists.

On the other hand, there are many factors that *can* be changed. Since the goal is to eliminate, or at least minimize, as many extraneous factors as possible, it is important to identify anything that you can change so it does not detract from the content of your pitch. Think of yourself as being in a race pushing a wheelbarrow full of bricks. The more bricks you remove, the faster you can go. For instance, you might be at a disadvantage if you are young, have full lips, and do not have wrinkles, at least according to Todorov's research. These are bricks you *cannot* remove. There are, however, bricks you *can* remove. The two simplest physical characteristics that you can modify are your hairstyle and wardrobe. And, believe it or not, wearing eyeglasses, even if they are not needed to correct your vision, can create a more a positive image.

Dr. Marianne LaFrance, a psychology professor at Yale University, authored a study in 2001 that related hairstyles to first impressions. She concluded that there is a perceived inverse relationship in hairstyles between attractiveness and intelligence for both men and women. For men, she found that medium-length, side-parted hair indicated intelligence and affluence, while long hair was viewed by most people as indicating brawn, with no brains, yet also a generally

[9] A. Todorov, C. Y. Olivola, R. Dotsch, and P. Mende-Siedlecki, "Social Attributions from Faces: Determinants, Consequences, Accuracy, and Functional Significance," *Annual Review of Psychology* 66, no. 1 (2015): 519–545.

good-natured person. Women with short, tousled hair were viewed as the most confident, intelligent, and outgoing, while women with medium-length, casual hair were viewed as intelligent and good natured. Long hair on women was viewed as the most attractive.[10]

Your clothing also conveys a tremendous amount of information that other people will use to build an impression of you. While there are numerous studies on the subject, we feel one is most representative. A group of researchers at the University of Hertfordshire in England and Istanbul Bilgi University in Turkey conducted a study in 2012 that produced surprising results. A total of 308 participants were shown pictures of a male model wearing a suit with his face obscured. In one of the pictures, the model was wearing a custom-made suit and in the other he was wearing a store-bought, "off-the-rack" suit. Both suits were the same color and fabric pattern. The study's participants were shown each image for five seconds and then were asked to rate the model's confidence, success, trustworthiness, salary, and flexibility, on a scale from 1 to 7. The model scored higher on all five attributes when he wore the custom suit. Although the participants viewed the pictures for only five seconds and the differences between the suits were very subtle, the meaningful difference in the rating indicates that clothing plays a large role in **subconscious perception** of personality traits.

Studies linking eyeglasses to perceived intelligence have been conducted since the early 1940s. The academic studies are consistent as they show *that although individuals who wear glasses are considered less physically attractive, they are perceived as being more intelligent.*

To demonstrate the subliminal power of these various attributes, look at the two pictures that follow. Quickly choose one of the two—whose stock idea would you be more likely to adopt? Zev on the left or the right?

---

[10] Marianne LaFrance, "First Impressions and Hair Impressions: An Investigation of Impact of Hair Style on First Impressions," February 2001.

You, and most portfolio managers, likely would pick Zev on the right. Ask yourself, why would that preference would exist? Probably because Zev on the left looks like he's just rolled in from a hard night of clubbing. Why should the analyst's looks make a difference if the content of the message is identical? Because it is vitally important to **look the part** and not have any extraneous factors detract from your message. It is like the envelopes we mention earlier in the chapter. Which one looks more appealing? They contain the exact same message, but the one of the right is clearly more appropriate for the situation.

That was an easy comparison. Let's try another. Make a quick decision—Zev on the left or Zev on the right?

The differences in this example are much subtler. By instinct, most senior portfolio managers will pick Zev on the right. At closer examination, you will probably notice the difference in the hair, the clothes, the glasses, and facial hair. While both appearances are acceptable, Zev on the left is probably more appropriate for his age, while Zev on the right is dressed more conservatively. It is important to ask, which mode of dress will minimize any extraneous factors you are trying to avoid?

Zev interned at Gabelli Funds, working in operations the summer between his junior and senior years of high school. Since Paul S. worked there as well, the impression Zev made would indirectly reflect on his dad. They had a discussion of how to dress before Zev started. Paul told Zev he would have to be clean shaven every day. Zev countered that all the interns his age didn't shave. Paul said to him, "What is socially acceptable really doesn't make a difference. The fact is that I'm 47, and it is not acceptable to me to go to work in the morning with three days of growth. And Mario is 73 and old school, and I am willing to bet that it is unacceptable to him as well. Mario might *say* he is fine with it, but subconsciously it will not look right to him. You dress and groom to make an impression on your boss, it makes no difference 'what everyone else is doing.'" Needless to say, Zev went to work each day clean shaven.

Acceptable dress in the workplace has evolved over time. For example, the "uniform" in investment banking has traditionally been a suit and tie. However, at one of the most respected investment banking firms in the industry today, its founder has set the dress code to what he feels is appropriate: suit but no tie. The best advice we can offer is to model your style after the person at the top. A recent *Wall Street Journal* article sums up this recommendation perfectly. "There's a tribal element. . . . It says, we're all going to wear the same thing, and it's going to be similar to whatever the leader wears."[11]

ADVICE TO STUDENTS

Paul S. often would give advice to students in his class on how to dress.[12] He would tell them that the goal with dressing is to avoid making any negative impression. Paul's simple test was that a half hour after you leave the meeting, whoever you met with should not remember what you were wearing. For men, this means a gray or blue suit, white or blue shirt, black belt, black socks, and black shoes, and then feel free to add a little color with your tie if you want. It also means clean shaven, conservative haircut, no fancy pens, no jewelry, and no cologne. And, aside from Jimmy Rogers and Chuck Royce, very few men can get away with a bow tie. Paul gives similar advice to women: wear a blue or black jacket and skirt with black shoes, and feel free to mix it up with colored shirts; wear simple jewelry, plain earrings, and no perfume; keep your hair short or pulled back and nails on the short side with a color that will not attract attention.

If you search the Internet for pictures of any recent US president, CEOs of a Fortune 500 company, or successful investors such as Bill Ackman, Dan Loeb, Barbara Marcin, Mario Gabelli, or Charlie Dreifus, to name a few, you will see they are all impeccably dressed in simple, although

---

[12] This story is a case of "do what I say, not what I do;" those who know Paul S. will laugh at the prospect of him giving advice on how to dress, as Paul's current wardrobe consists primarily of suits and ties from the late 1990s and it's arguable that they were not in style even when he bought them.

---

[11] Nandini D'Souza Wolfe, "Seven Office Menswear Dilemmas—and How to Manage Them," *Wall Street Journal*, April 13, 2017.

elegant, clothes, with dark suits, white or blue shirts, and understated ties, for the men, and attractive but conservative outfits for the women.

The best book to read on the subject, even though the most recent edition was written in 1988, is John T. Molloy's *Dress for Success*.[13] Molloy conducted several (nonscientific) studies in the 1970s showing how a person's clothing affected perception. In one example from the book, Molloy went to 25 preselected business offices with a copy of the *Wall Street Journal*,[14] asking the receptionist to allow him to deliver the paper personally to the individual in charge. He delivered the papers in a single morning when he wore a beige raincoat, but it took him a day and a half to deliver the 25 papers when he was wearing a black raincoat. Moral of the story, don't wear a black raincoat.

As for hairstyle, one of Paul's former students, David, worked for him as an intern in 2003. David had shoulder-length hair that Paul thought was unacceptable and dropped several not-so-subtle hints that if he wanted to be on Wall Street, Paul felt that David needed to get his hair cut.[15] The night before they were set to leave for a company visit, Paul finally said, "You gotta get those locks shorn. You can't come anywhere with me with that hair." The next morning David arrived at the office with an appropriately short haircut.

David launched his own hedge fund a few years later and became an adjunct professor at Columbia Business School. In preparing to write this story, Paul asked David if his "tough-love" approach helped. David responded, "It was fifteen years ago. As far as how I felt, you were right. I actually tell the story all the time, including to my students. What we wear, how we're groomed, what jewelry/watches we have on us, what we drive. . . . All of those items project an image. And I understood the image I was projecting wasn't necessarily in the best interest of my long-term career. I could have been stubborn and said, 'but I want long hair,' although, then I couldn't whine about not getting an opportunity (which you gave me!)"

---

[13] Interestingly, the *Wall Street Journal* article from which we quote had a sub-story titled "The Musty Smell of Success," which pokes fun at Molloy's book. The reporter, Jacob Gallagher, wrote, "Yet, much like a leisure suit, some of the advice dispensed by Mr. Molloy is utterly—rather than amusingly—out of touch." Gallagher lists 18 excerpts from Molloy's book that are obviously dated as the book was written in 1975. However, Gallagher is not writing to inform readers, but rather to sensationalize topics to sell papers. While there is no question that parts of the book are outdated, there are many timeless lessons if one reads between the lines, which is why we recommend reading it.

[14] For the younger readers, there was a time, in the very distant past, when the WSJ was not available online and only printed on paper from dead trees—and there was no color—the paper was published only in black and white.

[15] When asked to verify the validity of the story, David emailed back, "You may very well have been giving hints, but I was too dumb to pick up on them."

Also, as inconsequential as it might sound, show up to the meeting with just a single briefcase or small tote (no knapsacks or gym bags). Research shows that individuals who carry more than one item are perceived as disorganized.

Beware—Microexpressions Will Give You Away

There are other nonverbal characteristics that can influence perceived **credibility**, **capability**, and **likability**, including facial expressions, speed or hesitation of speech as well as tone and inflection of voice. For example, say that the portfolio manager asks you a question to which you don't know the answer and, in response, you show a look of surprise and hesitate as you respond. The portfolio manager will record your **nonverbal** reactions **subconsciously** and his perception of your **credibility** and **capability** will most likely decline. You might think, "Well, I won't look surprised nor have any hesitation in my voice when I answer." The problem is that it is extremely difficult to control your response because it is *subconscious and involuntary.*

Subconscious, involuntary changes in facial expressions are called **microexpressions** and last for less than a quarter of a second when they occur. They are usually triggered by an external event and convey an enormous amount of information about the emotions a person is experiencing. There are seven universal emotions: anger, disgust, fear, sadness, happiness, surprise, and contempt, and all trigger microexpressions when a person experiences them.

As an example, say you are at a picnic and a bee suddenly buzzes by your face. Without even knowing what the object is, your brain will recognize a threat and reflexively your hand will move to swat away the bee. You won't be aware that you had this reaction until after the fact. The reaction was a reflex. If someone took a picture of you at the exact moment that you raised your hand to swat away the bee, the look on your face probably would show a mix of surprise and fear. This facial response is a **microexpression**. It is involuntary and you cannot control it.

Similarly, if the portfolio manager asks you a question that you didn't anticipate and don't know the answer you likely will experience the same reaction you had with the bee, which is a combination of surprise and fear. Your face will reveal these emotions instantly and since they are **involuntary**, you won't be able to control them. Although your microexpression will last for *only* a split second, in all likelihood, the portfolio manager will register it, albeit subconsciously. He might respond reflexively with a microexpression of his own, revealing disgust and contempt. Subconsciously, you will notice *his* reaction, which escalates your nervousness and causes you to respond with a stutter, become flush, and break out in a sweat. In response, the manager subconsciously detects your body's response and the vicious cycle continues. That is, until someone breaks the silence with a verbal comment.

It is important to appreciate that **microexpressions** reveal critical **nonverbal** information to the other person and will, in most situations, influence their response to you. Unfortunately, there is little you can do to control your emotions and the information they convey through your facial expressions. The only practical way to prevent this behavior from occurring is to not be caught off-guard by questions the portfolio manager may ask. This insight reinforces why it's critically important for the analyst to understand the portfolio manager's criteria and anticipate critical issues and questions that he likely will raise during the pitch. In other words, do the work!

Nonverbal Signals Can Also Give You Away

Other nonverbal factors such as eye movement and body language can also reveal your emotional state. For instance, there is a high likelihood that you will be nervous in the meeting, which can result in rapid blinking, flustered speech, or poor posture. These behaviors send subtle, yet important cues to your audience about your heightened emotional state. Pacifying behaviors, such as biting your lip, adjusting your tie, fidgeting with your hands, playing with your hair, or touching your mouth or neck also show signs of nervousness and anxiety. Shrugging your shoulders indicates a lack of knowledge, and leaning back and crossing your arms shows discomfort. While it is extremely difficult to control microexpressions, you should try to minimize these behaviors as much as possible. Like your parents always told you, sit up straight, have good posture, and maintain eye contact when meeting someone new. And smile, although not too much, as that can indicate nervousness as well!

Anatomy of a Meeting

The purpose of a meeting is to get your idea adopted. It is important for you to be aware of different factors that can detract from the content of your pitch in that meeting. Certain factors, such as posture, dress, and the choice of wearing eyeglasses, are controllable and can enhance the content of your pitch. It is critical to understand when the portfolio manager is focused on extraneous nonverbal factors and when he is focused on your content.

Six Stages of a Meeting

To illustrate the importance of being aware of the balance between nonverbal factors and the content of your pitch, we separate a typical first encounter between an analyst and a portfolio manager into six different stages.

The "first glance" stage covers the moment the manager meets the analyst for the first time, much of which we have discussed already. The second stage covers "small talk," where pleasantries are exchanged as the analyst and portfolio manager shake hands and say hello to each other. The first two stages are similar because most of the communication is conveyed nonverbally, which forms the basis of the portfolio manager's **first impression**. As we highlight in lavender in Figure 12.8, none of the content of the message is conveyed in these stages. It is as if the manager is holding the "envelope" in his hands, evaluating whether he wants to open it.

The next three stages (which we discuss at length in this chapter as well as in Chapter 11), covers the **hook**, where the analyst introduces his idea; the **two-minute drill**, where the analyst presents his arguments; and, finally, several minutes of **Q&A**, where the portfolio manager probes and challenges the analyst's arguments. These middle three stages are similar in that the quality of the content (highlighted in yellow in Figure 12.8) is finally the focus of the interaction.

The last stage is when the analyst and portfolio manager say their goodbyes, and nonverbal communication once again plays a dominant role in the final interaction.

Figure 12.8   Six Stages of an Initial In-Person Meeting

Bud Fox's Initial Meeting with Gordon Gekko

In the movie *Wall Street*,[16] Bud Fox has hounded Gordon Gekko's secretary for three months to get an appointment with him. Fox shows up at Gekko's office on Gekko's birthday with a box of cigars as a present. After waiting several hours, Fox finally gets ushered into Gekko's office. Gekko is on the phone and glances at Fox. Within a split-second, Gekko has started his subconscious assessment of Fox's **credibility**, **capability**, and **likability**.

Gekko informs the people milling around his office as he gets off the phone, "This is the kid. Calls me 59 days in a row, wants to be a player." Then, turning to Fox, he says, "Oughta be a picture of you in the dictionary under persistence, kid." Clearly, Gekko's first impression of Fox was young, ambitious, and persistent. These are the qualities that got Fox into Gekko's office.

As Gekko is making these comments, a stupid-looking grin appears on Fox's face. At that point, in about four seconds, Gekko has crystallized his first impression of Fox.

---

[16] We encourage the reader to watch the movie clip before reading the following section. To see the clip, Google "Wall Street Bud Fox meets Gordon Gekko."

Next comes the small talk. Fox stands up as Gekko gets off the phone and says, "How do you do, Mr. Gekko? I'm Bud Fox." Fox has good eye contact and extends his hand to give Gekko a firm handshake. Gekko says, "Hope you are intelligent." And then, referring to the cigars, Gekko asks, "Where did you get these?" Fox replies, "I got a connection at the airport." Gekko responds, "So what's on your mind, kemosabe?" Fox is sitting down at that point. His shoulders are tense and his **microexpressions** convey nervousness and anxiety. Fox coughs and looks down before he speaks, revealing additional nonverbal information. Fox's voice is tentative and hesitant as he says, "I just want to let you know, Mr. Gekko, I read all about you at NYU Business, and I think you're an incredible genius and I've always dreamed of only one thing—to do business with a man like you." Gekko's expression is one of impatience and annoyance as he waits for Fox to finish his pandering. Fox has a deer-in-the-headlights expression on his face, and he seems out of place as he speaks to Gekko. Fox then looks bewildered when Gekko asks him questions about deals at his firm.

Gekko ends the small talk by cutting to the chase, "So what have you got for me, sport? Why are you here?" Fox stands up and snaps the paper in his hand as he launches into his pitch. His voice is suddenly strong and confident as he states, "Chart breakout on this one here. Whitewood-Young Industries. Low P/E, explosive earnings, 30% discount to book value, great cash flow, strong management, and a couple of 5% holders."

This scene illustrates the first three stages of the meeting structure presented in Figure 12.8. Gekko's initial impression of Fox before they even met was that the kid was young, persistent, and ambitious. However, Fox does not fare well when he finally meets Gekko in person. His hair is slicked back, he has a silly grin on his face, is wearing an inexpensive suit, and by his body language, looks uncomfortable and out of place. Fox's voice is hesitant and he conveys a lacks confidence as he engages with Gekko in small talk. Gekko **subconsciously** absorbs all this information, most of which is nonverbal and *extraneous to the actual investment ideas Fox is there to pitch.* However, Fox appears confident and assured when he launches into his pitch, while the mix of information Gekko processes shifts from nonverbal communications to the verbal content of his message.

Other Not So Obvious Barriers to Communication

There are a couple of additional potential obstacles that bear mention, albeit briefly. Although these barriers have nothing to do with the actual message and are *not specific to the analyst*, they need to be overcome nonetheless because they can prevent the portfolio manager from actually *hearing* the message.

The most apparent barrier is **physical**, and the most obvious one is noise. For instance, if you are trying to pitch your idea while there is a jackhammer on the street outside, the noise might be distracting enough that the portfolio manager cannot hear your pitch. In another situation, you might be at a business dinner with another person sitting between you and the portfolio manager, making it difficult for the manager to hear your pitch because of the actual physical distance between the two of you. Or, perhaps the ambient noise in the restaurant is so loud that the manager has trouble hearing you even if he is sitting right next to you.[17] The fix? Wait for a better time to present your idea or maneuver the manager to someplace quieter or more private where he is not distracted by the noise. Although these examples might seem obvious, they highlight the importance of your thinking about extraneous stimuli that can inhibit the portfolio manager's **receptivity** to your pitch.

The manager's **emotions** can also be an obstacle. Your message will not get heard if he is preoccupied, angry, or stressed. Pitching an idea to a portfolio manager right after the market's opening bell, when he is distracted by the start of the trading day and under assault by information coming at him from all directions, is not an ideal time to try to get his attention. Similarly, the anger and/or stress he is feeling from a disagreement with his wife or argument with a large client wanting to redeem their investment in the fund will prevent him from hearing your message. The fix? Wait for a better, calmer time to pitch your idea.

---

[17] For this very reason, Paul S. would often schedule lunch meetings at a small restaurant in midtown Manhattan called Teodora. The restaurant had a second floor that, although not well-known, was brightly lit and very quiet. In contrast, Paul would avoid Brasserie in the Seagram Building at all costs. The hardwood and glass décor at Brasserie produced horrible acoustics, making it difficult to hear someone speaking, even if they were sitting right next to you.

Language can be another obstacle to getting your message heard. This barrier can take several forms. It should be obvious that the portfolio manager will not understand you if you don't speak the same language. However, a less obvious problem is that even if fluent, an analyst communicating in a non-native tongue might have a limited vocabulary preventing him from using more nuanced or precise language. A thick accent can also be an impediment in the same way as a noisy room, in that the portfolio manager might have a hard time understanding what you are saying. Another language-based impediment is industry jargon. Although understanding the industry's technical terms may help you communicate the nuances of the business, the words could be foreign to the manager and make it difficult for him to understand your message.[18]

Although all three examples might seem fairly trivial, it is surprising how many times we have seen them violated in our careers. All three potential obstacles have easy fixes, yet young analysts oftentimes fail to recognize their importance and rarely address them directly.

How Do You Get to Carnegie Hall?

Everyone knows the answer to the classic joke. The same applies to pitching, whether you are pitching to a portfolio manager with whom you have worked for the past few years, in a stock pitching contest, your first stock in your new job, or in a job interview.[19] Practice, practice, and then, practice some more. Pitching well is a skill that requires time and experience to master. The analyst needs to

---

[18] Young analysts make this mistake all the time by throwing around terms, especially "acronyms," like NOPLAT, "normalized CASM," "OLED technology," and "SSSG." As a point of reference, after 65 years of combined teaching and work experience, the authors had to look up the definition of "NOPLAT" as they didn't know what the "L" stood for. FYI—NOPLAT is "net operating profit less adjusted taxes."

[19] It is important to recognize that *all* job interviews in the investment business are essentially stock pitches. The only thing that the portfolio manager cares about is whether the analyst can do the job. They are not professional interviewers. We commonly hear about interviews where the manager fumbles around with a resume in his hand, asking irrelevant questions about the analyst's education or former job, like "How did you like working for so and so?" until he stops himself, looks up, and says, "So what's your best idea?"

practice until the arguments seem natural and the evidence is clear in his mind. Although a comprehensive review of ways to rehearse effectively is beyond the scope of this discussion, we encourage anyone embarking on a career in the investment business to take the delivery of the message seriously. As we say in the book's introduction, not getting the idea into the portfolio is no different from not having a good idea in the first place.

Gems:

⬦ Always provide the portfolio manager with a "pitch pack." The pitch pack includes your slide presentation, any reports you have written, and the company's annual report, most recent 10Q, and latest earnings release. Portfolio managers often want to flip through the material during the meeting and appreciate having this information at their fingertips. You must make it easy for them, which you can do by serving your pitch on a silver platter with a big red bow.

⬦ It is important for the portfolio manager to understand what the company does and be able to put the business in context. Therefore, it is critical that the analyst explain the company's business simply and succinctly. If the business is complex, use pictures. As they say, "A picture is worth a thousand words."

⬦ To anticipate possible questions the manager might ask, it is important to identify any weaknesses in your arguments and which part is most likely to be attacked during the Q&A period: the evidence, warrant, or backing.

⬦ Since the goal is to eliminate, or at least minimize, as many extraneous factors as possible, it is important to try to alter anything that can be changed so it does not detract from the content of the pitch. Think of your being in a race pushing a wheelbarrow full of bricks. The more bricks you remove, the faster you can go.

⬦ It is important to appreciate that microexpressions reveal critical nonverbal information and will, in most situations, influence how other people respond to you. Unfortunately, there is little one can do to control their emotions and the information they convey through their facial expressions. The only practical way to avoid this behavior from occurring is to be prepared for any question that the portfolio manager might ask, which reinforces why it is critically important for the analyst to understand the manager's investment criteria and anticipate the critical issues that will likely arise concerning the investment idea. In other words, do the work!

Acknowledgments

This book would not have been written without considerable contribution from many different individuals, whom we want to thank personally.

First, we want to thank Professor Bruce Greenwald. No other individual has had a greater impact on both authors' understanding of the investing process than Professor Greenwald. He acted as an early mentor to both of us and was always quick to point out flaws in our thinking.[1] Professor Greenwald has supported both of our careers, while challenging us to grow as investors and professors. We cannot thank him enough for his continued friendship and guidance over the years.

We also want to thank Michael Mauboussin. Michael and Paul J. met when they were both young research analysts at First Boston Corp. Michael followed the food industry, while Paul followed technology companies. Although their primary research coverage was quite different, they quickly discovered that they both had a similar interest in valuation, strategy, shareholder value creation, and a myriad of other issues related to investing. Michael continues to be one of the most prolific writers on these topics and has a near-encyclopedic recall of journal articles, books, and other related publications. He was one of our go-to sources when we hit a roadblock with a thought or idea.

The authors thank the following individuals, all of whom patiently read multiple early drafts of the manuscript, spent countless hours on the phone discussing various topics and concepts, and

---

[1] For those who do not know Bruce, he is eager to point out flaws in *everyone's* thinking.

forced us to reach greater clarity in our explanations and writing: Jennifer Gallagher, Nick Gogerty, Pamela Johnson, Timir Karia, Marc Roston, and Michael Shearn.

The authors also thank the following individuals who helped us develop certain examples used in the book: Leigh Drogen, Ian Haft, Noah Snyder, Dan Krueger, Scott Page, and Ned Smith.

The authors thank the following individuals, all of whom read various sections of early drafts of the book and gave critically important and in-depth feedback: Chris Allwin, Vince Amabile, Jimmy Baker, Eric Ball, Charlie Dreifus,[2] Nick Galluccio, Michael Greiber, Ron Gutstein, Jeff Halis, Victoria Hart, Judd Kahn, James Kelly and the students in his investment classes at the Gabelli School of Business, Michael Mauboussin, Joe Meyerink, Scott Page, Brian Pellegrini, Steve Shaffer, Matt Teller, Liz Tikhonravova, and Arnie Ursaner.

The authors also thank the following individuals for their contribution to specific sections of the book: Nadia Alfridi, Nolan Dalla, Omar Dessouky, Chris Goulakis, Shane Heitzman, Sanjay Jain, Bradford Kirby, Evan Lustig, Amelia Manderscheid, Kyle Moran, Catherine Noble, Al Palombo, James Pan, Shane Parish, Regina Pitaro, Scott Powell, Bob Schneider, David Smith, Michael Steinhardt, and David Trainer.

The book is significantly better because of the contributions from these individuals.

The authors also thank the book's illustrator, Charlie Pendergraft, who worked countless hours under tight deadlines and had to suffer through our numerous change requests. His talent and creativity turned our ideas into reality. We also appreciate the legal assistance of Richard Stim, who provided guidance regarding copyright and permission issues that arose during this process.

We would also like to thank our extremely knowledgeable and reasonably priced lawyer, Paul Sennott, whom we recommend highly without the slightest hesitation. His professionalism, eye for detail, guidance, and responsiveness are beyond compare. We would also like to express our gratitude to acquisition editor at John Wiley & Sons, Bill Falloon, who went to bat for us more than once and

---

[2] Charlie gets additional thanks for giving us the idea to have "pearls of wisdom." Not only is Charlie a successful money manager at the helm of the Royce Special Equity Fund, he is one of the nicest people on Wall Street, which is a business where very few nice people exist.

held back his frustration when we missed yet another deadline. We also extend a special thanks to David Pugh who believed in and supported us throughout the process. We also thank other individuals at Wiley, including: Michael Henton (for helping create an amazing cover), Steven Kyritz, Kathryn Hancox, Judy Howarth, Nick Wehrkamp, and all the other people behind the scenes whose names were never divulged to us, but who helped with copyediting, image editing, and page layout.

Paul S. wants to personally thank people without whom this book would not have been possible: Glen Brooks, Paul Condzal, Susan Elliot, Jennifer Gallagher, Dan Iosifescu, and Alejandra Salaverria. He would also like to thank two people who were incredibly supportive: Mario Gabelli and Michael Price.

Paul J. wants to personally thank Pamela Johnson, William Kaplanidis, Timir Karia, Mary Lou La Pierre, Claire LeJuez, Jamie Lewis, Elizabeth Pappadopulos, Robert Siroka, and Myles Thompson, all of whom were wonderfully supportive throughout the three-year journey writing the book. Although there is no such thing as the perfect relationship, Paul thinks these individuals are all perfect in their own way. Thank you. Paul also thanks Elizabeth for introducing him to Starbucks green tea lattes, without which he might not have completed the book.

Finally, Paul would like to thank Paul for his intellect, curiosity, flexibility, perseverance, dedication, and friendship. We have challenged each other and stretched our limits in a process that has resulted in one of the most rewarding experiences in our careers. We are forever thankful to each other for such a gift.

Art Acknowledgments

The book's cover design was inspired by the illustration on the cover of the June 1937 issue of *Fortune* magazine, which was drawn by illustrator Antonio "Tony" Petruccelli (1907–1994).

Petruccelli was an accomplished, prolific, and highly acclaimed American illustrator. He designed 26 covers for *Fortune*, with his first illustration appearing in September 1933 and his last one published in 1945. Petruccelli also created for the magazine charts and diagrams, maps, illustrations, and caricatures. Interestingly, he designed the American Steel Industry commemorative stamp of 1957, in recognition of the 100th anniversary of the US steel industry.

In 1993, while rummaging through a bin containing old magazine covers at a flea market, Paul S. froze when he saw the *Fortune* magazine cover and instantly fell in love with it. He purchased the cover for $30, had it framed, and has hung it on his wall ever since. When thinking about possible cover designs for the book, the image seemed like an obvious choice.

Getting permission to use the illustration was no easy task. Paul S. contacted the Morris Museum in New Jersey, which had held a recent exhibition of Petruccelli's work. Through the museum's curator, Paul finally got in touch with Petruccelli's son Michael, and was granted permission. We thank Michael (and the entire Petruccelli family) for generously granting us permission to use the original illustration.

When the authors were brainstorming ideas for the design of the book's cover in March 2015, Paul S. showed Jen Gallagher a bunch of different design elements on the Internet that he liked, including Antonio Petruccelli's *Fortune* cover. Jen has had a lifelong passion for art and design. She attended the School of Visual Arts in New York City and studied archeology in Greece. Although she currently works in investment banking, she ran a successful custom invitation business for 11 years.

As Paul described the book, Jen took mental notes and started her own brainstorming. Using only Microsoft Word and images she collected on the Internet, Jen designed three cover mock-ups within a couple of hours. On the afternoon of April 4, 2015, she surprised Paul with the images below:

While Paul S. loved them all, he naturally gravitated toward the one with Petruccelli's ticker tape. Paul J. had the idea of having a design competition, but the contest never got off the ground. As part of the process, the illustrators at John Wiley took a stab at a cover design, which we show on the lower left. After some editing back and forth, we settled on the final cover image on the lower right, which, as you can see, is little changed from Jen's original design.

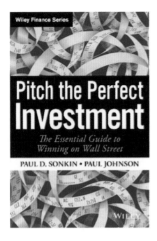 

While we created the diagrams ourselves, neither of us is an artist, therefore, the use of illustrations raised a critical issue as we felt the look and feel of the images needed to be consistent throughout the book. The only way to achieve that goal was to find an illustrator to create all of the images. In March 2016, Paul S. stumbled upon an illustrator, Charlie Pendergraft, on Instagram (@drawmecharlie), who Paul thought was very creative and reasonably priced. Over the course of a year, Charlie produced more than 300 illustrations that we have used in the book.

Charlie is an independent illustrator from Colorado Springs, CO. When asked to describe himself, he says that he "spends his time drawing comic greatness and drinking too much coffee." Not only is Charlie a professional artist, but he is a devoted father to three boys and an extremely talented piano player. He can be found at www.charlietheillustrator.com, or Google "draw me Charlie." The illustrations in our book are a departure from his usual commissions of voluptuous pinups. We think Charlie enjoyed his time working in the financial world, but then again, many of our images are a departure from what one would find in the standard investment book.

About the Authors

Paul D. Sonkin (New York, NY) is an analyst and portfolio manager at GAMCO Investors / Gabelli Funds. He is co-Portfolio Manager of the TETON Westwood Mighty Mites Fund, a value fund which primarily invests in micro-cap equity securities. Sonkin has over 25 years of experience researching small, micro and nanocap companies. Prior to analyzing stubs, spin-offs and micro-cap companies for GAMCO, Sonkin was for 14 years the portfolio manager of The Hummingbird Value Fund and the Tarsier Nanocap Value Fund. He holds an MBA from Columbia Business School and a BA in Economics from Adelphi University. For 16 years, Sonkin was an adjunct professor at Columbia Business School, where he taught courses on security analysis and value investing. For over 10 years, he was a member of the Executive Advisory Board of The Heilbrunn Center for Graham & Dodd Investing at Columbia Business School. Sonkin has extensive corporate governance experience having sat on six public company boards and is the co-author of *Value Investing: From Graham to Buffett and Beyond (2001)*.

Paul Johnson has been an investment professional for more than 35 years and currently runs Nicusa Investment Advisors. In his career, Johnson has been a top-ranked sell side analyst, a hedge fund manager, and an investment banker. As a portfolio manager, he invested in virtually all sectors of the economy and participated in more than 50 venture capital investments. Johnson has taught 40 semester-long graduate

business school courses on securities analysis and value investing to more than 2,000 students at Columbia Business School and Gabelli School of Business, Fordham University. Johnson received the Commitment to Excellence award in both 2016 and 2017 from the graduating class of Columbia Business School's Executive MBA program as well as the 2017 Columbia Business School's Dean's Prize for Teaching Excellence. He received the Gabelli School of Business graduate-level Dean's Award for Faculty Excellence in 2017. Johnson was a contributing annotator to The Most Important Thing Illuminated, by Howard Marks, co-author of the history of value investing in Columbia Business School: A Century of Ideas, and co-author of The Gorilla Game, Picking Winners in High Technology. Johnson has an MBA in Finance from the Executive Program at the Wharton School of the University of Pennsylvania and a BA in Economics from the University of California, Berkeley.

Index

demonstrating, in pitch preparation, 380

due to errors in incorporation, 293*f*

due to market inefficiency, 271*f*, 277*f*

and failure in wisdom of crowd, 177

illiquidity and investor neglect as cause of, 259

independence breakdown as cause of, 182, 183, 184*f,* 234–236, 234*f*

informational advantage with, 378, 378*f*

insufficient dissemination as cause of, 177–178, 178*f*

investor emotions as cause of, 225

and lack of diversity, 281–282, 282*f*

lack of diversity as cause of, 182, 183*f*

lack of domain-specific knowledge as cause of, 179, 179*f*

lack of incorporation as cause of, 188, 188*f*

and loss of crowd diversity, 236–237

and market efficiency, 268

reasons for, in pitch, 6–7

on variant perspective slide, 403

wisdom of crowds as cause of, 176

Missing information, in Steinhardt framework, 378

Mr. Market (concept), 223–226

Mity-Lite, 376–377

MKS Instruments, 166–167

Molloy, John T., 421

Monkees, 200

Monopoly, in business valuation, 85*t*

Mosaic theory, 372

Munger, Charlie, 68–69

Murray, Roger, 78, 131–132, 164, 233, 248–249

"The Musty Smell of Success" (Gallagher), 421

Mystery Ranch, 73

National Geographic, 313, 314

Navy SEALS, 362n.9

Needs, and feelings, 228

Negative excess returns, 103, 116

Negative space, identifying subjective criteria from, 364

Negative-sum game, 152

Neglect, investor, 259

Net income, 43–44, 44*t*

Net operating profit less adjusted taxes (NOPLAT), 428n.18

Network effects, as efficiency advantage, 93

Newport Corporation, 166, 166*f*

News and information media:
  influence on stock market of, 174
  systematic influence of, 246

Nice, as subjective criteria, 354

"No," as default response to pitch, 340n.1

Nobel Prize in Economic Sciences, 247, 248

No Bull (Steinhardt), 272–273

Noise:
  as communication barrier, 427
  false market signals as, 243, 244

"Noise" (Black), 243n.14

Noise traders, 243n.14

Nominal growth, 108–109, 109*t*

Nominal present value, of incremental growth, 111*t,* 114*t,* 115*t,* 118*t*

Nominal speeds, 108*t*

Non-material, nonpublic information, 158, 159*f*
  collected, in research, 289
  and quasi-public information, 161–162, 162*f*

Nonverbal communication:
  in meeting stages, 424, 425
  with microexpressions, 422–423
  in pitch delivery, 408–410, 422

NOPLAT (net operating profit less adjusted taxes), 428n.18

Normal distribution, 328

Normal distributions, 329–330, 329*f,* 330*f*

Numerical data, for quantitative criteria, 351